Russian Baptist Mission Theology in Historical and Contemporary Perspective

Andrey Kravtsev

© 2019 Andrey Kravtsev

Published 2019 by Langham Academic (Previously Langham Monographs)
An imprint of Langham Publishing
www.langhampublishing.org

Langham Publishing and its imprints are a ministry of Langham Partnership

Langham Partnership
PO Box 296, Carlisle, Cumbria, CA3 9WZ, UK
www.langham.org

ISBNs:
978-1-78368-747-3 Print
978-1-78368-748-0 ePub
978-1-78368-750-3 PDF

Andrey Kravtsev has asserted his right under the Copyright, Designs and Patents Act, 1988 to be identified as the Author of this work.

All Scripture quotations, unless otherwise indicated, are taken from the Holy Bible, New International Version®, NIV®. Copyright ©1973, 1978, 1984, 2011 by Biblica, Inc.™ Used by permission of Zondervan.

All rights reserved. No part of this publication may be reproduced, stored in a retrieval system or transmitted, in any form or by any means, electronic, mechanical, photocopying, recording or otherwise, without the prior written permission of the publisher or the Copyright Licensing Agency.

Requests to reuse content from Langham Publishing are processed through PLSclear. Please visit www.plsclear.com to complete your request.

British Library Cataloguing-in-Publication Data
A catalogue record for this book is available from the British Library

ISBN: 978-1-78368-747-3

Cover & Book Design: projectluz.com

Langham Partnership actively supports theological dialogue and an author's right to publish but does not necessarily endorse the views and opinions set forth here or in works referenced within this publication, nor can we guarantee technical and grammatical correctness. Langham Partnership does not accept any responsibility or liability to persons or property as a consequence of the reading, use or interpretation of its published content.

Dedicated to the pioneers of evangelical faith in Russia –
the men and women of God who often sacrificed
their freedom and lives for the sake of the gospel.
Your work has brought forth much fruit.

Contents

Acknowledgements xi
Abstract xiii
Abbreviations xv
Chapter 1 1
   Introduction
      A Brief Historical Overview 3
      The Current Socio-Political and Religious Context of Russia ... 8
      Research Problem 28
      Purpose of the Study 30
      Research Questions 30
      Definition of Terms 30
      Significance of the Research 32

Chapter 2 35
   The Development of Evangelical Mission Theology Since 1910
      A Historical Overview 35
      Evangelical Mission Theology in the Global Context 39
      The Essence of the Gospel 40
      The Church's Identity and Its Role in Mission 48
      Cultural Engagement in Mission 53
      Holistic Mission 66
      Concluding Summary 73

Chapter 3 77
   Russian Baptist Mission Theology in Context, 1867–1991
      Historical Roots of Russian Baptist Theology 77
      International Connections during This Period 80
      Russian Baptists' Missiological Convictions 82
      Revivalist Pietism: 1867–1905 83
          Historical Background 83
          The Nature of the Gospel 86
          The Identity and Purpose of the Church 88
          Cultural Engagement 91
          Holistic Mission 94
      Transformationist Pietism: 1905–1930 96
          Historical Background 96

	The Nature of the Gospel	98
	The Identity and Purpose of the Church	102
	Cultural Engagement	106
	Holistic Mission	109
Escapist Pietism: 1944–1991		112
	Historical Background	112
	The Nature of the Gospel	115
	The Identity and Purpose of the Church	120
	Cultural Engagement	124
	The View of Holistic Mission	128
Concluding Summary		133

Chapter 4 137

Conceptual Framework and Methodology

- Theoretical Framework 137
- Research Method 140
- Research Questions 141
- Research Population and Sample 141
- Research Procedures 142
- Validity and Reliability 143
- Research Delimitations 144
- Research Limitations 145
- Research Bias 145

Chapter 5 147

Research Findings, Part I: The Participants' Views on the Theology of Mission

- Introductory Comments 147
- The Contours of Russian Baptist Mission Theology 148
    - The Nature of the Gospel 148
    - The Kingdom of God 154
    - The Identity and Purpose of the Church 156
    - Cultural Engagement 159
    - Holistic Mission 171

Chapter 6 181

Research Findings, Part II: The Need for Revisions to Traditional Missiological Views and Ways of Introducing Them

- Group One: Revisions in the Traditionalist Perspective 182
    - Reflections on the Experience of Baptist Mission in Russia 182
    - Suggested Missiological Revisions 187
- Group Two: Revisions from the Innovators' Perspective 194

  Reflections on the Experience of Baptist Mission in Russia 194
  Suggested Missiological Revisions 208
  The Innovators on the Process of Revision 227

Chapter 7 231
Conclusions and Implications
  Summary of the Chapters..231
  The Answers to the Research Questions by Those Espousing the
   Traditionalist Paradigm 237
    The Contours of Russian Baptist Mission Theology.......................237
    Potential Missiological Revisions..239
  The Answers to the Research Questions by Those Espousing the
   Innovative Paradigm 240
    The Contours of Russian Baptist Mission Theology.......................240
    Potential Missiological Revisions..241
  Conclusions 243
  Implications 247
    Five Themes from Global Evangelical Missiology 253
    Approaches to Missiological Revisions 277
  Concluding Thoughts..280

Appendix 1 285
Informed Consent Form

Appendix 2 287
Interview Protocol

Appendix 3 289
Participants' Demographic Information

Appendix 4 291
A Missional Model of Theological Education

Bibliography..293

Acknowledgements

I am abundantly grateful to the individuals who made this research possible. First of all, I am thankful to my professors Craig Ott, Harold Netland, Robert Priest, and Tite Tiénou for many hours of instruction and for modeling a lifetime commitment to mission, academic excellence, and gracious humility. I am also thankful to my fellow students who enriched our learning experiences by their valuable insights from around the world. Last, but certainly not the least, I want to express my deep appreciation to the individuals, often anonymous, who generously extended their financial support throughout the years of my study at Trinity International University, and to my friends whose encouragement and prayers helped me to accomplish this project.

Abstract

Since the disintegration of the USSR and the arrival of religious freedom, many Russian Baptists have actively engaged in evangelism, church planting, and acts of social service. Today, twenty-five years later, the sweeping changes in Russian society invite reflection on the effectiveness of the past mission efforts and their possible adjustment in light of the current challenges in context. In this process, one can focus either on Baptist missionary methods or on the underlying theological principles and presuppositions that have directed their mission work. Lack of the academic literature on Russian Baptist mission theology suggests that these principles may not yet have been systematically analyzed or formally articulated.

This research uses qualitative methods to explore aspects of Russian Baptist mission theology as perceived by thirty key leaders of the Russian Union of Evangelical Christians-Baptists (RUECB). The study focuses, first, on their understandings of the gospel, the church, the nature of the church's mission, and the principles of cultural engagement. Second, it investigates their views regarding the need to introduce revisions to traditional missiological convictions in light of the current Russian context. One of the assumptions underlying this research is that Russian Baptists should see themselves as legitimate participants in missiological conversations with the global evangelical community. Hence, the principal background of the research is found in contemporary mission theologies working within the framework of the Lausanne Movement.

The findings reveal that the missiological thinking of the current Russian Baptist leadership – academic, denominational, and pastoral – reflects two distinct theological paradigms, which in this research are identified as "traditional" and "innovative." The traditional paradigm, with some modifications, closely corresponds to the otherworldly, dualistic, and inward-focused model which Russian Baptists developed during the late-Soviet period of their history. The innovative paradigm, on the other hand, is in many respects parallel to recent developments in global evangelical missiology with its more comprehensive view of the gospel, missional ecclesiology, critical cultural engagement, and a holistic understanding of mission. The final chapter of the research suggests five themes for further dialogue with the global evangelical community, which can facilitate the transition of Russian Baptist missiology from the late-Soviet model of eschatological escapism to those of a holistic, missional evangelicalism.

Abbreviations

AUCECB	All-Union Council of Evangelical Christians and Baptists
CRAC	Council of Religious Affairs and Cults
CRESR	Consultation on the Relationship between Evangelism and Social Responsibility
FSU	Former Soviet Union
ICCECB	International Council of Churches of Evangelical Christians-Baptists
IMC	International Missionary Council
LCWE	Lausanne Committee for World Evangelization
LOP	Lausanne Occasional Paper
LTWG	Lausanne Theology Working Group
NAE	National Association of Evangelicals
RST	Russian Synodal Translation of the Bible
RUECB	Russian Union of Evangelical Christians-Baptists
RUB	Russian Union of Baptists
RUGB	Russian Union of the Gospel Christians
RST	Russian Synodal Translation of the Bible (1876)
USSR	Union of the Soviet Socialist Republics
WCC	World Council of Churches
WEA	World Evangelical Alliance

CHAPTER 1

Introduction

The purpose of this research is to explore aspects of Russian Baptist mission theology in conversation with contemporary global evangelical missiologies working within the general framework of the Lausanne Movement. More specifically, I focus on the perceptions of four key missiological concepts (the gospel, the identity of the church, the nature of the church's mission, and the principles of cultural engagement) by leaders of the Russian Union of Evangelical Christians-Baptists (RUECB). The research also investigates these leaders' convictions regarding the need for and ways of introducing possible revisions to traditional missiological views in light of the current socio-political and religious contexts of Russia.

This book was written at a time when Russian Baptists are celebrating several important dates. Exactly one hundred fifty years ago, on 20 August 1867, the first Russian Baptist, Nikita Voronin, was baptized by German pastor Martin Kalweit in a small river near Tbilisi in the Caucasus. This event marked the official beginning of the Baptist faith in Russia.[1] The year 2017 also marks the five-hundredth anniversary of the Protestant Reformation, the movement of ecclesiastical restoration to which Russian Baptists look as their source and inspiration. And the year 2017 is the centennial year of the

---

1. Other groups that practiced believers' baptism had existed previously in Russia, including small groups of German Baptists who served expatriates and much larger communities of Mennonites. Although these descendants of German-Dutch Anabaptists were allowed to establish agricultural colonies in Southern Russia beginning in 1789, any proselytism among Orthodox peasants was strictly prohibited, so Mennonite churches consisted exclusively of German-speaking believers. The significance of Voronin's baptism was that he became the first known Baptist of Russian ethnicity. S. N. Savinskii, P. D. Savchenko, and I. P. Dik, eds., *Istoriia Evangel'skikh Khristian-Baptistov v SSSR [History of Evangelical Christians-Baptists in the USSR]* (Moscow: VSEKhB, 1989), 75.

Russian Revolution which introduced many tragic pages in the history of Russian Baptists and for decades defined the nature of their relationship with the state. Finally, the year 2017 marks a quarter of a century since the beginning of long-awaited freedom for evangelism and church planting in Russia.[2]

The need for this research stems, however, not only from these important dates, but also from the significant changes in the political, religious, and social landscape of Russia over the last two decades. It appears that today, one generation after the collapse of the USSR, the transition of Russia from the Soviet Empire to a nation-state, and from the ideological vacuum of the 1990s to a more or less established ideology, is largely over. In fact, it seems fair to say that Russian society is entering into a new, post-post-Soviet epoch.[3] Especially since the takeover of Crimea early in 2014, the social and political contours of a new Russia have become more apparent and distinct. Religiously, the majority of Russian population today identifies themselves as Christians, in stark contrast to the state atheism of the earlier period.[4] The rapid growth of evangelical churches characteristic of the decade of the 1990s has largely stopped or returned to pre-perestroika levels.[5] All these factors call for reflection on, and evaluation of, the past models, both theoretical and

---

2. Religious freedom was restored in Russia around 1988, but Baptists, by and large, became involved in active evangelism after the kickoff revival conference in Moscow led by Dr Billy Graham in the fall of 1992.

3. Piotr Dutkiewicz, Vladimir Kulikov, and Richard Sakwa, eds., *The Social History of Post-Communist Russia* (London; New York: Routledge, 2016); Igor Bobrov, "Pirrova Pobeda [A Pyrrhic Victory]," 2017, http://www.igorbobrov.com/2017/07/blog-post_4.html.

4. A 2012 survey by the Levada Center, an independent research group, suggests that 68 percent of Russians think of themselves as Orthodox Christians (against 56 percent in 2002) and 7 percent identify as Muslims (4 percent in 2002). Followers of Catholicism, Protestantism, and Judaism are 1 percent each. The number of atheists fell from 32 percent in 2002 to 19 percent in 2012. At the same time, only 4–6 percent of respondents regularly participate in the life of a religious community, which suggests that most Russians see their religiosity in terms of cultural or ethnic identification. Galina Gribanova, "Ethnic and Religious Relations in Russia Since the 1980s," in *The Social History of Post-Communist Russia*, ed. Piotr Dutkiewicz, Vladimir Kulikov, and Richard Sakwa (London; New York: Routledge, 2016), 222; cf. Boris Dubin, "Massovoe Pravoslavie v Rossii [The Mass Orthodoxy in Russia]," 2000, http://www.index.org.ru/journal/11/dubin.html; Nataliia Zorkaia, "Pravoslavie v Bezreligioznom Obschetve [The Orthodox Church in a Secular Society]," *Vestnik Obschestvennogo Mneniia [Messenger of Public Opinion]* 100, no. 2 (2009): 65–84.

5. Sergei Golovin, "The Missing Dimension of Evangelism in Post-Communist Society," *Religion in Eastern Europe* 28 (2008): 27; Alexander Yuchkovski, "A Comparison of the Evangelical Movement in Russia in the 1920s and the 1990s," (PhD diss., Oxford Centre for Mission Studies, 2014), 120.

practical, of Baptist mission in the country, with the purpose of adjusting and fine-tuning them in the changing socio-political and religious environment. This research focuses on the theoretical concepts that have undergirded the mission efforts of Russian Baptists.

A Brief Historical Overview

Although the focus of this dissertation is on the theology of mission, a short sketch of the history of the Baptist movement in Russia will provide the context for understanding the relationship between its social environment and its general outlook. The Russian Union of Evangelical Christians-Baptists is the oldest and second largest evangelical denomination in Russia. This movement was born in the second half of the nineteenth century thanks to the publishing of a Russian New Testament in 1822 and the mission work of German Baptists, Mennonites, and British revivalist preachers. Encouraged by the end of serfdom in 1861 and the opening of "people's schools" throughout the Empire, many religious seekers, who were repelled by the moral decadence of many among the Orthodox clergy, found alternative expressions of Christianity in evangelical pietism. The resulting groups of converts blossomed into a full-blown evangelical movement that grew from a handful of believers in the 1860s to about half a million baptized members in 1929.[6]

To describe the origin of the evangelical movement in Russia, Russian Baptist historians often use the metaphor of three independent tributaries fusing into an ever-widening stream. The first baptism in Tbilisi soon resulted in the organization of a small, specifically Baptist fellowship with Voronin as its first pastor. This church soon planted multiple daughter communities across the Caucasus region of Russia. Around the same time, in what is now southern Ukraine, the movement known as *Shtundism* began to grow through the influence of German Mennonite and Lutheran colonists. A third distinctive movement was born among aristocrats in the capital of the Russian Empire

---

6. Savinskii, Savchenko, and Dik, *Istoriia Evangel'skikh Khristian-Baptistov v SSSR [History of Evangelical Christians-Baptists in the USSR]*; Sergey Sannikov, ed., *Istoriia Baptizma [A History of Baptist Faith]* (Odessa: Bogomyslie, 1996); S. N. Savinskii, *Istoriia Evangel'skikh Khristian-Baptistov Ukrainy, Rossii, Belorussii: 1867–1917 [History of Evangelical Christians-Baptists of Ukraine, Russia, and Belarus: 1867–1917]* (St Petersburg: Bibliia dlia vsekh, 1999); Yuchkovski, "Comparison of the Evangelical Movement."

in 1874, when Lord Radstock, an Anglican revivalist preacher, arrived in St. Petersburg with an evangelistic mission. The present day Russian Union of Evangelical Christians-Baptists stands in direct continuity with all three of these initially unrelated groups.[7]

By the end of the first decade of the twentieth century these diverse groups of converts were formalized into two distinctive denominations, or *unions:* the Russian Union of Baptists (RUB) and the Russian Union of Gospel Christians (RUGC).[8] The former united the Baptist and Shtundist communities in Ukraine and the Caucasus, while the latter gathered together primarily those churches that had originated from the aristocrat-led movement in St Petersburg. Despite multiple attempts at unification into one denomination, the two unions remained separate and often competitive, largely because the much stricter Baptists had a hard time accepting the more "centered-set" views of the Gospel Christians. The latter allowed far more flexibility in relationships with other Christian groups, recognized (though did not practice) infant baptism during the initial years of their movement, did not require official ordination for administering baptism or presiding over the Lord's Supper, and in general had a looser attitude toward the standardization of doctrine and the achievement of uniformity. Their leadership belonged to a higher socioeconomic spectrum and were more "cosmopolitan" in their outlook.[9]

The growth rate of the two unions was phenomenal, especially after the Communist Revolution in 1917 and the subsequent decree on the separation of church and state. By 1907, Russian Baptists had two indigenous, locally

---

7. Savinskii, Savchenko, and Dik, *Istoriia Evangel'skikh Khristian-Baptistov v SSSR* [*History of Evangelical Christians-Baptists in the USSR*]; Sannikov, *Istoriia Baptizma* [*A History of Baptist Faith*]; Savinskii, *Istoriia Evangel'skikh Khristian-Baptistov Ukrainy, Rossii, Belorussii: 1867–1917* [*History of Evangelical Christians-Baptists of Ukraine, Russia, and Belarus: 1867–1917*]; Andrey P. Puzynin, *The Tradition of the Gospel Christians: A Study of Their Identity and Theology during the Russian, Soviet, and Post-Soviet Periods*, Kindle Edition (Eugene, OR: Pickwick, 2011).

8. They are sometimes referred to as "Evangelical Christians," but as Heather Coleman and Andrey Puzynin correctly observe, the term "Gospel Christians" is a more precise translation of the corresponding Russian term. Heather Jean Coleman, *Russian Baptists and Spiritual Revolution, 1905–1929* (Bloomington: Indiana University Press, 2005); Puzynin, *Tradition of the Gospel Christians*. This term is also helpful in distinguishing this group from broader global evangelicalism.

9. Catherine Wanner, *Communities of the Converted: Ukrainians and Global Evangelism* (Ithaca: Cornell University Press, 2007); Coleman, *Russian Baptists and Spiritual Revolution*; Puzynin, *Tradition of the Gospel Christians*.

supported mission agencies. They developed strong educational and financial partnerships with their fellow believers in the West and became members of the World Baptist Alliance at its very first congress in 1905. At the height of the movement in 1929 the two groups together included approximately 500,000 baptized believers and along with family members, represented a total community of as many as four million people.[10]

However, when Stalin solidified his power, evangelicals entered a decade of severe persecution which "remains their red or bloody decade without peer."[11] By the fall of 1929, the federal office of the Baptist Union in Moscow and all of the regional associations were closed, because all of their officials had been arrested. By the mid-thirties the total number of evangelicals was down to 250,000, and by the end of the 1930s the church had virtually ceased to exist as an institution. Most church buildings were expropriated by the authorities while large numbers of pastors were sent to labor camps or executed. All official religious life ceased.[12]

The state policies aimed at the eradication of the evangelical movement would perhaps have succeeded, had it not been for World War II. In 1944, the Soviet government designated the leaders of the Gospel Christians as the unifying center for the creation of a single government-controlled denomination, representing the merger of the two former denominations into a single body.[13] The resulting denomination took the name of the All-Union Council of Evangelical Christians and Baptists (AUCECB).[14] The new Union sought

---

10. During the first seven years of the Communist epoch (1917–1924), both Gospel Christians and Baptists increased their numbers almost fivefold. By 1924, the growth rate in Siberia was 10 percent annually, while in Ukraine it was 15 percent. Walter Sawatsky, *Soviet Evangelicals Since World War II* (Kitchener, ON; Scottdale, PA: Herald, 1981), 39. See also Sannikov, *Istoriia Baptizma [A History of Baptist Faith]*; Savinskii, *Istoriia Evangel'skikh Khristian-Baptistov Ukrainy, Rossii, Belorussii: 1867–1917 [History of Evangelical Christians-Baptists of Ukraine, Russia, and Belarus: 1867–1917]*; Wanner, *Communities of the Converted*; Yuchkovski, "Comparison of the Evangelical Movement."

11. Sawatsky, *Soviet Evangelicals*, 48.

12. Steve Durasoff, *The Russian Protestants* (Cranbury, NJ: Associated University Presses, 1969); Sawatsky, *Soviet Evangelicals*; Albert W. Olema, *History of Evangelical Christianity in Russia* (Dallas, TX: No Publisher, 1983); Coleman, *Russian Baptists and Spiritual Revolution*.

13. Most likely, the change in the state's policies during the War was precipitated by the Communist Party's intention "to channel the nation's religious forces" to serve patriotic causes during WWII. Durasoff, *Russian Protestants*, 99.

14. Soon, the "and" between "Evangelical (i.e. Gospel) Christians *and* Baptists" in the name of the denomination was replaced by a hyphen. The shortcut name "Baptist" became a

to stress its continuity with the past, but it was very much a new creation.¹⁵ In contrast to the vision of its founders, it was no longer a free association of churches, but a hierarchical structure that imposed an essentially "episcopalian" control system that governed in top-down fashion.¹⁶ The primary purpose of this "bureaucratic pyramid" was to "exercise significant oversight over evangelical life," allowing its leaders to suppress the evangelistic activity of its own members.¹⁷ The Union also developed its own eighty-page periodical, *Bratskii Vestnik* (The Brotherly Herald), which served as a key instrument for shaping the movement's theology and identity. Over the years, it helped formalize and institutionalize what up until then had been largely diverse, orally transmitted practices, agreed upon by local leaders.¹⁸

In the 1950s, the policies of Khrushchev that resulted in the reduction of the number of political prisoners led to the revitalization of Baptist communities, as many faithful and committed believers returned from labor camps and prisons. The new wave of explosive growth, however, prompted the state to tighten its regulation of local congregational life through much stricter control and the mandatory registration of local churches. Just as during Stalin's time, the Soviet government was still bent on the complete eradication of religion, but this time by means of propaganda, Communist indoctrination, and social ostracism.¹⁹ In 1961, the response to these governmental measures led to a

---

generic word for "evangelicals" in the Soviet Union, especially after the inclusion of Pentecostals in 1945; the Salvation Army, the so-called Free Darbyists, the Church of Christ, and Pentecostal Unitarians in 1946–1947; and the Mennonite Brethren in 1963. Savinskii, Savchenko, and Dik, *Istoriia Evangel'skikh Khristian-Baptistov v SSSR* [*History of Evangelical Christians-Baptists in the USSR*].

15. Sawatsky, *Soviet Evangelicals*, 16.

16. Alexey Sinichkin, *Vozrozhdenie Vopreki Bezbozhiiu* [*Revival Despite Godlessness*] (Korosten, Ukraine: Triada, 2015), 139.

17. Wanner, *Communities of the Converted*, 58; Sawatsky, *Soviet Evangelicals*; Sinichkin, *Vozrozhdenie Vopreki Bezbozhiiu* [*Revival despite Godlessness*].

18. Puzynin, *Tradition of the Gospel Christians*, 195–96; Wanner, *Communities of the Converted*, 59.

19. Lev Mitrokhin outlines two distinct periods in Soviet history with different approaches to church-state relations: the era of "militant atheism" (1920s–1930s) and the era of "scientific atheism" (1950s–1980s). During the first period persecution was more physical in nature, while during the second the state emphasized education as the means of cultivating "a new kind of man." Nevertheless, during both periods the government aimed at the eradication of religious "superstitions" as incompatible with the new social order. L. N. Mitrokhin, *Baptism: Istoriya i Sovremennost'* [*Baptists: History and Modernity*] (St. Petersburg: RKhGI, 1997), 42–62; Olena Panych, "Soviet Baptism after World War II: Rethinking the Concept of Church," in

deep split among Baptist believers, dividing them into two distinct groups: those who preferred to accept the obligation to register, and those who openly challenged the authorities by refusing to register.[20] The split remains in place until today with the second group, known as the International Council of Churches of Evangelical Christians-Baptists (ICCECB) remaining a small and internally focused group.[21]

After the disintegration of the Soviet Union in 1991, the associations of the AUCECB in the former Soviet republics withdrew their membership in the Union and created their own national unions. As a result, the AUCECB changed its name to the Russian Union of Evangelical Christians-Baptists (RUECB) and since then has remained one of the largest Protestant denominations in the country. The twenty-five years of religious freedom have witnessed active mission efforts by both foreign mission agencies and local workers. Hundreds of new churches or groups have been started.[22] Today, the RUECB includes about 1,800 communities in fifty-two regional associations with around 75,000 baptized members. Despite the growth, however, this number remains at approximately the same level of .05 percent of the Russian population where it was in 1992, and is today steadily declining.[23] One obvious reason for this decrease is the several waves of emigration to the

---

History and Mission in Europe: Continuing the Conversation, ed. Mary Raber and Peter F. Penner (Schwarzenfeld, Germany: Neufeld Verlag, 2011), 143.

20. Puzynin, *Tradition of the Gospel Christians*, 195; Tatiana Nikol'skaia, "Istoriia Dvizheniia Baptistov-Initsiativnikov [The History of the Baptist Initsiativniki Movement]," in *History and Mission in Europe: Continuing the Conversation*, ed. Mary Raber and Peter F. Penner (Schwarzenfeld, Germany: Neufeld Verlag, 2011), 111–140.

21. Olga Bokova, "Teologia Rossiiskikh Evangel'skikh Khristian-Baptistov Na Rubezhe XX i XXI Vekov [Theology of Russian Evangelical Christians-Baptists at the Turn of the Twenty-First Century]" (PhD diss., St. Petersburg State University, 2011). In the 1970s, a number of local communities detached themselves from the ICCECB to organize yet another Baptist group known as "autonomous Baptists." Neither of the two splinter groups is the focus of this research.

22. Based on her analysis of Baptist periodicals, Olga Bokova affirms that during 1992 about 9,700 new members joined the churches of the Union and eighty-nine new churches or groups were started in addition to the existing 891. By 1993 the RUECB had 73,741 members. In the period from 1994 to 1998, the growth was another six thousand members. By 1998, the number of newly planted churches was 230. By 2005, the growth largely came to a stop. Bokova, 15–16.

23. According to the official website of the RUECB, five thousand new members were baptized all over Russia in 1999, and the total membership reached 86,500. In 2008, the number of baptized persons was 551, almost nine times fewer, with total membership being 75,160. "Krizis Bogosluzheniia v Evangel'skikh Cerkviakh. Chto Dal'she? [The Crisis of Worship in Evangelical Churches. What's Next?]," 2009, https://baptist.org.ru/read/article/94462.

United States, Germany, and some other Western countries.[24] But as we shall see, most participants in this research agree that another major reason has been that Baptist mission efforts after 1992 were not as successful as expected. Today, when many Western missionary organizations are wrapping up their work in Russia, the reality is that there is little overall clarity or agreement as to how the Baptist mission to their compatriots should look going forward.

The Current Socio-Political and Religious Context of Russia

One of the missiological assumptions underlying this research is that a faithful missionary encounter with culture happens when a church community "embodies God's particular word of grace and judgment . . . within each culture, in its own speech and symbol."[25] From this perspective, to renew its mission efforts the church must not only faithfully articulate the gospel but also probe the reigning "story and fundamental assumptions of a specific culture."[26] It is therefore important to provide an analysis of the most important social developments in Russia that shape the ideological climate in which the mission of Russian Baptists is taking place. In addition, attention to the context may help to discern those areas where the church has tended to uncritically accommodate itself to cultural forces, thereby losing its countercultural stance.

On 18 March 2015, about 100,000 Russians flooded into Red Square in Moscow to celebrate the first anniversary of the takeover of Crimea. The crowd was waving Russian national flags and holding signs reading, "I am proud of my country," "Crimea is the birthplace of the Russian spirit," and "Putin is the savior of Russia." The celebration culminated in a short address by President Putin who said that the takeover of Crimea was "not about land mass of which we have plenty. It was rather about the very sources of our history, spirituality, and statehood; it was about those things that make us

---

24. Yuchkovski, "Comparison of the Evangelical Movement."

25. Lesslie Newbigin, *The Gospel in a Pluralist Society* (Grand Rapids, MI: Eerdmans, 1989), 152. See chapter 4 of this research for a more detailed presentation of the conceptual framework of the dissertation.

26. Michael W. Goheen, *Introducing Christian Mission Today: Scripture, History, and Issues*, Kindle Edition (Downers Grove, IL: IVP Academic, 2014), 4954–4956.

one people and a strong, united nation."[27] Why is the annexation of Crimea, which most of the world considers an act of aggression against another sovereign state, celebrated in Russia as an act of national glory? And how does the rise of Russian national consciousness which this event both catalyzed and symbolized shape the current social context in the country?

In the post-Communist transition from the Soviet empire to a nation-state, Russia has taken a significantly different path than many other former republics of the USSR. If the latter regarded their independence as a historical chance to build sovereign democratic states, for the vast majority of Russian citizens the disintegration of the USSR was accompanied by a tremendous sense of loss.[28] President Putin expressed this sentiment in his well-known comment that "the collapse of the Soviet Union was the main geopolitical disaster of the century . . . As for the Russian nation, it became a genuine drama."[29] For centuries, Russians in other parts of the Empire and later the Soviet Union behaved as if they were at home, ignoring the local cultures and languages and expecting the local peoples to adapt to Russian ways. In 1991, all of a sudden about 25 million ethnic Russians found themselves "abroad" in the now-independent states of the former Soviet Union which formerly were considered the outskirts of great Russia.[30] Dmitrii Furman[31] and Richard Sakwa[32] suggest that it was primarily this "generalized 'imperial' attitude" that made it difficult for Russians to identify with the Russian Federation as a separate homeland.[33]

---

27. Shaun Walker, "Russia Celebrates Anniversary of Crimea Takeover and Eyes Second Annexation," 2015, https://www.theguardian.com/world/2015/mar/18/russia-celebrates-anniversary-crimea-takeover-eyes-second-annexation.

28. Mikhail Gorshkov, "Twenty Years That Shook Russia: Public Opinion on the Reforms," in *The Social History of Post-Communist Russia*, ed. Piotr Dutkiewicz, Vladimir Kulikov, and Richard Sakwa (London; New York: Routledge, 2016), 95.

29. Vladimir Putin, "Annual Address to the Federal Assembly of the Russian Federation," 2005, http://kremlin.ru/events/president/transcripts/22931.

30. Interfax, "Alexander Chepurin: 'Za Predelami Rossii Seichas Prozhivaet Okolo 30 Millionov Nashikh Sootechestvennikov' [Alexander Chepurin: 'About 30 million of Our Compatriots Live Outside of Russia Now']," 2010, https://www.interfax.ru/interview/131938.

31. Dmitrii Furman, "Ot Rossiiskoi Imperii k Russkomu Demokraticheskomu Gosudarstvu [From the Russian Empire to a Russian Democratic State]," 2010, http://polit.ru/article/2010/12/08/furman/.

32. Richard Sakwa, "Nation and Nationalism in Russia," in *The SAGE Handbook of Nations and Nationalism*, ed. Gerard Delanty and Krishan Kumar (London: Sage, 2006), 410–424.

33. Sakwa, "Nation and Nationalism," 416.

Several other important factors must also be taken into account. The loss of superpower status and the humiliation of the geopolitical defeat in the Cold War; the collapse of the industrial complex and the unprecedented economic inequality caused by the failure of reforms; NATO wars in the former Yugoslavia, Afghanistan, and Iraq; and the promotion of a liberal agenda including LGBT propaganda – all of this played into the gradual disappointment of Russians with the new status quo and the ideals of Western democracy.[34] Inside the country, an ideological vacuum left by Communism was quickly filled with local ethnic and religious narratives, especially in predominantly Muslim regions such as Tatarstan, Chechnya, and Dagestan. Given the weak federal power, this posed the threat of the disintegration of the entire country.[35] By 1999, when Vladimir Putin came to power, there was a widespread desire to restore greater integrity to the state, which Putin was able to achieve through a combination of military actions and the construction of a top-down governing system (the so-called "power vertical"). His political success was propped up by extremely high oil prices ($143 per barrel in 2008 as compared to $18 in 1990), providing even greater contrast with the "disastrous 1990s" in the popular consciousness.[36]

In the minds of many Russians the takeover of Crimea in 2014 became a sure sign of Russia's resurgence on the international scene. The state-sponsored media interpreted it as a victory against the plot to weaken Russia through the Ukrainian coup d'état inspired by and manipulated from the West. Support for Putin rocketed from 60 percent to 86–88 percent.[37] Recent polls indicate that 83 percent of Russian citizens approve of Putin's leadership.

---

34. Natalya Tikhonova, "The Russian Roller Coaster: Changes in Social Structure in the Post-Communist Period," in *The Social History of Post-Communist Russia*, ed. Piotr Dutkievicz, Vladimir Kulikov, and Richard Sakwa (London; New York: Routledge, 2016), 130–150; Leonid Grigoriev, "Transformation: For the People or for the Elite?," in *The Social History of Post-Communist Russia*, ed. Piotr Dutkiewicz, Vladimir Kulikov, and Richard Sakwa (London; New York: Routledge, 2016), 81–94; Charles Clover, *Black Wind, White Snow: The Rise of Russia's New Nationalism* (New Haven: Yale University Press, 2016).

35. Gribanova, "Ethnic and Religious Relations."

36. Sakwa, "Nation and Nationalism," 417; Vladimir Popov and Piotr Dutkievicz, "A Time of Transition: Changes in Reality and Perceptions," in *The Social History of Post-Communist Russia*, ed. Piotr Dutkievicz, Vladimir Kulikov, and Richard Sakwa (London; New York: Routledge, 2016), 41–57.

37. "Iiul'skie Reitingi Odobreniia i Doveriia [July Ratings of Approval and Trust]," 2015, https://www.levada.ru/2015/07/23/iyulskie-rejtingi-odobreniya-i-doveriya-6/.

For the first time since 2008, a majority of Russians (73 percent) believe their country's leadership is leading them in the right direction, and they have confidence in the country's military (78 percent).[38] These numbers seem to suggest that the time of "a vague perception of themselves," when many Russians felt "confused, vacillating, insecure, and prone to negative self-identification," is being left behind.[39] President Putin has been able to provide them with "a unifying label," which people had been craving since the early 1990s, namely, the concept of a "great Russia."[40] As a result, after their disappointment with Communism and Western democracy, large masses of Russians now again feel that they belong to something significant, and they are willing to surrender to a leader who provides them with this collective frame of reference.[41]

In addition to perceptions of Russia as a "great country" and approval of its leader, another basic element of the "post-Crimean consensus" has been a strong anti-Western sentiment.[42] Over three-fourths of Russians are sure that their country has enemies and over half the population think that these enemies pose a real threat, according to a recent poll conducted by the Levada Center, an independent research group.[43] It is believed that Western countries led by America want to see Russia divided into smaller and weaker states in order to get access to its natural resources. Russian defense minister

---

38. Julie Ray and Neli Esipova, "Russian Approval of Putin Soars to Highest Level in Years," 2014, https://news.gallup.com/poll/173597/russian-approval-putin-soars-highest-level-years.aspx.

39. Anna Geifman and Yuri Teper, "Russia's New National Identity under Putin's Regime," *BESA Center Perspectives Paper* 279 (2014): 2, https://besacenter.org/perspectives-papers/russias-new-national-identity-putins-regime/.

40. Geifman and Teper, "Russia's New National Identity," 2.

41. As anthropologists observe, cultural traditions bestow a certain "pedigree" upon even "the most humble member" of a group, allowing him or her "to identify with heroic times, great deeds and a genealogy." Manning Nash, "The Core Elements of Ethnicity," in *Ethnicity*, ed. John Hutchinson and Antony D. Smith (Oxford: Oxford University Press, 1996), 27. A national self-identity, linked to a "valorized and idealized nation-state, provide[s] the person with a sense of agency and empowerment in realms apart from work, rather than powerlessness and submission." Langman, "Social Psychology of Nationalism," 74.

42. Alexei Levinson, "Proektsiia Rosii Na Zapad [Russia's Projection to the West]," 2017, https://www.vedomosti.ru/opinion/columns/2017/04/11/685051-proektsiya-rossii; Andrei Kolesnikov, "Russian Ideology after Crimea," 2015, https://carnegie.ru/2015/09/22/russian-ideology-after-crimea-pub-61350.

43. Artem Zhitenev, "Most Russians Feel Threat from External Enemies, Poll Shows," 2017, https://www.rt.com/politics/373929-most-russians-feel-threat-from/; Levada-Center, "Russia and the World," 2014, https://www.levada.ru/en/2014/10/22/russia-and-the-world/.

Sergey Shoigu complained recently that there are still so many citizens who are "blind" and must "recover their sight" to see the reality of the NATO threat at Russia's western borders.⁴⁴ Besides the direct military threat, the so-called Arab Spring and the "colored revolutions" in some East European countries are seen as part of a conspiracy aimed at replacing independent governments with pro-Western leaders in the process of building a total "hegemony" of the West.⁴⁵

This anti-Western narrative, according to political expert Lilia Shevtsova, has become the most important element of self-legitimization by the Russian ruling elite and the primary justification for the way it rules both inside and outside the country.⁴⁶ In the area of external politics, Russia seems to have taken a course that aims at the restoration of power balance in what since 1991 has been a unipolar world. While the USSR can hardly be restored, Moscow strives to transform much of the territory lost into a zone of privileged Russian interests.⁴⁷ There is also a search for potential allies of the Russian government with its conservative moral and social agenda among anti-Western political parties in Europe and beyond.⁴⁸ Whether feasible or not, the stated ideal is some form of division of spheres of influence similar to the post-WWII agreements between the superpowers.⁴⁹ This makes Russian political discourse

---

44. Pavel Felgengauer, "Vostochnyi Flang Trebuet Peremen [The Eastern Wind Requires Changes]," 2017, https://www.novayagazeta.ru/articles/2017/07/01/72978-vostochnyy-flang-trebuet-peremen.

45. Lyndon LaRouche, "Colored Revolutions 'Illegal Warfare Under International Law and Federal Constitution,'" 2014, https://larouchepac.com/20141103/colored-revolutions-illegal-warfare.

46. Lilia Shevtsova, "Udar Po Modeli Suschestvovaniia Rossii [A Blow at Russia's Model of Existence]," 2017, https://nv.ua/opinion/shevcova/udar-po-modeli-sushchestvovanija-rossii-1209848.html.

47. Walter Laquer, "After the Fall: Russia in Search of a New Ideology," *World Affairs* 176, no. 6 (2014): 71–77.

48. Gustav Gressel, "Fellow Travelers: Russia, Anti-Westernism, and Europe's Political Parties," 2017, https://www.ecfr.eu/publications/summary/fellow_travellers_russia_anti_westernism_and_europes_political_parties_7213?utm_content=buffer72a49&utm_medium=social&utm_source=twitter.com&utm_campaign=buffer.

49. Sergei Lavrov, "Remarks and Answers to Media Questions at the Primakov Readings International Forum, Moscow, June 30, 2017," 2017, http://www.mid.ru/foreign_policy/news/-/asset_publisher/cKNonkJE02Bw/content/id/2804842?p_p_id=101_INSTANCE_cKNonkJE02Bw&_101_INSTANCE_cKNonkJE02Bw_languageId=en_GB; Clover, *Black Wind, White Snow.*

almost completely focused on America "with the rest of the world just being an appendix to Russian-American bipolarity."[50]

In internal politics, the anti-Western narrative justifies firm control of the mass media, the suppression of political opposition, tight control of the candidate list on all levels of elections, and restrictive policies against NGOs. In the words of Charles Clover, "alternative interpretations" of political events in the state-controlled media make many Russians live in an "upside-down world," where black is white and white is black.[51] In fact, it has become common to refer to Russia's "weaponizing [of] misinformation" in order to create a "post-truth age."[52] The government is investing billions of dollars in such media as *Russia Today*, *Sputnik*, and Russian internet organizations that disseminate Kremlin viewpoints and half-truths outside the country. These media are "skillful at intermixing news and opinion, and often aim, at a minimum, to confuse the information space."[53]

Since 2014, freedom of expression has been significantly curtailed through a system of strict forms of punishment, including criminal prosecution, and pressure on independent media outlets has increased drastically.[54] Due to the notorious "foreign agent law" passed on 13 July 2012, basically any NGO that has the potential to influence public opinion can now be accused of political interference and stigmatized as an agent of foreign powers.[55] On a popular level, there is a widespread conviction that individuals and organizations that are not in complete agreement with current Russian politics are instruments for advancing foreign agendas. The notion of "national traitors," or a "fifth

---

50. Shevtsova, "Udar Po Modeli Suschestvovaniia Rossii [A Blow at Russia's Model of Existence]," n.p.

51. Clover, *Black Wind, White Snow*, 18.

52. Andrei Kolesnikov, "The October Revolution in Post-Truth Russia," 2017, https://carnegie.ru/2017/03/28/october-revolution-in-post-truth-russia-pub-68456; Samuel Osborne, "Russia 'Weaponising Misinformation' to Create 'Post-Truth Age' and Destabilise the West, Defence Secretary Warns," 2017, https://www.independent.co.uk/news/world/europe/russia-weaponising-misinformation-destabilise-west-nato-cyber-attacks-michael-fallon-a7560481.html; Ingo Mannteufel, "Vladimir Putin's Post-Truth Year of Success," 2016, https://www.dw.com/en/opinion-vladimir-putins-post-truth-year-of-success/a-36914293; Natalia Roudakova, *Losing Pravda. Ethics and the Press in Post-Truth Russia* (Cambridge: Cambridge University Press, 2017).

53. Andrey Makarychev, "The Russian World, Post-Truth, and Europe," 2017, http://www.ponarseurasia.org/memo/russian-world-post-truth-and-europe.

54. Kolesnikov, "Russian Ideology After Crimea."

55. Human Rights Watch, "Russia," 2017, https://www.hrw.org/europe/central-asia/russia.

column," introduced by President Putin in his "Crimea speech" in 2014, has since become a common element of public discourse.[56] The majority political party (not accidentally called "United Russia") has successively employed Cold War-era stereotypes to develop the personality cult of Vladimir Putin as the "national leader" and to impose uniformity through repressive legislation in the religious and political arenas.[57]

There is a debate among Western authors on whether the reemerging Russian nationalism is primarily defensive or offensive in nature. Some argue that Crimea was a justifiable one-off response to Ukrainian and Western provocation. The West needlessly soured its relations with Russia by expanding into territories that the Kremlin had abandoned after the collapse of Communism and unfairly demonized Vladimir Putin. So instead of fighting a new cold war, Western leaders should recognize the traumas the Russian people have been through and allow them to get on with restoring their historic heritage.[58] This perspective, however, not only ignores the legitimate issue of the self-determination of the former Soviet republics, but also

---

56. Vladimir Putin, "Address by President of the Russian Federation," 2014, http://en.kremlin.ru/events/president/news/20603; John R. Schindler, "Putin's Orthodox Jihad," 2014, http://www.interpretermag.com/putins-orthodox-jihad/.

57. Sakwa, "Bringing the People Back In," 290. See also a fascinating study by Valeria Kasamara and Anna Sorokina from the Moscow Higher School of Economics demonstrates that some form of social consensus regarding how Russians see themselves and others has emerged across all social strata. In this research they compared the political views of more than thirty members of parliament and almost a hundred homeless people and discovered close similarities both in the content and stylistics of the two groups. The three basic ideas on which the participants agree are: (1) the national exclusivity of Russians as a "special people" with a "special spirit"; (2) the perception of Russia as a "great country" that should play a leading role in global politics and economics, and which other countries should treat with fear and respect; and (3) the perception of most other countries as enemies or competitors of Russia. V. A. Kasamara and A. Sorokina, "Imperial Ambitions of Russians," *Communist and Post-Communist Studies* 45, no. 3–4 (2012): 279–288.

58. Henry A. Kissinger, "To Settle the Ukraine Crisis, Start at the End," 2014, https://www.washingtonpost.com/opinions/henry-kissinger-to-settle-the-ukraine-crisis-start-at-the-end/2014/03/05/46dad868-a496-11e3-8466-d34c451760b9_story.html?noredirect=on; Peter Hitchens, "The Cold War Is Over," 2016, https://www.firstthings.com/article/2016/10/the-cold-war-is-over; Christian Osthold, "Nur Wenn Europa eine Voraussetzung Beachtet, Kann Seine Ukrainepolitik Erfolg Haben [Only if Europe Takes into Account One Prerequisite Can Its Ukraine Policy Succeed]," 2017, https://www.focus.de/politik/experten/osthold/ukraine-konflikt-nur-wenn-europa-eine-voraussetzung-beachtet-kann-seine-ukrainepolitik-erfolg-haben_id_7523140.html.

demonstrates a lack of understanding that Putin is driven by an ideological agenda which considers the West a permanent threat.[59]

Charles Clover, in his well-documented research, describes the current version of Russian nationalism as "Eurasianism."[60] Originally developed in the 1920s as an apocalyptic vision by a group of Russian emigrant thinkers, it has been further elaborated over the last two decades by people like Alexander Dugin, a former professor at Moscow State University.[61] According to Dugin, the salvation of Russia lay in turning away from democratic liberalism and reestablishing repressive central control in order to bring into existence a multi-national, but distinctly Russian and non-Western geopolitical empire, "Eurasia." Running through the book is the idea that the Cold War was in reality the continuation of a permanent conflict between two geographical and civilizational realities – the world's greatest land power, Eurasia, and its natural opponent of "Atlantic" sea power, represented first by Britain and then by the USA. In statecraft there are no rules other than a drive for conquest; slogans such as "human rights" or "democracy" are mere window dressing and propaganda. Under their guise, the United States is working right now to destroy its foe.[62]

The geopolitical implications of this view of the world are being further developed by a number of political experts, writers, journalists, and politicians (e.g. the *Izborsk Club*) and popularized through the *Tsargrad* TV channel, talk shows, rock concerts, and even bike shows.[63] Moreover, Clover argues that the key ideas of Eurasianism are becoming increasingly manifest in Vladimir Putin's speeches, including his rejection of the concept of "nation-state" in

---

59. Schindler, "Putin's Orthodox Jihad"; Mark Movsesian, "Putin: Ideological, Not Irrational," 2014, https://www.firstthings.com/blogs/firstthoughts/2014/05/putin-ideological-not-rational; Edward Lucas, "The Realism We Need," 2016, https://www.firstthings.com/web-exclusives/2016/10/the-realism-we-need.
60. Clover, *Black Wind, White Snow*.
61. A. G. Dugin, *Osnovy Geopolitiki [The Basics of Geopolitics]* (Moscow: Arktogeya, 1997).
62. Dugin; Clover, *Black Wind, White Snow*.
63. Areg Galstyan, "Third Rome Rising: The Ideologues Calling for a New Russian Empire," 2016, https://nationalinterest.org/feature/third-rome-rising-the-ideologues-calling-new-russian-empire-16748. The Russian right wing is an endless list of individuals and small groups, of splits, reunions, and changing views. Besides the philosopher Alexander Dugin, some of the best known personalities are writer Alexander Prokhanov, scientist Zhores Alferov, and priest Ivan Okhlobystin. "Izborskii Klub [The Izborsk Club]," accessed 12 June 2017, https://izborsk-club.ru/.

favor of "civilizational state" and the vision of the Eurasian Union of the former Soviet states.[64]

For our purposes it is important to pay attention to the religious dimension of this ideology. A key role in shaping the underlying outlook belongs to the Russian Orthodox Church, which has stepped to the fore of social life and is backing the government's agenda with its own interpretation of Russian history and Russia's unique mission. To outline Orthodoxy's ideological function in today's Russia, I will refer to the ideas of three Western authors: Samuel Huntington, Adrian Hastings, and Jonathan Haidt; and three Russian Orthodox authors and speakers: Patriarch of Moscow Kirill; archpriest Vsevolod Chaplin, who served as the Chairman of the Synodal Department for Cooperation between the Church and Society from 2009 until 2015; and bishop Tikhon Shevkunov, who is often referred to as the personal confessor of Russian President Vladimir Putin.

In his book on religion and nationalism, Hastings identified several important ways in which the Christian faith has historically contributed to the growth of national self-consciousness: it sanctifies the origins of a nation; it contributes to the mythologization of threats to national identity; it uses the Bible as the mirror through which to imagine and create a Christian nation; and it constructs a unique national destiny – the claim to be a chosen people, a holy nation with some special mission to fulfill.[65] Donald Fairbairn observes that within Orthodox autocephalous churches especially, "the belief frequently arises that the nation or ethnic group stands in a special relationship with God."[66]

In particular, the development of what is known as "the Russian idea" goes back to the fall of Constantinople to the Turks in 1453. In 1510, the monk Philotheus penned his famous address to the Tsar, arguing that "two Romes have fallen, but the third stands," thereby suggesting that Moscow should take

---

64. Vladimir Putin, "Vystuplenie na Zasedanii Valdaiskogo Kluba [The Speech at the Valdai Club]," 2013, https://rg.ru/2013/09/19/stenogramma-site.html. Clover, *Black Wind, White Snow*.

65. Adrian Hastings, *The Construction of Nationhood: Ethnicity, Religion and Nationalism* (Cambridge: Cambridge University Press, 1997), 185–98; cf. Rogers Brubaker, "Religion and Nationalism: Four Approaches," *Nations and Nationalism* 18, no. 1 (2012): 16.

66. Donald Fairbairn, *Eastern Orthodoxy through Western Eyes* (Louisville, KY: Westminster John Knox, 2002), 145.

up where the Roman and the Byzantine empires left off. This view later grew into the conviction that the Russian nation is a "God-bearing people" and that the Russian Empire has been entrusted with a unique mission to be the sole guardian of the true Christian faith.[67] While under atheistic pressure the church was effectively marginalized, after the collapse of the USSR it became possible to speak about this mission once again.

In 1996, Huntington observed that in the post-Cold War era people were "discovering new but often old identities and marching under new but often old flags which lead to wars with new but often old enemies."[68] In particular, he noted that Russians were "mobilizing and marching" behind the symbols of their new (and old) cultural identity. Huntington also emphasized that a "central axis of post-Cold War world politics is . . . the interaction of Western power and culture with the power and culture of non-Western civilizations."[69] Recently, Jonathan Haidt attempted to explain some of the tensions along this axis using Richard Shweder's tripartite theory of morality.[70] Haidt contrasted Western cultures characterized by individualism and secularism with those that emphasize an "ethic of community" and an "ethic of divinity" more than an "ethic of autonomy." In other words, these cultures see people principally as members of collectives – families, tribes, and nations – with strong claims to loyalty, and hold that people's principal duty is to God, not themselves. "In such societies," Haidt writes, "the personal liberty of secular Western nations looks like libertinism, hedonism, and a celebration of humanity's baser instincts."[71]

It is instructive to observe how both the "Russian idea" and the concept of the "clash of civilizations" come to the surface in the rhetoric of the top Orthodox clergy. During the prolonged debates over the adoption of new national symbols – the flag, emblem, and new national anthem – it was Patriarch

---

67. Fairbairn, *Eastern Orthodoxy*, 146, 149.

68. Samuel P. Huntington, *The Clash of Civilizations and the Remaking of World Order* (New York: Simon & Schuster, 2011), 20.

69. Huntington, *Clash of Civilizations*, 29.

70. Richard A. Shweder et al., "The 'Big Three' of Morality (Autonomy, Community, Divinity) and the 'Big Three' Explanations of Suffering," in *Morality and Health*, ed. Allan M. Brandt and Paul Rozin (New York: Routledge, 1997), 119–72.

71. Jonathan Haidt, *The Righteous Mind: Why Good People Are Divided by Politics and Religion* (New York: Pantheon Books, 2012), 100.

Kirill of Moscow who suggested to President Putin the idea of adopting a modified version of the Soviet anthem that would seek to reconcile all political generations.⁷² The result became what Sakwa calls a "syncretic Russian national identity" that draws on all phases of Russian history.⁷³ The period of ancient Rus is seen as the time of "faith," the imperial period as the development of "statehood," and the Soviet period as the time of "justice," as well as of industrialization, the victory over Nazism, and the conquest of space.

This holistic view of Russian history emphasizes the victories of the great nation in each period and explains its defeats by the intrigues of either external or internal adversaries. At the same time, the atrocities connected to its long history of authoritarianism and military expansionism are denied, diminished, or written off as a necessary evil.⁷⁴ One of the key promoters of such a mythologized view of Russian history on popular level has been Vladimir Medinsky, the Minister of Culture of the Russian Federation since 2012. In his doctoral dissertation, he claimed that "weighing on the scales of Russia's national interests creates an absolute standard of the truthfulness and reliability of historical research."⁷⁵ In response to his critics from the academic community, he recently published an article in a national newspaper in which he affirms that "there is no reliable [knowledge of the] past, because five minutes after an event happens, it begins to exist [merely] as an interpretation . . . He who controls history, controls the future."⁷⁶ With such a methodological approach, history turns into an easy-to-absorb ideological product that is "legitimized by constant references to the past, glorious traditions, and occasionally fictional historical events."⁷⁷

---

72. Kirill, "Interview," 2015, http://vlasti.net/news/209489.

73. Sakwa, "Nation and Nationalism in Russia," 420.

74. Evgeny Morozov, "Russia: Ideology Becomes a Mash-Up," 2008, http://www.opendemocracy.net/article/russia-theme/russia-ideology-becomes-a-mash-up; Alec Luhn, "Stalin, Russia's New Hero," *The New York Times*, 2016, https://www.nytimes.com/2016/03/13/opinion/sunday/stalinist-nostalgia-in-vladimir-putins-russia.html.

75. A. Anikin et al., "O Metodakh Nauchnogo Issledovaniia i Dissertatsii V.R. Medinskogo [About the Research Methodology and Dissertation of V.R. Medinsky]," 2016, https://www.kommersant.ru/doc/3127495.

76. Vladimir Medinsky, "Interesnaia Istoriia [An Interesting Story]," 2017, https://rg.ru/2017/07/04/vladimir-medinskij-vpervye-otvechaet-kritikam-svoej-dissertacii.html.

77. Kolesnikov, "Russian Ideology After Crimea," n.p.

In a book that deals with the issues of human rights and personal dignity from an Orthodox perspective, Patriarch Kirill desribes the world in terms of two antagonistic systems. The struggle between them is "the most fundamental conflict of our present era."[78] "Eastern Christian civilization" arose under the influence of Orthodoxy and displays "the unconditional primacy of [the] spiritual over [the] material, of self-sacrifice over the desire for worldly success, of the common interest over private concerns, [and] of loyalty to truth and ideals over everyday advantage and earthly well-being."[79] In contrast, Western liberal civilization grows out of secularism and rejection of the normative status of Christian tradition. Ironically, its beginnings go back to the Protestant Reformation with its "rejection of the absolute authority of the Church in interpreting Holy Scripture."[80] The inevitable result was doctrinal and then moral relativism. In essence, this culture is nothing but "pagan anthropocentrism" in which individual freedom is the highest value.[81] Without a concept of sin, individual freedoms and the emphasis on human rights lead to the liberation of sinful passions from all moral conventions and norms.

This binary view of the world may sound rather simplistic in that the Patriarch consider neither the complexity of Western culture nor the variety of Western Christianity, but it clearly reflects key traditional themes of the "Russian idea": the spiritual superiority of the Russian people, collectivism and the primacy of the state over the individual, and the view of Westerners as this-worldly and materialistic. These ideas also increasingly influence Russian politics as President Putin adopts the rhetoric of civilizational struggle and even claims occasionally that Russians, with their unique and powerful "genetic code" and spirituality, possess better souls and moral values than self-indulgent Westerners.[82] A general acceptance of this framework by the

---

78. Kirill, *Freedom and Responsibility: A Search for Harmony, Human Rights and Personal Dignity* (London: Darton, Longman and Todd, 2011), 1.

79. Kirill, *Freedom and Responsibility*, 71. Many of its fundamental moral values are in essential agreement with those of other traditional world religions, such as Islam, Buddhism, and Judaism. Russian Muslims are therefore seen by Kirill as allies of Orthodox Christianity in this clash of civilizations.

80. Kirill, 55.

81. Kirill, 6.

82. Vladimir Putin, "Stenogramma [Transcript]," 2014, https://www.tvc.ru/news/show/id/37458.

majority of Russians will have direct bearing on whether Western ideas of liberal democracy will be seen as applicable or even relevant in Russia in the future.[83]

Closely related to the concept of "Eastern Christian civilization" is Patriarch Kirill's idea of *Russkii Mir*, or "the Russian world." This concept denotes a combination of linguistic, cultural, and religious elements that have created Russian civilization with its unique spiritual and cultural values. According to the Patriarch, the "Russian world" embraces the Eastern Orthodox Slavs (Russians, Ukrainians, and Belarusians) and those non-Slavic people who share Russian culture and the Orthodox faith.[84] Russia, therefore, has a special "mission of enlightenment" toward compatriots abroad.[85] Although presented as a spiritual rather than political space, this concept has served as an ideological underpinning of Putin's project of the Eurasian Customs Union – a military and economic association of Russia, Ukraine, and Belarus designed as an alternative to the European Union.[86] After Russia failed in its efforts to make Ukraine join the bloc in 2014, the concept of the "Russian world" became a key ideological element in the mobilization of Russian proxies for the military conflict in eastern Ukraine.[87]

---

83. Sakwa, "Nation and Nationalism in Russia," 419. In a recent statement, Bishop Hilarion Alfeyev, the Chairman of the Department of External Church Relations of the Patriarchate of Moscow, affirmed that "as history has demonstrated, autocracy has more advantages than any election-based form of government." A tsar, he continued, receives his "lifelong [ruling] mandate not merely from voters, but from God himself through the Church." Sergey Bolotov, "Mitropolit Illarion Posovetoval Rossii Absolyutnuyu Monarkhiyu [Metropolitan Hilarion Advised Russia an Absolute Monarchy]," 2017, https://www.ridus.ru/news/256104. If a restoration of the monarchy should ever take place in Russia, it will most likely mean a complete divorce from the ideals of democracy and, perhaps, will lead to the revision of the current constitution which many right-wing Russians consider artificial and imposed on them by the West in the 1990s. Maria Lipman, "How Russia Has Come to Loathe the West," 2015, https://www.ecfr.eu/article/commentary_how_russia_has_come_to_loathe_the_west311346.

84. Kirill, "Russkii Mir eto Osobaiia Tsivilizatsiia Kotoruiu Neobkhodimo Sberech [The Russian World is a Special Civilization That Must be Preserved]," 2014, http://www.patriarchia.ru/db/text/3730705.html.

85. DECR Communication Service, "VII Russian World Assembly Opens in St. Petersburg," 2013, https://mospat.ru/en/2013/11/04/news93676/.

86. Paul L. Gavrilyuk, "The President and the Patriarch: An Alliance over Ukraine?," 2014, https://www.firstthings.com/web-exclusives/2014/04/the-president-and-the-patriarch.

87. Cyril Hovorun, "Interpretiruia Russkii Mir [Interpreting the Russian World]," 2015, http://www.russ.ru/Mirovaya-povestka/Interpretiruya-russkij-mir; Sijbren De Jong, "Why Countries Are Not Rushing to Join Putin's Union," 2016, https://euobserver.com/opinion/133574. According to Hovorun, the practical power of this idea is comparable to the

According to Patriarch Kirill, unless the church enters the battle of civilizations, it cannot accomplish its mission of individual and communal transformation.[88] In this process, the church's main partner is the state whose task is "to ensure the implementation of God's law in public life and the protection of the faith" using all necessary means, including coercion. The idea of the *symphony* of church and state that goes back to the sixth novella of Emperor Justinian remains the Orthodox ideal for Russian society. Kirill is aware that in the past this ideal was never implemented in full, yet he insists that this "[does] not signify [the] rejection by Russia of the concept itself."[89] The task of the church in this partnership is to "establish in our people an understanding of the Orthodox faith as a norm of life" so that all areas of life will be shaped by its value system.[90] The ultimate goal is comprehensive: to produce "a Christian way of government, way of being society, economy, culture, science – in short, to Christianize life in all its manifestations."[91]

In keeping with this goal, the church has been taking successful steps to penetrate the military and the state education system. The supporters of this process emphasize the benefits of cultivating morality and patriotism in students and military personnel, whereas its opponents insist that "the growing clericalization of society" violates the constitutional principle of an ideologically neutral state.[92] This process is gaining momentum, however, because the current Russian political leadership seems bent at making the

---

power of other ideologies that provoked twentieth-century conflicts in Europe. He goes so far as to draw parallels between the nineteenth century trajectory of the "German world" and the current trajectory of the "Russian world": "In their initial stages, both . . . exploited language as soft power to facilitate the unification of the politically fragmented German and Russian ethnic spheres. At a later stage, they instrumentalized language and gradually turned it into a political instrument for the unification of *Völker*. In both cases, language became a foundation of neo-imperial projects. Both projects exploited moral agendas to claim superiority over other nations. The church contributed to the achievement of this goal and significantly enhanced the neo-imperial ideology. All this eventually ended up in bloodshed." Hovorun, "Interpretiruia Russkii Mir [Interpreting the Russian World]."

88. Kirill, *Freedom and Responsibility*, 45, 106.

89. Kirill, 46; cf. David Satter, "Putin Runs the Russian State – and the Russian Church Too," 2009, https://www.forbes.com/2009/02/20/putin-solzhenitsyn-kirill-russia-opinions-contributors_orthodox_church.html.

90. Kirill, 11.

91. Kirill, 18.

92. Clifford J. Levy, "Welcome or Not, Orthodoxy Is Back in Russia's Public Schools," *The New York Times*, 2007, sec. Europe, https://www.nytimes.com/2007/09/23/world/europe/23russia.html; Alexander Eremin and Sergei Oscmachko, "The Education Activity of

Orthodox Church the de facto state religion. Whether he sincerely believes Orthodox teachings or not, Vladimir Putin considers them a "spiritual shield" that Russia needs in addition to its nuclear shield.[93]

It comes as no surprise, therefore, that the idea that Russia stands or falls on its religion was also the central premise of a controversial but widely promoted documentary, "The Fall of the Empire: The Lesson of Byzantium," produced by Putin's alleged confessor Tikhon Shevkunov in 2008. In it, he argues that the key elements of the success and longevity of the Byzantine Empire were a strong centralized state, resistance of the West, the symphony of church and state, and harsh suppression of separatist and sectarian movements. Shevkunov explicitly suggests these emphases as a political program for contemporary Russia.[94] He is also well-known for his effective popularization of the ideals of Orthodox spirituality. In his 2011 bestseller *Everyday Saints* (English translation published in 2012), Shevkunov depicts the life of monastic communities with their virtues of humility, manual work, total self-denial, and unconditional submission to the hierarchy. For those living in the world, however, spirituality means complete dependence on one's confessor, partaking in the church's sacraments, and occasional pilgrimages to holy places. The book reflects strong eschatological pessimism with regard to the conditions of society, public morality, and politics, and almost total lack of interest in implications of one's faith beyond personal religiosity and salvation in the hereafter.[95]

The social and political thought of Kirill and Tikhon is fairly moderate in comparison to that of the prominent adherent of radical anti-Westernism Vsevolod Chaplin. This influential priest who is a frequent guest on television and radio programs argues that the "third Rome" has the ability to liberate humanity from "the civilization of narrow elites" that is attempting to

---

the Russian Orthodox Church in the Contemporary Transcultural Space of Russia," *Procedia* 237 (2017): 1475–81.

93. John R. Schindler, "Why Vladimir Putin Hates Us," *Observer* (blog), 2016, https://observer.com/2016/11/why-vladimir-putin-hates-us/.

94. Cyril Hovorun, *Ukraiinska Publichna Teologiia [Ukrainian Public Theology]* (Kyiv: Dukh i Litera, 2017), 49.

95. Tikhon Shevkunov, *Everyday Saints* (Dallas, TX: Pokrov, 2012); Ilya Iliukovich, "Krestyianstvo Ili Khristianstvo: Sotsialnye Aspekty Sovremennogo Pravoslaviya [Peasants or Christians: Social Aspects of Contemporary Orthodox Faith]," 2017, https://ahilla.ru/krestyanstvo-ili-hristianstvo-sotsialnye-aspekty-sovremennogo-pravoslaviya/.

take control of the global population.⁹⁶ For this, Russians must stand against "present-day Western civilization which is not the true West that was also created by Christianity."⁹⁷ Chaplin believes that

> Russia is the center, and maybe the only center, of the world . . . We have often, at the price of our own lives . . . stopped all global projects that conflicted with our conscience, with our vision of history and, I would say, with God's own truth. Such was Napoleon's project; such was Hitler's project. We will stop the American project too.⁹⁸

Chaplin's name figures prominently in research by Russian social scholar Boris Knorre on the "theology of war" in post-Soviet Orthodoxy.⁹⁹ Along with several other Orthodox priests and activists, Chaplin develops a justification of war from a religious perspective. By projecting spiritual warfare into the political area, these thinkers advance the idea of "Holy Russia" as the eschatological *katekhon* that will fight against the powers of the Antichrist. In the meantime, Russians must resist the decadent, postmodern West as Satan's project, designed to subvert traditional religion and family life with its liberal agenda. Despite anything Russia's "historical enemies and their propaganda" might say, Chaplin claims, Russian civilization is "truly Christian, always ready to stand up for itself and not give a single chance to the enemies of the people."¹⁰⁰

---

96. Tatiana Zavalishina, "Vsevolod Chaplin: 'Ostanovili Gitlerovskii Proekt, Ostanovim i Amerikanskii!' [Vsevolod Chaplin: 'We Stopped the Nazi Project and We Will Stop the American One!']," 2014, https://www.business-gazeta.ru/article/122025.

97. Paul Goble, "'We Stopped Hitler and We Can Stop the Americans,' Aide to Patriarch Kirill Says," 2014, https://www.eesti.ca/we-stopped-hitler-and-we-can-stop-the-americans-aide-to-patriarch-kirill-says/article43959.

98. "Church Spokesman: Russia Has Messianic Mission to Stop 'American Project,'" The Moscow Times, 2014, http://themoscowtimes.com/news/church-spokesman-russia-has-messianic-mission-to-stop-american-project-42577.

99. Boris Knorre, "The Culture of War and Militarization within Political Orthodoxy in the Post-Soviet Region," *Transcultural Studies* 12, no. 1 (2016): 15–38.

100. Paul Goble, "Moscow Archpriest Calls for New Death Squads to Destroy 'Traitor-Emigres,'" *Euromaidan Press* (blog), 2017, http://euromaidanpress.com/2017/03/11/moscow-archpriest-calls-for-new-death-squads-to-destroy-traitor-emigres-euromaidan-press/. Archpriest Chaplin is also well-known in Russia for his call for the creation of special death squads to kill those émigrés who are seen as traitors and enemies of the Russian Federation, and for his comment that from a biblical point of view, "there is nothing wrong with eradicating a

Thus, in sum, following the annexation of Crimea in March 2014, Russian society has been embracing an increasingly conservative and nationalistic outlook. Seeing themselves as confined to a besieged fortress, surrounded by external enemies, and faced with a domestic fifth column, the people of Russia "have thrown their support behind the commander of the fortress, President Vladimir Putin."[101] David Schindler describes this "virulent ideology" as an "explosive amalgam of xenophobia, Chekism and militant Orthodoxy which justifies the Kremlin's actions and explains why the West must be opposed at all costs."[102] While it might be too early to call this outlook, which is still in the making, a full-fledged "ideology," its main contours are more or less clear.[103] Moreover, given the economic crisis in which Russia now finds itself due to Western sanctions, we might expect even more Russians to turn to this worldview which "resonates with their nation's history and explains the root of their suffering."[104]

While there is a positive side to these developments in that the post-Communist chaos and ethnic disunity are being left behind, there are also serious concerns. The first is a potential danger of sliding into radical nationalism.[105] Whenever the notion of a "sacred" community is extended to embrace a whole nation, while simultaneously excluding the faithful from other Christian groups and other nations, the universal gospel story is compromised by local religious myths. In this scheme, the nation is what demands unquestioned and uncompromising loyalty. The world is viewed in terms of "two irreconcilable and warring camps – one's own nation in opposition to all other nations – where the latter are . . . one's implacable enemies."[106] The war

---

certain number of internal enemies." Valentin Baryshnikov, "For the Church, Violence Is the Norm," 2017, https://therussianreader.com/tag/juvenile-justice/.

101. Kolesnikov, "Russian Ideology After Crimea," n.p.

102. Schindler, "Putin's Orthodox Jihad," http://www.interpretermag.com/putins-orthodox-jihad/.

103. Schindler, "Putin's Orthodox Jihad."

104. Schindler.

105. Gribanova, "Ethnic and Religious Relations," 225.

106. Steven Elliott Grosby, *Nationalism: A Very Short Introduction*, Kindle Edition (Oxford: Oxford University Press, 2005), 232.

in eastern Ukraine, under the banner of "civilizational" and religious struggle, may be the first but quite likely not the last fruit of these developments.[107]

Second, the recent Russian patriotism that takes pride in selectively interpreted history is directed mainly toward the past and is neglecting the future. It tends to conserve current social, economic, and political models and ignores demands for modernization.[108] The system is simply not designed for change; the very idea of reforms is bound by the fears of another "perestroika" and of disintegration. In Ekaterina Schulman's words, in today's Russia "the values of security and preservation radically prevail over the values of progress and development. In this, both the authorities and citizens unite: everyone is afraid of the future which they see in terms of threats and challenges and . . . not of opportunities for improvement that tomorrow can bring."[109] But when a state ideology is founded on a country's past glory and offers no overriding concept for the future, it may have a decidedly limited life span.[110] The question is whether the ruling elite will have a supply of reformist ideas when the demand for them from below becomes really strong, or whether they will be tempted "to explain all [the] problems by 'malicious schemes' of its external and internal enemies" as has often been the case in the past.[111]

The developing social and economic stagnation is further exacerbated by paternalistic thinking and widespread social passivity among Russians. Research by Kasamara and Sorokina shows that there is a common dream

---

107. Donald Fairbairn reminds us that religious nationalism is not a product of mature Orthodox doctrine. Fairbairn, *Eastern Orthodoxy*, 146. Russian Orthodox theologian John Meyendorff challenged the church-state alliance as rooted in "a strong emphasis on an 'already realized' eschatology" and warned about nationalism "making use of the Church in order to achieve its own goals." John Meyendorff, *Byzantine Theology: Historical Trends and Doctrinal Themes* (New York: Fordham University Press, 1979), 2017; John Meyendorff, *Catholicity and the Church* (Crestwood, NY: St. Vladimir's Seminary Press, 1983), 139. Alexander Schmemann's work demonstrated how the "victory of theocratic dream" and the upsurge of national and religious consciousness has often turned "into a triumph for the Moscow autocracy" with all its cruelty and imperial conquests. Alexander Schmemann, *The Historical Road of Eastern Orthodoxy* (Crestwood, NY: St. Vladimir's Seminar Press, 1977), 313. Vladimir Solovyov exposed the nature of "Byzantism" as a form of caesaropapism in which the church is basically subdued to a totalitarian state and loses its prophetic voice. Vladimir Solovyov, *Freedom, Faith, and Dogma*, ed. Vladimir Wozniuk (Albany, NY: State University of New York Press, 2008).

108. Sakwa, "Bringing the People Back In," 289.

109. Sergei Medvedev, "Futurophobia," 2017, https://www.svoboda.org/a/28538329.html.

110. Kolesnikov, "Russian Ideology After Crimea."

111. Gribanova, "Ethnic and Religious Relations," 225.

across all social strata of a "tsar father" figure who consolidates all power in his hands and always works hard to "help simple people." At the same time, the research participants complain that Russian society is experiencing a moral crisis characterized by a lack of mutual trust, low solidarity, and a prevailing attitude of "every man for himself."[112] The lack of horizontal connections and self-organization beyond nuclear family ties has been noted by other authors.[113] Some suggest that such an "atomization of society" has been traditionally imposed by the ruling elites to keep the population easily controllable and dependent on the state.[114]

One result of this passivity is that individual or social initiatives that are not initiated or sanctioned by the authorities tend to be looked upon with suspicion.[115] Lev Gudkov of the Levada Centre, an independent polling and research organization, connects this mentality with the concept of *homo sovieticus*.[116] In 1989, when a group of sociologists led by Yuri Levada began to study what they called the Soviet Man, an artificial construct characterized by paternalism, suspicion and isolationism, they expected it to vanish in the near future. Unfortunately, the Soviet "mental software" has proved much more durable. The primary reason is that the central pillars of Soviet totalitarian rule, such as the intelligence services, the army, the prosecutor's office,

---

112. Kasamara and Sorokina, "Imperial Ambitions of Russians."

113. Boris Dubin, "Pravoslavie i Natsional'naia Identichnost: Neotraditsionalistskoe Znachenie Very [The Russian Orthodoxy and National Identity: A Neo-Traditionalist Meaning of Faith]," *Vestnik Obschestvennogo Mneniia [Messenger of Public Opinion]* 71, no. 3 (2004): 35–44; Zorkaia, "Pravoslavie v Bezreligioznom Obschetve [The Orthodox Church in a Secular Society]"; Alexander Akhiezer, Igor Klyamkin, and Igor Yakovenko, *Istoriia Rosii: Konets Ili Novoye Nachalo? [History of Russia: The End or A New Beginning?]* (Moscow: Liberalnaya Missiya, 2013); Natalia Kovalyova, *Unlearning the Soviet Tongue: Discursive Practices of a Democratizing Polity* (London: Lexington Books, 2014).

114. Zorkaia, "Pravoslavie v Bezreligioznom Obschetve [The Orthodox Church in a Secular Society]"; Igor Bobrov, "Pochemu Rossiiskii Politicheskii Rezhim Prevraschaet Grazhdan v Iskliuchionnykh [Why Russian Political Regime Deprives Citizens of Their Rights]," 2017, http://www.igorbobrov.com/2017/07/blog-post.html.

115. This is not to say that no forms of social life are active in Russia. In fact, as Sakwa observes, civil society has thrived in the Putin years, but of a peculiar sort. Independence and autonomy is constrained, but the regime itself sponsors forms of civil society activism that advances its goals. Sakwa, "Bringing the People Back In," 290.

116. L. Gudkov, B. Dubin, and N. Zorkaya, *Postsovetskiy Chelovek i Grazhdanskoe Obschestvo [The Post-Soviet Person and Civil Society]* (Moscow: Moscow School of Political Research, 2008); Max Bears, "Homo Sovieticus: Twelve Traits of a Soviet Man," 2014, http://bearsandvodka.com/homo-sovieticus.

and the judiciary system, persist. The schools, the national media, and the conscript army are reproducing the values and practices of the Soviet Union.[117] In fact, in the new ideological climate, *homo sovieticus* has acquired some new characteristics such as cynicism and aggression.[118]

The third major concern is that this outlook nurtures intolerance to dissent, whether political or religious. In particular, evangelicals are increasingly perceived as adherents of a "foreign religion" and as collaborators with the West. Apparently, some of these fears were behind the bill on traditional religions adopted in 1997, which distinguished between two categories of religious denominations, each having a different legal status and different rights.[119] Among Christian denominations, only the Orthodox Church was given the status of a traditional religion (along with Judaism, Islam, and Buddhism). Catholics, Protestants, and even breakaway Orthodox movements were listed among "non-traditional religious groups," and all but Catholics are often referred to as "sects." In July 2016, new anti-missionary legislation was passed. Although it was presented under the pretext of being aimed against terrorism, a year later more than one hundred court cases demonstrate that it has, in fact, been used primarily against evangelical missionary outreach in Russia.[120] On 20 April 2017, the Supreme Court placed a ban on the Jehovah's

---

117. This point finds support in social research by others. Thelen and Coulson in their analysis of the Russian national character conclude that Russians obey authority without question and are accustomed to centralized decision making. Shawn Thelen and Kevin Coulson, "Russian National Character: An Application of Clark's Comprehensive Framework," *The Marketing Management Journal* 12, no. 1 (2002): 19–31. Prasnikar, Pahor, and Svetlik find that Russians are accustomed to the state taking care of people and believe that the leaders could not be contested. Janez Prasnikar, Marko Pahor, and Jasna V. Svetlik, "Are National Cultures Still Important in International Business? Russia, Serbia, and Slovenia in Comparison," *Management* 13, no. 2 (2008): 1–26. Fernandez, Carlson, Stepina, and Nicholson in their study of cultural values in eight countries – Chile, China, Germany, Japan, Mexico, Russia, United States, Venezuela, and Yugoslavia – conclude that respondents from Russia score the highest on the dimension of power distance. Denise R. Fernandez et al., "Hofstede's Country Classification Twenty-Five Years Later," *The Journal of Social Psychology* 1 (1997): 43–54.

118. Sergei Gogin, "Homo Sovieticus: Twenty Years after the End of the Soviet Union," *Russian Analytical Digest* 109 (2012): 12–15; Lev Gudkov, "Russian Cynicism: Symptom of a Stagnant Society," 2013, http://www.opendemocracy.net/od-russia/lev-gudkov/russian-cynicism-symptom-of-stagnant-society.

119. Mark Elliot and Sharyl Corrado, "The 1997 Russian Law on Religion: The Demographics of Discrimination," 1999, http://www.eastwestreport.org/articles/ew07101.htm.

120. The distribution of New Testaments, public preaching of the gospel, and even invitations through social media to attend evangelical services have been criminalized. Victoria

Witnesses' work in Russia and ordered all the property of the organization to be confiscated by the state.[121] Given the fact that the State Duma (Parliament) recently put together a group of experts to "improve" the current legislation on religious freedom, there are concerns that some other groups may experience a similar fate.

Responses to these developments in the evangelical community have been rather diverse. Some groups prefer to ignore them as long as they do not interfere with their own daily routine. Some lean toward quietism, appealing to biblical texts such as Proverbs 28:28 ("When the wicked rise to power, people go into hiding"). Some choose cautious conformism and send official letters to the President to assure him of their loyalty. There are many who uncritically and even enthusiastically support both Russian military actions abroad and the persecution of Jehovah's Witnesses as "heretics." A few voices, however, have openly condemned the military crimes and the recent limitation of religious freedom. The overall impression is that many church leaders are trying to make sense of these developments so that they could appropriately adjust their ministry and mission in the current situation.

Research Problem

This research examines the theological concepts undergirding Russian Baptist mission efforts in the current Russian context and evaluates them against the background of global evangelical mission theologies. During the Soviet era, when Baptists were almost completely isolated from developments in evangelical mission theology in the West, they developed an idiosyncratic understanding of the gospel, the church, and mission.[122] For decades, this understanding served as the guiding tradition for Baptist communities in Russia. When the Soviet Union fell and Christians were granted religious freedom, the Russian Baptists' traditional understanding of mission simultaneously

---

Arnold, "Russia: 'Anti-Missionary' Punishments Full Listing," 2017, http://www.forum18.org/archive.php?article_id=2306.

121. Kate Shellnutt, "Russia Bans Jehovah's Witnesses as Extremists," 2017, https://www.christianitytoday.com/news/2017/april/russia-bans-jehovahs-witnesses.html.

122. Sawatsky, *Soviet Evangelicals*; Wanner, *Communities of the Converted*.

stimulated and hindered their missional engagement with society.[123] Since that time, Russian Baptists have also been interacting with a number of Western and international approaches to mission. These contacts, however, have been largely focused on right-wing evangelical groups in the USA and Germany that have a similar missiological outlook.[124] The available missiological literature has been either limited or unclaimed.

This study assumes that Russian Baptists are an integral part of the worldwide evangelical movement, and are thus called to become legitimate participants in the global evangelical missionary conversation. Since 1974, one of the benchmarks in the development of a global evangelical theology of mission has been the Lausanne Movement whose statements from the Congresses of 1974, 1989, and 2010 serve as the recognized mouthpiece of the evangelical mission tradition.[125] The Movement represents a broad spectrum of international evangelicalism and has been known for a distinctively evangelical, yet balanced, dialogical theology. Lausanne missiology has been willing to adopt biblical insights from all branches of the global church, both evangelical and counciliar. According to the introduction to the most recent statement of the Cape Town Commitment, its authors also actively partnered with the World Evangelical Alliance in each stage throughout the process. As a result, "The leaders of the WEA are in full agreement with both the Confession of Faith and the Call to Action."[126]

Although some developments within the Lausanne Movement have not been uncontroversial and not all issues are completely resolved, it represents a certain form of evangelical consensus on mission that is widely recognized around the world. For this reason, the Lausanne primary documents will constitute the principal background for this study. In what follows, I adopt the perspective of Lausanne as my theological framework for the assessment

---

123. John E. White, "Three Periods of Awakening in Eastern Slavic Lands," *Theological Reflections* Special Issue (2013): 244–258.

124. Puzynin, *Tradition of the Gospel Christians*; Gennagii Sergienko, "Nevyuchenyie Uroki Proshlogo [Unlearned Lessons of the Past]," 2011, http://gazeta.mirt.ru/stat-i/cerkov/post-1431/.

125. Goheen, *Introducing Christian Mission Today*, 2759.

126. Doug Birdsall and Lindsay Brown, "Foreword," in *The Cape Town Commitment: A Confirmation of Faith and a Call to Action*, ed. Julia Cameron (Peabody, MA: Hendrickson, 2011), 5.

of Russian Baptist missiology and for making recommendations in the final chapter. I will also refer to the work of some prominent missiologists who either represent a broad evangelical camp (Wilbert Shenk, Michael Goheen, and Christopher Wright) or have exerted a strong outside influence on the development of evangelical mission theology (Lesslie Newbigin and David Bosch).

Purpose of the Study

The purpose of this research is twofold: (1) to investigate the selected Russian Baptist leaders' perceptions of the gospel, the church, culture, and mission in their present socio-political context; and (2) to explore the leaders' views regarding the need to revise traditional Russian Baptist mission thinking, the potential for this to happen, and possible ways of introducing missiological changes.

Research Questions

1. How do some of the most influential Russian Baptist leaders understand the following issues?

- The nature of the gospel
- The church's identity and purpose
- Christian cultural engagement
- Holistic mission

2. What missiological revisions, if any, do these leaders deem necessary in the current socio-political and religious contexts of Russia?

- Possible inadequacies of traditional formulations
- Specific areas and issues to reconsider
- Potential strategies / obstacles in the process of introducing missiological revisions

Definition of Terms

Theology of mission, as understood in this research, denotes "theological reflection on the *nature* and *task* of mission" which examines its "theological foundations, guidelines, and dimensions."[127] Methodologically, mission theology is an integrative discipline that arises in "dialogue between biblical text and missionary context" as the church seeks to understand and fulfill God's purposes in the world.[128] Wilbert Shenk adds the historical experience of the church as another essential element of mission theology, and highlights its practical orientation in that it seeks to "give guidance to the church in fulfilling its missionary calling."[129] All four dimensions of mission theology will be important for this study. Given the fact that Russian Baptist missiology has not yet been formally articulated, Charles Van Engen's definition will also be helpful for the analytical part of this research.[130] He describes mission theology as a deeper-level reflection on "the presuppositions, assumptions, and concepts undergirding mission theory."

Evangelical. For this research, I have adopted David Bebbington's description of evangelicalism as a movement molded in its early period by leaders such as Jonathan Edwards, John Wesley, and George Whitefield, and characterized by the four marks of conversionism, activism, biblicism, and cruciocentrism.[131] When describing Western mission theology, the term denotes the evangelical Protestant tradition of mission that took shape during the second half of the twentieth century in opposition to the ecumenical Protestant tradition. Recent studies of Russian Baptists demonstrate that although their narratives of self-identity have sometimes depended on "geopolitical fluctuations" between Western and Orthodox (or Soviet) civilizations, the four marks

---

127. Craig Ott and Stephen J. Strauss, *Encountering Theology of Mission: Biblical Foundations, Historical Developments, and Contemporary Issues* (Grand Rapids, MI: Baker Academic, 2010), xix.

128. Ott and Strauss, *Encountering Theology of Mission*, xix.

129. Wilbert R. Shenk, "Recasting Theology of Mission: Impulses from the Non-Western World," in *Landmark Essays in Mission and World Christianity*, ed. R. L. Gallagher and P. Hertig (Maryknoll, NY: Orbis Books, 2009), 131.

130. Charles Van Engen, "Theology of Mission," in *Evangelical Dictionary of World Missions*, ed. A. Scott Moreau (Grand Rapids, MI: Baker Academic, 2000), 949.

131. David Bebbington, *Evangelicalism in Modern Britain: A History from the 1730's to the 1980's* (New York: Routledge, 1989), 3–19; David Bebbington, "Introduction," in *Evangelicalism: Comparative Studies of Popular Protestantism in North America, the British Isles, and Beyond, 1700–1990*, ed. Mark A Noll, David Bebbington, and George A Rawlyk (New York: Oxford University Press, 1994), 3–18.

of evangelicalism have remained definitive in their theology and church life from the movement's inception through the present.[132]

Mission paradigm. In his theory of scientific revolutions, Thomas Kuhn defined a paradigm as "the entire constellation of beliefs, values, techniques, and so on shared by the members of a given community."[133] From this perspective, the paradigm is not only the prevailing scientific theory, but the entire worldview in which it was formulated. Hans Küng applied Kuhn's insight to the analysis of Christian history, using the concept of paradigm in the basic sense of models of interpretation of the Christian.[134] Later, David Bosch in his now classic work[135] used this notion for the study of the historical transformations of mission models in church history.[136] In post-Soviet theological studies, Andrey Puzynin employed Küng's distinction between macro-, meso- and micro-paradigms as a heuristic device for understanding the development of the theological tradition of the "Gospel Christians" in Russia.[137] In this research, I apply the notion of paradigms and micro-paradigms to the analysis of the specifically *mission* theology of Russian Baptists.

Finally, the word *mission* in this research refers primarily to Russian Baptists' efforts to make the gospel known to their own compatriots rather than to cross-cultural evangelism or church planting.

Significance of the Research

This study aims at filling a gap in both the academic literature on Russian Baptist mission theology and in mission practice. While there has been a steady growth of quality literature on Baptist history, little research has been

---

132. Puzynin, *Tradition of the Gospel Christians*, 141; Gregory L. Nichols, *The Development of Russian Evangelical Spirituality: A Study of Ivan V. Kargel (1849–1937)*, Kindle Edition (Eugene, OR: Pickwick, 2011).

133. T. S. Kuhn, *The Structure of Scientific Revolutions* (Chicago, IL: University of Chicago Press, 1970), 175.

134. Hans Küng, *Theology for the Third Millennium: An Ecumenical View* (London: Harper Collins, 1991); Hans Küng and David Tracy, eds., *Paradigm Change in Theology: A Symposium for the Future* (Edinburgh: T&T Clark, 1989).

135. David J. Bosch, *Transforming Mission: Paradigm Shifts in Theology of Mission*, Twentieth anniversary edition (Maryknoll, NY: Orbis Books, 2011).

136. cf. Stephen B. Bevans and Roger Schroeder, *Constants in Context: A Theology of Mission for Today* (Maryknoll, NY: Orbis Books, 2004).

137. Puzynin, *Tradition of the Gospel Christians*.

done on their theology and, especially, on the theological aspects of their mission.[138] Lack of academic literature hinders awareness of the fact that missional engagement with society is always shaped by certain theological assumptions about the nature of the gospel, the church, and culture that develop in response to specific historical contexts.[139] As a result, traditional assumptions tend to be elevated to the status of unquestioned orthodoxy with little felt need for their revision. This study aims at providing Russian Baptist educators, pastors, and missionaries with an opportunity to critically evaluate the dominant mission models in light of the denomination's own history and the global evangelical consensus.

Articulating traditional missiology and letting it enter into dialogue with the global evangelical community might also help in overcoming unnecessary theological barriers to missionary partnerships between Russian Baptists and other evangelical groups in a country where the total evangelical population is a tiny minority.[140] It can also contribute to the development of fruitful partnerships between Russian Baptist leaders and international mission agencies and churches. Over the last two decades, Russian Baptists' educational and missionary partnerships have tended to be limited to North American evangelical fundamentalist groups, whereas the broader evangelical community

---

138. In fact, the concept of "mission theology" is rarely used in either the academic or ecclesiastical discourse of Russian Baptists. The word "theology" is understood as referring almost exclusively to systematic or dogmatic, and, increasingly, to biblical theologies. Without belittling the importance of recent studies, the fact is that available research focuses more on the history and practice of missions than on theology of mission. Some helpful recent studies that deal with aspects of mission theology include the following: Walter Sawatsky and Peter F. Penner, eds., *Mission in the Former Soviet Union* (Schwarzenfeld, Germany: Neufeld Verlag, 2005); Puzynin, *Tradition of the Gospel Christians*; Mary Raber and Peter F. Penner, eds., *History and Mission in Europe: Continuing the Conversation* (Schwarzenfeld, Germany: Neufeld Verlag, 2011); Alexey Sinichkin, *Vsio Radi Missii [Everything for the Sake of Mission]* (Irpen: Dukhovnoe Vozrozhdenie, 2011); Sinichkin, *Vozrozhdenie Vopreki Bezbozhiiu [Revival despite Godlessness]*; Yuchkovski, "Comparison of the Evangelical Movement"; Mary Raber, "Ministries of Compassion among Russian Evangelicals, 1905–1929" (PhD diss., Wales University, 2014); Peter Penner et al., eds., *Novye Gorizonty Missii [New Horizons of Mission]* (Cherkassy: Colloquium, 2015); John E. White, "An Analysis of Factors behind the Surge in Ukrainian Evangelical Missionaries from 1989–1999" (PhD diss., Biola University, 2016).

139. David J. Bosch, *Witness to the World: The Christian Mission in Theological Perspective* (Eugene, OR: Wipf & Stock, 1980), 24.

140. Alexander Zaychenko, "Sila i Slabost' Sovremennogo Rossiiskogo Protestantisma [Strengths and Weaknesses of Russian Protestantism Today]," 2011, http://gazeta.mirt.ru/stat-i/obschestvo/post-1014/; Sawatsky and Penner, *Mission in the Former Soviet Union*.

represented in the Lausanne Movement has been largely ignored.[141] With the financial and theological backing of Western churches, these conservative groups tend to define the theological agenda for the Union as a whole.

My hope is that this research will assist Russian Baptist pastoral, denominational, and educational leaders in building a more holistic missional vision as they develop missionary structures and strategies for the changing Russian society. Theological convictions about the gospel, church, and culture will directly impact the way Russian Baptists fulfill their mission. The ultimate goal of this research is therefore to contribute to a discussion that will hopefully lead Russian Baptists to a renewed missionary encounter with culture.

---

141. As Andrei Puzynin observes, "Anglo-American fundamentalism has been playing the most influential role in reshaping the identity, theology, and practices of the [Baptist] tradition during the post-Soviet period." Puzynin, *Tradition of the Gospel Christians*, 283.

CHAPTER 2

The Development of Evangelical Mission Theology Since 1910

This chapter outlines the basic contours of global evangelical mission theology as a major conversation partner for the Baptist mission in Russia. In what follows, I will first present a historical overview of the development of evangelical missiology in over a century beginning with the World Missionary Conference in Edinburgh (1910) and culminating in the Lausanne III Congress in Cape Town (2010). Then I will focus on contemporary formulations of the four theological issues that are central for this research: (1) the nature of the gospel; (2) the church's identity and its role in mission; (3) cultural engagement; and (4) holistic mission.

A Historical Overview

The 1910 World Missionary Conference in Edinburgh represented, in David Bosch's words, "the all-time highwater mark in Western missionary enthusiasm, the zenith of the optimistic and pragmatist approach to missions."[1] Theologically, however, the conference was the last evidence of the Protestant consensus on mission that had led the church through the great missionary movement of the nineteenth century. Although by 1910 the theological consensus was already eroding, Protestants generally still saw mission as the geographic spread of the Christian faith, in which the main role was given to mission agencies and societies.[2] Under the influence of theological liberalism

---

1. Bosch, *Transforming Mission*, 346.
2. Craig Ott, "Introduction," in *The Mission of the Church: Five Views in Conversation*, ed. Craig Ott (Grand Rapids, MI: Baker Academic, 2016), xii.

and the social gospel, the International Missionary Council (IMC, formed in 1921) gradually developed a trajectory of mission in which social, economic, and political issues came to dominate the agenda. This development resulted in growing controversies within Protestant denominations, until eventually Western Protestantism entered into an era of polarization between its ecumenical and evangelical wings.[3]

Evangelicals remained part of the IMC through the first half of the twentieth century, but many of them withdrew after the IMC joined the World Council of Churches (WCC) in 1961. While the IMC focused on mission as political and economic liberation, evangelicals focused on conversion and church planting as the primary goals of mission.[4] By the second half of the century, evangelicals articulated their theology of mission in rather "narrow, clearly definable categories," placing world evangelization at the top of their agenda.[5] The central task of mission was understood to be the conversion of souls, discipleship, and church planting. The concept of the kingdom of God, which is central for the gospel, was understood largely in otherworldly terms.[6]

This missionary tradition continued to develop through a series of consultations, beginning with the Wheaton and Berlin Congresses, both held in 1966. During the 1960s and through the end of the 1980s the Church Growth Movement led by Donald A. McGavran emphasized even more strongly evangelism and church growth as the central tasks of mission. Although that movement has since lost much of its influence, many of its fundamental concepts "left an indelible mark on evangelical missiology."[7] Another important development in the middle of the 1970s was the emergence of Ralph Winter's Frontier Movement, focused on the evangelization of "unreached

---

3. Bosch, *Transforming Mission*; Ott, "Introduction"; Andrew F. Walls, *The Missionary Movement in Christian History: Studies in the Transmission of Faith* (Maryknoll, NY: Orbis Books, 1996).

4. Roger E. Hedlund, *Roots of the Great Debate in Mission* (Madras, India: Evangelical Literature Service, 1981); Bosch, *Transforming Mission*; Goheen, *Introducing Christian Mission Today*; Ott and Strauss, *Encountering Theology of Mission*.

5. Charles Van Engen, *Mission on the Way: Issues in Mission Theology* (Grand Rapids, MI: Baker Book House, 1996), 130.

6. Goheen, *Introducing Christian Mission Today*.

7. Ott, "Introduction," xxiii.

peoples."⁸ Overall, the evangelical theology of mission kept developing and consolidating primarily in response to and, to a large degree, over against conciliar missiological thought.⁹

The growing disillusionment over the WCC's formulations of mission reached a climax in 1974 when Billy Graham initiated the first Lausanne Congress on World Evangelization in Lausanne, Switzerland. The goal of what later became known as the Lausanne Movement was to reach "a definitive evangelical consensus on the nature of Christian mission."¹⁰ The Congress produced the Lausanne Covenant which aimed to provide evangelicals with self-understanding and express their commitment to world evangelization. In Michael Goheen's words, the Lausanne Congress "prove[d] to be the defining event of the evangelical mission tradition," and the Lausanne Covenant "has continued to play an authoritative role in defining the Evangelical tradition of mission for almost four decades."¹¹ The catchphrase that has guided this tradition is "the whole church taking the whole gospel to the whole world."¹²

Between the first Congress and the next major meeting in Manila in 1989 (Lausanne II) a series of issues-based gatherings took place, chief among them being consultations on gospel and culture, on unreached peoples, on simple lifestyle, and on holistic mission. Lausanne II produced the Manila Manifesto, which is essentially an "elaboration of the Lausanne Covenant . . . fifteen years later."¹³ This "public declaration" of evangelical convictions about mission consists of two parts. In the first part, twenty-one affirmations are stated. In the second part, those affirmations, in keeping with the Lausanne

---

8. Ralph D. Winter, "The Highest Priority: Cross-Cultural Evangelism," in *Let the Earth Hear His Voice: International Congress on World Evangelization, Lausanne, Switzerland*, ed. J. D. Douglas (Minneapolis, MN: World Wide Publications, 1975), 213–258.

9. Harold Lindsell, "Philosophy of Christian Mission," in *The Theology of the Christian Mission*, ed. Gerald H. Anderson (New York: McGraw-Hill, 1961), 242; Bosch, *Transforming Mission*; Goheen, *Introducing Christian Mission Today*.

10. Ott, "Introduction," xxiii–xxiv.

11. Goheen, *Introducing Christian Mission Today*, 2744–2749.

12. The Lausanne Movement, "About the Movement," accessed 25 July 2017, https://www.lausanne.org/about-the-movement.

13. John Stott, ed., *Making Christ Known: Historic Mission Documents from the Lausanne Movement, 1974-1989* (Grand Rapids, MI: Eerdmans, 1996), xx; David Parker, ed., "A Commentary of the 'Manila Manifesto,'" *Evangelical Review of Theology* 14 (1990): 236; Robert J. Schreiter, "From the Lausanne Covenant to the Cape Town Commitment: A Theological Assessment," *International Bulletin of Missionary Research* 35 (2011): 88–89.

slogan, are elaborated on in three sections: "The Whole Gospel," "The Whole Church," and "The Whole World." Finally, in 2010, Lausanne III was convened in Cape Town, South Africa. This last Congress produced the Cape Town Commitment, which consists of two parts. Part I is a confession of faith (entitled "For the Lord We Love") and Part II is a commitment to action (entitled "For the World We Serve"). Building on both the Lausanne Covenant and the Manila Manifesto, the Cape Town Commitment articulates the evangelical vision of participation in God's "integral mission" to the world.[14]

Although evangelical mission theology is far from being monolithic and includes diverse perspectives on multiple issues, the Lausanne Committee for World Evangelization (LCWE, founded in 1974) has significantly contributed to the development and consolidation of evangelical mission thinking.[15] In particular, the Lausanne Covenant has become a symbol of evangelical identity and a catalyst for evangelical cooperation worldwide.[16] The Lausanne Movement has thus become "the recognized mouthpiece of the Evangelical tradition of mission," and its documents and meetings provide us with "a window into its theology."[17] Three primary documents from the Lausanne Movement are especially important for this study: the Lausanne Covenant (1974), the Manila Manifesto (1989), and the Cape Town Commitment (2010).[18] Certain occasional papers will also be referenced when necessary.

---

14. The Lausanne Movement, "The Cape Town Commitment," 2011, https://www.lausanne.org/content/ctc/ctcommitment.

15. Back in 1980, Bosch identified at least six different groups of evangelicals. Bosch, *Witness to the World*, 30. Since then, evangelical Christianity has grown even more diverse, not only in North America and Western Europe, but in Latin America, sub-Saharan Africa, Asia, and Oceania. Timothy C. Tennent, *Invitation to World Missions: A Trinitarian Missiology for the Twenty-First Century*, Kindle Edition (Grand Rapids, MI: Kregel, 2010), 17.

16. James A. Scherer and Stephen B. Bevans, eds., *New Directions in Mission and Evangelization* (Maryknoll, NY: Orbis Books, 1992).

17. Goheen, *Introducing Christian Mission Today*, 2760.

18. John R. W. Stott, ed., "The Lausanne Covenant with an Exposition and Commentary," in *Making Christ Known: Historic Mission Documents from the Lausanne Movement, 1974–1989* (Grand Rapids, MI: Eerdmans, 1996), 1–55; John R. W Stott, ed., "The Manila Manifesto: An Elaboration of the Lausanne Covenant Fifteen Years Later," in *Making Christ Known: Historic Mission Documents from the Lausanne Movement, 1974–1989* (Grand Rapids, MI: Eerdmans, 1996), 225–248; Julia Cameron, ed., *The Cape Town Commitment: A Confirmation of Faith and a Call to Action* (Peabody, MA: Hendrickson, 2011).

Evangelical Mission Theology in the Global Context

Over the last forty years, evangelical missiology has been increasingly taking into account the input of non-Western churches as well as changing world realities. The three Lausanne Congresses brought together thousands of leaders from all around the globe, and the movement's documents reflect this diversity. Preliminary discussions concerning its latest statement, the Cape Town Commitment, took place at a gathering of eighteen theologians drawn from every continent, and it includes insights drawn from regional consultations of leaders in the majority world.[19] The social, political, economic, and cultural challenges the global church faces have also led to the rethinking of traditional formulations.[20] Timothy Tennent speaks of the need for the "readjustment and reassessment" of missions in light of seven major shifts in the world today. He sees the "seven megatrends" below not as separate, but as "related to, intertwined with, and built upon the others":[21]

1. The collapse of Christendom;
2. The rise of post-modernism in theology, the church, and culture;
3. The collapse of the "West-Reaches-the-Rest" paradigm;
4. The changing face of global Christianity, or the "Walls shift";[22]
5. The emergence of a fourth brand of Christianity (the Pentecostal movement);
6. Globalization: immigration, urbanization, and new technologies;
7. A deeper, post-denominational ecumenism.[23]

Michael Goheen also gives attention to changing global realities, but he stresses the collapse of colonialism in the last century, the staggering social and economic problems that afflict our world, the soaring population increase of the last century, a resurgence of religions around the world, and tectonic shifts in Western culture.[24] He also takes into account changes in the

---

19. Birdsall and Brown, "Foreword," 4.

20. The impetus seems first to have come from the mainline missiologist David Bosch, who believed that the need for a new theological paradigm in mission stemmed from several major changes in the world after World War II. Bosch, *Transforming Mission*.

21. Tennent, *Invitation to World Missions*, 104–105.

22. Walls, *Missionary Movement*.

23. Tennent, *Invitation to World Missions*, 70–474.

24. Goheen, *Introducing Christian Mission Today*, 303.

global church, such as the numerical growth of the church in the Southern Hemisphere, the decline of the Western church, and the Western church's "deep compromise to the secular humanist worldview of Western culture."[25] Likewise, the Preamble to the Cape Town Commitment gives attention to the impact of the following trends: globalization, the digital revolution, the changing balance of economic and political power in the world, global poverty, war and ethnic conflict, the ecological crisis, and climate change.[26]

All these developments have established a new context for mission today, in which the church is called to proclaim and demonstrate the unchanging reality of the gospel. This context is important to keep in mind for understanding the current formulations of the four aspects of evangelical mission theology that are central for this research.

The Essence of the Gospel

Salvation. The gospel is the good news of salvation which God in Christ offers to humanity. What this salvation includes, however, has been understood in a variety of ways. In the traditional Western Protestant view of mission, salvation was seen as "the redemption of individual souls in the hereafter, which would take effect at the occasion . . . of the death of the individual believer."[27] From this perspective, at the center of the gospel stands Christ's substitutionary death on the cross. Individuals are saved from eternal punishment when they put their trust in this sacrifice for their sins. The most well-known conservative evangelist of the past century, Billy Graham, summarized the message of the gospel and the ensuing view of the church's mission in his keynote address at Lausanne in 1974 as follows: "Jesus Christ, very God and very Man, died for my sins on the cross, was buried, and rose the third day."[28]

---

25. Goheen, 242.

26. Cameron, *Cape Town Commitment*, 6.

27. Bosch, *Transforming Mission*, 386. Bosch traces this emphasis back to D. L. Moody (1837–1899) for whom sin was exclusively an individual affair, with the sinner standing alone before God. Bosch, 408. Goheen observes that this approach to evangelism was deeply shaped by the Enlightenment paradigm that succumbed to privatism and individualism. Goheen, *Introducing Christian Mission Today*, 2784.

28. Billy Graham, "Why Lausanne?," in *Let the Earth Hear His Voice: International Congress on World Evangelization, Lausanne, Switzerland*, ed. J. D. Douglas (Minneapolis, MN: World Wide Publications, 1975), 25.

Accordingly, "evangelism and the salvation of souls is the vital mission of the church."

With regard to social involvement, this view assumed a distinction (whether explicit or implicit) between the "horizontal" or "external" aspects of missionary work (charity, education, medical help) and its "vertical" or "spiritual" elements (such as preaching, the sacraments, and church attendance). Even though historically the church has performed remarkable service in caring for the sick, the poor, and orphans, as well as in education, in agricultural instruction, and the like, works of compassion were seen as "either a by-product of salvation or a bridge to preaching the good news that leads to salvation."[29] These were "auxiliary services" whose purpose was "to dispose people favorably toward the gospel" and thereby prepare the way for the work of "the real missionary, namely, the one who proclaimed God's word about eternal salvation."[30] Inevitably, such an understanding of salvation led to a "preoccupation with narrowly defined ecclesiastical activities," complicating the involvement of believers in society, which was thought to have nothing to do with salvation.[31]

The Enlightenment challenged this spiritual and otherworldly view of salvation and introduced the idea of progress that could be achieved by human capability. The theologically liberal wing of Protestantism increasingly adjusted its understanding of salvation to this development while trying to retain vestiges of Christian teaching. It emphasized social, political, and economic action, with an insufficient critique of modern progress. This "uneasy combination" can be seen in the notion of the "comprehensive approach" introduced at the meeting of the International Missionary Council in Jerusalem in 1928.[32] In reaction to liberal formulations, evangelicals tended to emphasize only one major goal of mission, namely, the "salvation of individual souls."[33] The concept of sin was increasingly limited to the individual, with little interest in how it is embodied in oppressive and unjust structures.

---

29. Goheen, *Introducing Christian Mission Today*, 2585.
30. Bosch, *Transforming Mission*, 386.
31. Bosch, 386.
32. Goheen, *Introducing Christian Mission Today*, 2586.
33. Van Engen, *Mission on the Way*, 130; John F. Walvoord, "The Theological Basis for Foreign Missions," in *Facing the Unfinished Task: Messages Delivered at the Congress on World Missions*, ed. Mary Bennett (Grand Rapids, MI: Zondervan, 1961), 244.

Attempts at political liberation were often equated with the "social gospel" and dismissed. However, as Michael Goheen observes, in the final analysis, both the ecumenical tradition and the evangelical tradition became "equally captive to modernity with a spiritualized and privatized gospel."[34]

Already in the 1970s in many mission circles, both evangelical and conciliar, attempts were made to develop a more holistic understanding of salvation which would embrace both present and future salvation, evangelism and social concern, and political and economic action.[35] Today, when missiologists speak of the gospel as "comprehensive," "integral," "holistic," or "total," they are pointing to the desire to overcome the "inherent dualisms of the past—individual and society, soul and body, present and future, vertical and horizontal, evangelism and seeking justice, word and deed."[36] In the ecumenical tradition, a holistic understanding of salvation tends to be formulated with the help of a "comprehensive Christology," as suggested by Bosch. For him, dualistic views of salvation focus on only one aspect of Christ's person and work. Instead, he says, "the emerging paradigm" in mission must adopt a christological framework that "makes the *totus Christus* – his incarnation, earthly life, death, resurrection, and parousia – indispensable for church and theology."[37] Evangelical theologians tend to develop a holistic view of the gospel based on the theme of the kingdom of God as the irrupting reign of God and the lordship of Christ in all realms of life.[38]

The Kingdom of God. Traditionally, the concept of God's kingdom in evangelical circles has tended to be understood as a future or inner spiritual reality which is experienced by Christian believers.[39] This futurist, millennial view

---

34. Goheen, *Introducing Christian Mission Today*, 2595.

35. Bosch, *Transforming Mission*, 399.

36. Goheen, *Introducing Christian Mission Today*, 2597–2600; Bosch, *Transforming Mission*, 391.

37. Bosch, 391.

38. George Eldon Ladd, *A Theology of the New Testament* (Grand Rapids, MI: Eerdmans, 1974); Christopher J. H. Wright, *The Mission of God: Unlocking the Bible's Grand Narrative* (Downers Grove, IL: IVP Academic, 2006); Howard A. Snyder, *Models of the Kingdom* (Nashville, TN: Abingdon, 1991); Ott and Strauss, *Encountering Theology of Mission*; Goheen, *Introducing Christian Mission Today*.

39. Snyder, *Models of the Kingdom*; John Corrie, "Kingdom of God," in *Dictionary of Mission Theology: Evangelical Foundations*, ed. John Corrie, Samuel Escobar, and Wilbert R. Shenk (Nottingham, England: IVP Academic, 2007), 196; C. René Padilla, *Mission Between the Times: Essays on the Kingdom* (Carlisle, UK: Langham Monographs, 2010), 9–10. Howard

of the kingdom, on the one hand, has served as a strong motif for world evangelization.[40] On the other hand, such a narrow view of the kingdom has limited the scope of salvation to a private experience focusing primarily on obtaining eternal life in heaven after one's death. This inner and spiritual understanding of the kingdom has also served to justify the traditional understanding of the church's mission as the salvation of souls through evangelism and church planting.[41]

One reason for this narrowing was a reaction against the ecumenical usage of the concept of the kingdom. Johannes Hoekendijk affirmed that the kingdom of God can be realized outside of the church, in the social and political realms. He argued that "Church-centric missionary thinking is bound to go astray because it revolves around an illegitimate center."[42] No wonder the concept of the kingdom, as Ralph Winter notes, was "almost totally banned from Evangelical circles for at least 50 years. Only recently has this word, so prominent in [the] NT, been recovered as some expositors have written books about the kingdom of God and tried to bring it back into the fold."[43] In fact, as late as 1982, Arthur P. Johnston, in his plenary paper for the CRESR in Grand Rapids, described the kingdom of God in predominantly spiritual terms: "[T]he kingdom of God is the present inner rule of God in the moral and spiritual dispositions of the soul with its seat in the heart. God does rule as King in the lives of those 'born again.'"[44]

Snyder observes that this view of the kingdom "tends to see present 'blessings' . . . in rather personal, private, and self-centered terms . . . [which] fits well with the ruggedly individualistic, private enterprise mind-set that has characterized much conservative Protestantism." Snyder, *Models of the Kingdom*, 54–55.

40. The premillennialist hope of the second coming of Christ and the new kingdom "lent a strong, almost desperate urgency to gospel proclamation." Van Engen, *Mission on the Way*, 130–131.

41. Padilla, *Mission Between the Times*, 9.

42. Johannes Christiaan Hoekendijk, "The Church in Missionary Thinking," *International Review of Mission* 41 (1952): 332; Johannes Christiaan Hoekendijk, *The Church Inside Out* (Philadelphia, PA: Westminster, 1964), 38.

43. Ralph D. Winter, "The Future of Evangelicals in Mission," in *Missionshift: Global Mission Issues in the Third Millennium*, ed. David J. Hesselgrave and Ed Stetzer (Nashville, TN: B&H Academic, 2010), 180.

44. Arthur F. Johnston, "The Kingdom in Relation to the Church and the World," in *Word and Deed: Evangelism and Social Responsibility*, ed. Bruce Nichols (Exeter, Devon: Paternoster, 1985), 128.

Since the 1970s and 1980s, evangelicals have begun gradually to articulate their mission theology in relation to the kingdom theme. As Van Engen puts it, "We cannot fully understand the breath or depth of the congregation's mission unless we see it in relation to the kingdom of God in the world."[45] The impetus initially came from the realm of biblical studies and affected missiology through the work of George Eldon Ladd, Johannes Blauw, Arthur F. Glasser, Howard A. Snyder, René Padilla, Orlando Costas, Ken Gnanakan, and Charles Van Engen.[46] Today, many evangelical missiologists agree that the kingdom of God is the "starting point" for understanding the gospel – its "center" and the "orienting point of mission."[47] The kingdom is seen, overall, as the "divine intent to bring all things under [God's] rule, to reconcile all things to himself, to restore that which is fallen and corrupted, and to overthrow all powers in opposition to him and his reign of peace, joy, and righteousness."[48] The church as the people of the kingdom becomes its "living sign and an instrument." As kingdom people, they are called to live in this interim age "under Christ's lordship and work for the cause of holiness, righteousness, and justice in all their relationships and in the world."[49]

For a balanced view of the church's mission, understanding the tension between the historical and eschatological manifestations of the kingdom is important. In this regard, Oscar Cullmann's salvation-historical approach remains helpful. He suggested a way to reconcile theologically the nature

---

45. Charles Van Engen, *God's Missionary People: Rethinking the Purpose of the Local Church* (Grand Rapids, MI: Baker Book House, 1991), 101.

46. George Eldon Ladd, *The Gospel of the Kingdom: Scriptural Studies in the Kingdom of God* (Grand Rapids, MI: Eerdmans, 1959); Johannes Blauw, *The Missionary Nature of the Church: A Survey of the Biblical Theology of Mission* (New York: McGraw-Hill, 1962); Arthur F. Glasser, "The Evolution of Evangelical Mission Theology Since World War II," *International Bulletin of Missionary Research* 9 (1985): 9–13; Snyder, *Models of the Kingdom*; C. René Padilla, "Evangelism and the World," in *Let the Earth Hear His Voice: International Congress on World Evangelization, Lausanne, Switzerland*, ed. J. D. Douglas (Minneapolis, MN: World Wide Publications, 1975), 116–146; Orlando E. Costas, *The Church and Its Mission: A Shattering Critique from the Third World* (Wheaton, IL: Tyndale House, 1974); Kenneth Romesh Gnanakan, *Kingdom Concerns: A Biblical Exploration Towards a Theology of Mission* (Bangalore: Theological Book Trust, 1989); Charles Van Engen, *The Growth of the True Church: An Analysis of the Ecclesiology of Church Growth Theory* (Amsterdam: Rodopi, 1981).

47. Goheen, *Introducing Christian Mission Today*, 1527; Ott and Strauss, *Encountering Theology of Mission*, 86.

48. Ott and Strauss, 86–87.

49. Ott and Strauss, 105.

of the kingdom's fulfillment in history as "already-but-not-yet."[50] This view influenced both Leslie Newbigin and David Bosch, whose influential writings, in turn, have served as an important shaping influence on many conciliar, Roman Catholic, and evangelical theologies of mission.[51] For evangelicals, keeping this tension in mind helps maintain balance between eschatological hope, on the one hand, and advocating the values of the kingdom in society at large, on the other. Thus, Padilla, in response to Johnston's interiorized view of the kingdoms, observes: "The eschatological tension between the *already* and the *not yet* – a tension that is taken for granted throughout the New Testament – disappears [in this view] and the possibility of understanding the kingdom of God . . . as the basis for the Christian mission is thus removed."[52]

At Lausanne I the motif of God's kingdom as the goal and foundation of God's mission was brought out by René Padilla, Andrew Kirk, and an ad hoc group formed by Radical Discipleship.[53] Despite the tendency of many evangelicals to emphasize the futility of moral or political improvement in the present age, the Lausanne Covenant affirmed both an eschatological framing of mission and the need to be involved in God's work in the world until the *parousia*. Article 15 of the Covenant reads: "We believe that the interim period between Christ's ascension and return is to be filled with the mission of the people of God, who have no liberty to stop before the end."[54] This formulation reflects the fact that in the tension between the "already" and the "not yet" of the kingdom the church serves as its anticipation and instrument.

---

50. Oscar Cullmann, "Eschatology and Missions in the New Testament," in *The Theology of the Christian Mission*, ed. Gerald H. Anderson (Nashville, TN: Abingdon, 1961), 42–54.

51. Bosch frequently admits his indebtedness to Cullmann's perspective on eschatology. Bosch, *Transforming Mission*, 130, 496, 523.

52. Padilla, *Mission Between the Times*, 10.

53. Padilla, "Evangelism and the World"; Peter Beyerhaus, "World Evangelization and the Kingdom of God," in *Let the Earth Hear His Voice: International Congress on World Evangelization, Lausanne, Switzerland*, ed. J. D. Douglas (Minneapolis, MN: World Wide Publications, 1975), 283–302; J. Andrew Kirk, "The Kingdom of God and the Church in Contemporary Protestantism and Catholicism," in *Let the Earth Hear His Voice: International Congress on World Evangelization, Lausanne, Switzerland*, ed. J. D. Douglas (Minneapolis, MN: World Wide Publications, 1975), 1071–1080; Ad Hoc Group, "Theology and Implications of Radical Discipleship," in *Let the Earth Hear His Voice: International Congress on World Evangelization, Lausanne, Switzerland*, ed. J. D. Douglas (Minneapolis, MN: World Wide Publications, 1975), 1294–1296.

54. Stott, "Lausanne Covenant," 53.

Ken Gnanakan describes the implications of kingdom theology for the church's mission as "actualization" and "declaration": "Mission involves the declaration of God's purposes for the establishing of his Kingdom by a people who in an anticipatory sense actualize this kingdom.[55] This infers a total involvement of the church in God's total mission." Since the kingdom of God involves a comprehensive restoration of creation, including cultural and societal renewal, the church in the "already-not-yet" is to be a preview of that restoration.[56] The Manila Manifesto describes the church's relationship to the kingdom of God in similar terms: "The church is intended by God to be a sign of his kingdom, that is, an indication of what human community looks like when it comes under his rule of righteousness and peace."[57]

It is important to keep in mind, however, that the concept of God's kingdom may run the risk of becoming a "catchall to justify any good work, any spiritual ministry, any economic or political agenda, any new strategy of 'mission.'"[58] For this reason it is important not to lose the eschatological and christological perspectives on the kingdom. Ultimately, the hope of mission lies not in successful human efforts, but in "the final intervention of God himself with Christ's return and the fullness of the kingdom."[59] Acts of mercy and justice cannot be identified with God's reign; rather, they are signs of the coming kingdom. Until Christ comes back, the kingdom of God is manifested only where Christ's lordship is confessed and acknowledged. This is not to say that the kingdom is coextensive with the church. Rather, it means that the gospel is Christ-centered and that one cannot preach the kingdom without the King.[60]

---

55. Gnanakan, *Kingdom Concerns*, 119.

56. Goheen, *Introducing Christian Mission Today*, 4236–4239.

57. Stott, "Manila Manifesto," 241.

58. Ott and Strauss, *Encountering Theology of Mission*, 88.

59. Ott and Strauss, 89, 155.

60. Ladd, *Gospel of the Kingdom*; J. Verkuyl, *Contemporary Missiology: An Introduction* (Grand Rapids, MI: Eerdmans, 1978), 198; Van Engen, *God's Missionary People*; Tim Chester, "Church Planting: A Theological Perspective," in *Multiplying Churches: Reaching Today's Communities through Church Planting*, ed. Stephen Timmis (Fearn, Tain: Christian Focus, 2000), 23–46; Tormod Engelsviken, "*Missio Dei*: The Understanding and Misunderstanding of a Theological Concept in European Churches and Missiology," *International Review of Mission* 92 (2003): 481–497; Milfred Minatrea, *Shaped by God's Heart: The Passion and Practices of Missional Churches* (San Francisco, CA: Jossey-Bass, 2004); Richard Yates Hibbert, "The Place

Three current models of the gospel. As a result of the theological developments of the last forty years, the evangelical community today is far from uniform in how the gospel is understood. Ronald Sider identifies the three most common evangelical approaches to understanding the gospel, which he labels as the "Individualistic Model," the "Radical Anabaptist Model," and the conservative sub-type of the "Dominant Ecumenical Model."[61] The first group is represented by Billy Graham and generally follows the traditional paradigm described above. The second places more emphasis on persons-in-community with a greater emphasis on the church as part of the gospel. In this view Christians are called to demonstrate that it is now possible by grace to live in a new society in which all relationships are being redeemed – personal, economic, and social.[62] The third group espouses a broader view of the gospel in which the redemptive work of Christ has cosmic implications. In the person and work of Jesus Christ God is restoring his rule over the whole creation and over every aspect of human life.[63]

Today, it is the third model that is gaining more and more ground, not least due to the influence of so-called "missional hermeneutics" and authors such as Tom Wright, Michael Goheen, and Christopher Wright, who is also the principal author of the Cape Town Commitment.[64] Evangelicals in this group remain committed to the uniqueness of Christ and the importance of explicit faith in Christ for individual conversion. Sider's labeling of this model as

---

of Church Planting in Mission," *Evangelical Review of Theology* 33 (2009): 316–331; Ott and Strauss, *Encountering Theology of Mission.*

61. Ronald J. Sider, *Good News and Good Works: A Theology for the Whole Gospel* (Grand Rapids, MI: Baker Book House, 1999), 27–31.

62. John Howard Yoder, *The Politics of Jesus* (Grand Rapids, MI: Eerdmans, 1972); Stanley Hauerwas and William H. Willimon, *Resident Aliens: Life in the Christian Colony* (Nashville, TN: Abingdon, 1989).

63. Anthony A. Hoekema, *The Bible and the Future* (Grand Rapids, MI: Eerdmans, 1979); Albert M. Wolters, *Creation Regained: Biblical Basics for a Reformational Worldview* (Grand Rapids, MI: Eerdmans, 2005); Richard J. Mouw, *He Shines in All That's Fair: Culture and Common Grace* (Grand Rapids, MI: Eerdmans, 2001); Cornelius Plantinga, *Engaging God's World: A Christian Vision of Faith, Learning, and Living* (Grand Rapids, MI: Eerdmans, 2002).

64. N. T. Wright, *Surprised by Hope: Rethinking Heaven, the Resurrection, and the Mission of the Church* (New York: HarperOne, 2008); N. T. Wright, *The Day the Revolution Began: Reconsidering the Meaning of Jesus's Crucifixion* (New York: HarperOne, 2016); Michael W. Goheen, *A Light to the Nations: The Missional Church and the Biblical Story* (Grand Rapids, MI: Baker Academic, 2011); Goheen, *Introducing Christian Mission Today*; Wright, *Mission of God*; Christopher J. H. Wright, *The Mission of God's People: A Biblical Theology of the Church's Mission* (Grand Rapids, MI: Zondervan, 2010).

"ecumenical" therefore simply reflects the fact of Bosch's "new convergence": its proponents recognize that the traditional interpretation of salvation has proven inadequate, biblically and practically. More and more evangelicals today are subscribing to Bosch's comment made a quarter of a century ago:

> We cannot . . . simply return to the classical interpretation of salvation, even if that position upholds and defends elements which remain indispensable for a Christian understanding of salvation. Its problem lies, first, in the fact that it dangerously narrows the meaning of salvation, as if it comprises only escape from the wrath of God and the redemption of the individual soul in the hereafter and, second, in that it tends to make an absolute distinction between creation and new creation, between well-being and salvation.[65]

The Church's Identity and Its Role in Mission

One of the crucial problems of Christian missiology during the second half of the twentieth century was the question of how to accomplish a "successful transition from an earlier *church-centered* theology of mission to a *kingdom-oriented* one without the [loss] of missionary vision or [the] betrayal of biblical content."[66] The concept of *missio Dei*, despite much confusion about the meaning of term, has served as the most effective means to accomplish this transition.

Missio Dei. This idea was first explicitly formulated at the 1952 conference of the IMC in Willingen, Germany, to help articulate the conviction that neither the church nor any other human agent can ever be considered the author

---

65. Bosch, *Transforming Mission*, 390.

66. James A. Scherer, "Church, Kingdom, and Missio Dei: Lutheran and Orthodox Correctives to Recent Ecumenical Mission Theology," in *Good News of the Kingdom: Mission Theology for the Third Millennium*, ed. Charles Van Engen, Dean S. Gilliland, and Paul Pierson (Eugene, OR: Wipf & Stock, 1993), 82.

of mission.⁶⁷ As Bosch puts it, mission "has its origin in the heart of God."⁶⁸ In the 1960s, the concept of *missio Dei* was popularized through George Vicedom's *The Mission of God: An Introduction to a Theology of Mission*.⁶⁹ Lesslie Newbigin's work also greatly contributed to the popularization of the concept as well as its missiological implications regarding the nature and purposes of the church.⁷⁰ Johannes Blauw developed his idea of the missionary nature of the church on the concept of *missio Dei*.⁷¹ On the whole, since Willingen the understanding of mission as *missio Dei* has been gradually embraced by virtually all Christian persuasions, including the conciliar, evangelical, Roman Catholic, and Eastern Orthodox traditions.⁷²

However, in the 1960s the question of how to interpret the *missio Dei* concept caused sharp debates. As Charles Van Engen points out, "the meaning of 'mission' and the theological understanding of *missio Dei* underwent a

---

67. One of the first theologians to articulate the missiological implications of the doctrine of the Trinity was Karl Barth, who discussed this issue in a paper presented at the Brandenburg Missionary Conference in 1932 (Bosch, *Transforming Mission*, 381). Neither he nor the IMC Willingen conference in 1952 used the term itself. Nevertheless, the text of "The Missionary Calling of the Church" from Willingen explicitly affirms the idea of God's mission: "The missionary movement of which we are part has its source in the Triune God Himself" (International Missionary Council, *Missions under the Cross: Addresses Delivered at the Enlarged Meeting of the Committee of the International Missionary Council at Willingen, in Germany, 1952; With Statements Issued by the Meeting*, ed. Norman Goodall [London: Edinburgh House, 1953], 189).

68. Bosch, *Transforming Mission*, 384.

69. Georg F. Vicedom, *The Mission of God: An Introduction to a Theology of Mission* (Saint Louis, MO: Concordia, 1965).

70. Lesslie Newbigin, *The Relevance of Trinitarian Doctrine for Today's Mission* (London: Edinburgh House, 1963); Lesslie Newbigin, *The Open Secret: An Introduction to the Theology of Mission* (Grand Rapids, MI: Eerdmans, 1995); Lesslie Newbigin, "What Is a Local Church Truly United?," in *Growing Together in Unity: Text of the Faith and Order Commission on Conciliar Fellowship*, ed. Choan-Seng Song (Geneva: Christian Literature Society, 1978), 149–164; Newbigin, *Gospel in a Pluralist Society*. Although Newbigin did not claim to be an evangelical, he was sometimes scathingly critical of the liberal theology of the WCC, and he positively evaluated developments in evangelical mission theology. In one quotation he says, "I do not want to endorse all that is done by the churches and movements that bear the name 'evangelical' . . . [but] it is a very important fact that these bodies are the ones that are growing and showing increasing breadth of vision in their approach to the whole range of contemporary human problems, while the bodies that hold the doctrinal position represented in this book are largely in decline." Lesslie Newbigin, "Ecumenical Amnesia," *International Bulletin of Missionary Research* 18, no. 1 (1994): 4.

71. Blauw, *Missionary Nature of the Church*.

72. Bosch, *Transforming Mission*, 390–391; Scherer, "Church, Kingdom, and Missio Dei," 86–88; Engelsviken, "*Missio Dei*," 490.

radical shift very soon after this initial expression – a shift that brought about the opposite of what was originally intended."[73] In ecumenical theology, this concept was expressed in stark contrast to Blauw's use of it for the articulation of the missionary nature of the church. In his book *The Church Inside Out*, Johannes Hoekendijk argued that making the church the primal locus of God's mission narrows the concept of the kingdom of God.[74] Instead, *missio Dei* should be regarded as God's activity in the world outside the church.

As a result, the concept of *missio Dei* received two primary, and significantly different, interpretations, which caused some confusion in Protestant missiology.[75] Engelsviken calls these two understandings "*missio Dei specialis*" and "*missio Dei generalis*."[76] "*Missio Dei specialis*" is the "classical" understanding of God's mission, referring to the redemptive work of God through the church, whereas "*missio Dei generalis*" focuses on God's work in the social and political spheres, outside the church. In the latter view, the role of the church is understood as discerning what God is doing in the world and participating in it.[77] In the ecumenical theology of the 1960s, this latter view became predominant, while "*missio Dei specialis*" was marginalized.[78] Naturally, the concept of the church and its role in mission were also pushed aside and downplayed.

In evangelical mission theology, however, this secularized understanding of God's mission as the process of historical transformation was rejected in favor of a more biblical and robust understanding of *missio Dei*. The Trinitarian basis of mission was explicitly introduced by John Stott and others at the 1974 Lausanne conference.[79] In his plenary address, "The Biblical Basis of

---

73. Van Engen, *Mission on the Way*, 152.

74. Hoekendijk, *The Church Inside Out*.

75. Engelsviken, "*Missio Dei:*," 481–497; Jacques Matthey, "Missiology in the World Council of Churches: Update, Presentation, History, Theological Background and Emphases of the Most Recent Mission Statement of the WCC," *International Review of Mission* 90 (2001): 429–430; Ott and Strauss, *Encountering Theology of Mission*, 65.

76. Engelsviken, 489.

77. Matthey, "Missiology," 429.

78. Matthey, 429–430; Goheen, *Introducing Christian Mission Today*, 2719–2722.

79. John Stott, "The Biblical Basis of Evangelism," in *Let the Earth Hear His Voice: International Congress on World Evangelization, Lausanne, Switzerland*, ed. J. D. Douglas (Minneapolis, MN: World Wide Publications, 1975), 65–78; Howard Snyder, "The Church as God's Agent in Evangelism," in *Let the Earth Hear His Voice*, 327–360; Stott, "Lausanne Covenant," 28.

Evangelism," John Stott defined the concept of mission in relation to "a sending God":

> "Mission" is an activity of God arising out of the very nature of God. The living God of the Bible is a sending God, which is what "mission" means. He sent the prophets to Israel. He sent his Son into the world. His Son sent out the apostles, and the seventy, and the church. He also sent the Spirit to the church and sends him into our hearts today.[80]

Later, at the 1999 Iguassu Consultation, the importance of basing missiological theory and practice on a Trinitarian understanding of mission was again emphasized.[81] Since then, the Trinitarian understanding of mission has been reaffirmed in post-Lausanne evangelical theologies.[82] The most important implication of the *missio Dei* concept is that mission came to be understood as rooted in divine initiative and character. In fact, "the whole story of the Bible can be understood in terms of God's sending activity."[83] If before mission was commonly understood in either soteriological (as salvation of individuals from eternal damnation) or ecclesiastical categories (as the expansion of the church or of a specific denomination), in the new paradigm, mission is almost universally seen as being derived from the very nature of God.[84] Thus, it was "put in the context of the doctrine of the Trinity, not of ecclesiology or soteriology."[85]

In relation to ecclesiology, one crucial implication of the *missio Dei* is that it makes the church missionary in its own nature: God's mission defines both the church's identity and the scope of its mission. In Bosch's words, "The *missio Dei* institutes the *missiones ecclesiae*. The church changes from

---

80. Stott, "Biblical Basis of Evangelism," 66.

81. Samuel Escobar, "Evangelical Missiology: Peering into the Future at the Turn of the Century," in *Global Missiology in the 21st Century: The Iguassu Dialogue*, ed. William David Taylor (Grand Rapids, MI: Baker Academic, 2000), 101–122; William David Taylor, ed., *Global Missiology in the 21st Century: The Iguassu Dialogue* (Grand Rapids, MI: Baker Academic, 2000), 19.

82. Stott, "Manila Manifesto," 238; The Lausanne Movement, "The Cape Town Commitment."

83. Ott and Strauss, *Encountering Theology of Mission*, 62.

84. Craig Ott describes this turn as a "Copernican revolution" in the understanding of mission. Ott and Strauss, 62.

85. Bosch, *Transforming Mission*, 381.

being the sender to being the one sent."[86] As Scherer profoundly observes, abandoning the church-centered framework "in no way implies forsaking the church's mission, but [it is] rather a re-visioning of that mission from a fresh biblical, missiological, and above all, eschatological point of view."[87] The *missio Dei* concept defines the content of the mission of the church in light of what God is doing in the world. As John Stott puts it: "[T]he mission of the church arises from the mission of God and is to be modeled on it. 'As the Father has sent me,' Jesus said, 'even so I send you.'"[88] The church's mission, therefore, should be modeled after the ministry of Christ whose person and work stands at the center of God's redemptive plan.[89]

The missionary nature of the church is unambiguously affirmed in the Lausanne Covenant: "A church that is not a missionary church is contradicting itself and quenching the Spirit."[90] God's people are both "called out from the world and sent back" into the world "to be his servants and witnesses."[91] The church therefore stands "at the very center of God's cosmic purpose" as "his appointed means" for spreading the gospel and extending the kingdom.[92] The centrality of the church in God's plan means, first of all, that the church does not exist for its own sake: "The church is not an afterthought, not merely a place where individual Christians happen to meet for mutual encouragement. It is the object of Christ's love and the instrument of his service in the world."[93] The idea of an "instrument," in turn, broadens the church's mission beyond the verbal proclamation of the gospel:

> The church has not only a witnessing or participating function in what God is doing in the world, but it has a sacramental or instrumental function, in that the mission of God is carried out in and through the church as its primary locus. The deeper theological reason for this is that humans are saved only by faith in

---

86. Bosch, 361.
87. Scherer, "Church, Kingdom, and Missio Dei," 85.
88. Stott, "Biblical Basis of Evangelism," 66.
89. cf. Newbigin, *Gospel in a Pluralist Society*, 118; Bosch, *Transforming Mission*, 403–404; Wright, *Mission of God's People*, 46.
90. Stott, "Lausanne Covenant," 49.
91. Stott, 9.
92. Stott, 28.
93. Ott and Strauss, *Encountering Theology of Mission*, 22.

Christ, and that this faith comes by hearing the gospel, preached in word and deed (cf. Rom 10:13–15; 15:18–20).[94]

Leslie Newbigin often used three particular nouns to describe the church in its relationship to culture: the sign, instrument, and foretaste of God's kingdom in the world.[95] Since then, this idea has been adopted by a number of evangelical missiologists, even if the exact wording differs.[96] The Cape Town Commitment reflects the three aspects of this understanding of the church when it describes the people of God as "the most vivid present expression of the kingdom of God" who exist to "proclaim and demonstrate the gospel" and "to participate in the transforming mission of God within history."[97]

Cultural Engagement in Mission

The missionary nature of the church, in Bosch's words, "evokes intentional, that is direct involvement in society."[98] In other words, it requires the church's double orientation, to God and to the world. The people of God are called to mediate his blessing to the nations, so their life is to be directed outward for the sake of the world.[99] What this engagement means theologically and practically, however, has caused much debate and disagreement over the two millennia of Christian history.

In his seminal work on *Christ and Culture*, Richard Niebuhr identified five historical patterns of relationships between the church and culture.[100] Multiple studies on the topic that followed Niebuhr have built on his taxonomy as axiomatic, elaborated it further, or questioned its accuracy. More recently, evangelical scholar D.A. Carson and pastor Timothy Keller came up with four rather than five views on Christ and culture, dismissing the "Christ of culture" approach as sub-Christian.[101] Craig A. Carter, whose profound criticism of

---

94. Engelsviken, "*Missio Dei*," 485–486.
95. Newbigin, *Gospel in a Pluralist Society*, 233; Newbigin, *Open Secret*, 110.
96. Goheen, *Light to the Nations*; Goheen, *Introducing Christian Mission Today*, 4065.
97. The Lausanne Movement, "The Cape Town Commitment."
98. Bosch, *Transforming Mission*, 364.
99. Goheen, *Light to the Nations*, 191–192.
100. Helmut Richard Niebuhr, *Christ and Culture* (New York: Harper, 1956).
101. D. A. Carson, *Christ and Culture Revisited* (Grand Rapids, MI: Eerdmans, 2008); Timothy Keller, *Center Church: Doing Balanced, Gospel-Centered Ministry in Your City*, Kindle

Niebuhr's work was that Niebuhr assumed that the era of "Christendom" was still in place, suggested his own typology, which includes six approaches.[102] James Hunter used a sociological rather than historical approach to identify three contemporary models of cultural engagement in North America, in contrast to which he then proposed his own model.[103] Admittedly, none of the taxonomies can do justice to all historical and biblical themes, yet they remain helpful as heuristic devices. Overall, they suggest that historically the church has tended either to identify with culture, to separate from it, or to develop various forms of engagement with it.

Evangelical tradition has absorbed multiple historical influences, and it displays, to use Nicholas Wolterstorff's terms, both *avertive* forms of Christianity (especially in its pietistic expressions, which have greatly influenced Russian Baptists) and its opposite – *world-formative* ones (especially those churches influenced by the Reformed tradition). The former reflects dualistic thinking which distinguishes within reality the realm of the sacred from the realm of the secular. The world outside the church is perceived as a hostile power, and the fundamental goal of life is seen as turning away from the inferior realm so as to attain closer *relationships* with the higher reality, God. In the latter, one seeks reformation of the inferior realm in *obedience* to God, rather than acquiescing to it or turning away from it. Instead of looking at the totality of God's creation through the lens of the fall, this view emphasizes the goodness of God's creation and the continuity of cultural efforts in the new creation.[104] Thus, in avertive religion one "desires to become a vessel of God" and in the world-formative religion one "desires to become an instrument of God."[105]

In recent decades several distinctive evangelical positions have been articulated that deserve to be briefly presented here. The first approach aims at changing culture for Christ. Tim Keller lumps together in this group

---

Edition (Grand Rapids, MI: Zondervan, 2012).

102. Craig A. Carter, *Rethinking Christ and Culture: A Post-Christendom Perspective* (Grand Rapids, MI: Brazos, 2006).

103. James Davison Hunter, *To Change the World: The Irony, Tragedy, and Possibility of Christianity in the Late Modern World* (New York: Oxford University Press, 2010).

104. Bosch, *Transforming Mission*, 367; Niebuhr, *Christ and Culture*, 188.

105. Nicholas Wolterstorff, *Until Justice and Peace Embrace* (Grand Rapids, MI: Eerdmans, 1983), 11.

(which he calls "transformationists") such movements as the Christian Right (Jerry Falwell), Christian Reconstructionism (Rousas Rushdoony), and the "Kuyperian" neo-Calvinists (Anthony Hoekema, Nicholas Wolterstorff, Francis Schaeffer, Albert Wolters, Charles Colson, Alvin Plantinga, Craig Bartholomew, and Michael Goheen).[106] The differences in this camp mostly have to do with strategies of cultural change, in that some groups see government and politics as the primary instruments, while others emphasize the role of education, the media, economics, and the arts. Yet all of them believe that redemption in Christ empowers the church "to be nothing less than God's agents in building a new Christian culture."[107] So Christians should work "to help bring Christ's restoration to the entire creation order."[108]

A rather different, if not opposite, approach gained popularity shortly before the first Lausanne Congress in 1974. It was formulated by John Howard Yoder, a prominent Mennonite theologian and ethicist who wrote from an Anabaptist perspective. For him, Jesus was "the bearer of a new possibility of human, social, and therefore political relationships," first in his own person, and then through the creation of "a new kind of community leading to a radically new kind of life."[109] The church is thus a counter-cultural community, a "sample of humanity within which . . . economic and racial differences are surmounted."[110] The primary task of the church, as God's "pilot project," is to *be* the church God intends, by imitating Christ's style of life of which the cross is the culmination.[111] By its very existence this community presents a social alternative to the reigning structures and so "challenges the system as no mere words ever could."[112]

Yoder's thought, albeit with somewhat different emphases, was further developed by Stanley Hauerwas and William H. Willimon. Writing from within the cultural and social context of post-Christendom society, they claim

---

106. Keller, *Center Church*.

107. Charles W. Colson and Nancy Pearcey, *How Now Shall We Live?* (Wheaton, IL: Tyndale House, 1999), 279.

108. Colson and Pearcey, *How Now Shall We Live?*, xiii.

109. Yoder, *Politics of Jesus*, 63.

110. Yoder, 154.

111. John Howard Yoder, *The Royal Priesthood: Essays Ecclesiological and Ecumenical* (Grand Rapids, MI: Eerdmans, 1994), 126.

112. Yoder, *Politics of Jesus*, 40.

that Scripture "shows us the world to be alien, an odd place where what makes sense to everybody else is revealed to be opposed to what God is doing among us."[113] The authors are harshly critical of almost every aspect of Western culture, especially of the values and institutions of North American capitalist democracy, produced by "the liberalism of the Enlightenment."[114] They disparage its rationality, its concept of justice, civil religion, the notion of individual rights and freedom, the idea of the nation state, and, most of all, its secularism.[115] Even working for peace is of no value because it is done for "idolatrous reasons . . . namely, the anxious self-interested protection of our world as it is."[116] In fact, the world's morality at its highest, for instance, as expressed in Kant, could be described as "demonic."[117]

The church living in this environment is portrayed with the help of metaphors as an exilic people living in a foreign land: "resident aliens," "strangers in the strange land," "one culture in the middle of another," a "new polis," and "a social alternative" to the world.[118] Rather than making the world a better place to live in, the church should focus on the spiritual formation of its members, i.e., discipleship. The goal of this process is seen in the "production of people who more closely resemble, in their life-style, beliefs, and values, disciples of Jesus."[119] To achieve this purpose, the church has to renounce any forms of "accommodationist" thinking in its apologetics, preaching, worship, pastoral care, and theological education. Whenever the church is faithful to its calling, it "confronts the world with a political alternative the world would not otherwise know."[120] Therefore, the formation of God's people in the church can be legitimately called the main "political task of the church."[121]

---

113. Hauerwas and Willimon, *Resident Aliens*, 75.
114. Hauerwas and Willimon, 49.
115. Hauerwas and Willimon, 50, 156, 159.
116. Hauerwas and Willimon, 89.
117. Hauerwas and Willimon, 102.
118. Hauerwas and Willimon, 11, 12, 30.
119. Hauerwas and Willimon, 105.
120. Hauerwas and Willimon, 41.
121. Hauerwas and Willimon, 48.

Another distinctive evangelical perspective, though not as common or well-known, is offered by David VanDrunen and Michael Horton.[122] It aims to present a biblical alternative to the concept of the redemptive transformation of culture espoused by representatives of neo-Calvinism, the New Perspective on Paul, and the Emerging Church movement.[123] For VanDrunen and Horton, the whole concept of cultural transformation is misguided and is not true to Scripture. The alternative is found in the doctrine of the "two kingdoms," which he traces back to Augustine's concept of the "two cities." According to this doctrine, "God is not redeeming the cultural activities and institutions of this world, but is preserving them through the covenant he made with all living creatures through Noah in Genesis 8:20–9:17 . . . Simultaneously, God is redeeming a people for himself, by virtue of the covenant made with Abraham."[124]

In this theology, the so-called "cultural mandate" (Gen 1:28) was never actually intended for all people, because it was limited exclusively to the first human, Adam, and had a specific purpose: "By a divine covenant, Adam's righteous cultural labors would have earned him a share in the eschatological world-to-come."[125] The first Adam failed terribly, so God sent a second and last Adam, Jesus Christ, who took upon himself Adam's responsibility and fulfilled the original task once and for all. As a result, God "does not call [Christians] to engage in cultural labors so as to earn their place in the world-to-come. We are not little Adams."[126] As for the people of God who in this view are directly identified with the redemptive kingdom, their chief action takes place in the church, whereas all the other institutions or cultural activities are secondary.[127] In fact, all of that "will come to an abrupt end, along with this present world as a whole" when Christ ushers in the new heaven

---

122. David VanDrunen, "The Two Kingdoms and the Ordo Salutis: Life beyond Judgment and the Question of a Dual Ethic," *Westminster Theological Journal* 70 (2008): 207–224; David VanDrunen, *Living in God's Two Kingdoms: A Biblical Vision for Christianity and Culture*, Kindle Edition (Wheaton, IL: Crossway, 2010); Michael S. Horton, "How the Kingdom Comes," *Christianity Today* 50, no. 1 (2006): 44–45.

123. Wright, *Surprised by Hope*; Brian D. McLaren, *Everything Must Change: Jesus, Global Crises, and a Revolution of Hope* (Nashville, TN: Thomas Nelson, 2007).

124. VanDrunen, *God's Two Kingdoms*, 15.

125. VanDrunen, 27.

126. VanDrunen, 28.

127. VanDrunen, 102.

and new earth.[128] Until then, Christians are to live like exiles in the midst of "Babylon," acknowledging both "spiritual antithesis and cultural commonality" with the present world order.[129]

James Hunter in his important book describes common evangelical approaches to cultural engagement in North America and brings them together into three broad categories: "defensive against" (e.g. the Christian Right), "relevance to" (the Christian Left), and "purity from" culture (the neo-Anabaptists). He carefully evaluates, both theologically and sociologically, their assumptions and impact, and concludes that strategies of cultural change based on any of them ultimately fail to achieve their purpose. The primary reason for this failure lies in a mistaken understanding of two core concepts, culture and power. The popular evangelical view of culture as a worldview or the values in the hearts and mind of individuals that are manifest through the choices we make reflects the strong influence of idealism and individualism and is fundamentally flawed.[130]

Hunter develops an alternative view of culture in which it is seen as "a system of truth claims and moral obligations" that is rooted in history and "embedded in very powerful institutions, networks, interests, and symbols."[131] Therefore, the deepest forms of cultural change typically occur from the "top down," through the work of elites, or cultural "gatekeepers," who provide creative direction and management within spheres of social life. Also, evangelicals typically think of power primarily in political terms, regardless of whether they strive to obtain or renounce it. For Hunter, however, what counts for culture change is cultural (or symbolic) and social power. In this regard, American evangelicalism is weak and divided. Yet without attention to this factor, Christians will not engage the culture effectively.[132]

Hunter's alternative model of cultural engagement is called a "theology of faithful presence." It begins with an acknowledgement of God's faithful presence with us and his call to us is to be faithfully present to him and others

---

128. VanDrunen, 29.
129. VanDrunen, 73–74, 99.
130. Hunter, *To Change the World*, 272.
131. Hunter, 32, 44.
132. Hunter, 32–92.

in return.¹³³ The practice of faithful presence requires rejection not only of "the Constantinian temptation" of political domination, but also models of being defensive against, isolated from, or absorbed into the dominant culture. This model affirms the centrality of the church as a community that offers an alternative formation to what is offered by popular culture. Based on the incarnation of Christ, it requires that the church live within a dialectic of *affirmation* and *antithesis* toward culture.¹³⁴ Through this, the church strengthens its healthy qualities and humbly criticizes and subverts its most destructive tendencies.¹³⁵

Thus, unlike some versions of the neo-Calvinist theology of culture, this model avoids the imagery of dominion and conquest. Its primary purpose is not to change the world per se, but rather to worship and honor God in all it does. In fact, the language of conquest exposes what Hunter calls *politicization*, or the proclivity to think of the Christian faith and its engagement with the culture around it in political terms. In Hunter's view, politicization has "delimited the imaginative horizon through which the church and Christian believers think about engaging the world and the range of possibilities within which they actually act.... It is essential, however, to demythologize politics, to see politics for what it is and what it can and cannot do and not place on it unrealistic expectations."¹³⁶ Instead, a theology of faithful presence

> obligates us to do what we are able, under the sovereignty of God, to shape the patterns of life and work and relationship – that is, the institutions of which our lives are constituted – toward a shalom that seeks the welfare not only of those of the household of God but of all. That power will be wielded is inevitable. But the *means of influence* and the *ends of influence* must conform to the exercise of power modeled by Christ.¹³⁷

From this perspective, the critical tension between *affirmation* and *antithesis* is the key for biblically informed cultural engagement for the sake of

---

133. Hunter, 240–242.
134. Hunter, 281.
135. Hunter, 285.
136. Hunter, 185–186.
137. Hunter, 254; emphasis original.

the gospel. A similar idea is expressed under different names by many other theologians, both mainline and evangelical. Andrew Walls views the whole span of Christian history as "a battleground for two opposing principles" – the *indigenizing* principle and the *pilgrim* principle, which are in constant tension, because both originate from the gospel itself.[138] Newbigin speaks of an unbearable tension in the life of the church as it seeks to avoid both syncretism and irrelevance at the intersection of the gospel and the cultural worldview.[139] Howard Snyder speaks of "the redemptive tension" of the church's double orientation[140], and Bosch applies his concept of "creative tension" to the church's stance between complete identification with the world's agenda and a form of escapism that "makes a mockery of the true claims" of Christianity.[141] Goheen repeatedly speaks of "affirmation and critique," "embrace and rejection," and "solidarity" with, and "antithesis" toward, culture.[142]

The first Lausanne Congress in 1974 did not discuss in depth the issue of gospel and culture theologically, although there was a general awareness of "the problems raised by culture."[143] In the years following the congress, the Movement would pay more attention to these problems. Thus, in 1978, the Willowbank international consultation on Gospel and Culture, sponsored by the Lausanne Theology and Education Group, further explored the implications of the Covenant with regard to culture. The consultation produced the Willowbank report (LOP 2) that made a significant contribution to an evangelical understanding of the relationship between gospel and culture in several areas. First, it suggested a definition of culture which "offered hope for the possibility of an open and fruitful discussion among evangelicals worldwide."[144] Second, it emphasized the need for humility on the part of the messengers of the gospel. And third, it clearly delineated the

---

138. Walls, *Missionary Movement*, 7.

139. Lesslie Newbigin, *Foolishness to the Greeks: The Gospel and Western Culture* (Grand Rapids, MI: Eerdmans, 1986); Newbigin, *Gospel in a Pluralist Society*.

140. Howard Snyder, *Liberating the Church: The Ecology of Church and Kingdom* (Eugene, OR: Wipf & Stock, 1983), 29.

141. Bosch, *Transforming Mission*, 373–377.

142. Goheen, *Introducing Christian Mission Today*, 4815.

143. Stott, *Making Christ Known*, xv.

144. Tite Tiénou, "Gospel and Cultures in the Lausanne Movement," in *The Lausanne Movement: A Range of Perspectives*, ed. Lars Dahle, Margunn Serigstad Dahle, and Knud Jørgensen (Eugene, OR: Wipf & Stock, 2014), 164.

nature and content of the gospel. According to John Stott, the importance of the Willowbank report was that it had carefully considered the influence of culture in six areas – "in the writers and the readers of the Bible (since they and we are both culturally conditioned), in the preaching and the receiving of the Bible (contextualization and conversion), in the formation of the church and in ethical behavior."[145]

Robert Schreiter observes within Lausanne theology after 1974 a move away from the original statement with regard to human culture and the world.[146] Thus, in the Lausanne Covenant, the church is set over against the world, which flows from the Covenant's interpretation of the fall in Genesis 3. Manila generally maintains this stance, but also positively emphasizes the importance of engaging the world. Cape Town takes a much different approach by "framing the biblical narrative of God's action in the world with the theme of love."[147] Harold Netland, however, disagrees with Schreiter in that Cape Town represents a fundamental shift in evangelical theology of mission. Although the Commitment does extol love for the world of nations and cultures, the original Covenant also had positive things to say about culture. In addition, the Cape Town Commitment speaks rather clearly about sin and evil in the world.[148] From this perspective, therefore, the perceived change is not a deviation from the original commitments, but rather maturation in understanding.

Likewise, the tension between "solidarity" and "antithsis" has been clearly reflected in the Lausanne primary documents. The Covenant states: "We confess with shame that we have often denied our calling and failed in our mission, by becoming conformed to the world or by withdrawing from it."[149] The Manila Manifesto emphasizes the side of the tension in which conservative evangelicals were historically weak: "We deeply regret that many of our congregations are inward-looking, organized for maintenance rather than mission, or preoccupied with church-based activities at the expense of

---

145. Stott, *Making Christ Known*, xvii.

146. Schreiter, "From the Lausanne Covenant."

147. Schreiter, 90.

148. Harold Netland, "The Cape Town Commitment: Continuity and Change," in *The Lausanne Movement: A Range of Perspectives*, ed. Lars Dahle, Margunn Serigstad Dahle, and Knud Jørgensen (Eugene, OR: Wipf & Stock, 2014), 429.

149. Stott, "Lausanne Covenant," 9.

witness. We determine to turn our churches inside out."[150] The Cape Town Commitment longs to see the gospel "embodied and embedded in all cultures, redeeming them from within." Love to God's world, however, "includes critical discernment," for "all cultures show not only positive evidence of the image of God in human lives, but also the negative fingerprints of Satan and sin" (I.7).[151]

The critical question, therefore, is how to discern between the cultural good and the effects of sin in culture. This requires the concept of a biblical worldview based on the entire narrative of Scripture. John Stott was one of the earliest evangelical theologians to propose a fourfold scheme of biblical history: the creation ("the good"), the fall ("the evil"), redemption ("the new"), and the consummation ("the perfect").[152] Stott believed that this framework "supplies the true perspective from which to view the unfolding process between two eternities, the vision of God working out his purpose . . . a way of integrating our understanding, [and] the possibility of thinking straight, even about the complex issues."[153] D.A. Carson, in his elaboration of the "Christ-and-culture" theme, also takes into account the major turning points of redemptive history. He affirms that these so-called "non-negotiables" of biblical theology "must control our thinking *simultaneously* and *all the time.*"[154] Likewise, the Cape Town Commitment sees the Bible as the "universal story of creation, fall, redemption in history, and new creation." This "overarching narrative" provides Christians with a "coherent biblical worldview and shapes [their] theology."[155]

---

150. Stott, "Manila Manifesto," 242.
151. The Lausanne Movement, "The Cape Town Commitment."
152. John Stott, *Issues Facing Christians Today* (Grand Rapids, MI: Zondervan, 1984).
153. Stott, *Issues Facing Christians Today*, 64.
154. Carson, *Christ and Culture Revisited*, 59. Emphasis original.
155. The Lausanne Movement, "The Cape Town Commitment." In thinking about culture it is also important to take into account the fact that God's missionary purposes are cosmic in scope, concerned with the renewal of all creation, and not just the salvation of fallen humanity. Wright, *Mission of God*, 67; Stuart Murray, *Church Planting: Laying Foundations*, Kindle Edition (Scottdale, PA: Herald, 2001), 403. This emphasis on the comprehensive scope of redemption is an important complement to Stott's and Carson's rather chronological turning points.

A comprehensive framework for cultural engagement can be found in the notion of missionary encounter with culture.[156] According to Goheen, it is based on recognition of the fact that human life, by its very nature, is culturally embodied, which means that anti-cultural stances are misguided. A polemical opposition to culture that seeks to displace the dominant public narratives with one that is Christian is equally misguided, because any culture retains much creational good. A missionary encounter happens when the church lives fully in the biblical story and interprets its culture in the light of that story. By faithfully embodying the gospel, the church challenges the idolatrous cultural story and offers the gospel as a counter-story, as a credible alternative way of life. This will challenge the foundational beliefs shared by a cultural community and call for radical conversion as an invitation to understand and live in the world in the light of the gospel. The struggle, therefore, is to find a faithful way that is embodied and expressed within the culture.[157]

In his seminal article "Can the West be Converted?," Newbigin discusses what is necessary for an "effective missionary encounter" with Western culture.[158] Much of the article is devoted to the contours of a new apologetic that challenges the neutrality of secular reason. In the conclusion Newbigin lists several additional elements, namely (1) the "declericalizing" of theology so that it is done in the public rather than private sector; (2) the recovery of the teaching of the kingdom of God as the restoration of the whole creation rather than the survival of individual souls; (3) a humble post-Christendom stance which understands the "difference between bearing witness to the truth and pretending to possess the truth"; (4) a unified church which radically breaks with denominationalism; (5) the need to learn how to listen to the voice of the global church; and (6) the need for courage in wrestling against the spiritual powers behind the cultural forces. Elsewhere, Newbigin speaks of three other essential elements of this encounter: (7) a counter-cultural church community that serves as "the hermeneutic of the gospel"; (8) earning

---

156. Newbigin, *Foolishness to the Greeks*; Wilbert R. Shenk, *Write the Vision: The Church Renewed* (Valley Forge, PA: Trinity Press International, 1995); Keller, *Center Church*; Goheen, *Introducing Christian Mission Today*.

157. Goheen, *Introducing Christian Mission Today*, 4919.

158. Lesslie Newbigin, "Can the West Be Converted?," *International Bulletin of Missionary Research* 11, no. 1 (1987): 2–7. In view of globalization processes, many of his observations are highly relevant for the global church in other cultures as well.

the right to be heard through willingness to serve others sacrificially; and (9) transforming culture through equipping the laity to bring the implications of their faith into their public callings.[159]

Bosch spells out his vision for mission in the post-Christian West along similar lines. In dealing with culture, the church must first of all avoid two opposing errors: trying to re-create a Christian society (the mistake of Christendom) and withdrawing from society into the "spiritual realm" (the mistake of modernity). Second, Christians must learn how to challenge publicly and prophetically the idol of autonomous reason and its results. Third, local churches must become contrast societies or countercultures that demonstrate to society what human life would look like if it was free from the idols of race, wealth, sex, power, and individual autonomy. These communities model an alternative society by allowing the gospel to shape how they live in the world. This will require equipping the laity for their public callings. Finally, the church needs to cultivate life-shaping worship that nurtures the life of mission, and to model as much unity between churches as is practically possible.[160]

Wilbert Shenk describes missionary encounter with culture as the church turning outward out of concern for the welfare of all people rather than being focused inward on individual spiritual and personal concerns.[161] This presupposes two essential tasks. First, the church must develop a deep consciousness of its own missional identity; and second, the church must foster an outward-facing mission consciousness.[162] As a result, however, the church will have to live in "an inescapable tension with the sociopolitical order."[163] Building on the legacy of Newbigin and Shenk, Michael Goheen believes that the missionary encounter with culture requires the recovery of three things: an awareness of the public truth of the gospel of the kingdom, a recognition and acceptance of the missional nature of the church, and a commitment to

---

159. Newbigin; Keller, *Center Church*, 7324.

160. David J. Bosch, *Believing in the Future: Toward a Missiology of Western Culture* (Valley Forge, PA: Trinity Press International, 1995).

161. Wilbert R. Shenk, "Missionary Encounter with Culture," *International Bulletin of Missionary Research* 15 (1991): 104–109; Shenk, *Write the Vision*.

162. Shenk, *Write the Vision*, 87, 94.

163. Wilbert R. Shenk, *Changing Frontiers of Mission* (Maryknoll, NY: Orbis Books, 1999), 128.

engage in missional analysis of Western culture. He categorizes these three tasks correspondingly as theological, ecclesiological, and cultural.[164]

One result of a successful missionary encounter with culture will be the contextualization of the gospel; that is, its expression in terms of a particular culture as well as the transformation of certain aspects of that culture.[165] Scott Moreau[166] suggests a model of "comprehensive contextualization" which covers the seven dimensions of religion (doctrinal, mythic, ethical, social, ritual, experiential, and material) noted earlier by religious scholar Ninian Smart.[167] Some other missiologists point out that contextualization should go beyond the sphere of religion: it should aim at the faithful living out of the gospel "across the whole spectrum of human life in the midst of a culture shaped by a different set of religious beliefs."[168] Darrell Whiteman[169] describes the goal of contextualization as "presenting Christianity in such a way that it meets people's deepest needs and penetrates their worldview."[170] Critical contextualization is therefore "an ongoing process . . . that can lead to a better understanding of what the lordship of Christ and the kingdom of God on earth are about."[171]

Finally, several authors stress the fact that a missionary encounter with culture will bring suffering to the church.[172] In the post-Christendom context, Christians should understand that "witness (marturia) means not dominance and control but suffering."[173] When the church is faithful to the gospel, its life and witness "will overturn the world's most fundamental beliefs," challenging

---

164. Goheen, *Introducing Christian Mission Today*, 4956.

165. Paul G. Hiebert, "Critical Contextualization," *International Bulletin of Missionary Research* 11, no. 3 (1987): 104–112; Paul G. Hiebert, *Anthropological Reflections on Missiological Issues* (Grand Rapids, MI: Baker Book House, 1994); Bosch, *Transforming Mission*.

166. Scott Moreau, "Contextualization That Is Comprehensive," *Missiology: An International Review* 34, no. 3 (2006): 325–335.

167. Ninian Smart, *Dimensions of the Sacred: An Anatomy of the World's Beliefs* (Berkeley: University of California Press, 1996).

168. Goheen, *Introducing Christian Mission Today*, 4764–4766.

169. Darrell L. Whiteman, "Contextualization: The Theory, the Gap, the Challenge," *International Bulletin of Missionary Research* 21 (1997): 2–7.

170. Whiteman, "Contextualization," 2.

171. Hiebert, "Critical Contextualization," 111; Hiebert, *Anthropological Reflections*, 92.

172. Newbigin, "Can the West Be Converted?"; Shenk, "Missionary Encounter with Culture"; Wright, *Mission of God's People*; Goheen, *Introducing Christian Mission Today*.

173. Newbigin, "Can the West Be Converted?," 7.

the ruling powers. As a result, "there will be conflict and suffering for the Church."[174] Louis Berkhof reminds us that there are two ways by which the church may avoid this clash with society: sacralization and secularization.[175] Although "sacralization" – that is, when the church is concerned only for its own institutional life – looks more pious and respectable than outright secularization, in the final analysis it is no less unfaithful than the latter. Each is a different form of the church's refusal to embrace its missionary calling.[176]

Holistic Mission

In his now-classic work, David Bosch observes that "the relationship between the evangelistic and the societal dimensions of the Christian mission constitutes one of the thorniest areas in [the] theology and practice of mission."[177] This is certainly true with regard to the issue of holistic, or integral, mission. The term usually means mission that is concerned with "the whole scope of human need,"[178] or with "transforming the whole of creation, the whole person, body, mind, and spirit."[179] This approach to mission, therefore, strives to integrate evangelism, or what the church says, and social responsibility, or what the church does.[180]

By the end of the nineteenth century the liberal social gospel and the evangelical revivalist tradition arrived at two different views of mission that developed in counterpoint to one another. By the 1930s, partially in reaction to the emphasis on socio-political action for justice, dominant in liberal

---

174. Newbigin, *Gospel in a Pluralist Society*, 107, 136.

175. Hendrikus Berkhof, *Christian Faith: An Introduction to the Study of the Faith* (Grand Rapids, MI: Eerdmans, 1979).

176. Goheen, *Introducing Christian Mission Today*, 1289–1291.

177. Bosch, *Transforming Mission*, 392.

178. Christopher J. H. Wright, "Holistic Mission," 2012, http://www.wycliffe.net/missiology?id=2723.

179. Brian E. Woolnough and Wonsuk Ma, eds., *Holistic Mission: God's Plan for God's People* (Eugene, OR: Wipf & Stock, 2010), xi.

180. Las Newman, "Foreword," in *Holistic Mission: God's Plan for God's People*, ed. Brian Woolnough and Wonsuk Ma (Eugene, OR: Wipf & Stock, 2010), ix–x; Ronald J. Sider, Philip N. Olson, and Heidi Rolland Unruh, *Churches That Make a Difference: Reaching Your Community with Good News and Good Works* (Grand Rapids, MI: Baker Book House, 2002). Lausanne Occasional Paper 21 divides the social dimension of mission into two primary forms: social service (or acts of mercy) and social action (or acts of justice). I will adopt this division for the presentation of research findings in later chapters.

circles, and partially due to the influence of premillenialism and individualism, the evangelical community in the West largely reduced the church's task in mission to the verbal proclamation of the gospel.[181] The notion of sin was reduced to individual disobedience, and, accordingly, salvation was seen as individual conversion that led to eternal life in heaven after one's death.[182]

In the late 1940s, Carl Henry challenged what he described as "the uneasy conscience" of fundamentalism, calling on evangelicals to undertake social action, to engage with the culture, and to speak out publicly against social evils.[183] Gradually, a "new social conscience" began to develop and, by the middle of the 1970s, most evangelicals recognized social concern as a legitimate part of mission.[184] Already in 1966 this change was apparent at the World Congress on Evangelism in Berlin, where the social dimensions of the gospel were explored in several papers. That same year the Wheaton Declaration called upon evangelicals to engage in social action and to be actively involved in the pursuit of justice.[185] However, it was the Lausanne Congress on World Evangelization (LCWE, 1974) that most decisively marked the turn toward holistic mission in evangelical missiology. Although the Lausanne Covenant explicitly rejected conciliar formulations of mission and prioritized evangelism over social concern, it unambiguously called on the church to see social action as part of its duty. The Lausanne Covenant reads:

> We express penitence . . . for having sometimes regarded evangelism and social concern as mutually exclusive. Although reconciliation with other people is not reconciliation with God, nor is social action evangelism, nor is political liberation salvation, nevertheless we affirm that evangelism and socio-political involvement are both part of our Christian duty. For both are

---

181. This turn has sometimes been referred to as the "great reversal." David O. Moberg, *The Great Reversal: Evangelism Versus Social Concern* (Philadelphia, PA: Lippincott, 1972).

182. Richard Lovelace, "Completing an Awakening," *The Christian Century* 98, no. 9 (1981): 298; Bosch, *Transforming Mission*; Goheen, *Introducing Christian Mission Today*; Ott and Strauss, *Encountering Theology of Mission*.

183. Carl F. H. Henry, *The Uneasy Conscience of Modern Fundamentalism* (Grand Rapids, MI: Eerdmans, 1947).

184. Goheen, *Introducing Christian Mission Today*, 3769.

185. Ott and Strauss, *Encountering Theology of Mission*, 139.

necessary expressions of our doctrines of God and man, our love for our neighbor and our obedience to Jesus Christ.[186]

In light of the prevalent evangelical understanding of mission as evangelism and church planting, this view was indeed revolutionary. The fresh rediscovery of the church's broader mission reflected the new theological understanding of *missio Dei*. Moreover, during the Congress, a group of participants called for an even stronger stance on social involvement in an ad hoc paper entitled "Theology and Implications of Radical Discipleship."[187] Members of this group which included René Padilla, Samuel Escobar, Orlando Costas and others criticized the Covenant for minimizing social concern. Later, John Stott also changed his mind on the issue. One year after the Congress he wrote: "I now see more clearly that not only the consequences of the commission but the actual commission itself must be understood to include social as well as evangelistic responsibility, unless we are to be guilty of distorting the words of Jesus."[188] In the decade following Lausanne I a significant amount of literature by various evangelical theologians advocating holistic mission was published.[189]

Eight years later, the LCWE-sponsored international Consultation on the Relationship between Evangelism and Social Concern (CRESR) took place in Grand Rapids, Michigan. In the words of Craig Ott, this was perhaps "the most significant" event aimed at clarifying the evangelical position regarding the place of social action in mission.[190] The resulting report, which was a compromise statement after much bitter debate, maintained the priority of evangelism over social action, but also described their relationship as "partnership" and "marriage" in which social action is a consequence of, a bridge

---

186. Stott, "Lausanne Covenant," 24.

187. Ad Hoc Group, "Radical Discipleship."

188. John Stott, *Christian Mission in the Modern World* (Downers Grove, IL: IVP Academic, 1975), 23.

189. Costas, *Church and Its Mission*; Orlando E. Costas, *Christ Outside the Gate: Mission Beyond Christendom* (Maryknoll, NY: Orbis Books, 1982); Samuel Escobar and John Driver, *Christian Mission and Social Justice* (Scottdale, PA: Herald, 1978); William A. Dyrness, *Let the Earth Rejoice! A Biblical Theology of Holistic Mission* (Westchester, IL: Crossway, 1983); C. René Padilla, "Response," in *In Word and Deed: Evangelism and Social Responsibility*, ed. Bruce Nicholls (Grand Rapids, MI: Eerdmans, 1985), 133–134.

190. Ott and Strauss, *Encountering Theology of Mission*, 140.

to, and a partner of evangelism.[191] In 1989, the Manila Manifesto confirmed the commitment of the Lausanne Covenant to social justice, as well as its prioritizing of evangelism over social concern. The document articulated the strong conviction that "the biblical gospel has inescapable social implications," and that the proclamation of God's kingdom "necessarily demands the prophetic denunciation of all that is incompatible with it."[192] In the spirit of the first Lausanne conference, the Manifesto repented of the traditional dualistic thinking and practice in evangelical mission: "We repent that the narrowness of our concerns and vision has often kept us from proclaiming the lordship of Jesus Christ over all of life, private and public, local and global."[193]

The third Lausanne Congress in Cape Town marked "the consolidation of [the] recovery" of an integrated and holistic understanding of mission.[194] The Cape Town Commitment roots the church's mission in *missio Dei* and views it as "the integration of evangelism and committed engagement in the world."[195] Following the Micah Network Declaration on Integral Mission (2001), the Commitment adopts the term "integral" as basically synonymous with "holistic":

> Integral mission means discerning, proclaiming, and living out, the biblical truth that the gospel is God's good news, through the cross and resurrection of Jesus Christ, for individual persons, and for society, and for creation. All three are broken and suffering because of sin: all three are included in the redeeming love and mission of God: all three must be part of the comprehensive mission of God's people.[196]

On the whole, as Las Newman observes, "One of the most important developments in contemporary Christian missiology is the recovery of a theology of mission in the late twentieth century that integrates faith and life,

---

191. Lausanne Committee for World Evangelization, "Evangelism and Social Responsibility: An Evangelical Commitment (LOP 21)," 1982, https://www.lausanne.org/content/lop/lop-21.

192. Stott, "Manila Manifesto," 236–237.

193. Stott, 237.

194. Cameron, *Cape Town Commitment*; Christopher Wright in praise for Woolnough and Ma, *Holistic Mission*.

195. The Lausanne Movement, "The Cape Town Commitment."

196. The Lausanne Movement.

word and deed, proclamation and presence."[197] In this regard, there has been a certain moderation in both evangelical and conciliar missiological positions, resulting in a measure of convergence between them. While in evangelical circles the pendulum has swung back to a more holistic perspective of mission, in ecumenical circles recognition of the church's role and the importance of evangelism in mission have become more prominent.[198]

However, not all evangelicals have welcomed the emerging view of holistic mission. Arthur P. Johnston insisted that "Historically the mission of the church is evangelism alone."[199] For Donald McGavran, evangelism and church planting remained primary, if not the only proper definition of mission, although he did believe these would lead to personal and social change.[200] Contrary to Stott, David Hesselgrave argued that the Great Commission, as it appears in Matthew 28:18–20, rather than the version found in John 20:21 is Christ's ultimate statement on mission.[201] He has advocated the traditional view of "prioritism" which does not rule out social action in mission, but prioritizes evangelism and church planting.[202] John MacArthur, who has exerted tremendous influence on Russian Baptists and has become *the* Bible expositor for many of them, claims:

> God's purpose in this world – and the church's only legitimate commission – is the proclamation of the message of sin and

---

197. "Foreword" to Woolnough and Ma, *Holistic Mission*, ix.

198. Bosch, *Transforming Mission*, 399; Ott and Strauss, *Encountering Theology of Mission*, 137. A more comprehensive perspective on mission was reflected in the recent World Council of Churches conference 2013 in Busan, South Korea. "Adopted Documents and Statements," World Council of Churches, accessed 26 June 2017, https://www.oikoumene.org/en/resources/documents/assembly/2013-busan/adopted-documents-statements.

199. Arthur P. Johnston, *The Battle for World Evangelism* (Wheaton, IL: Tyndale House, 1978), 18.

200. Donald A. McGavran, *Understanding Church Growth* (Grand Rapids, MI: Eerdmans, 1970); Arthur F. Glasser and Donald A. McGavran, *Contemporary Theologies of Mission* (Grand Rapids, MI: Baker Book House, 1983).

201. David J. Hesselgrave, "Redefining Holism," *Evangelical Missions Quarterly* 35 (1999): 278–284.

202. David J. Hesselgrave, *Paradigms in Conflict: Ten Key Questions in Christian Missions Today* (Grand Rapids, MI: Kregel, 2005).

salvation to individuals, whom God sovereignty redeems and calls out of the world.[203]

Christ did not come to promote some new social agenda or establish a new moral order. He did come to establish a new spiritual order, the body of believers from throughout the ages that constitutes his church . . . In the truest sense, the moral, social, and political state of a people is irrelevant to the advance of the gospel. Jesus said that His kingdom was not of this world.[204]

Many evangelicals today continue to criticize the Lausanne commitment to "holistic mission."[205] Moreover, among those who do accept a broader view of mission, debates persist on the nature of the connection between the gospel and social action. As Harvie Conn points out, "The fact remains that we are far from a holistic solution that integrates the two components . . . Two abstractions do not make a whole. But two are better than one."[206] Craig Ott observes that the debate is complicated and problematic in at least two ways. First, many advocates of holistic mission come from contexts where injustice and poverty are strong concerns. Their opponents, on the other hand, fear that the church's mission can be watered down or hijacked by other agendas, such as social justice.[207] Second, the two positions are often "not as far apart in practice as they are in the rhetoric."[208]

Obviously, the fear that *missio Dei* may become divorced from the Great Commission is a legitimate concern. In fact, "Mission that does not explicitly

---

203. John MacArthur, *The Vanishing Conscience: Drawing the Line in a No-Fault, Guilt-Free World* (Dallas, TX: Word Publishing, 1994), 12.

204. John MacArthur, *Why Government Can't Save You* (Dallas, TX: Word Publishing, 2000), 11–12.

205. Kevin DeYoung and Greg Gilbert, *What Is the Mission of the Church? Making Sense of Social Justice, Shalom, and the Great Commission* (Wheaton, IL: Crossway, 2011); Christopher R. Little, "The Case for Prioritism," in *Controversies in Mission: Theology, People, and Practice of Mission in the 21st Century*, ed. Rochelle Cathcart Scheuermann, Kindle Edition (Pasadena, CA: William Carey Library, 2016), 11–28; Jonathan Leeman, "Soteriological Mission: Focusing in on the Mission of Redemption," in *Four Views on the Church's Mission*, ed. Jason S Sexton and Stanley N. Gundry (Grand Rapids, MI: Zondervan, 2017), 17–45.

206. Harvie M. Conn, *Evangelism: Doing Justice and Preaching Grace* (Grand Rapids, MI: Zondervan, 1982), 62.

207. In the famous words of Stephan Neill, "If everything is mission, then nothing is mission." Stephen Neill, *Creative Tension* (London: Edinburgh House, 1959), 81.

208. Ott and Strauss, *Encountering Theology of Mission*, 143–144.

bring the good news of God's salvation in Jesus Christ to the world cannot be considered biblical mission."[209] Therefore, evangelicals usually agree on the importance of evangelism and many believe it is important and faithful to the spirit of the Lausanne Covenant to give evangelism the highest priority in the church's mission.[210] From this perspective, social action is either a consequence of evangelism or a bridge to it.

Some, however, see both as equal partners. Goheen finds the solution to "the unbiblical dichotomy" between the two tasks in "a return to the gospel and mission in the way of Jesus."[211] The gospel of the kingdom defines the church's mission as participation "in God's mission to restore the whole creation and all of human life."[212] From this perspective, the central reality is neither word nor act but "the total life of a community enabled by the Spirit to live in Christ, sharing his passion and the power of the resurrection."[213] Based on the fourfold scheme of biblical history, Christopher Wright also develops a comprehensive picture of the whole of God's people participating in the whole of God's mission. This holistic picture of mission can be summarized using three sets of key phrases from the Lausanne Covenant:

> *The whole gospel* as the message of the transformation of every area of human life contaminated by sin.
>
> *The whole world.* A holistic mission aims at the restoration of human nature in all its fullness: physical, intellectual, emotional, and social. It also restores the four fundamental human relationships: with God, self, others, and the rest of creation.

---

209. Ott and Strauss, 113.

210. DeYoung and Gilbert, *What Is the Mission of the Church?*, 248–249. Ronald Sider suggests several ways in which evangelism is, and should remain, primary over social action in mission: logically, ontologically, and in terms of the use of resources. Sider, *Good News and Good Works*, 165–171.

211. Goheen, *Introducing Christian Mission Today*, 3867.

212. Goheen, 4063–4066.

213. Goheen, 3873–3876. This approach echoes Bosch's conviction that evangelism and social action are not "separate components or parts of mission, but dimensions of the one, indivisible mission of the Church." Bosch, *Transforming Mission*, 81.

The whole church. The whole gospel based on the whole biblical story involves the whole church to play different roles in the mission of God's people to the world.[214]

Craig Ott offers a solution by framing the church's responsibility in terms of two mandates: the *creation* mandate and the *gospel* mandate.[215] The former (also called the cultural or social mandate) is based on common grace and general revelation and describes the ethical obligations of Christians and non-Christians alike. The latter is given only to Christians. These two mandates represent very different kinds of activities and concerns, and the distinction between them should be maintained. Otherwise social responsibility tends to redefine evangelism (as in conciliar mission) or the creation mandate tends to be "reduced to a tool of the gospel mandate."[216] At the same time, Ott believes that the gospel mandate is more fundamental, because "only through reconciliation with God can the creation mandate be fulfilled in the deepest sense."[217] Like the approaches of Goheen and Wright, this view expresses God's concern for the totality of human life and creation, yet attempts more explicitly to keep the centrality of the cross in the church's mission.[218]

Concluding Summary

During much of the period since 1910, evangelical missiology has been taking shape in polemical confrontation with ecumenical Protestant mission thinking, rejecting many of its formulations and yet adopting some of its important, biblical insights. The theological developments that climaxed in the Cape Town Commitment were far from being smooth and uncontroversial; in fact, even today there are issues that remain unresolved. Overall, however, despite the controversies and narrow concerns, it has been a path of fresh discoveries, leading toward a fuller appreciation of the gospel. In particular, these insights include the *missio Dei* concept (although with a distinctively different interpretation), the missionary nature of the church, and the importance of

---

214. Wright, *Mission of God's People*, 43, 272.
215. Ott and Strauss, *Encountering Theology of Mission*.
216. Ott and Strauss, 153; Sider, *Good News and Good Works*.
217. Ott and Strauss, 155.
218. Ott and Strauss, 155–156.

holistic mission (with the priority of evangelism over social service).[219] As a result of these "birth pangs" there emerged a certain consensus among many evangelicals in key areas of mission theology. Another important factor has been the growing role of the global church and non-Western theology. Indeed, over this period of history, evangelical missiology has grown from being an exclusively Western effort to a truly global enterprise.

By the end of the twentieth century, the traditional evangelical understanding of mission (which Goheen describes as "dualistic, individualist, and otherworldly"[220]) was giving way to a new paradigm of *integral* mission. While it is hardly possible to speak about complete evangelical agreement on mission, certain contours of this new paradigm can be more or less clearly recognized. With regard to the understanding of the gospel, the concept of salvation as exclusively spiritual and future has given way to the concept of the salvation of the whole person, both present and future. The emphasis on individual conversion is now balanced by the communal aspect of the gospel, which sees the church as the new humanity in Christ. Kingdom theology has also highlighted the cosmic aspect of salvation which includes social and cultural renewal, however provisional and imperfect it may be during the interim period between the "already" and the "not yet."

With regard to evangelical understandings of the church, their emphasis has shifted from seeing it as a repository of the saved to its being the sign, instrument, and foretaste of the kingdom. The grand story of the Bible makes the church missionary at its very core. Not only are the people of God "called out" from the world in preparation for the transition to heaven; they are also "sent" into the world to continue the mission of Israel and of Jesus. This, in turn, presupposes the church's involvement with the world, which is found in critical and creative tension between affirmation and critique, solidarity and alternative. It is not enough for the church to guard its purity from contamination by the fallen world; it is called to serve as a model of a renewed human society. Socially, culturally, economically, and politically, the church is called to provide an alternative to the existing world order. Its mission is founded on God's comprehensive plan of restoration which embraces individuals,

---

219. Other areas of influence have been contextualization and interreligious dialogue.
220. Goheen, *Introducing Christian Mission Today*, 1450.

society, culture, and ecology, and shows itself in the words, deeds, and total life of the church. As God's primary instrument in mission, the church is to become the locus of the missionary encounter between the gospel and a particular culture.

For most of the period under consideration, Russian Baptists were isolated from these developments. Their experiences in their particular socio-political and religious contexts shaped a distinctive understanding of mission, which, while not always explicitly articulated, served as a guiding vision in their mission efforts. In the following chapter I will look more closely at how the story and the content of Russian evangelical mission theology were unfolding from the inception of the movement in 1867 to the collapse of the Soviet Union in 1991.

CHAPTER 3

Russian Baptist Mission Theology in Context, 1867–1991

Historical Roots of Russian Baptist Theology

In her research on the early Baptists in Russia, Heather Coleman affirms that "There is virtually no published scholarly work on the Russian Baptists in English."[1] Although Walter Sawatsky correctly points out that Coleman exaggerates the case, her observation is still true with regard to Russian Baptist theology and missiology in particular.[2] The most thorough analysis of Russian Baptist doctrinal convictions to date was attempted more than forty years ago by Alexander de Chalandeau,[3] but as Andrey Puzynin correctly observes, his research was based almost exclusively on the study of the AUCECB's official magazine *Bratskii Vestnik* and, on the whole, is incomplete and under-researched.[4]

---

1. Coleman, *Russian Baptists and Spiritual Revolution*, 7.

2. Walter Sawatsky, "Review of Russian Baptists and Spiritual Revolution 1905–1929," ed. Heather J. Coleman, *Religion in Eastern Europe* 26 (2006): 58. For a variety of reasons, the Eastern (including Russian) Orthodox Church did not produce formal theology of mission either. The general environment in communist lands was not conducive to reflection on mission. cf. Ott, "Introduction," xxvi; Edward Rommen, "A Sacramental Vision Approach," in *The Mission of the Church*, ed. Craig Ott (Grand Rapids, MI: Baker Academic, 2016), 69–90.

3. Alexander De Chalandeau, *The Theology of the Evangelical Christians-Baptists in the USSR as Reflected in the Bratskii Vestnik* (Chicago, IL: Harper and Co, 1978).

4. Puzynin, *Tradition of the Gospel Christians*, 216. For instance, Chalandeau completely misses the adoption of dispensational eschatology after World War II, which arguably was the main theological turn in Russian Baptist theology during the last century.

An important area in which debates continue among scholars has to do with whether Russian evangelicalism should be seen as a unique movement rooted in Eastern Orthodox spirituality or as an imported sect of entirely non-Russian origin. One perspective has tended to downplay the international connections and influences in order to protect the Baptists from Russian Orthodox and Soviet accusations of being a branch of Western Christianity. Instead, Baptists are seen as a "synthesis of Western Protestantism [and] Russian-Ukrainian piety."[5] The other perspective tends to emphasize the Western roots of Russian Baptists. Andrei Puzynin in his research argues that regardless of the constant modifications of their narratives of self-identity, along with "the fluctuations in the geopolitical force field," the Baptist tradition continued to move along the trajectory of Anglo-American evangelicalism to which it owes its existence. The key identifiers of Western evangelicalism – biblicism, crucicentrism, conversionism, and activism – have not undergone any changes since the late nineteenth century.[6] Puzynin supports his case by demonstrating how Russian Baptists abundantly borrowed from Western evangelical historiography, theology, spirituality, hymnody, Bible study methods, leadership structures, and finances.

While it is true that Western evangelicalism served as a primary catalyst and model for the Baptist movement in Russia, multiple scholars and observers have noted the distinctive character of Russian Baptist spirituality, which they often connect to the Russian Orthodox soil and context in which it developed. It is generally acknowledged that the ground for the evangelical awakening in Russia had been prepared by "the deep spirituality of the Russian Orthodox God-seekers" who were disappointed with the formality and moral decay of the dominant state church.[7] This quest for an alternative spirituality

---

5. Walter Kolarz, *Religion in the Soviet Union* (London: Macmillan, 1961), 283; J. A. Hebly, *Protestants in Russia* (Grand Rapids, MI: Eerdmans, 1976); Savinskii, Savchenko, and Dik, *Istoriia Evangel'skikh Khristian-Baptistov v SSSR* [*History of Evangelical Christians-Baptists in the USSR*]; Savinskii, *Istoriia Evangel'skikh Khristian-Baptistov Ukrainy, Rossii, Belorussii: 1867–1917* [*History of Evangelical Christians-Baptists of Ukraine, Russia, and Belarus: 1867–1917*]; M. S. Karetnikova, *Al'manakh Po Istorii Russkogo Baptizma* [*The Reader on the History of Russian Baptists*] (St Petersburg: Bibliia dlia vsekh, 1999).

6. Puzynin, *Tradition of the Gospel Christians*, 141, 191; cf. Paul D. Steeves, "The Russian Baptist Union, 1917–1935: Evangelical Awakening in Russia" (PhD diss., University of Kansas, 1976); Coleman, *Russian Baptists and Spiritual Revolution*, 96.

7. Sawatsky, *Soviet Evangelicals*, 14; cf. Hebly, *Protestants in Russia*; Savinskii, Savchenko, and Dik, *Istoriia Evangel'skikh Khristian-Baptistov v SSSR* [*History of Evangelical Christians-*

took its specific shape in the second half of the nineteenth century, when it was cross-pollinated with Pietist-Revivalist and Anabaptist traditions.[8]

In particular, strong influences initially came from the Keswick movement and some of its enthusiastic teachers such as D. L. Moody, R. A. Torrey, A. B. Simpson, and George Müller.[9] During its four years of publication (1907–1910), the RUB journal *Baptist* published forty-five articles by these and other foreign writers, who thus became indirect teachers of Russian evangelicals. In addition to the emphasis on dramatic experiences of conversion and personal holiness, the Keswick movement transmitted to Russian Baptists dispensational theology, with its premillennial eschatology and pre-critical methods of biblical interpretation.[10] Organizationally, the Union of Gospel Christians led by Ivan Prokhanov not only relied on Western teachers and preachers, but also copied Western institutions such as the Evangelical Alliance and the YMCA.

Walter Sawatsky argues that through Russian and Ukrainian Mennonites and Shtundists, "it is possible to trace direct continuous roots back to the Anabaptists of the 16th century."[11] The primary theological marks of Anabaptism among Russian Baptists are a strict belief in the separation of church and state, the concept of a "church of only the regenerated," church discipline, and responsible discipleship. Pacifism used to be another mark inherited from Anabaptism, but under pressure from the Soviet authorities, Baptist

---

Baptists in the USSR]; Savinskii, *Istoriia Evangel'skikh Khristian-Baptistov Ukrainy, Rossii, Belorussii: 1867–1917 [History of Evangelical Christians-Baptists of Ukraine, Russia, and Belarus: 1867–1917]*; Karetnikova, *Al'manakh Po Istorii Russkogo Baptizma [The Reader on the History of Russian Baptists]*; Geoffrey H. Ellis and L. Wesley Jones, *The Other Revolution: Russian Evangelical Awakenings* (Abilene, TX: ACU Press, 1996); Mark J. Harris, "Historical Perspectives on the Evangelistic Theology and Methodology of Russian Baptists," 1999, http://cvi2.org/pages/harris/harris_russian_baptist_evangelistic_history_1999.pdf.

8. Mikhail Ivanov, "Sovremennye Tendentsii v Bogoslovii Rossiyskikh Evangel'skikh Khristian-Baptistov [Contemporary Trends in the Theology of Russian Evangelical Christians-Baptists]" (PhD diss., RANEPA, 2012).

9. Sawatsky, *Soviet Evangelicals*, 17; Puzynin, *Tradition of the Gospel Christians*, 19, 340.

10. Nichols, *Russian Evangelical Spirituality*; Puzynin, *Tradition of the Gospel Christians*.

11. In fact, the first president of the Russian Baptist Union in 1884 was a German Mennonite, Johannes Wieler. In the 1920s, the influence continued through a number of Mennonite evangelists and teachers at Ivan Prokhanov's Leningrad Bible school, through British and North American Baptists, and through the incorporation of the so-called Brotherly Mennonites into the AUCECB in the 1950s. Sawatsky, *Soviet Evangelicals*, 339; cf. Johannes Dyck, "Elements of Post-Gulag Mennonite Theology: View of an Eyewitness," in *History and Mission in Europe: Continuing the Conversation*, ed. Mary Raber and Peter F Penner (Schwarzenfeld, Germany: Neufeld Verlag, 2011), 207.

leaders were forced to officially renounce it in the early 1920s.¹² Perhaps the most important influence of Anabaptism can be discerned in the fact that the pietistic message of personal salvation on the Russian soil bore the fruit of alternative communities with their strong shared life, rather than merely a number of individual converts.

The Orthodox influence can be recognized in some distinctive features of Russian Baptist soteriology, such as the emphasis on repentance from sin more than reliance on the finished work of Christ and the concept of working together with God in living out the Christian life.¹³ It is also reflected in the "temple-centered" character of Baptist church life, in the melancholic character of, and the emphasis on the mysticism in, their worship, as well as in the dramatization of the physical aspect of Christ's suffering in their practice of the Eucharist and in their deep reverence toward the bread and wine. Some also see the influence of Orthodoxy in their loose attitude toward formal theologizing.¹⁴ In ecclesiology, there is a tendency to base pastoral authority on an institutional rather than charismatic foundation, which seems to reflect the Orthodox concepts of priesthood and apostolic succession. Michael Ivanov and J. A. Hebly also mention the important contribution of the semi-Orthodox *Molokan* sect from which most early Baptist converts came.¹⁵ In particular, they highlight the Molokan belief in salvation by both faith *and* works and their extreme anti-cultural stance.

International Connections during This Period

In contrast to the nationalistic isolation of the Russian Orthodox Church, the first Russian Baptists regarded themselves as part of the worldwide evangelical movement for which foreign ties were natural. Both the RUB and RUGC were incorporated into the Baptist World Alliance at its first congress in London in

---

12. Sawatsky, *Soviet Evangelicals*, 37.
13. Harris, "Historical Perspectives," 5.
14. Sawatsky, *Soviet Evangelicals*, 107, 342; Fairbairn, *Eastern Orthodoxy*.
15. Ivanov, "Sovremennye Tendentsii v Bogoslovii Rossiyskikh Evangel'skikh Khristian-Baptistov [Contemporary Trends in the Theology of Russian Evangelical Christians-Baptists]," 19; Hebly, *Protestants in Russia*, 79.

1905.[16] However, beginning in the late 1920s, Baptist leaders found themselves "charged with anti-Soviet activity [and with] spying for a foreign country . . . Soviet evangelicals became isolated."[17] There were virtually no foreign contacts until 1954, when Russian Baptists were allowed to begin rebuilding former connections. In 1955, Yakov Zhidkov, a key leader of the AUCECB, became a vice president of the Baptist World Alliance, and in 1962 he was elected to the European Baptist Federation executive committee. That same year, the AUCECB joined the World Council of Churches – just one year after the Russian Orthodox Church had done so.

The role of the AUCECB within the WCC was not significant, however. The AUCECB was not involved in world missions nor did its representatives make notable contributions to theological discussions. Their presence in international religious organizations largely served the purpose of highlighting the "Sovietness" of evangelicalism in the USSR and of advocating for the Soviet government's interpretation of religious freedom. During WCC meetings, Soviet representatives regularly voted as a bloc on all decisions, including against numerous resolutions that might have been perceived as critical of the Soviet Union.[18] Moreover, Baptist membership in the WCC led to growing discord within the Union. The more conservative circles within the AUCECB had deep fears regarding any ecumenical involvement – fears which were fed both by the leaders of the splinter group and by Western fundamentalist radio preachers who typically "identified the World Council with the Babylonian whore which is to lead the church astray in the end times."[19] But in the end, the AUCECB had no option but to remain a member.

The Union was also occasionally allowed to invite foreign guests, including Billy Graham in 1982 and 1984. However, considering the extensive travels and connections of the AUCECB's top leaders, it is notable that no representative of the Union was able to participate in the World Congress on Evangelism in Berlin in 1966 or in the Lausanne Congress on World Evangelization in

---

16. In the next congress of 1911, the chair of the RUGC, Ivan Prokhanov, was elected as one of the Alliance's vice presidents. Wanner, *Communities of the Converted*, 23.

17. Sawatsky, *Soviet Evangelicals*, 360.

18. Wanner, *Communities of the Converted*, 64; Sawatsky, *Soviet Evangelicals*, 368; Puzynin, *Tradition of the Gospel Christians*, 195.

19. Sawatsky, *Soviet Evangelicals*, 369.

1974.[20] Sawatsky suggests that evangelical organizations appeared to "represent interests which Soviet authorities [did] not wish to encourage." For instance, the fact that the NAE regularly issued anti-communist resolutions was one of several barriers to relationships.[21]

Russian Baptists' Missiological Convictions

In the rest of this chapter, I will look at the shaping and transformations of the four key aspects of Baptist mission theology (the nature of the gospel, the church's identity and purpose, the view of cultural engagement, and holistic mission) in their historical context. It is now common to divide this rather eventful period from the origin of Baptist movement in the Russian Empire through the collapse of the USSR into several stages, typically based on the status of church and state relations. In this research I divide it into three stages and suggest that, from the perspective of mission theology, each stage represented the dominance of a different missiological micro-paradigm within a broader paradigm of evangelical pietism (for different approaches to setting time frames see Savinskii, Plett, Puzynin).[22]

Certainly it should be borne in mind that the three micro-paradigms cannot be viewed as mutually exclusive or limited only to their specific time frames. As Bosch reminds us, a new theological paradigm does not necessarily cancel the old ones, and in ordinary life people often straddle two theological paradigms at the same time.[23] Nevertheless, at each stage one particular set of convictions moved to the foreground, overshadowing the others. I identify these three micro-paradigms as *revivalist* (1867–1905), *transformationist*

---

20. Alexander Karev, who served as general secretary of the AUCECB for twenty-seven years, represented the union on thirty-nine journeys abroad. He served as the Soviet Union's representative in the World Peace Council, the Soviet Council of Peace, The Peace Trust, the Institute of Soviet-American Relations, and the World Council of Churches. Puzynin, *Tradition of the Gospel Christians*, 196; Wanner, *Communities of the Converted*, 58.

21. Sawatsky, *Soviet Evangelicals*, 383.

22. Savinskii, *Istoriia Evangel'skikh Khristian-Baptistov Ukrainy, Rossii, Belorussii: 1867–1917 [History of Evangelical Christians-Baptists of Ukraine, Russia, and Belarus: 1867–1917]*; S. N. Savinskii, *Istoriia Evangel'skikh Khristian-Baptistov Ukrainy, Rossii, Belorussii: 1917–1967 [History of Evangelical Christians-Baptists of Ukraine, Russia, and Belarus: 1917–1967]* (St Petersburg: Bibliia dlia vsekh, 2001); I. P. Plett, *Istoriia Evangel'skikh Khristian Baptistov s 1905 Po 1944 God [The History of Evangelical Christians-Baptists in 1905–1944]* (Moscow: ICCECB, 2001); Puzynin, *Tradition of the Gospel Christians*.

23. Bosch, *Transforming Mission*, 173–175.

(1905–1930), and *escapist* (1944–1991). The dates indicate that there is a fourteen-year break between the second and the third periods. During this time, Russian Baptists were experiencing brutal persecution and repression. Theologically, it was a time of forging the new paradigm, but its explicit articulation and general acceptance would not take place until the Baptist movement emerged from persecution and received legal status again in 1944. My arguments for the time frames are presented in the text below and are summarized in the conclusion of this chapter.

Revivalist Pietism: 1867–1905

Historical Background

To appreciate the power and attraction of the evangelical faith in Russia during this period, it is important to keep in mind that until 1905 national differences among multiple ethnicities of the Empire were seen as including a religious dimension, which was thought to be inherited and unalterable. As the established church of the Empire, the Russian Orthodox Church asserted that the Eastern Slavic world was its "canonical territory," and it relied on the state to retain the faithful by charging that apostasy equaled treason to the tsar and the motherland. Only Orthodox authorities could register marriages, births, and deaths, which meant that practitioners of minority faiths were not considered married, so that their children were viewed as illegitimate and ineligible for admittance to Orthodox-run schools. Any form of "proselytism" was prohibited and open manifestation of "sectarian faith" in publications, processions, and open-air preaching was criminalized.[24]

Religious life, however, felt the influence of the social, political, and intellectual turmoil that followed the reforms by Alexander II – particularly the emancipation of serfs in 1861. Rapid industrialization, the growth of literacy, and the transformations of the traditional social order led to the emergence of "new ... personal identities, the creation of a public sphere and civic culture, [and] debates over the notion and nature of citizenship."[25] The Bible in

---

24. Wanner, *Communities of the Converted*, 21–22; Ellis and Jones, *The Other Revolution*, 62; Coleman, *Russian Baptists and Spiritual Revolution*.
25. Coleman, 3.

vernacular Russian became available to the masses for the first time.[26] These tremendous changes raised sharp questions about religion and its place in private life, public discourse, and state structures. The role of the state church as the only legitimate spiritual choice for citizens was questioned. Atheistic and socialist theories captured the minds of a growing number of students and of the educated elite. Ellis and Jones summarize the spirit of the epoch as follows:

> A sterile Orthodox Church, compromised from its inception with entanglements in a "kingdom of this world," was an empty option for the nobility, alienated from the intelligentsia, and without answers for the peasantry . . . In reaction, materialistic ideologies were spawned which readily fed radical minds but which were patently empty of moral and spiritual values. Their ends could be gained only through revolution and internecine struggle.[27]

After Alexander II was killed in 1881 in the streets of St Petersburg by a bomb thrown by a member of the revolutionary "People's Will," the next monarch was determined not only to preserve but to intensify the dominance of imperial rule by repressing all opposition. The heightened expectations of the people were frustrated. In the less than forty years that followed, Russia saw radical political transformations climaxing in the replacement of the tsarist regime in 1917, first by the provisional democratic government and then by the Bolsheviks.[28]

It is against this background of repressive collectivism that the message of the first evangelicals must be understood. They boldly proclaimed the

---

26. The New Testament in the Russian language was first published in 1822 by the Russian Bible Society, which owed its existence to liberal influences that Alexander I brought from Western Europe after the victory over Napoleon Bonaparte. When Orthodox reaction set in, the Bible Society was closed by tsarist order in 1826, but Bible translation and distribution never ceased entirely. Between 1814 and 1826 about half a million copies of the New Testament were distributed in forty-one languages of the Empire, and a Russian translation of the complete Bible was finished in 1876 after the Bible Society was reopened in 1856. I. A. Chistovich, *Istoriia Perevoda Biblii Na Russkii Iazyk [The History of the Russian Translation of the Bible]* (Moscow: AFI, 2012).

27. Ellis and Jones, *The Other Revolution*, 63.

28. W.E. Mosse, "Alexander II, Emperor of Russia," 2016, https://www.britannica.com/biography/Alexander-II-emperor-of-Russia.

reality of personal conversion and a sense of devotional nearness to God that did not require the mediation of the church.[29] New converts celebrated their right to read and interpret the Bible for themselves. Russian peasants, workers, and members of high society flocked to hear evangelical preachers, and multiple groups met for Bible study and prayer, with some participants experiencing ecstasies. New believers were welcomed into voluntary pietistic groups that celebrated a personal relationship with God and viewed themselves as an alternative to the "people's church." Heather Coleman's analysis of multiple conversion narratives from that time paints compelling pictures of individuals who found the means for self-expression and growth within a new kind of community.[30]

In searching for the nature of the Baptist mission theology of this period, it makes sense to turn primarily to the St Petersburg wing of the movement (the "Gospel Christians"). Its aristocratic leaders articulated and widely publicized their views through the "Society for the Advancement of Spiritual-Ethical Reading" that they founded in 1876. By 1884 the Society published and distributed all over Russia more than one million pieces of literature.[31] In fact, in many parts of Russia it was the only literature available for learning purposes. The St Petersburg leaders also played a key role in several attempts to unite the diverse groups. Moreover, sixty years later it was the leaders of the Gospel Christians who became the leadership core of the restored AUCECB.

Theologically, two key persons stand out at the earliest stage of the movement: the British evangelist Lord Radstock (1833–1913) and his Russian convert Vasiliy Pashkov (1831–1902). Radstock's arrival in 1874 in the capital of Russia at the invitation of members of high society marked the beginning of the "drawing room" revival.[32] But it was Colonel Pashkov who became the soul of the movement after Radstock left Russia in 1878.[33]

---

29. Wanner, *Communities of the Converted*, 26; Sawatsky, *Soviet Evangelicals*, 31.

30. Coleman, *Russian Baptists and Spiritual Revolution*.

31. Durassoff, *Russian Protestants*, 44.

32. The revival caused a significant public resonance that stirred prominent Russian thinkers such as Feodor Dostoevsky, Leo Tolstoy, and Nikolai Leskov to address this public phenomenon in their writings.

33. Sharyl Corrado, "The Philosophy of Ministry of Colonel Vasiliy Pashkov" (MA thesis, Wheaton College, 2000).

The Nature of the Gospel

Puzynin, in his in-depth analysis of Radstock's views, argues that his premillennial holiness theology and pre-critical method of biblical interpretation were typical of the Anglo-American evangelicalism of the second half of the nineteenth century. The gospel he preached focused on the themes of God's love, the fallen condition of individuals, and the possibility of personal justification and regeneration through faith in Christ's work for sinners as testified to in Scripture. Overall, Radstock's message was marked with a strong "revivalist emphasis on the personal and affective conversion experience and a subsequent life of complete devotion to Christ in light of his imminent advent."[34]

Radstock was not deeply concerned about doctrine or theology. He was a sort of evangelical mystic who emphasized a personal relationship with Christ and answered prayers.[35] As Russian writer Nikolai Leskov observed, the sentimental nature of his spirituality had power to attract people to Christ.[36] He avoided theological debates and announced the "simple message of the gospel." In the Orthodox environment, the most controversial aspect of his teaching was his belief in justification by faith and assurance of salvation. It alarmed priests in the city who believed that such ideas would lead to licentious living.[37] However, Radstock insisted that true regeneration has experiential dimensions and is accompanied by receiving God's power to overcome sin in one's personal life. In fact, his emphasis on personal holiness for everyday living in the world visibly contrasted with the Orthodox concept of spirituality that was largely confined to monastic life.[38]

Another alarming aspect of his preaching was his view of the church. While he did not explicitly reject the need for sacraments, liturgy, or clergy for salvation, he "felt that the formalism in the existing organized churches had

---

34. Puzynin, *Tradition of the Gospel Christians*, 17.

35. Puzynin, 202–207.

36. "His ideas are shaky, but his spirit is splendid ... 'In studying the feeling of Radstock, I myself sense that the man is in love with Christ,' one person who knows him well said to me, and this must be true. Radstock is in love, and this feeling is almost irresistible." N. S. Leskov, *Schism in High Society: Lord Radstock and His Followers*, trans. James Y. Muckle (Nottingham: Bramcote, 1995), 23.

37. Corrado, "Philosophy of Ministry," 63–64; Ellis and Jones, *The Other Revolution*, 84.

38. Edmund Heier, *Religious Schism in the Russian Aristocracy 1860–1900: Radstockism and Pashkovism* (The Hague, Netherlands: Martinus Nijhoff, 1970), 66.

become a dominating factor which overshadowed the essence of faith and the true Christian spirit."[39] Radstock believed in the Bible as the only authoritative text and never explicitly referred to any denominational tradition in his preaching. Thus, the revival he spurred was a Bible-born and Bible-centered movement from its inception.[40] Obviously, this vision differed sharply from Orthodox beliefs, as voiced, for instance, by the chief procurator of the Most Holy Governing Synod, K.P. Pobedonostsev, in 1884. He insisted that "the Church alone possesses the full, clear, catholic interpretation of the whole [biblical] text . . . and everyone who separates himself from the church, or sets himself up [as] a preacher, becomes a sectarian.."[41] One of Pobedonostsev's predecessors, Count Protasov (the chief procurator from 1836 to 1855), actually stopped the printing of the Bible in vernacular Russian as harmful in a country that was full of sects and almost illiterate.

Scholars agree that Colonel Pashkov's soteriology was similar or even "identical" to Radstock's.[42] The center of his teaching was also found in justification by grace, the unconditional love of God, and the personal appropriation of salvation by faith. From the very beginning, the Gospel Christians exhibited a strong missionary zeal and promoted the notion that every Christian was an evangelist. One of the common topics of their leadership meetings was the question of how to evangelize millions of Orthodox Russians who, for Radstock and his followers, were unregenerate people in need of salvation.[43]

Similar processes were going on in the Baptist and Shtundist communities in the south of the country. At the first Baptist congress of 1884 in Novovasilievka (Odessa region, Ukraine) that brought together forty representatives from thirteen churches, mission was central to the whole event. Johan Wieler, the chair of the conference, suggested a fourfold "scale of priorities" for the emerging Baptist communities: (1) visiting and strengthening small communities of believers located far from the centers; (2) stimulating

---

39. Heier, *Religious Schism*, 46.

40. Hebly, *Protestants in Russia*, 82–83; Ellis and Jones, *The Other Revolution*.

41. From a private letter sent to Tsar Alexander II, dated 10 May 1880. In it, he asked the Emperor to move urgently against the "heresy of Pashkovism" and "send Pashkov away from Russia.." Heier, *Religious Schism*, 125–127.

42. Gregory L. Nichols, "Pashkovism: Nineteenth Century Russian Piety" (MA thesis, Wheaton College, 1991), 85, 99; Puzynin, *Tradition of the Gospel Christians*.

43. Harris, "Historical Perspectives," 10.

and encouraging a "missionary mood" among the brothers and sisters; (3) strengthening love and unity in local communities; and (4) evangelizing "unconverted souls." The importance of missions on the congress' agenda can be seen in the fact that its decisions regarding local mission work were passed as mandatory for every church, whereas doctrinal and organizational decisions were passed as advisable.⁴⁴ To facilitate the emerging work of evangelism and church planting, a missionary committee with a missions fund was established, and eight full-time *blagovestnik* (evangelists) were selected. As a result, in spite of repressions from the state and Orthodox clergy, the number of Baptists in Ukraine alone grew from 2,006 in 1884 to 4,670 in 1893.⁴⁵

The Identity and Purpose of the Church

The sources of that period emphasize that Radstock had no intention of initiating a new denomination in Orthodox Russia.⁴⁶ As an Anglican, he did not practice believers' baptism and his early converts typically did not sever their ties with Orthodoxy. In fact, his and his early followers' ultimate purpose was to stimulate the spiritual renewal of the Orthodox Church; they wanted to "revive neglected Christian ideals . . . from within."⁴⁷ What defined the Christian community for them was the mystical union of the Holy Spirit who tied the universal church together in love rather than by a code of doctrine. The true church was a fellowship of born-again Christians who come together to study the Word of God in the spirit of mutual love. Accordingly, Radstock accepted infant baptism as legitimate and did not regard formal membership as essential, because it is a personal relationship with Christ that makes

---

44. Sinichkin, *Vsio Radi Missii [Everything for the Sake of Mission]*, 178; Johannes Dyck, "Zavisimost' Nezavisimosti: Obshchina v Zhizni Evangel'skogo Bratstva Rosii v Period Ego Stanovleniia, 1870–1887 [Dependence of Independence: The Local Church in the Life of the Evangelical Union of Russia at the Stage of Its Formation, 1870–1887]," in *Avtonomia Pomestnoi Tserkvi: Materialy Simposiuma [Local Church Autonomy: Proceedings of Symposium]*, ed. Sergey Sannikov (Odessa: Dukhovnoe Vozrozhdenie, 2009), 275–294.

45. Savinskii, *Istoriia Evangel'skikh Khristian-Baptistov Ukrainy, Rosii, Belorussii: 1867–1917 [History of Evangelical Christians-Baptists of Ukraine, Russia, and Belarus: 1867–1917]*.

46. So Leskov in his analysis of the movement says, "If schism is conceived as [a] complete split from the Church . . . this is not a schism . . . The whole of the Radstockist movement is a group of people who like to discuss the Word of God, salvation and justification . . . They are still in the church and will not be separated from it." Leskov, *Schism in High Society*, 106–108.

47. Heier, *Religious Schism*, 108; Nichols, "Pashkovism," 82; Ellis and Jones, *The Other Revolution*, 85; Hebly, *Protestants in Russia*, 80; Coleman, *Russian Baptists and Spiritual Revolution*, 17.

one a Christian.[48] Accordingly, in the first years there was no question of an organized congregational alliance among the Gospel Christians.[49]

Under the leadership of Pashkov, however, the movement gradually began to develop a distinct identity, distancing itself from the state church. Puzynin explains this in terms of Pashkov's view of Orthodoxy as a deviation from biblical truth, as a dead church founded on human traditions. The result was a drift "from pietism as a religion of the heart to the ecclesiology of evangelical restorationist-primitivism, with its vision of establishing a primitive Apostolic church."[50] Many other authors, however, emphasize that it was primarily the combined power of the state and the established church that pushed evangelical communities to clarify who they were. In a sense, rejection and persecutions became instrumental in driving them to form a separate identity.[51] In J. C. Pollock's words, "what might have been a reformation within the Church, was forced to be a sect outside it."[52]

In any case, Pashkov eventually came to the conclusion that Russia needed a spiritual transformation that would lead to the replacement of Orthodoxy by an evangelical form of Christianity. This change of paradigm was marked by the introduction of rebaptism and of weekly breaking of bread among the members of the community. Infant baptism was now seen as a "human teaching."[53] Pashkov himself was rebaptized around 1881, and he later baptized a number of Molokans in Southern Ukraine in 1881. His life purpose now became to bring together diverse evangelical groups. With this goal in mind he convened the first congress that brought together representatives of all evangelical currents in the Empire in 1884. Although the discussions did not reach consensus in all matters of theology and worship, the sense of unity in one new movement was overwhelming.[54] Unfortunately, Pashkov's vision was never realized in his lifetime, because later that same year he was deported from Russia.

---

48. Nichols, "Pashkovism," 92–93, 102; Heier, *Religious Schism*, 45.

49. Hebly, *Protestants in Russia*, 68.

50. Puzynin, *Tradition of the Gospel Christians*, 22; cf. Nichols, "Pashkovism," 103–106.

51. Hebly, *Protestants in Russia*, 58; Coleman, *Russian Baptists and Spiritual Revolution*, 14.

52. John Charles Pollock, *The Faith of the Russian Evangelicals* (New York: McGraw-Hill, 1964), 68.

53. Puzynin, *Tradition of the Gospel Christians*, 91, 112.

54. Heier, *Religious Schism*, 142.

The Baptist communities in the south, from the outset, held a very different view of the church. Under the influence of German Baptists and particularly of Johann Gerhard Onken (1800–1882), they practiced baptism by full immersion as a sign of spiritual regeneration.[55] Adult baptism initiated the converts into a local congregation made up of those who had had a personal conversion experience. Through continuous church discipline, their communities sought to maintain a regenerate membership.[56] The first congregation in Tbilisi was modeled after German Baptist communities and, in turn, became the organizational model for all other Baptist communities in Russia.[57] Its future pastor and also future leader of the RUB, Vasily Pavlov, was sent to Hamburg Baptist Seminary, where he became "a favorite pupil of Onken."[58]

On the one hand, Baptists, just like the Gospel Christians, were inspired by the New Testament vision of a primitive church. On the other hand, they tended to view themselves as a movement of local congregations, rather than as an expansion of the universal church. They saw their mission, therefore, as that of restoring the local church to its pristine purity, rather than as a spiritual transformation of established ecclesiastical structures.[59] In their zeal for maintaining purity of membership they manifested a "distinctively sectarian characteristic."[60] In fact, the main reason why the first congress convened by Pashkov in 1884 was unable to unite the diverse groups was the Baptists' refusal to take communion with paedobaptists.[61] Socially, Baptists were much more homogeneous as a "purely peasants' and workers' sect."[62] This also set them apart from the diverse and primarily aristocrat-led Gospel Christians, with their "centered-set" view of Christianity. In fact, for the latter, unity was not uniformity. In the words of Count Modest Korf, another prominent convert of Radstock in St Petersburg who was present at the congress in 1884,

---

55. The first Baptist converts in Tbilisi were from a Molokan background who had not been baptized anyway, because Molokans did not practice Orthodox-style infant baptism.

56. Coleman, *Russian Baptists and Spiritual Revolution*, 14; Hebly, *Protestants in Russia*, 57.

57. Yuchkovski, "Comparison of the Evangelical Movement," 34; Alexander Nagirnyak, *Podvizhniki Very [Devotees of Faith]* (Kiev: Knigonosha, 2014), 201.

58. Ellis and Jones, *The Other Revolution*, 72.

59. Steeves, "Russian Baptist Union," 485.

60. Nichols, "Pashkovism," 106.

61. Olema, *History of Evangelical Christianity*, 74.

62. Heier, *Religious Schism*, 135; Corrado, "Philosophy of Ministry," 188; Durassoff, *Russian Protestants*, 46.

Christians should seek unity "in spirit and in truth" rather than in "the single understanding of dogma."[63]

The third, mostly peasant, group of Shtundists in Ukraine initially viewed themselves as a biblical movement within the Orthodox Church and did not separate from it even when severe persecutions against them began.[64] But as they became acquainted with believers' baptism, they developed a critical attitude toward the official church as a nominal church, in contrast to the fellowship of born-again Christians. In November 1772, the Shtundists of Chaplinka village respectfully deposited their home icons at the bell tower of the church, thereby "formally acknowledging a break with the State Church."[65] Prior to his deportation, Pashkov actively worked among Ukrainian peasants. After he had to leave Russia, the more solidly organized Baptists attracted the "unorganized masses of ecclesiastically uprooted Shtundists" and these groups largely joined the ranks of the Baptist Union.[66] Just as was the case with the Gospel Christians, the "blind anger of the priests killed any hope that Shtundism [might] become a reformation within the Orthodox Church."[67]

Cultural Engagement

Even though Radstock's message focused primarily on the vertical aspects of the gospel, he explicitly taught new converts that new life in Christ should affect all their relationships – personal, vocational, social, etc. It was thought that the ever-increasing number of individual conversions would ultimately lead to the reformation of all of Russia "on a religious and moral basis."[68] Pashkov inherited from Radstock this passion to bring the entire population of Russia to evangelical faith and moral transformation.[69] The primary

---

63. V. A. Stepanov, "Sankt-Peterburgskii Syezd Evangel'skikh Veruiuschikh 1884 Goda: Mify, Facty, Uroki [The Congress of Evangelical Believers in St Petersburg in 1884: Myths, Facts, Lessons]," 2016, http://bit.ly/2lFHUYP.

64. Hans Brandenburg, *The Meek and the Mighty: The Emergence of the Evangelical Movement in Russia* (New York: Oxford University Press, 1977), 76; Hebly, *Protestants in Russia*, 50; A. I. Mitskevich, *Istoriia Evangel'skikh Khristian-Baptistov [A History of Evangelical Christians-Baptists]* (Moscow: RSEKhB, 2007), 33; Yuchkovski, "Comparison of the Evangelical Movement," 33.

65. Hebly, *Protestants in Russia*, 55.

66. Hebly, 57, 72; cf. Ellis and Jones, *The Other Revolution*, 69.

67. Pollock, *Faith of the Russian Evangelicals*, 64.

68. Heier, *Religious Schism*, 29.

69. Corrado, "Philosophy of Ministry," 185.

instrument in the process was seen to be the spread of literacy. It was common knowledge that a sectarian, regardless of his or her social background, quickly learned to read because the reading of the Gospels became their spiritual nourishment. Pashkov personally financed the publication of the *Russian Workman* magazine and multiple pamphlets which were distributed free of charge or for the minimum cost of a half to one kopek.[70]

Another powerful instrument was the visible demonstration of equality and brotherhood across ethnic and social lines among the Gospel Christians. Many authors point out that this kind of egalitarianism was a defining characteristic of the Pashkovite movement.[71] In the strictly hierarchical Russian society, with ten clearly defined *soslovie* (or strata), one's official social identity was determined by the circumstances of their birth.[72] At the meetings of Pashkovites, however, every stratum of Russian society was present, which was indeed unusual and often misinterpreted.[73] They turned their ballrooms and mansions into prayer rooms occupied by the nobility together with their servants and others of humble origin. In fact, evangelical egalitarianism may be seen as the first serious attempt in Russia to bridge the social gap which rigidly separated the masses from the privileged groups.[74]

The third instrument of the spiritual transformation of Russia employed by the Pashkovite groups was their active involvement in responding to social needs (which will be considered in the section on holistic mission below). The three strategies together had an enormous effect on Russia. Without having a definite social program as did the revolutionaries, and merely promoting "evolutionary change with the Bible as their guidance," the Pashkovites by 1884 were the only group of all the social and religious societies of the 1880s "capable of initiating large-scale changes" within the Russian empire.[75] It is very likely, as Russian historian Paul Miliukov observed, that had the tsarist

---

70. Heier, *Religious Schism*, 121.

71. Yuchkovski, "Comparison of the Evangelical Movement," 32; Ellis and Jones, *The Other Revolution*, 77–78; Corrado, "Philosophy of Ministry," 187.

72. Coleman, *Russian Baptists and Spiritual Revolution*, 4.

73. The ober-procurator Pobedonostsev basically lumped Pashkov together with socialists. For him, there appears to have been no difference between threats coming from either the religious or political manifestations of opposition to Orthodox civilization. Puzynin, *Tradition of the Gospel Christians*, 77.

74. Heier, *Religious Schism*, 48, 110; Ellis and Jones, *The Other Revolution*, 94.

75. Heier, 136.

government not taken measures to limit Pashkovite and other evangelical influence, a Russian reformation "would have been an accomplished fact."[76]

It should be noted, however, that not all evangelical groups were alike in their views on cultural engagement. Most groups in Ukraine and southern Russia consisted mostly of peasants or members of formerly persecuted semi-Orthodox sects.[77] Among Baptists, most early converts came from the Molokans. Coleman portrays the Molokans as a "sect with Quaker-like beliefs,"[78] and Hebly characterizes them as "very conservative and puritanical," taking "no part in the general cultur[al] life around them."[79] For these groups it was natural to lean toward individualized spirituality, introversion, and isolation from the sinful world. Hebly observes that Shtundists and Baptists at that stage did not pursue political interests or social reforms; above all else they simply "wanted to remain true to their faith and preach the gospel as they had come to know it."[80]

Hence, as far as cultural engagement is concerned, Russian evangelicals from the very beginning manifested two different approaches. As we will see later, depending on the social and political environment, one or the other tendency would come to the fore in the future. At the same time, Coleman profoundly observes that by their very existence in the politically and religiously totalitarian environment, Baptist communities, based on voluntary membership, democratic organization, and intellectual egalitarianism, made it possible to "envision a social and political space where people could live and make choices according to their individual convictions."[81] Their religious ex-

---

76. P. N. Miliukov, *Russia and Its Crisis* (New York: Collier Books, 1962), 100.

77. Sinichkin, *Vozrozhdenie Vopreki Bezbozhiiu [Revival despite Godlessness]*, 91.

78. Coleman, *Russian Baptists and Spiritual Revolution*, 15.

79. Hebly, *Protestants in Russia*, 79. Their self-identity had been shaped primarily over against the state church which, in their view, mixed the pure "milk of the Word of God" (1 Pet 2:2) with human philosophies and institutions. (The name *Molokan* comes from the Russian word for *milk*.) It is possible, however, that the name was given to them because they refused to abstain from dairy products during Orthodox Lent. "Dukhovnyie Khristiane (Molokane) [The Spiritual Christians (The Molokans)]," accessed 25 June 2017, http://molokan.narod.ru/index_long.html.

80. Hebly, *Protestants in Russia*, 61.

81. Coleman, *Russian Baptists and Spiritual Revolution*, 223.

perience was a ferment that eventually moved evangelicals to demand and live out "an alternative vision of society to that sponsored by the Russian state."[82]

Holistic Mission

As was already mentioned, one common accusation against the Gospel Christians' belief in justification by faith was that this teaching would inevitably lead to licentiousness.[83] Yet even their opponents had to admit that converts were typically known for their morally transformed lives and generous charity. Writing about Radstock's influence on the aristocrats of the capital, Dostoevskii comments that while he "found nothing special" in his evangelistic preaching, the man "performs miracles over human hearts." The converts "are looking for the poor in order, as quickly as possible, to bestow benefits upon them; they are almost ready to give away their fortunes."[84] As a foreigner, Radstock was not able to become as actively involved in social work in Russia as he had been in England,[85] so it was up to Pashkov and other Russian converts, many of whom were of high standing with the government and had vast amounts of wealth, to develop this aspect of the movement.[86]

Theologically, Pashkov saw good works as both an expression of gratefulness to God and the fruit of the Spirit expected of all Christians.[87] While good deeds could not help one earn salvation, their absence testified to "departure from [the] faith itself."[88] Following in the footsteps of Pashkov, who devoted his enormous personal wealth and full energies to the cause, many began helping the poor spiritually and materially. Heier describes this as follows:

---

82. Coleman, 222.

83. Corrado, "Philosophy of Ministry," 66.

84. F. M. Dostoevskii, *Dnevnik Pisatelia Za 1876 g [A Writer's Diary for 1876]*, 1879 ed. (St Petersburg: Tipografiia Iu. Shtaufa, n.d.), 87; Quoted in Raber, "Ministries of Compassion," 36.

85. He grew up in a family that turned from high society to the Plymouth Brethren movement and donated money to reach out to the poor. His mother was active in the slums of London rescuing prostitutes. As a family, they sponsored a home for recent immigrants in London and a home for girls in Paris. Mark Myers McCarthy, "Religious Conflict and Social Order in Nineteenth-Century Russia: Orthodoxy and the Protestant Challenge, 1812–1905" (PhD diss., University of Notre Dame, 2004), 51–52.

86. Nichols, "Pashkovism," 109–110.

87. Leskov, *Schism in High Society*.

88. Corrado, "Philosophy of Ministry," 66.

A sense of brotherhood, the great ethical ideal of Christianity – that of personal service and help – was developing among the high society of St. Petersburg... Many began petitioning for those who were in difficulty with the authorities. District visiting among the poor in factories, in hospitals, and in prisons [was] initiated, hospitals and schools were built on country estates, and lodging houses and inexpensive tearooms for the poor were established in the capital.[89]

While the Gospel Christians stressed the primacy of evangelism, works of charity always accompanied their sharing of the gospel. They supported food pantries, opened schools and orphanages, created workplaces for the poor, rehabilitated alcoholics, built shelters for homeless women and prostitutes, sponsored reading materials and libraries for the masses, opened Bible schools teaching an ethical lifestyle, established nursing homes for the elderly, organized technical schools for uneducated young people, visited prisoners, and established scholarships for university students from poor families.[90] Their charity work was a major reason why people flocked to the Pashkovite prayer meetings: it was clear that these people truly obeyed Christ's teachings by caring for the welfare of their fellow Russians. As Heier puts it, "The purely religious propaganda, the preaching of 'love thy neighbor' by these aristocrats would have meant very little had their ideas not resulted in practical application, not only in fraternal behavior towards the lower classes, but also in extensive philanthropic work."[91]

Some historians go so far as to suggest that the evangelical revival in the final quarter of the nineteenth century, had it gathered enough momentum,

---

89. Heier, *Religious Schism*, 48.

90. Viacheslav Tsvirin'ko, "Missiia Pervykh Evangel'skikh Dvizhenii v Rossiiskoi Iimperii i SSSR [Mission of the First Evangelical Movements in the Russian Empire and the USSR]," in *Novye Gorizonty Missii [New Horizons of Mission]*, ed. Peter Penner et al. (Cherkassy: Colloquium, 2015), 197; Nichols, "Pashkovism," 110; Savinskii, Savchenko, and Dik, *Istoriia Evangel'skikh Khristian-Baptistov v SSSR [History of Evangelical Christians-Baptists in the USSR]*; Sinichkin, *Vsio Radi Missii [Everything for the Sake of Mission]*; Raber, "Ministries of Compassion." Nichols observes a strong similarity between the innovative social work in Russia and the social work by evangelicals in the West, such as was done in England through the Evangelical Alliance, the Midway Conference, and later the Keswick Conference. Nichols, *Russian Evangelical Spirituality*, 110.

91. Heier, *Religious Schism*, 113.

might have "deflected the course of Russian history."[92] In stark contrast to the socialist agenda of "what's yours is mine," the Pashkovites demonstrated the philosophy of Jesus, or "what's mine is yours."[93] It is said that General Feodor Trepov, the Governor of St Petersburg from 1873 to 1878, exclaimed on one occasion, "If Pashkov succeeds, we are all saved!"[94] From this perspective, the evangelical movement was perhaps the only alternative to the Communist Revolution. Unfortunately, in the 1880s and 1890s, the possibility of a national reformation was rejected and suppressed by the monarchical state, inspired by the nationalistic state church. As a result, the initiative was now passing to atheistic extremists. Echoing the words of Russian thinker Nikolay Berdyaev, Olema and Pollock observe that Communism became "the fruit of Christian failure."[95]

After the exile of Pashkov from Russia in 1884, the evangelical movement entered into a phase of strong governmental repression and control. The vacuum of leadership and crystallized doctrine was filled by invited Baptist preachers who gradually transformed the open-minded movement into a more sectarian shape. The emergence of a new generation of leaders such as Johann Kargel (1849–1937), Vasilty Pavlov (1854–1924), and Ivan Prokhanov (1869–1935) brought with it centralized leadership and clearly defined theology that would serve the movement during the next period of new opportunities.

Transformationist Pietism: 1905–1930

Historical Background

On 17 April 1905, Tsar Nicholas II signed the Edict of Religious Toleration, which marked a significant shift in religious policy. Later that same year, the Toleration Act was superseded by the Manifesto of 17 October 1905, which granted citizens freedom of the press, freedom to organize societies

---

92. Pollock, *Faith of the Russian Evangelicals*, 69; Miliukov, *Russia and Its Crisis*, 100.
93. Corrado, "Philosophy of Ministry," 189.
94. Heier, *Religious Schism*, 113.
95. Nicolas Berdyaev, *The Origin of Russian Communism* (Ann Arbor, MI: University of Michigan Press, 1960); Pollock, *Faith of the Russian Evangelicals*, 74; Olema, *History of Evangelical Christianity*, 162.

and meetings, freedom to engage in political activities, and the free practice of religion. With some setbacks during WWI and the afflictions of the civil war of 1918–1920, this freedom continued until Stalin's anti-religious legislation of 1929. In the wake of these developments, Russian evangelicals embarked on twenty-five years of intense missionary activity, publishing work, and the organizational consolidation of their movement. The Communist Revolution in October 1917 and the resulting decree on the separation of church and state sounded for many evangelicals like "a charter of liberties for all religious groups that had seen discrimination and persecution under the old partnership of tsar and Orthodoxy."[96] By all means, the years between 1917 and 1929 became the time of the greatest freedom, the broadest opportunities, and the most active work in which Russian evangelicals had ever engaged, or would engage in after that. In fact, this period is sometimes referred to as their "golden decade."[97]

Theologically, three names stand out during this period: Ivan Prokhanov, Johann Kargel, and Vasiliy Pavlov. The first two were leaders and organizers of the Gospel Christians, while the third was a leader of the Baptist Union. While only Kargel can be considered properly a theologian among them, they all wrote multiple articles and pamphlets whose influence endured long after they passed away. In 1909, Prokhanov wrote the Confession of Faith that was accepted by the Union of Gospel Christians as their official creed. In 1906, Pavlov translated and edited for Russian needs the so-called Hamburg Confession that had been put together by Johannes Gerhard Onken in 1847. It was then republished by Nikolay Odintsov in 1928 and remained authoritative until 1966, when Kargel's Confession, originally written in 1913, was adopted by the AUCECB as its formal confession. Kargel's creed retained this status through 1985, when the current confession was adopted. In this way, Kargel's theology would become definitive for the next, late Soviet, period of Russian Baptist history. In what follows, I will attempt to trace the transformations of the four key aspects of theology of mission during this period.

---

96. Wanner, *Communities of the Converted*, 21.
97. Sawatsky, *Soviet Evangelicals*, 47.

The Nature of the Gospel

In their understanding of salvation, Russian evangelicals remained faithful to the original pietistic concept that had been shaped over against Russian Orthodox theology and practice. Perhaps, most vividly this can be seen in Ivan Prokhanov's autobiography.[98] The state church, he says, taught

> that the tsar was far and God was too high, that he was a severe judge, and that no one could directly approach God, that one must do it through the ranks of priests and saints . . . that man is justified and saved by his works, but at the same time . . . that no one can know on earth that he is saved . . . [The clergy] omitted and lost the whole gospel, the source of joy and life, and left their people in the darkness of hopeless life of spiritual pessimism and everlasting fear: no salvation, no eternity.[99]

In contrast to this view of Christianity, evangelicals proclaimed "justification by faith, salvation by Christ's death on the cross, purification from sin by the blood of Jesus Christ, spiritual regeneration (new birth), the forgiveness of sins directly by God, [and] the work of the Holy Spirit in the hearts of men."[100]

Vasiliy Pavlov in his Confession of Faith also explicates his view of the gospel against the background of Orthodox sacramentalism:

> Christ does not need mediators for his grace, which he communicates directly by touching [the] human soul by his Spirit . . . This is our main principle that completely eradicates clericalism and ritualism . . . No mediation of a church mechanism [sic], whatever it is called: priesthood, sacraments, rites or rituals, is important [for salvation] . . . because this does not agree with the Holy Scriptures.[101]

This period, however, saw one important development which deserves special attention. In the atmosphere of newfound freedoms and opportunities,

---

98. Ivan Prokhanov, *In the Couldron of Russia: 1869–1933* (New York: All-Russian Evangelical Christian Union, 1933).

99. Prokhanov, *Couldron of Russia*, 24.

100. Prokhanov, 24.

101. Quoted in Nagirnyak, *Podvizhniki Very [Devotees of Faith]*, 235; cf. Olema, *History of Evangelical Christianity*, 92.

Ivan Prokhanov developed a truly holistic understanding of the gospel which brought Colonel Pashkov's earlier vision to its logical completion. Prokhanov's view of the gospel is best expressed in his article "New Life in the Gospel."[102] In it, he describes the gospel metaphorically as "the all-renewing stone" that "recreates anew everything it touches."[103] What the Bible calls conversion should be seen as a double process: first, the gospel renews the believer's internal life, making him or her a new creature; and second, it renews their external life. The gospel transforms one's mind, family life, social relationships, work ethics, creativity, and aesthetics. It renews cities and villages, industries and technology, science, arts, music, and architecture. Prokhanov claims that the "essence of Evangelical Christianity," just as of the first Christianity in its time, is "the proclamation of the great teaching of the gospel about the full and constant renewal of human life."[104]

What undergirded Prokhanov's optimism about the power of the gospel were not only the new social conditions, but also his postmillennial eschatology.[105] He believed that new life in Christ eventually "restores all aspects of the spiritual person in their full perfection as we had it before the fall." The Christian ideal, therefore, is to "bring Christ down to earth through reaching his likeness in humans."[106] In the final pages of his autobiography he enthusiastically calls on his readers to "take the old and yet eternally new gospel as the foundation of [their] life and to rebuild it in accord with the teaching of Jesus Christ, and the earth and heaven will be new." As a result, God himself would "create a new and happy life in our country."[107] It is go-

---

102. Ivan Prokhanov, *Novaya Ili Evangel'skaya Zhizn [New Life in the Gospel]* (Moscow: Logos, 2009).

103. Prokhanov, *Novaya Ili Evangel'skaya Zhizn [New Life in the Gospel]*, 96.

104. Prokhanov, *Couldron of Russia*, 102.

105. Most likely, he developed it during his three and a half years in Western Europe from 1895 to 1899. While he did not earn a theological degree, he had the opportunity to attend classes in theological colleges in Bristol, London, Berlin, and Paris. In particular, he was able to listen to lectures given by Adolf von Harnack at the University of Berlin in 1898, and spent a semester at the Faculty of Protestant Theology in Paris. This gave Prokhanov "at least a superficial acquaintance with the European theology of the time." Puzynin, *Tradition of the Gospel Christians*, 129.

106. Prokhanov, *Couldron of Russia*, 110.

107. Prokhanov, 270.

ing to be a time when "love will rule in this life, and God himself will be the king, for God is love."[108]

Prokhanov's understanding of the gospel was met, to say the least, with much criticism and skepticism, especially in Baptist circles.[109] In the follow-up to his programmatic article, Prokhanov identified these skeptics as "pessimists" and went on to rebuff the four most common objections to his ideas. In his view, they were based on a superficial reading of the following biblical maxims:

1. Christians are "aliens and strangers in the world" (1 Pet 2:2);
2. They must "set their minds on things above, not on earthly things" (Col 3:2);
3. There "will be terrible times in the last days" (2 Tim 3:1);
4. The "present heavens and earth are reserved for fire" (2 Pet 3:7)[110]

Baptists generally felt more at home with the soteriological emphases of Johann Kargel who focused on Radstock's idea of the higher Christian life through full consecration and the filling of the Spirit.[111] The roots of this tradition go back to the evangelical holiness stream of spirituality, but it was uniquely articulated and mediated through Johann Kargel.[112] Nichols summarizes his view of the Christian life as follows:

> Kargel . . . called people to personal trust in Jesus Christ for both justification and sanctification; focused in his teaching on "abiding in Christ" in order to live a life of victory; stressed the power of the Holy Spirit; and saw the life of discipleship as involving following Christ on the pathway of suffering.[113]

---

108. Prokhanov, *Novaya Ili Evangel'skaya Zhizn [New Life in the Gospel]*, 124.

109. Mitskevich, *Istoriia Evangel'skikh Khristian-Baptistov [A History of Evangelical Christians-Baptists]*, 278; Sannikov, *Istoriia Baptizma [A History of Baptist Faith]*, 367; N. V. Potapova, *Evnagel'skoe Khristianstvo i Baptism [The Gospel Christians and Baptists]*. Vol. 1 (Yuzhno-Sakhalisnk: SachGU, 2014), 135; Nagirnyak, *Podvizhniki Very [Devotees of Faith]*, 28.

110. Prokhanov, *Novaya Ili Evangel'skaya Zhizn [New Life in the Gospel]*, 125–130.

111. Nichols, "Pashkovism," 102.

112. Puzynin, *Tradition of the Gospel Christians*; Nichols, *Russian Evangelical Spirituality*, 148–149; Miriam Kuznetsova, "Early Russian Evangelicals (1874–1929): Historical Background and Hermeneutical Tendencies Based on I. V. Kargel's Written Heritage" (PhD diss., University of Pretoria, 2009).

113. Nichols, *Russian Evangelical Spirituality*, 153–155.

Kargel was also heavily influenced by the dispensationalist thought of the Darby school. His premillennial, pretribulational eschatology was first explicitly articulated in the creed which he wrote in 1913 and, later, in his commentary on the book of Revelation, which remained practically the only exposition of the book available to Russian Baptists through the end of the 1980s. In this regard, his theology stood in sharp contrast with Prokhanov's convictions.

Despite the different emphases, evangelism remained the highest priority for both unions throughout this period. Believers took very seriously the motto "Every Christian (or Baptist) a missionary!"[114] In 1907, Baptists launched a missionary society in Rostov, and later that same year another one in Omsk. In 1921, the 24th Congress of Russian Baptists announced that "evangelism is the most important work of our spiritual life. Any form of our organization should be considered valuable only inasmuch as it contributes to the successful preaching of the Gospel."[115] By the end of 1923, Baptists had sixty-five fully supported evangelists, and about one thousand more worked as volunteers. Many evangelical preachers conducted evangelistic meetings in the open air or in rented theaters, restaurants, university classes, etc.

As a result, this period saw enormous growth of the Baptist and Gospel Christian movements. According to reports from the All-Russia Congress of Baptists in 1911, the union then included fifty thousand members.[116] By June 1928, the Baptist Union of Russia had two hundred thousand baptized members (a fourfold growth in seventeen years!), four thousand local churches, and nine hundred ordained pastors. The Gospel Christians, under the leadership of Prokhanov, whom Durasoff aptly characterizes as an "aggressive leader" and "master organizer," grew from 8,472 members in 1914 to about 250,000 in 1922. By 1928 they had over six hundred missionaries dispatched all across the Soviet Union.[117]

In view of this enormous growth, it is not surprising to read in Prokhanov that "We began to spiritually conquer the whole of Russia, and we would have

---

114. Prokhanov, *Couldron of Russia*, 64; Olema, *History of Evangelical Christianity*, 167; Wanner, *Communities of the Converted*, 25; Nagirnyak, *Podvizhniki Very [Devotees of Faith]*, 249.

115. Sinichkin, *Vsio Radi Missii [Everything for the Sake of Mission]*, 183.

116. Sinichkin, 181.

117. S. Bolshakoff, *Russian Nonconformity: The Story of "Unofficial" Religion in Russia* (Philadelphia: Westminster, 1950), 119; Durassoff, *Russian Protestants*, 56; Olema, *History of Evangelical Christianity*, 76.

covered the whole territory but for the interference of atheism."[118] A similar confidence was expressed by the Baptist leader Pavel Ivanov-Klyshnikov at the 1928 Baptist World Congress in Toronto. He stated optimistically: "The Russian people represent the most fruit-bearing spiritual ground among the peoples of the whole world. It is a people of God-seekers . . . We observe signs of a great awakening."[119] Similar sentiments were expressed by external observers as well. The president of the British Baptist Union, J.H. Shakespeare, expected in 1911 that "when Russia becomes the most Baptist country in the world, outside America, it will mark a turning point in the history of Europe."[120] However, by the end of the 1920s this optimism was replaced by the realization that the government made it its agenda to completely eradicate evangelical Christianity and was preparing measures of repression.

The Identity and Purpose of the Church

Both the RUB and the RUGC finally received the opportunity to function legally, and they were officially organized during this period. Already in 1905 the first attempts were made to unify the two groups into one body, with the last unsuccessful attempt taking place in 1920. In addition to the personal traits and ambitions of the leadership of both groups, part of the reason why this did not happen lay in their different theological conceptions of the church. Prokhanov saw the church as an instrument and sign of God's kingdom. He mildly criticized the emphasis on higher spirituality that was popular among many evangelicals, emphasizing instead the practical aspects of the Christian life:

> Some persons who love Christ's teachings understand them in a narrow sense of spiritual contemplation . . . They like to be caught emotionally aflame, but their life hardly goes beyond that . . . While [all of this] is necessary, our primary purpose in this life is not rest, but a hard and constant work of God's construction . . . The Christian sees every labor, spiritual or physical,

---

118. Prokhanov, *Couldron of Russia*, 155.
119. Durassoff, *Russian Protestants*, 74.
120. Coleman, *Russian Baptists and Spiritual Revolution*, 7.

as participation in the great work of his Creator and Savior in renewing the life of humanity.[121]

Elsewhere, Prokhanov defined God's work as "lessening any evil in political and social life through the example of love and prayer in order to contribute to the triumph of good, freedom, justice, and peace."[122] He was convinced that visible, tangible signs of a transformed, alternative lifestyle have "a tremendous power of example and are a new object lesson and incentive to the highest living instead of merely existing from one day to the next, as the vast majority of Russians did in past years."[123] When Christians bear their testimony by a "truly successful life in the midst of poverty and degradation," they become "a living witness" to the power of the gospel.[124]

In his efforts to restore, as he saw them, original apostolic Christianity, Prokhanov also exhibited a strong "ecumenical drive for an enlarged fellowship."[125] The Baptist sectarian tendencies "were too rigid to him."[126] From his perspective, organizational unity was necessary only for the purpose of mission and evangelism and should be based on freedom, equality, and mutual interdependence without the requirement of dogmatic uniformity in all matters.[127] In his letter to Pashkov who lived in Paris at that time (May 1898), he wrote:

> The Christian work should be based on the requirements of Christ's love which is the only source of the Church's strength on the earth, rather than on dogmatic formulations which erect boundaries . . . The plurality of opinions concerning secondary issues does not destroy but actually embellishes the spiritual unity of different communities within evangelical Christianity . . .

---

121. Prokhanov, *Novaya Ili Evangel'skaya Zhizn* [*New Life in the Gospel*], 105.

122. Prokhanov, 157.

123. Ivan Prokhanov, *Ateism Ili Evangelie?* [*Atheism or the Gospel?*] (Moscow: VSEKh, 1933), 22.

124. Prokhanov, *Ateism Ili Evangelie?* [*Atheism or the Gospel?*], 23.

125. Prokhanov, 23.

126. Durassoff, *Russian Protestants*, 55; Olema, *History of Evangelical Christianity*, 76.

127. Prokhanov, *Novaya Ili Evangel'skaya Zhizn* [*New Life in the Gospel*], 155; Durassoff, *Russian Protestants*, 62; Mitskevich, *Istoriia Evangel'skikh Khristian-Baptistov* [*A History of Evangelical Christians-Baptists*], 135, 141.

> There is no better joy ... than to discover the spiritual unity of God's children in diverse ecclesiastical traits.[128]

His vision of restored Christianity embraced all churches that were built on the biblical gospel. Hence, Prokhanov envisioned a union embracing all Russian Protestants through which he hoped to effect a reformation in Russia. In addition to his attempts to see the two evangelical groups unite, in 1921 he published an appeal to the leadership of the so-called Living Church (a reform movement within the Russian Orthodox Church supported by the Bolsheviks). The essence of "The Gospel Call," as he called it, was first to announce forgiveness of the Orthodox clergy, now devoid of the support of the state, for their long-standing persecution of religious minorities, and second, to encourage them to become evangelical in the most important matters of theology and ecclesiastical practice.[129]

Baptists during that period, however, firmly held to their convictions of the church as a local community, pastored by properlyordained ministers. They followed their strict order of worship and discipline. Under the leadership of Dey Mazaev who held key leadership positions in the Baptist Union for almost thirty years, Baptists insisted on closed communion and imposed the name "Baptist" on the projects of the united body, which for the Gospel Christians sounded non-Russian. In Sawatsky's summary:

> From the Baptist point of view it was clear that ... they had a greater claim to biblical truth than any other church body. A committed Baptist could not conceive of any other reason for rejecting Baptist distinctives than willful disobedience of the commands of Jesus. Therefore, renunciation of Baptist distinctives was apostasy and with apostates no fellowship could be possible.[130]

---

128. Quoted in M. Y. Zhidkov, "Edinstvo vo Khriste [Unity in Christ]," *Bratskii Vestnik [Brotherly Herald]* 1 (1985): 52.

129. Yuchkovski, "Comparison of the Evangelical Movement," 48; Puzynin, *Tradition of the Gospel Christians*, 159.

130. Sawatsky, *Soviet Evangelicals*, 83.

It was primarily this attitude that, coupled with a number of other factors, prevented attempts at unification after 1920.[131] In addition, Kargel, who was Prokhanov's associate in the RUGC, thought that Baptist principles could not be compromised by ecumenical contacts with the Russian Orthodox Church.[132] As a result, even those limited contacts with the Living Church that Prokhanov managed to establish met with disapproval on the part of both the more conservative wing of Orthodoxy and the Baptists.[133] Exacerbated by the political intrigues of the Bolsheviks to split the Russian Orthodox Church, the development of these relations finally came to a stop.[134]

Baptists were also critical of Prokhanov's vision of comprehensive gospel renewal. For people such as Dey Mazaev, that vision was little more than a form of utopia. Mazaev saw the church as "the instrument [for] saving... souls on earth in order to lead them to the heavenly kingdom of God."[135] The *Baptist* magazine, edited by Mazaev, published a number of articles against the Gospel Christians, and, according to the memoirs of long-standing AUCECB leader Arthur Mitskevich, Baptist members "were all taught to despise Prokhanovism."[136] The diverse emphasis can be seen in the different ultimate goals of each group at that time. If Prokhanov strived toward seeing Russia become a nation of evangelical Christianity, Mazaev taught that "mass conversions are hardly desirable or helpful, because many new members who have not yet imbibed our teaching, can influence our communities toward making decisions which are immature, or even inimical to our church order."[137]

---

131. In particular, Hebly pays attention to the personal motives of Prokhanov and Mazaev, observing that both leaders "tended to be somewhat authoritarian." Hebly, *Protestants in Russia*, 97.

132. Yuchkovski, "Comparison of the Evangelical Movement," 63.

133. Savinskii, *Istoriia Evangel'skikh Khristian-Baptistov Ukrainy, Rossii, Belorussii: 1917–1967 [History of Evangelical Christians-Baptists of Ukraine, Russia, and Belarus: 1917–1967]*, 97; Nagirnyak, *Podvizhniki Very [Devotees of Faith]*, 287.

134. D. Pospielovsky, *Russkaia Pravoslavnaia Tserkov' v XX Veke [The Russian Orthodox Church in the Twentieth Century]* (Moscow: Respublika, 1995), 89–102.

135. Nagirnyak, *Podvizhniki Very [Devotees of Faith]*, 27–28; Potapova, *Evnagel'skoe Khristianstvo i Baptism [The Gospel Christians and Baptists]*. Vol. 1.

136. Mitskevich, *Istoriia Evangel'skikh Khristian-Baptistov [A History of Evangelical Christians-Baptists]*, 155, 278.

137. Sawatsky, *Soviet Evangelicals*, 54.

Cultural Engagement

Speaking about the Gospel Christians, Hebly finds it rather remarkable that a group coming out of persecution was capable of developing a very broad vision of church and society. Their pietistic roots, he affirms, had not produced a "narrow-minded, introverted mentality," but rather an awakened Christianity with "a strong sense of calling with respect to social problems."[138] Many leaders of the movement saw the breaking of the old social and political order as an "opportunity for spiritual renewal, even a moral resurrection of the people that would result in a new encompassing spiritual community."[139] Ivan Prokhanov's grand vision basically meant living one's whole life – personal, social, and cultural – in new ways in Christ, the risen Lord who rules all things. In his brochure "Atheism or the Gospel," the leader of the RUGC articulated the main aspects of his vision:

- Love [for] God, our neighbors and even our enemies.
- [Broad] participation . . . in education and the sciences. There must not be a single illiterate man or woman among us. We must produce great scientists.[140]
- The gospel must find expression in the development of [the] arts, such as literature, music, architecture, painting, sculpture, etc.
- The gospel must bring its influence to bear on all branches of labor, to produce love of work [and] the faithful performance of all duties [and] to improve and perfect industry by the application of new inventions and methods of work.
- There must be improvement in all branches of agriculture, livestock raising, poultry, fruit, wheat, rye, etc. These must be developed to the point of winning prizes in agricultural fairs.
- Our houses in villages, towns, and cities must be surrounded by green vegetation, with plenty of flowers and with "kitchen gardens" at the rear, all so outstanding and different from the average that passerby will say: "A Gospel Christian lives here."

---

138. Hebly, *Protestants in Russia*, 93.

139. Wanner, *Communities of the Converted*, 31.

140. Elsewhere he writes, "At least half of the students in the Academy of Sciences must consist of Evangelical Christians." Quoted in Hebly, *Protestants in Russia*, 93.

- ... Absolute forbearance from things superfluous and unnecessary to our health should be promoted. [But] ... full teetotalism and the complete absence of narcotics ... can be realized only on the basis of moral and spiritual regeneration ...
- All [aspects of] the practical everyday life of the Gospel Christian and our congregations must be so ordered that "neither may there be among them any that lack." (Acts 4:34)[141]

At the congress of the RUGC in 1926 it was resolved that the Gospel Christians would dedicate themselves, in the midst of the Russian people, to "a new lifestyle founded on the gospel."[142] As seen from the above, this meant more than the conversion of individuals; it was the "penetration of all sectors of human life with the spirit of the gospel."[143] Prokhanov believed that the gospel "will remedy all the evils from which the Russian people are suffering" and that "faith in the gospel is ... the victory that overcomes the world."[144]

In the new situation of freedom, Prokhanov and others tried to bring the evangelicals' voice to the public square. In March 1917 he created *Voskresenie* (the Resurrection) political party and, although his effort was unsuccessful, his name was placed on the ballot for a seat in St Petersburg as a Christian Democrat candidate.[145] The party platform addressed a wide range of issues, such as the right to strike, an eight-hour workday, the right to education, and the right to pensions for the retired. Russia was seen as a federal state, in which regions would have some degree of autonomy. On the international stage, the party proposed the creation of a world union of states, which would regulate international affairs. Despite Prokhanov's expectations, however, the RUGC Congress in May 1917 did not approve having that party represent the union. The ensuing debates demonstrate the difficulty of defining the correct boundaries between faith and politics.[146]

---

141. Prokhanov, *Ateism Ili Evangelie? [Atheism or the Gospel?]*, 22–23; quoted in Nichols, "Pashkovism," 111–112.

142. Mitskevich, *Istoriia Evangel'skikh Khristian-Baptistov [A History of Evangelical Christians-Baptists]*, 258–261.

143. Hebly, *Protestants in Russia*, 92.

144. Prokhanov, *Couldron of Russia*, 206, 257.

145. Yuchkovski, "Comparison of the Evangelical Movement," 51; Durassoff, *Russian Protestants*, 52.

146. Yuchkovski, 51.

Some Baptist leaders also used the new opportunities to publicize their social and political views. In June 1917, Pavel Pavlov (the son of Vasily), in his editorial for the first issue of *Slovo Istiny* (The Word of Truth) newspaper, argued that Christianity should not be passive and distant from people's lives but practical and real, with concrete goals focused on particular aspects of people's daily lives.[147] Together with Mikhail Timoshenko, Pavlov published a document called "The Political Demands of Baptists," in which they advocated the separation of church and state; freedom of assembly, union, speech, and publication; equality for all citizens, regardless of nationality; and freedom of worship and propagation for all confessions that do not contradict generally accepted morals.[148] Vasily Pavlov in his article on the separation of church and state articulated the "Baptist ideal" in the public square as follows: "a free church in a free state."[149] Dey Mazaev, a Baptist leader and prosperous farmer, was elected to one of the three North Caucasus seats in the State Duma, or Parliament.

During the seven-month period between the liberal and Communist revolutions of 1917, it became common for the leaders of both unions to use the language of "spiritual revolution" in their preaching, publications, and public addresses.[150] In essence, this expression was another name for the long-standing idea of a Russian reformation, yet the choice of the term reflected both an adjustment and an alternative to the current social trends.[151] On the one hand, it linked political and religious liberation and hence blurred "the lines between the sacred and the profane, between religious and social thought."[152] On the other hand, it indicated that political revolution alone is not enough; it must be accompanied by faith in the gospel and spiritual regeneration.

It was also not uncommon for evangelicals to present themselves and their system of church organization as a model for the new era in Russia, in terms of both democratic organization and the resolution of class tensions.

---

147. Pavel Pavlov, "K Momentu [To the Moment]," *Slovo Istiny* [*The Word of Truth*] 1 (1917): 2; Yuchkovski, 63.

148. Wanner, *Communities of the Converted*, 32.

149. Vasily Pavlov, *Baptisty: Tzerkov i Gosudarstvo* [*Baptists: Church and State*] (Moscow: Logos, 2004), 128.

150. Coleman, *Russian Baptists and Spiritual Revolution*, 137–143.

151. Prokhanov, *Couldron of Russia*, 7.

152. Coleman, *Russian Baptists and Spiritual Revolution*, 143.

In his public speeches during 1917, Pavel Pavlov claimed that among Russian Baptists, "present class dissension is reconciled – the poor and the rich consider themselves brothers."[153] He added that, like all other progressive liberation forces in the country, the Baptists also "strive for socialism," but theirs, he said, was "not based on seizure, built on the declaration of another's property to be one's own." Rather, their shared communal life was flowing from the "moral perfection" they were able to achieve through the experience of spiritual revolution.[154] Caught up in the enthusiasm of the revolutionary era, evangelical leaders confidently proclaimed that the revolution of the Spirit, accompanied by the triumph of true science and progress and political revolution, would lead to the complete transformation of culture by the gospel and to the full liberation of humanity from all kinds of bondage, both spiritual and physical.[155]

Holistic Mission

In her important dissertation, Mary Raber presents a comprehensive picture of the evangelicals' compassionate ministries during the period from 1905 to 1929.[156] She discerns three primary patterns in their work: (1) aid within the evangelical communities, with the establishment of dedicated funds and the organization of church-based institutions; (2) urban rescue ministries and involvement in the temperance movement; and (3) the establishment of economic communities during the 1920s that were expected ultimately to abolish poverty altogether. The former two were represented largely by Baptist leaders such as Dey Mazaev, Vasilii Pavlov, Wilgelm Fetler, and Ivan Prokhanov, whereas the last one was an emphasis of the Gospel Christians and I. Prokhanov. Although each of these areas of service was quite distinct, they were all supported by the same set of theological convictions regarding the power of the gospel to eradicate human suffering, and regarding the Christian responsibility to witness both in word and deed. They taught that compassion was the concern of all members of the church, regardless of their economic status or age.[157]

---

153. Quoted in Coleman, 142.
154. Coleman, 142.
155. Coleman, 142.
156. Raber, "Ministries of Compassion."
157. Raber; cf. Nagirnyak, *Podvizhniki Very [Devotees of Faith]*, 22, 109.

Whereas subsidiary groups within the church had long been "a sectarian feature," the unique innovation during this period was the establishment of faith-based artisan cooperatives and agricultural communes.[158] In keeping with their collectivistic ideology, the Soviet government granted religious minorities free land and large estates to develop exemplary collective farms, especially during the so-called New Economic Policy of 1921–1928. Even though the government was fostering sectarianism as a "means to its own ends," including the rebuilding of the economy after the devastating wars of 1914–1921 and the weakening of the Orthodox Church, evangelicals enthusiastically responded to this invitation.[159] Economic communes functioning according to the principles of "Christian socialism" were established across Russia.[160] By 1925, Gospel Christians boasted close to a hundred communes, and about twenty-five more were associated with the Baptist Union.[161] In fact, inspired by the success of these communes, Prokhanov and other leaders of the RUGC contemplated the vision of building an exemplary city, *Evangelsk*, or the City of the Sun, in Siberia toward the end of the 1920s. While this city was never built, because of a governmental decision to terminate the project, the expectation was that it would reflect the ideal of Christian communal life governed by restored Apostolic Christianity.[162]

This "marriage" did not last long, however. First, the evangelical communities were conspicuously more successful than the Bolshevik farms, where members lacked "the motive of mutual love."[163] As Hosking points out, this experiment made it painfully obvious that the Baptists' principles – hard work, self-discipline, sobriety, and mutual aid – were "closer to the official morality which the Communists preached but did not practice."[164] But the deeper reason for the breach in the partnership was that evangelicals did not

---

158. Pollock, *Faith of the Russian Evangelicals*, 82.

159. Yuchkovski, "Comparison of the Evangelical Movement," 82.

160. Hebly, *Protestants in Russia*, 92; Pollock, *Faith of the the Russian Evangelicals*, 81; Coleman, *Russian Baptists and Spiritual Revolution*, 175.

161. Coleman, 175.

162. Yuchkovski, "Comparison of the Evangelical Movement," 86; Durassoff, *Russian Protestants*, 84; Olema, *History of Evangelical Christianity*, 177.

163. Pollock, *Faith of the Russian Evangelicals*, 81; Nichols, "Pashkovism," 96.

164. Geoffrey A. Hosking, *The First Socialist Society: A History of the Soviet Union from Within* (Cambridge, MA: Harvard University Press, 1992), 238; cf. Pollock, 80.

acknowledge the Marxist theory of social transformation. While there was much overlap in the evangelical and Bolshevik endorsement of such values as egalitarianism, collectivism, and social justice, the means by which each group was trying to achieve them were completely opposite. The Communists wanted to change social conditions in order to produce a new kind of human person, whereas evangelicals believed that only spiritually transformed persons can change society. Both Pavlov and Prokhanov openly affirmed this:

> We must tell people that the new age can come only through born-again people, that only Jesus is the righteous Ruler, that all the methods of producing new people without the gospel are not sufficient, that we know the secret and the power to transform life, that only regenerated humanity is the new humanity, and that the only way to make the social fruit good is to make the social tree good first.[165]

> It would be pointless to change the outward conditions of human life and not to reform humans spiritually. Political and social activists can work out ideal reforms for the outward life of men, but they cannot change a wicked man into a good one ... For the political revolution to succeed in the state, it is necessary for every man and woman to undergo a spiritual revolution, to overthrow sin and give the first place to God in every heart.[166]

It was this refusal by evangelicals to comply with the all-pervasive ideology and renounce their communal life based on biblical convictions that earned them the full wrath of the Soviet authorities after 1929. Despite the pressure of the state propaganda machine, they rejected the "relegation of religion to a private sphere by maintaining vibrant communities that promoted an alternative moral order."[167]

By the end of the 1920s, when the Communists announced their plans to launch rapid industrialization, forced collectivization, and a cultural revolution, the evangelical community represented a fast-growing society that was parallel to, but ideologically incompatible with, the Soviet socialist one. In

---

165. Pavlov, *Baptisty: Tzerkov i Gosudarstvo* [*Baptists: Church and State*], 78.
166. Prokhanov, *Novaya Ili Evangel'skaya Zhizn* [*New Life in the Gospel*], 174.
167. Wanner, *Communities of the Converted*, 52.

fact, its existence became "an emblem for the party leaders of the limits of their control over society and their failure to rapidly transform social values and behavior."[168] In addition, both Bolsheviks and evangelicals were "conversion-driven" toward the rest of the Russian population: what the Communists saw as the raw material for building the society of the future, evangelicals viewed as a vast mission field for the advancement of the kingdom of God. All this challenged the Bolsheviks to "define the limits of social autonomy" in the emerging society built on atheist and materialist doctrine.[169]

On 8 April 1929, a new law, "On Religious Associations," was issued. It deprived all religious groups of the right to form any children's, youth or women's meetings, Bible studies, literary, handiwork or labor gatherings, reading rooms, libraries, etc. All mutual-aid funds, cooperatives, and any other economic activities that were not directly related to "satisfying religious needs" were forbidden. The law thus effectively eliminated all aspects of religious community life except for the actual worship service.[170] In 1930, the last congresses of both the RUGC and the RUB took place, after which official religious life came to an end, or went underground. During the following decade, at least twenty-two thousand evangelicals were sent to Siberian prison camps, many of whom did not make it back home.[171]

Escapist Pietism: 1944–1991

Historical Background

In 1944, the Baptists and Gospel Christians were again allowed to exist legally, but now as a single, unified denomination, under the strict control of the government. The law of 1929 remained in effect, so concessions granted to religious groups were matters of expediency and not of law. The newly created All-Union Council of Evangelical Christians-Baptists (AUCECB) was now subordinate to the state Council of Religious Affairs and Cults (CRAC). It is essential to take into account several important developments during

---

168. Coleman, *Russian Baptists and Spiritual Revolution*, 199–200.
169. Coleman, 200.
170. Ellis and Jones, *The Other Revolution*, 175; Coleman, 217.
171. Insur Shamgunov, "Listening to the Voice of the Graduate: An Analysis of Professional Practice and Training for Ministry in Central Asia" (PhD diss., University of Oxford, 2009), 17.

this period in order to understand the transformations that Russian Baptist missiology underwent at that time.

First, the new denomination was structured as a "bureaucratic pyramid, which would exercise significant oversight over evangelical life."[172] A centralized, three-layered hierarchy took the place of a previously loose association of churches. The decisions of the leadership council in Moscow were implemented in a top-down fashion through a network of regional superintendents (the so-called senior presbyters). As Alexey Sinichkin observes, "The government imposed on Baptists an episcopal system which was totally alien to their principles."[173] This gave the CRAC a lever for managing the entire denomination through a narrow circle of its leaders.[174]

Second, the law of 1929 continued to be strictly enforced with respect to church life. Sunday schools, home Bible study groups, youth and women's gatherings, and relief funds were forbidden. Ministry by traveling preachers was prohibited: only ordained pastors with a special license from the council had the right to visit other churches. All activities of local churches were to take place only within their church buildings, and the definition of these activities was narrowed to the "administration of cultic rites."[175]

Third, by means of a centralized magazine, *Bratskii Vestnik* (Brotherly Herald) and a hymnal edited by the CARC, church services were increasingly standardized, as the same liturgical elements were introduced in every local church. The intention behind this was to make the churches rigid and inflexible, in order ultimately to "strip Baptists of any traits attractive to the masses."[176] Since the magazine was the only available teaching tool until the launching of correspondence courses in 1968, it also helped create a rather uniform dogmatic understanding in Baptist churches all over the USSR. The government's purpose behind these tactics was to "refocus [Baptist]

---

172. Wanner, *Communities of the Converted*, 58.

173. Sinichkin, *Vozrozhdenie Vopreki Bezbozhiiu [Revival despite Godlessness]*, 139.

174. Panych, "Soviet Baptism," 149, 152. The statute of the new denomination simply declared that what had previously been an *executive* board now had the authority of a *governing* body. Also, the practice of holding regular congresses was abolished, which basically made the governing body irremovable.

175. Coleman, *Russian Baptists and Spiritual Revolution*, 217.

176. This and the following quote come from reports by the CARC officials to the Soviet Council of Ministers in 1947. Quoted in Sinichkin, *Vozrozhdenie Vopreki Bezbozhiiu [Revival despite Godlessness]*, 143.

propaganda from widening their numbers to deepening spirituality inside their communities and self-perfection." As a result of all these developments, the interchurch structure that had initially been established to facilitate mission was now becoming a superstructure that would work to restrain it.

Theologically, the most important turn took place with regard to the doctrine of eschatology. Coming out of their harsh experiences in the 1930s, Soviet evangelicals rejected the modernistic postmillennialism of Prokhanov and appropriated the dispensational premillennialism of Kargel as their default teaching. Andrey Puzynin identifies this turn as "the major theological development" of the period and notes several factors that precipitated it: (1) the atheistic government's suppression of religion; (2) the restoration of the state of Israel in 1948; and (3) the heated atmosphere of the Cold War with its danger of nuclear engagement between the world superpowers.[177] Greg Nichols adds socio-political pessimism as another factor: under Stalin's leadership, Russian evangelicals could not perceive that the world was becoming a better place.[178] As a result, the more pessimistic premillennial view of Kargel gained adherents and by the middle of the century completely replaced Prokhanov's postmillennialism.

Puzynin observes how this theological development resulted in a significant change in the dynamics of Russian Baptist spiritual life.[179] If Prokhanov's earlier vision was oriented toward the past ideal of Apostolic Christianity and was restorationist in its core, Kargel expected the invisible return of Christ at any moment and promoted a futurist interpretation of the Book of Revelation. What became central from this perspective were sanctification and constant readiness to meet the Lord, rather than evangelism or social involvement. As we shall see later, this change had important missiological implications.

The last important development worth noting for our purposes is the schism in the union in the early 1960s that led to the creation of a separate Baptist denomination in Russia. In the summer of 1960, the AUCECB dispatched a secret letter of instructions to the senior presbyters, warning them about "unhealthy missionary tendencies" in local churches. The letter ordered that membership drives "must be decisively terminated" and called on pastors

---

177. Puzynin, *Tradition of the Gospel Christians*, 240.
178. Nichols, *Russian Evangelical Spirituality*, 6512–6515.
179. Puzynin, *Tradition of the Gospel Christians*, 177.

to adhere strictly to the Soviet anti-religious legislation of 1929.[180] More detailed instructions included discouraging the baptism of candidates under the age of thirty, prohibiting the ministry of traveling preachers/evangelists, and stopping parents from bringing their children under the age of eighteen to church services. In response, a dissident group called the *Initsiativniki* condemned the council for allowing themselves to "be governed according to the prescriptions of outsiders." By this, they claimed, the council leaders were "ruining the church inside."[181] Yakov Zhidkov, who was the chair of the AUCECB between 1944 and 1968, and other leaders defended the Soviet requirements on the grounds that they enabled candidates for water baptism to be sufficiently mature.[182] The dissident group disagreed, however, and spearheaded the breakaway of about 10 percent of the membership. This bitter division was accompanied by controversies regarding the relationship between church and state and the interpretation of Romans 13 and other relevant texts of Scripture.[183] I will deal with this important debate in more detail later in the section on holistic mission.

In view of these developments, it is critical to distinguish between the official confessions of faith and the actual practice of Baptist churches during this period. On the one hand, official creeds remained basically intact from the previous stage, except for the premillennial turn. On the other hand, as I will attempt to demonstrate in the remaining part of this chapter, significant transformations in the everyday life of local communities in their context make it legitimate to speak about the formation of a distinctive missiological micro-paradigm during these decades. In this research, I identify it as eschatological *escapism*. Below, I will look at the transformation of the four key aspects of mission theology during this period.

The Nature of the Gospel

Among the distinctive soteriological emphases that developed during these decades, the foremost were the stress on sanctification and holy living, the

---

180. Sawatsky, *Soviet Evangelicals*, 107; Nikol'skaia, "Istoriia Dvizheniia Baptistov-Initsiativnikov [The History of the Baptist Initsiativniki Movement]."

181. Olema, *History of Evangelical Christianity*, 190.

182. Durassoff, *Russian Protestants*, 107; Olema, 189.

183. Durassoff, 200.

intensity of the eschatological hope, and the positive view of suffering.[184] Already in 1946, Yakov Zhidkov, the first president of the AUCECB, in his letter to American Baptists, underlined the primacy of sanctification as the main focus of the denomination:

> The spiritual depth, purity, and holiness of life of our churches and members – this is what occupies the first place in our educational work. We do not hunt for numbers . . . Numbers interest us very little and we are not especially concerned with statistics of our membership. This is a specific feature of ours, and we do not consider it a bad one. The purity of the church and the high Christian life of its members are most important for us.[185]

It is not surprising that visiting a number of Baptist churches in the USSR thirty years later, Walter Sawatsky observed that the bulk of their preaching was primarily "inward-oriented, seeking to meet [the] spiritual needs of believers."[186] In terms of content, it focused on salvation through spiritual regeneration and sanctification in light of Christ's second coming.[187] Sawatsky suggested that this "soteriological preoccupation" was explained primarily by the long experience of persecutions along with the ravages of revolutions and wars.[188]

The second key emphasis during this period was on the eschatological rapture and the hope of heaven.[189] As noted by another visitor to the USSR, for Russian Baptists eternal life when God would wipe away all tears from their eyes was "a vivid certainty."[190] Their prayers often had an eschatological dimension and their hymnody was replete with references to the hope of Jesus coming soon to "take his own from the earth."[191] In fact, Sawatsky's impression was that the prayers for the quick return of Christ were essentially

---

184. Dyck, "Post-Gulag Mennonite Theology," 206.
185. Quoted in Hebly, *Protestants in Russia*, 117–118.
186. Sawatsky, *Soviet Evangelicals*, 339–341, 109.
187. Hebly, *Protestants in Russia*, 113.
188. Sawatsky, *Soviet Evangelicals*, 345.
189. Dyck, "Post-Gulag Mennonite Theology," 206; Panych, "Soviet Baptism," 154–155.
190. Pollock, *Faith of the Russian Evangelicals*, 100.
191. Yuchkovski, "Comparison of the Evangelical Movement," 137.

"appeals to cut short their life on earth," this vale of tears.[192] Given that this hope was escapist in nature and was accompanied by deep pessimism about the socio-political order, Gennady Sergienko identifies it as "apocalyptic" rather than "eschatological."[193]

Closely related to apocalyptic thinking was another development at that time which Yuchkovski describes as a "theology of suffering,"[194] and Constantine Prokhorov describes as "the way of tears."[195] This concept goes back to Johann Kargel for whom the acceptance of suffering for the sake of Christ was a positive mark of true faith and a means of attaining future glory.[196] In Kargel's thought, suffering confirms that the believer is on the true and narrow way of Christ and allows the believer to participate in Christ's holiness.[197] From this perspective, suffering has a positive value as God's instrument of sanctification and, to a certain extent, is even desirable. Some Baptist leaders came to speak of the experience of persecution as being of greater value than, for instance, the knowledge of theology. It was common to refer to it as the "Siberian seminary."[198]

Another important theological development of this period was parallel in certain respects to what Mark Noll and some other Western scholars describe as "naïve biblicism."[199] Evangelicalism in Russia had been a biblical movement from the very beginning; it strongly affirmed the ability of every person to understand the Scriptures with the help of the Holy Spirit, and it showed great reverence toward the biblical text. During this period, however, when

---

192. Sawatsky, *Soviet Evangelicals*, 353.

193. Gennagii Sergienko, "Baptisty i Obshcestvo [Baptists and Society]," 2011, http://www.mbchurch.ru/publications/articles/15/5892/.

194. Yuchkovski, "Comparison of the Evangelical Movement," 136.

195. Constantin Prokhorov, *Russian Baptists and Orthodoxy, 1960-1990* (Carlisle, UK: Langham Monographs, 2013), 326.

196. Sawatsky, *Soviet Evangelicals*, 337–358.

197. Nichols, *Russian Evangelical Spirituality*, 6687–6690.

198. Yuchkovski, "Comparison of the Evangelical Movement," 136.

199. Mark A. Noll, *The Scandal of the Evangelical Mind* (Grand Rapids, MI: Eerdmans, 1994); Mark A. Noll, "The Peril and Potential of Scripture in Christian Political Witness," in *Christian Political Witness*, ed. George Kalantzis and Gregory W. Lee (Downers Grove, IL: IVP Academic, 2014), 35–55; Kevin J. Vanhoozer, "May We Go beyond What Is Written After All? The Pattern of Theological Authority and the Problem of Doctrinal Development," in *The Enduring Authority of the Christian Scriptures*, ed. D. A. Carson (Grand Rapids, MI: Eerdmans, 2016), 747–794.

Baptists had essentially no access to either their own theological education or to the products of Western biblical studies, the text of the only available Russian translation – the so-called Synodal Bible (RST) – became for them the inerrant word of God, which was interpreted literally and dogmatically.[200]

One the one hand, this uncritical biblicism in their circumstances contributed to biblical faithfulness. In 1964, Pollock observed that in the USSR "you either have a transformative faith or you have no faith" at all, and a decade later Hebly added that "an adjusted cultural Christianity would not endure" there for very long.[201] On the other hand, a negative effect of naïve biblicism was that in the absence of a theological dialogue with any tradition beyond their own, Russian Baptists had come to identify uncritically their traditional interpretations and theological viewpoints with biblical theology as such. The distance between the text and the interpreter was not perceived; the literal reading of the Bible was taken at face value and equated with the "plain" meaning of the text. In the words of the Russian Baptist scholar Nikolay Kornilov, Baptists tended to see the Bible as a "set of fixed truths given in the past once and for all," and proof-texting often eliminated the need for deep thinking.[202] The situation was exacerbated by the almost complete blockage of access to secular higher education for evangelical believers.

In sum, the excessive emphases on eschatology and sanctification in the post-war period stand in stark contrast to the primarily social and evangelistic concerns of the 1920s. In fact, the values of the earlier period were sometimes intentionally degraded and replaced.[203] Yakov Zhidkov discouraged evangelistic preaching, affirming that "it is our fundamental task to instruct those already believing."[204] The *Brotherly Herald* in 1947 referred positively to the

---

200. Dyck, "Post-Gulag Mennonite Theology," 203–204; Ales Dubrovsky, "Bogoslovskii Fundamentalism Kak Tormoziaschiy Faktor v Razvitii Evangel'skikh Tserkvey Postsovetskogo Perioda [Theological Fundamentalism as A Constraining Factor in the Development of Evangelical Churches in the Post-Soviet Period]," in *Dvatsat' Let Religioznoy Svobody i Aktivnoi Misii [Twenty Years of Religious Freedom and Active Mission]*, ed. Mikhaiil Cherenkov (Kiev: Dukh i Litera, 2011), 27–44.

201. Pollock, *Faith of the Russian Evangelicals*, 92; Hebly, *Protestants in Russia*, 116.

202. Nikolai Kornilov, "Kakogo Roda Bogoslovie Nam Nuzhno? [What Kind of Theology Do We Need?]," *Put' Bogopoznaniia [Way of Knowledge of God]* 6 (2000): 15.

203. Nagirnyak, *Podvizhniki Very [Devotees of Faith]*, 262.

204. Y. I. Zhidkov, "Staryi God i Novyi God [The Past Year and the New Year]," *Bratskii Vestnik [Brotherly Herald]* 1 (1949): 5.

reduction in the number of water baptisms as compared with 1945 and 1946, when thousands of people coming out of the terrible experience of war were joining local churches (increasing church membership by as much as 30 percent annually in some parts of the country). The editors saw this reduction in the number of baptisms as the successful outcome of the leadership's "serious warning . . . to strive more towards depth rather than width, just like 'a man building a house, who dug down deep.'"[205] The work of attracting new members was depicted as "an extreme" that leads to a dangerous disregard for the "deepening of spiritual life." The "quietness" and "prayerful godliness" of church buildings was to be preferred over "the noise of public baptisms." Instead of "hunting for numbers," ministers should focus rather on the "quality" of members.[206]

Officially, the AUCECB leadership explained their position by emphasizing the danger of accepting immature persons who might harm both the work of God and themselves. In part, this concern was justified, given the inadequate discipleship efforts during the earlier period, which contributed to a massive falling away from membership during Stalin's purges of the 1930s. Less explicit, but possibly also a factor, was a desire to protect local communities from the infiltration of informants. At the same time, when seen within the context of the relationship with the government during that period, these efforts obviously went hand in hand with the state's policy of redirecting Baptist work from an external focus to an internal one. It seems that under immense pressure from the CRAC, the leaders of the union chose to enjoy limited religious freedom rather than no freedom at all.[207]

---

205. Y. I. Zhidkov, "Nash Otchet [Our Report]," *Bratskii Vestnik [Brotherly Herald]* 1 (1947): 15–16.

206. Y. I. Zhidkov, "Vzglyad Nazad [Looking Back]," *Bratskii Vestnik [Brotherly Herald]* 1 (1948): 6.

207. Pollock, *Faith of the Russian Evangelicals*, 143. The following quotation from Alexander Karev, the general secretary of the ACUECB, is illustrative both in terms of its content and its metaphorical style that avoids the direct naming of problems, a style that is still common among many Baptist leaders. Explaining to other members of the council in December 1959 why the anti-evangelism letter must be sent to senior presbyters, he said: "In recent years we have experienced some flooding [i.e. mass conversions] . . . People of a different ideology [i.e. Communist Party] cannot take it easy. Besides, this flooding should concern us as well. Any flood lifts and disperses mud and dirt: a lighthearted attitude toward the opposite sex, dishonesty in dealing with church finances, new kinds of fish among our members. The Council [CARC] is letting us know that we should return to our banks." Quoted in Mitskevich, *Istoriia Evangel'skikh Khristian-Baptistov [A History of Evangelical Christians-Baptists]*, 325–326.

This is not to say, however, that evangelism as such was completely superseded by other concerns. Since the propagation of the faith outside of church buildings was illegal, it became a common practice to preach evangelistic sermons during worship services. Typically, one of the three or four sermons every Sunday was directed at the conversion of unbelievers, whether visitors or, much more often, believers' family members.[208] Christians were prompted to invite their neighbors and colleagues to attend services. Thus, as Pollock rightly notes, evangelism for Russian Baptists was more the work of congregations than of individuals. Believers were encouraged not so much to evangelize openly as to live lives of transparent integrity and "goodness of character and action" that would show outsiders the beauty of Christ's teaching.[209]

The Identity and Purpose of the Church

Doctrinally, no essential changes in ecclesiology can be discerned during this period as Baptists remained faithful to their original primitivist vision of the church. Yet the shift of emphasis from evangelism to sanctification was increasingly finding its way into the official statements of the union. Thus, in Johann Kargel's confession, which served as the official statement of faith of the AUCECB from 1966 until 1985, the local church, as part of the one universal church, is said to exist for the following purposes: (1) demonstrating the unity of the saved; (2) worshipping God together; (3) building up members in their knowledge of God and in the perfection of the life of faith, and (4) extending the kingdom of God on earth.[210] In the 1985 Confession of Faith, which remains the official statement of the RUEBC, the local church is described as "the gathering of regenerated souls tied together by one confession of faith . . . united for serving God together and for the satisfaction of their spiritual needs."[211] The reference to evangelism ("extending the kingdom of God" in Kargel) in this later document becomes even less explicit, whereas the internal needs of Baptist communities become more pronounced.

---

208. Harris, "Historical Perspectives," 11.

209. Pollock, *Faith of the Russian Evangelicals*, 102–105, 107; Dyck, "Post-Gulag Mennonite Theology," 207.

210. Johann Kargel, "Verouchenie Evangel'skikh Khristian [The Confession of Faith of the Gospel Christians]," *Bratskii Vestnik [Brotherly Herald]* 4 (1966): 16.

211. AUCECB, "Verouchenie Evangel'skikh Khristian-Baptistov [The Confession of Faith of Evangelical Christians-Baptists]," *Bratskii Vestnik [Brotherly Herald]* 4 (1985): 43–44.

From the accounts of visitors and academic studies, it is possible to observe a number of social characteristics of Baptist churches in the Soviet Union at the time. At least five of them, in my view, have a direct bearing on the (re)shaping of Baptist missiology during the period, even if this connection was not explicitly articulated. First, given the fact that all religious gatherings in private homes were illegal, the activities of local churches became limited almost exclusively to church worship services. Pollock points out that for the Russian Baptist, "life centers around his church."[212] A decade later, Hebly adds that it is "in the services that the life of the church expresses itself."[213] Visitors were often impressed by the lively atmosphere at crowded services that lasted between two and three hours, with most church members perceived as active and involved.

It is only natural that in the hostile social atmosphere of the time, members looked for emotional support and self-expression in the company of like-minded believers. A local Baptist community was "the citadel of faith and fellowship" for its members.[214] In the *Brotherly Herald,* a common metaphor for the church at that time was "the inn where the Good Samaritan brought the wounded man," and believers were encouraged to make it "a warm and comfortable place where our spiritual needs could be fully met."[215] No wonder, in the late 1970s Sawatsky would make the following observation: "The average evangelical knows no social life besides the church."[216]

Second, the sociological makeup of Baptist communities during this period became largely level and homogeneous. Unlike the diversity of the early evangelical movement, which encompassed peasants (Shtundists), upper or middle class townsfolk (Baptists), and the aristocracy (the Gospel Christians), with a significant proportion of the latter in leadership, state pressure now guaranteed that believers would remain in the lower class and be uneducated. In the mid-1960s Pollock observed that "academic or professional qualifications are comparatively few among sectarians, who are found mostly in the

---

212. Pollock, *Faith of the Russian Evangelicals,* 97, 102.
213. Hebly, *Protestants in Russia,* 110.
214. Pollock, *Faith of the Russian Evangelicals,* 102.
215. Zhidkov, "Staryi God i Novyi God [The Past Year and the New Year]," 4.
216. Sawatsky, *Soviet Evangelicals,* 111.

ranks of plain toilers."²¹⁷ The upper classes were forcibly eliminated in the thirties, and when new elites were developing in the following decades, access to that status through higher education was blocked for confessing believers.²¹⁸ Andornoviene and Parushev suggest that Russian Baptists developed their notoriously negative attitude toward secular education as a rationalization of this blockage.²¹⁹ In many cases, however, even when it was possible for them to enter universities, evangelicals often rejected such opportunities because of the atheistic and ideological nature of state-sponsored education.²²⁰

Third, the primary, although not exclusive, source of new members was the families of believers themselves, especially after the post-WWII wave of conversions in the late 1940s receded.²²¹ Typically, Baptists held strictly to the custom of endogamy within their own denomination. A positive aspect of this development was that converts had already been socialized in the specific subculture of Baptist communities and therefore had few difficulties in the subsequent discipleship process. On the other hand, as Michael Nevolin points out, these people had "little experience of relating to the people outside of their ecclesiastical microcosm."²²² All of this contributed to the widening of the cultural distance between Baptists and their unchurched contemporaries. Sawatsky mentions, for instance, the problem of "an ingrown cliché language" that got in the way of communication with outsiders.²²³

Fourth, the Baptists' belief in a regenerate church membership required strict discipline, which often resulted in a struggle with legalism and hasty excommunications. Visitors frequently commented positively on the Baptists'

---

217. Pollock, *Faith of the Russian Evangelicals*, 116.

218. Yuchkovski, "Comparison of the Evangelical Movement."

219. Lina Andornoviene and Parush R. Parushev, "Church, State, and Culture: On the Complexities of Post-Soviet Evangelical Social Involvement," *Theological Reflection* 3 (2004): 194–212.

220. Yuchkovski, "Comparison of the Evangelical Movement," 185.

221. cf. Nagirnyak, *Podvizhniki Very [Devotees of Faith]*, 225.

222. Michael Nevolin, "Dvadtsat' Let Svobody: Dostizheniya i Problemy [Twenty Years of Freedom: Achievements and Problems]," in *Dvatsat' Let Religioznoy Svobody i Aktivnoi Misii [Twenty Years of Religious Freedom and Active Mission]*, ed. Mikhaiil Cherenkov (Kiev: Dukh i Litera, 2011), 10; cf. Bokova, "Teologia Rossiiskikh Evangel'skikh Khristian-Baptistov Na Rubezhe XX i XXI Vekov [Theology of Russian Evangelical Christians-Baptists at the Turn of the Twenty-First Century]."

223. Sawatsky, *Soviet Evangelicals*, 355, 439.

"strong moral discipline"[224] but negatively on their "legalism."[225] Harris points out that areas many in the West would consider gray were starkly black and white for Russian Baptists. External issues such as dressing and grooming oneself conservatively tended to become hard and fast rules within Baptist communities. Prohibitions against wearing earrings or makeup, smoking, drinking (even in moderation), going to movies, and dancing of any sort "became central to Baptist spirituality."[226] These rules emphasized the contrast between the Christian's lifestyle and that of the world and maximized the distance between the believer and the unbeliever.[227]

Finally, both insiders and outsiders frequently observed parallels between the Soviet system of governance and Baptist approaches to leadership. Yuchkovski goes as far as to speak about the "totalitarian mentality of evangelical ministers" and "a structure similar to the one Communists had."[228] Other authors speak less strongly about the "institutionalization" and "bureaucratization" of leadership.[229] The fact is that unlike the former RBU and RUGC, the first leaders of the AUCECB were initially installed by the authorities rather than elected by representatives from the churches, even though most of them had been in various leadership positions in their unions prior to WWII.[230] The senior (or regional) presbyters were in turn appointed by the union leadership in a top-down fashion. While this practice was abolished in 1966 following strong pressure from the *Initsiativniki*, still a major goal of denominational leadership was to ensure that the legislation of 1929 was carefully observed at the local church level. In this way, state control became a form of a selection grid which guaranteed that often at the top of the leadership pyramid were those disposed to loyalty and conformity rather than those who had the necessary spiritual credentials.[231]

Overall, the social dynamics outlined above seriously affected Baptist engagement with society and significantly altered their pre-war mission-focused

---

224. Pollock, *Faith of Russian Evangelicals*, 96.
225. Brandenburg, *Meek and the Mighty*, 151.
226. Harris, "Historical Perspectives," 6–7.
227. Harris, 14; Dyck, "Post-Gulag Mennonite Theology," 210.
228. Yuchkovski, "Comparison of the Evangelical Movement," 117.
229. Nagirnyak, *Podvizhniki Very [Devotees of Faith]*, 264–269.
230. Panych, "Soviet Baptism," 147.
231. Nagirnyak, *Podvizhniki Very [Devotees of Faith]*, 269.

outlook. Even a fairly sympathetic observer, Katherine Wanner, found in typical Baptist churches shortly after the fall of the Iron Curtain "communities characterized by a closed system of membership, a deep suspicion of outsiders, hierarchical understandings of authority, a highly literal interpretation of the Bible, and an austere communal ethos."[232] It is important to keep in mind that many of these developments had been intentionally programmed and consistently enforced by the government. In his well-documented article on relationships between Baptist leaders and the CRAC in the post-war period, Sinichkin cites a quotation from a letter by Ivan Polyansky, the chair of the CRAC between 1944 and 1956.[233] This official lists several measures the council had taken to intentionally inhibit the growth of Baptist churches. In particular, "Centralization has been enforced, services are being standardized, multilayered hierarchy is being built, sectarian pastors and preachers are becoming professionals, etc." The irony is that over time, some of these impositions from the outside found their theological rationalizations inside Baptist circles.

Cultural Engagement

Russian Baptist attitudes toward the broader culture during this period were defined mainly by two key factors: the hostility of the atheistic society toward religion and the apocalyptic outlook of the believers themselves. As was already shown, Prokhanov and many other early evangelicals with their Christian socialism agenda were not principally seeking cultural isolation. But by the end of the 1930s general culture, including education, the media, the arts, films, theaters, and later, television, was completely determined by Marxist-Leninist ideology. Official Soviet propaganda aimed to portray Baptists as "inhumane and backward-thinking sectarians" who met in small houses of prayer at the outskirts of towns to pray and to join in "minor-key songs performed by ten or twenty elderly people."[234]

Due to both the external pressure and the internal protective drive, evangelicals soon found themselves in the ghetto of their own culture. In the effort to maintain a distance from the surrounding culture, Baptists naturally

---

232. Wanner, *Communities of the Converted*, 64.
233. Sinichkin, *Vozrozhdenie Vopreki Bezbozhiiu [Revival despite Godlessness]*, 141.
234. Sergienko, "Baptisty i Obshcestvo [Baptists and Society]."

became more secretive and cloistered. Hebly correctly points out that Baptists could preserve their identity only by resisting the spiritual and cultural pressures of their environment. In this situation, it is quite fair to defend the proposition that "there is strength in isolation."[235] New believers typically would be expected to join in this separation from the world and the Baptist community was thus gradually becoming more and more ingrown.[236] In fact, no one would be baptized until they had severed basically all of their ties and old friendships outside the church circle.[237]

In preaching, culture was portrayed primarily, and often exclusively, in negative terms. Yuchkovski lists several metaphors and preaching clichés that were employed to portray the world. Some of the most common were "the darkness of unbelief," "the valley of tribulation," and "the spiritual desert."[238] Relationships with outsiders were often condemned on the basis of the biblical maxim that "friendship with the world is enmity toward God" (Jas 4:4). In spite of repeated calls by the central leadership of the AUCECB for believers to soften their attitudes toward popular culture, public celebrations, movies, television, etc.,[239] the atheist researcher A. Klibanov in 1960 concluded that the sermons in local Baptist churches were largely eschatological and differed fundamentally from the materials found in the official publications of the AUCECB.[240]

As a result, by the end of the Soviet period Russian Baptists had developed an attitude that is described by various scholars as a "fortress mentality,"[241]

---

235. Hebly, *Protestants in Russia*, 114.

236. Harris, "Historical Perspectives," 6.

237. Dyck, "Post-Gulag Mennonite Theology," 207–208; Yuchkovski, "Comparison of the Evangelical Movement," 170.

238. Yuchkovski, 136.

239. Here are two typical examples of such admonitions: "We must follow our country's order for all its citizens . . . by participating in community holidays, demonstrations, meetings, etc." Y. I. Zhidkov, "Nashi Prazdniki [Our Celebrations]," *Bratskii Vestnik [Brotherly Herald]* 2 (1946): 14–15; and "There are among us some individual believers who, regrettably, are strangers to all that is new and useful in the area of culture. They are accustomed to count all that is worldly to be sin," A. I. Mitskevich, "Derzhis' Obraztsa Zdravogo Ucheniia [Keep the Pattern of Sound Teaching]," *Bratskii Vestnik [Brotherly Herald]* 1 (1960): 53, 55.

240. L. N. Mitrokhin, "Izuchenie Sektanstva v Tambovskoi Oblasti [The Study of Sects in Tambov Province]," *Voprosy Filosofii [Issues of Philosophy]* 1 (1960): 145.

241. Olga Bokova, "Sovremennye Rossiyskie Evangelskie Khristiane-Baptisty: Sotsialnaia Struktura i Ideologiia [Contemporary Russian Evangelical Christians-Baptists: Social Structure

"standing outside the general culture,"[242] or "living outside of history."[243] Missiologically, this stance had at least four major implications. First, it tended to deeply alienate evangelicals from their own culture and society. Not only was Soviet culture considered "worldly," but the whole heritage of classic Russian literature, music, and the arts was often disregarded, unless these reflected specifically religious themes.[244] Yuchkovski and Bokova suggest that this alienation had prepared many evangelicals for the sweeping emigration that followed the lifting of the Iron Curtain, when at least five hundred thousand Russian religious emigrants left the country.[245] Since many of them did not feel closely connected to the country of their origin anyway, they left without an afterthought precisely when unprecedented opportunities for evangelism and social involvement were available once again.

Second, this attitude significantly contributed to the development of an anti-intellectual stance among Russian Baptists.[246] The initially natural suspicion toward secular thought and education eventually was given a theological rationale. Biblical texts such as "knowledge puffs up" (1 Cor 8:1) or "not many of you are wise by human standards" (1 Cor 1:26) were commonly used to set worldly education against the spiritual wisdom that comes from the humble reading of the Bible and godly living. Sergienko goes so far as to affirm that in the traditional Baptist culture, "ignorance and mediocrity were lifted to the status of virtues," which, he argues, even today remains a serious barrier for attracting educated and deeply thinking individuals to Baptist churches.[247]

---

and Ideology]," *Gosudarstvo, Religiia, Tserkov v Rossii i Za Rubezhom [State, Religion and Church in Russia and Abroad]* 3 (2009): 36; Harris, "Historical Perspectives," 14.

242. Hebly, *Protestants in Russia*, 114.

243. Sergienko, "Baptisty i Obshcestvo [Baptists and Society]."

244. Sergienko.

245. Yuchkovski, "Comparison of the Evangelical Movement;" Bokova, "Teologia Rossiiskikh Evangel'skikh Khristian-Baptistov Na Rubezhe XX i XXI Vekov [Theology of Russian Evangelical Christians-Baptists at the Turn of the Twenty-First Century]."

246. Vladimir Solodovnikov, "Marginalizatsionnye Tendentsii v Sovremennom Rossiiskom Protestantisme i Perspektivy Ikh Preodoleniia [Tendencies Toward Marginalization in Contemporary Russian Protestantism, and the Prospects of Their Overcoming]," in *Krizisnye Iavleniia v Sovremennom Rossiiskom Protestantisme i Sposoby Ikh Preodoleniia [The Crisis Henomena in Contemporary Russian Protestantism and the Ways of Dealing with Them]*, ed. Vladimir Solodovnikov (Moscow: SEKhR, 2008), 7–20.

247. Sergienko, "Baptisty i Obshcestvo [Baptists and Society]."

Third, living in a cultural ghetto led to the "freezing" of certain expressions of Baptist faith and practice, granting them the semi-sacred status of *the* Christian culture. Thanks to the centralization of the Union, its publications, and interchurch connections, by the end of the 1980s certain exegetical approaches, theological understandings, liturgical forms, aesthetic elements, and standards of behavior became uniform and were commonly accepted. Deviation from these established beliefs and practices usually "was viewed as sin."[248] In the absence of a theological tradition which would encourage both maintaining the doctrinal core and adjusting to the changing cultural context, there was no outside perspective to critically evaluate these expressions scripturally and theologically.[249]

Finally, the emphasis on the injunction "not [to] love the world or anything in the world" (1 John 2:15) produced a form of spirituality characterized by the emphasis on *negative* aspects of holiness and the Christian life. The portrait of an ideal believer was painted largely "from the opposite": a good Christian was someone who did not smoke or drink, watch movies or go to the theater, or read newspapers or books (except for the Bible). In Sergienko's acute words: "The apocalyptic paradigm . . . [has] only two colors: black and white, with no shades or nuances . . . We knew very well what Christians were not supposed to do, but had little idea of what their positive influence in society might be."[250] This picture contributed to the formation of a specific type of evangelical believers whom Bokova identifies as "traditionalists":

> The traditionalists prefer to stay insulated within their own subculture. They tend to understand the Christian dialogue with society [only] as calling people to repentance, not as rethinking culture from a Christian perspective or seeking in it what is in harmony with their faith. . . . They strictly distinguish things Christian from those un-Christian, and do not think it is possible to borrow anything from secular culture or knowledge

---

248. Yuchkovski, "Comparison of the Evangelical Movement," 117.
249. Sergienko, "Baptisty i Obshcestvo [Baptists and Society]."
250. Sergienko.

for . . . use in the church. New things or ideas tend to be rejected as "people pleasing."[251]

In her more recent research, she suggests that this type of believers still dominates post-Soviet Baptist communities, which, of course, is hard to verify empirically.[252]

The View of Holistic Mission

During the purges of the 1930s, the government successfully crushed all previous Christian efforts to reform society.[253] In the process, the increasingly totalitarian state completely replaced independent social work and charity efforts with state-operated structures. The anti-religious legislation of 1929 made it illegal for the church to carry on any charitable activity or to use funds for any purpose beyond needs related to the "performance of cultic rites."[254] As a result, the omnipotent state "left but a very small space" in society for the hardly tolerated church.[255]

Through the governing body of the Baptist Union in Moscow, the CARC used the *Brotherly Herald* to indoctrinate believers with the idea that social work was now a function of the state and that Christians did not need to engage in it. In his 1969 report at the 40th Congress of the AUCECB, Alexander Karev, the chair of the Union, announced that all forms of social activity such as caring for orphans, the sick, the aged, and the needy "have been taken over by the state which is fully carrying out this grand task . . . Therefore the church has no need to conduct this function."[256] A year later, he published an editorial that glorified Lenin and the socialist political system as "a world

---

251. Bokova, "Sovremennye Rossiyskie Evangelskie Khristiane-Baptisty: Sotsialnaia Struktura i Ideologiia [Contemporary Russian Evangelical Christians-Baptists: Social Structure and Ideology]," 37.

252. Bokova, "Teologia Rossiiskikh Evangel'skikh Khristian-Baptistov Na Rubezhe XX i XXI Vekov [Theology of Russian Evangelical Christians-Baptists at the Turn of the Twenty-First Century]."

253. Nichols, "Pashkovism," 111.

254. Ellis and Jones, *The Other Revolution*, 175.

255. Hebly, *Protestants in Russia*, 180.

256. A. V. Karev, "Doklad General'nogo Sekretaria VSEKhB [The Report of the General Secretary of the AUCECB]," *Bratskii Vestnik [Brotherly Herald]* 2 (1970): 40.

without human exploitation, unemployment and economic crises; a world in which social justice reigns."[257]

The new situation in which evangelicals now found themselves was also pushing them to rethink their former conceptions of the kingdom of God. If for the evangelicals of the 1920s postmillennial convictions served as "an engine for . . . social and political activity," now the kingdom was increasingly being seen as spiritual, internalized, and future in nature.[258] In their publications, Baptist leaders presented Christianity as a religion focusing exclusively on non-earthly matters, because in this form it, apparently, could be tolerated by the state. The textbook on dogmatic theology that was used at the correspondence courses in 1968–1989 identifies three loci of the kingdom: (1) in human hearts as "the kingly power of Christ over the souls of men who have willingly subordinated themselves to the laws of the heavenly kingdom"; (2) in the church where "the kingdom is realized, and through which its power expands to new souls"; and (3) in the new heaven and new earth in the eschaton.[259] The primary texts that define the nature of the kingdom are: "My kingdom is not of this world" (John 18:36); "The kingdom is within you" (RST: "inside you," Luke 17:21)[260]; and "The kingdom of God is not a matter of eating and drinking, but of righteousness, peace and joy in the Holy Spirit" (Rom 14:17). In the present, the kingdom is "hidden, invisible" reality which has basically no social implications beyond the personal godly walk of Christians. The church's work has to do with the "issues of internal spiritual life," while the state takes care of the political, social, cultural, and other aspects of the earthly lives of its citizens.[261]

Two other factors which contributed to the abandoning of holistic mission, especially at the grassroots level, were eschatological pessimism and the theology of suffering. Neither provided theological incentives to engage in

---

257. A. V. Karev, "Rozhdenie Novogo Mira [The Birth of a New World]," *Bratskii Vestnik [Brotherly Herald]* 2 (1970): 6.

258. Puzynin, *Tradition of the Gospel Christians*, 177.

259. The materials used for the correspondence courses were compiled by Russian authors, but they generally reflect a dependence on the resources of the Moody Bible Institute. Puzynin, xxxix.

260. Bible quotations marked RST are from the Russian Synodal Bible. This version is in the public domain.

261. A. M. Bychkov and A. I. Mitskevich, *Dogmatika [Dogmatic Theology]* (Moscow: VSEKhB, 1970).

changing the world; on the other hand, both helped Baptists to adjust to the changing socio-political context by providing biblical explanations for their situation. Sawatsky ties all three elements together when he observes that the emphasis on a "spiritual kingdom" was both the result of Baptists' "adoption of dispensational theology" and reflected "the changed meaning ... this principle had undergone following the Stalinist persecutions."[262] Sergienko exposes the implications of Soviet Baptists' eschatological outlook:

> While helping the believer to stoically endure all the calamities of the present existence, the apocalyptic mindset suggested that what he or she experienced was a norm rather than an exception. Life in this world is not going to become better; instead, the closer the coming of Christ is, the worse the condition of the world must become.[263]

Present hardships, therefore, are not injustices to be set right, but God-ordained instruments of spiritual growth. They help believers bear spiritual fruit and achieve Christlikeness which, according to Johann Kargel, is "the only reason why He does not take us immediately to glory after our conversion."[264]

Thus, in sum, after WWII Russian Baptists significantly revised their forerunners' grand vision of the spiritual transformation of Russia. The task of evangelicals in the country was now seen in "finding ways to survive by being good citizens, demonstrating an excellent work ethic, and worshipping in compliance with the restrictions that existed at the time."[265] Commenting from this perspective on the evangelistic, social, and political activism of the churches in North America, AUCECB leader Alexei Bychkov compared them to the biblical Martha: they are "not taking much time to sit and reflect at the feet of Jesus, but always working and inviting people to serve on committees,

---

262. Sawatsky, *Soviet Evangelicals*, 350; cf. Dyck, "Post-Gulag Mennonite Theology," who speaks of the "post-Gulag" theology of Russian Mennonites.

263. Sergienko, "Baptisty i Obshcestvo [Baptists and Society]."

264. Johann Kargel, *Sobranie Sochinenij [Collected Works]* (St Petersburg: Bibliia dlia vsekh, 1927), 49.

265. Yuchkovski, "Comparison of the Evangelical Movement," 134.

subcommittees, and sub-subcommittees... Soviet churches look more like Mary – quiet and reflecting."²⁶⁶

Finally, the issue of the Baptists' view of the state during this period deserves a brief treatment. Although a detailed study of the conflict with the *Initsiativniki* (now a separate denomination with virtually no connections to the RUECB) is beyond the scope of this dissertation, the AUCECB's perceptions of church and state were largely shaped over against the position of the splinter group. It is important, therefore, to provide a summary of the debate.

When at the end of the 1950s the government again strengthened its pressure on the churches, the leadership of the AUCECB chose to cooperate actively with the CARC. They insisted that the churches' activities are exclusively spiritual, whereas in earthly matters Christians, as citizens of their fatherland, must be compliant to the civil authorities. According to Mikhail Zhidkov, to love one's country meant to obey all the laws and directives of the government.²⁶⁷ Alexander Karev taught that "motherland is the state and the powers and laws, and it is also the task of the Christian to have a right relationship to powers."²⁶⁸ Alexey Bychkov claimed that Baptists were "happy to find themselves in their country as good patriots."²⁶⁹

In response, the *Initsiativniki* refused to comply with the letters of instruction from the AUCECB. Theologically, they emphasized Acts 5:29 and the priority of obedience to God in cases when the government's requirements contradicted the word of God as they understood it. In their preaching they used biblical examples of saints who challenged the powers, such as the Hebrew midwives in Egypt, Shadrach, Meshach and Abednego in Babylon, Queen Esther in Persia, the apostles in Acts, etc.²⁷⁰ It is important to note, however, that they were not opponents of the political regime as such. While they were, most likely, some of the first people in the Soviet Union

---

266. Quoted in Sawatsky, *Soviet Evangelicals*, 355.

267. Y. I. Zhidkov, "Khristianin i Rodina [The Christian and the Motherland]," *Bratskii Vestnik [Brotherly Herald]* 1 (1945): 7.

268. A. V. Karev, "Khristianin i Rodina [The Christian and the Motherland]," *Bratskii Vestnik [Brotherly Herald]* 3 (1970): 52.

269. Alexei Bychkov, "Otchetnyi Doklad General'nogo Sekretaria VSEKhB A.M. Bychkov [The Report by the General Secretary of the AUCECB A.M. Buchkov]," *Bratskii Vestnik [Brotherly Herald]* 1 (1975): 42.

270. Gennady Kriuchkov, *Tol'ko Khristos [Only Christ]* (Moscow: CCECB, 2001), 22.

ever to organize political protest actions and publish their own underground magazine, they were not aiming at political change.[271] Rather, the *Initsiativniki* resisted the government's interference in church affairs and insisted on the actual observance of Article 124 of the Soviet Constitution that guaranteed freedom of conscience and the separation of church and state.[272] Therefore, even if they can be seen as a prophetic voice of the church at that time, this should be taken in a narrowly religious, and not the social or political sense of the term. Nor did they emphasize mission; rather, what they called to was a renewal in the church in terms of sanctification and rededication.[273]

The theological position of the AUCECB was based on texts such as Romans 13:1–7, 1 Peter 2:13–17, and Jesus's instructions in Matthew 22:21 to give to Caesar what is Caesar's. Unlike their opponents who emphasized the powers' tendency to resist God, they interpreted Romans 13 in the sense that the powers-that-be are *personally* ordained to this position by God as his "vessels." In the words of Yakov Dukhonchenko, "the leaders of the state fulfill what God's hand and his will had decided beforehand should happen."[274] Since "the king's heart is in the hand of the Lord" (Prov 21:1), the implication is that whatever comes from the powers comes, in a sense, from God and

---

271. On 16 May 1966, five hundred believers from all parts of the country began a two-day demonstration next to the building of the Central Committee of the Communist Party. The leaders of the demonstration were later given prison terms. In 1970, Lidia Vins founded a group called the Council of Prisoners' Relatives which produced a bulletin documenting all known prisoners, including details of their arrests, trials, and treatment in prison. When the Vins family was later deported together with other dissidents in an exchange for Soviet spies held in the West, Grigory Vins was received by President Jimmy Carter. Wanner, *Communities of the Converted*, 65.

272. Hebly, *Protestants in Russia*, 156–159; Nagirnyak, *Podvizhniki Very [Devotees of Faith]*, 124.

273. Sawatsky, *Soviet Evangelicals*, 177. In the post-Soviet period, the *Initsiativniki* movement adopted an extremely anti-cultural stance, turning into an increasingly closed and separatist community. The long-time leader of the movement, Gennady Kriuchkov, taught that "culture has always been a competitor of God's word" and "sin is the fruit of culture." Kriuchkov, *Tol'ko Khristos [Only Christ]*, 56–57. In her research, Bokova concludes that remaining a sect has become the very core of the group's identity to such a degree that many of them seem to actually long for persecutions. Bokova, "Teologia Rossiiskikh Evangel'skikh Khristian-Baptistov Na Rubezhe XX i XXI Vekov [Theology of Russian Evangelical Christians-Baptists at the Turn of the Twenty-First Century]," 156.

274. Y. K. Dukhonchenko, "Prakticheskaya Khristianskaya Zhizn [Practical Christian Living]," *Bratskii Vestnik [Brotherly Herald]* 4 (1985): 32.

must be obeyed.[275] Obviously, from this perspective, any protest is disobedience before God.[276] For the leaders of the AUCECB, the *Initsiativniki* were little more than schismatic dissenters who were destroying the church's unity and disobeying the government. Their sufferings and imprisonments were typically written off as resulting from their own faults.[277]

Lastly, it is important to note that in contrast to the AUCECB leaders who tended to entirely and uncritically support the state, at the local church level general isolation from Soviet society resulted in deep apoliticism. Pastors and preachers carefully avoided "earthly" political issues in their preaching. In the late 1970s, Sawatsky was hoping that "One of the results of the increased Western and ecumenical influences, perhaps also of their own Bible study, will be to move them beyond an apolitical position that is content to maintain its religious ritual."[278] While that was hardly possible in the USSR, he was asking rhetorically what path Baptists would choose should freedom ever come: "Will they move further in the direction of an uncritical support of the state, or will they perform a prophetic role?"[279]

Concluding Summary

In this chapter I have looked at the development of Russian Baptist mission theology between 1867 and 1991. Although the Baptist movement in Russia was not uniform and reflected divergent mission approaches from the very beginning, I suggested that in each of its three historical periods a distinctive missiological micro-paradigm dominated. Based on my analysis, I identified the first period (1867–1905) as that of "Revivalist pietism." At that stage, Protestant ideas shaped by British revivalism were brought to Russia and found fertile ground there. The pietistic, non-sectarian perspective of revivalism allowed "born-again" believers to stay for some time within the

---

275. Perhaps this can be seen as another instance of the influence of Russian Orthodox tradition on Baptist theology.

276. Brandenburg, *Meek and the Mighty*, 199–200; Nagirnyak, *Podvizhniki Very [Devotees of Faith]*.

277. Mitskevich, *Istoriia Evangel'skikh Khristian-Baptistov [A History of Evangelical Christians-Baptists]*, 325, 383; I. G. Ivanov, "Tridtsat' Let Vmeste [Thirty Years Together]," *Bratskii Vestnik [Brotherly Herald]* 1 (1975): 18–24.

278. Sawatsky, *Soviet Evangelicals*, 447.

279. Sawatsky, 447.

Orthodox Church, as they were hoping to reform it from the inside. The movement exhibited a strong missionary drive and was holistically oriented. Its grand vision was the complete renewal and transformation of all spheres of Russian society – spiritual, social, economic, and political.

At around the same time, two other forms of Protestantism were breaking ground in Russia, as Baptists and Mennonites with their Shtundist groups experienced success. Unlike the largely aristocratic-led Gospel Christians in St Petersburg, these groups drew converts mostly from among peasants and formerly Orthodox sectarians. Under the influence of German Baptists, they integrated their members into a previously developed system of membership and ordination that from the very beginning had a separate identity from the Orthodox Church. Baptists and Shtundists (the two groups soon merged) held to a more otherworldly conception of salvation, and to a more church-centered rather than socially and culturally active view of the Christian life.[280]

In the second period (1905–1930), designated here as that of "Transformationist pietism," both groups experienced tremendous growth and organizational success. The grand vision of Colonel Pashkov and the Gospel Christians took on new life under the strong leadership of Ivan Prokhanov. Evangelical leaders, including some Baptists, became active proponents of a holistic gospel that went along with the social and political currents of the time. They actively promoted the vision of "Spiritual Revolution," hoping to see Russia as a whole transformed by the gospel. Missionary and social work were the primary areas of focus of both denominations at the time. Inspired by their vision of a Russian reformation, evangelicals openly expressed their political and social demands for change. However, as the Bolsheviks were pursuing total ideological control over the minds of the Russian people, they saw the evangelical faith as a major competitor. After the anti-religious legislation of 1929 was enforced, a decade of harsh persecution followed.

In the final period (1944–1991), which I identified as that of "Escapist pietism," Baptists emerged out of fiery persecutions as a newly created

---

280. As we have seen, throughout their history in Russia Baptists would remain divided into two primary groups based on two different views of church and culture. Even after the artificial unification of the two groups by the authorities in 1944, they would soon be divided again, based on two different views of church and state.

denomination under the strict control of the government. Adjusting to the atmosphere of "scientific atheism," with its extreme social ostracism, they revised much of their earlier missiological vision. Although doctrinally the only significant change was the adoption of dispensational eschatology, a significant shift in emphases can be discerned along the "church-gospel-culture" axis. In this chapter, I have attempted to demonstrate that the implications of this shift for the life of the Baptist churches in Russia were so profound that it is totally legitimate to speak about a different missiological microparadigm. Since this model presents the primary context for the following chapters, it would be helpful to summarize it here by means of the following ten propositions:

1. The gospel is the message of the salvation of the soul in the hereafter and the means of spiritual regeneration for a personal relationship with the Lord in the present.
2. The kingdom of God is an otherworldly and future realm which now works within the hearts of believers through the Spirit.
3. Culture and society are fallen and irredeemable powers, destined to destruction along with the rest of the material creation. Christians must separate themselves from them.
4. The church is the people of God called out of the sinful and perverse world. A local church is the Christian's true family, a safe haven, protecting and supporting them on the way to heaven in a spiritually hostile environment.
5. The purpose of the Christian life is personal sanctification in preparation for the rapture. Spirituality focuses on the avoidance of sin and bearing the fruit of the Spirit, not on vain and unbiblical attempts to transform the world.
6. Evangelism is understood as the proclamation of personal reconciliation with God addressed to those present in church services. Outside the church, verbal evangelism is discouraged and understood primarily as showing outsiders the beauty of Christ's teaching through the goodness of one's character and action.
7. As the government took it on itself to care for the needy, the church relegated all social work to the state, except for members'

mutual help.
8. The conflict with the unregistered Baptists over the proper relationship of the churches to the government led to the refinement of a semi-sacred view of the state and the complete loss of prophetic voice in society.
9. Socially, relationships became limited largely to those within the group. New members came primarily, though not exclusively, from Baptist families.
10. Organizationally, an initially spontaneous movement with charismatic leadership gave place to an institutionalized denomination with a centralized administrative structure and strictly defined worship expressions and church order.

The new opportunities for mission work that emerged in Russia with the collapse of the Communist regime found most Baptist churches in the country with this missiological outlook, or one similar to it. At the same time, thousands of Western Protestant missionaries flooded into the former Soviet Union to spread the gospel of Jesus Christ, bringing with them fresh visions and funds for the launching of mission ventures, theological schools, Christian publishing houses, social services, construction projects, etc. Russian Baptists entered into a period of international partnerships. In chapters 5 and 6, I turn to interviews to explore the missiological convictions of the current Baptist leadership in comparison with the late Soviet paradigm of eschatological escapism. In what ways and how significantly have the contours of Russian Baptist mission theology changed as a result of their mission efforts, international contacts, exposure to theological literature and education, and a different socio-political context?

CHAPTER 4

Conceptual Framework and Methodology

Theoretical Framework

The theoretical framework of this dissertation is built around several key concepts. The first, and central, concept is Lesslie Newbigin's vision of the church's missionary encounter with culture.¹ A missionary encounter includes more than the verbal proclamation of the gospel: it occurs when the church embodies its comprehensive demands as an alternative way of life to the culture in which it is set.² In order to live holistically as a faithful witness, foretaste, and instrument of the kingdom, the church must first of all recover the fullness of the gospel as the true story of the world and "indwell" this story, letting it shape the way it understands the world and lives in it. In this way, the church will challenge the axioms of the reigning cultural story.³ Building on Newbigin's ideas, Wilbert Shenk proposes two urgent tasks for the renewal of the Western church's missionary encounter with culture: (1) to nurture a deep consciousness of the church's missional identity as a "people living out the fundamental role and purpose, [which is] mission," and (2) to foster an outward mission consciousness by becoming "self-critically aware of the 'kingdom of the Western world' which is counterposed to the reign of God."⁴

---

1. Newbigin, *Foolishness to the Greeks*.
2. Newbigin, 1; Newbigin, *Gospel in a Pluralist Society*, 152; Goheen, *Introducing Christian Mission Today*, 4913.
3. Newbigin, *Foolishness to the Greeks*; Newbigin, *Gospel in a Pluralist Society*.
4. Shenk, *Write the Vision*, 87, 94.

Based on Newbigin's vision and Shenk's proposal, Michael Goheen suggests that for any church community to renew its missionary encounter with culture, it needs to focus on three primary tasks: (1) a *theological* task that faithfully articulates the gospel of the kingdom; (2) an *ecclesiological* task that explores the missional identity of the church; (3) and a *cultural* task that probes the story and fundamental assumptions of a specific culture.[5] This dissertation focuses on the themes of the gospel, the church, culture, and mission in the current Russian context. Ultimately, my purpose is to explore how well Russian Baptist leaders are addressing (or are failing to address) the tasks that are needed for the church's missionary encounter with Russian culture today.

The second concept is Paul Hiebert's notion of the global church as a hermeneutical community.[6] In view of the purpose of mission to incarnate the gospel in particular cultures without falling captive to their underlying worldviews, there is a need for continuing dialogue between local and global mission theologies.[7] In Hiebert's words, "Local churches have the right to interpret and apply the gospel in their contexts, but also a responsibility to join the larger church community around the world in seeking to overcome the limited perspectives each brings, and the biases each has that might distort the gospel."[8] The developments in global evangelical missiology over the last hundred years serve as the principal background for this research. Russian Baptist mission thinking is analyzed and articulated here not only to be understood, but to be evaluated against the mission thinking of others in the global evangelical community. As a legitimate part of global evangelicalism, Russian Baptists should also be participants in its theological conversations.

Third, the nature of missiology as an integrative discipline defines the method and the contents of this dissertation. In its reflection on the message of the gospel in local contexts, missiology draws on four primary sources:

---

5. Goheen, *Introducing Christian Mission Today*, 4954–4956.

6. Paul G. Hiebert, *The Missiological Implications of Epistemological Shifts Affirming Truth in a Modern/Postmodern World* (Harrisburg, PA: Trinity Press International, 1999), 112; Paul G. Hiebert, *The Gospel in Human Contexts: Anthropological Explorations for Contemporary Missions* (Grand Rapids, MI: Baker Academic, 2009), 183.

7. Tite Tiénou and Paul G. Hiebert, "Missional Theology," *Missiology: An International Review* 2 (2006): 219–238; Walls, *Missionary Movement*.

8. Hiebert, *Gospel in Human Contexts*, 29.

Scripture, theology, church history, and social studies.[9] In Hiebert's words, it strives to integrate data from the study of "both divine revelation and human contexts, each conducted in both synchronic and diachronic fashion."[10] This dissertation looks at the diachronic development of both global evangelical mission theology and Russian Baptist missiology, and presents a synchronic analysis of current Baptist mission thinking in the socio-political context of today's Russia. Although this research focuses on a synchronic approach (interviews), it assumes that contexts are always shaped by history.

Fourth, this dissertation is concerned with the theology of mission at the level of "basic presuppositions" and "underlying principles which give direction to our ecclesiastical activities."[11] Even though in the case of Russian Baptists these presuppositions might not yet have been formally or systematically articulated, Bosch reminds us that behind every missionary enterprise in every epoch there is theological reflection. There is simply no mission without theology.[12] My task here is to analyze these assumptions, describe them, and let them enter into dialogue with global evangelical mission theology. In a sense, I focus on what Richard Lints and Timothy Keller describe as a "theological vision," or the middle space between doctrinal beliefs and ministry methods.[13] According to Keller, a theological vision is a "deeper level . . . reflect[ion] on our theology and our culture to understand how both of them shape our ministry."[14] For this purpose, a qualitative approach designed "to achieve an understanding of how people make sense out of their lives, delineate the process . . . of meaning-making, and describe how people interpret what they experience" seems fitting and appropriate.[15]

---

9. Alan R. Tippett, "Missiology, A New Discipline," in *The Means of World Evangelization: Missiological Education at the Fuller School of World Mission*, ed. Martin Alvin (Pasadena, CA: William Carey Library, 1974), 25–31; Wright, *Mission of God*; Robert J. Priest, "What in the World Is Missiology!?," 2012, http://static1.squarespace.com/static/56dee43ee321400514f98522/t/575c3b17e707eb73521a574c/1465662232210/4+MISS+401+Mag+4.pdf.

10. Hiebert, *Gospel in Human Contexts*, 35.

11. Bosch, *Witness to the World*, 24; cf. Van Engen, "Theology of Mission," 949.

12. Bosch, 24.

13. Richard Lints, *The Fabric of Theology: A Prolegomenon to Evangelical Theology* (Grand Rapids, MI: Eerdmans, 1993); Keller, *Center Church*.

14. Keller, 17.

15. Sharan B. Merriam, *Qualitative Research: A Guide to Design and Implementation* (San Francisco, CA: Jossey-Bass, 2009), 14.

Fifth, I use the concept of theological paradigms and micro-paradigms as a heuristic device for understanding the historical transformations of Russian Baptist mission theology. This concept was originally used by Thomas Kuhn in relation to scientific paradigms, which he defined as "the entire constellation of beliefs, values, techniques, and so on shared by the members of a given community."[16] David Bosch, in his now-classic work on the historical transformations of mission models, applied this notion to the study of paradigm changes in Christian history.[17] In this study, I focus on theological paradigms as patterns of theological understanding, both historical and current, of the four interrelated elements of mission theology: the gospel, the church, the nature of the church's mission, and the principles of cultural engagement. I suggest that from a missiological point of view the relatively short history of Baptists in Russia can be seen as a progressive replacement of three different theological micro-paradigms within a broader paradigm of evangelical pietism.

Research Method

This study seeks to investigate aspects of the Russian Baptists' mission theology in conversation with contemporary global evangelical mission theologies, working within the general framework of the Lausanne movement. Because Russian Baptists have few written or published sources on the theology of mission, the primary source will be interviews with Baptist leaders. The study employs basic qualitative research methods that aim at "uncovering the meaning for those involved."[18] Qualitative research assumes that persons' subjective meanings are influenced by social and historical contexts, as they "are formed through interaction with others . . . and through historical and cultural norms that operate in individuals' lives."[19] In the analysis of data, my task is to discover regular themes and patterns of understanding that appear in the responses of selected Baptist leaders, as well as in their relevant sermons

---

16. Kuhn, *Structure of Scientific Revolutions*, 175.

17. Bosch, *Transforming Mission*.

18. Juliet M. Corbin and Anselm L. Strauss, *Basics of Qualitative Research: Techniques and Procedures for Developing Grounded Theory* (Los Angeles, CA: Sage, 2008), 16.

19. John W. Creswell, *Qualitative Inquiry and Research Design: Choosing among Five Traditions* (Los Angeles, CA: Sage, 2007), 21.

and conference addresses, in historical and current official statements by the union, and in the curricula of its five leading seminaries. The open-ended questions in the interview were designed to obtain both the leaders' own understanding of specific theological themes as well as their responses as to how these themes are framed in contemporary evangelical mission theologies and in the Lausanne primary documents.

Research Questions

1. How do some of the most influential Russian Baptist leaders understand the following issues?

- The nature of the gospel
- The church's identity and purpose
- Christian cultural engagement
- Holistic mission

2. What missiological revisions, if any, do these leaders deem necessary in the current socio-political and religious contexts of Russia?

- Possible inadequacies of traditional formulations
- Specific areas and issues to reconsider
- Potential strategies / obstacles in the process of introducing missiological revisions

Research Population and Sample

The population of this study is active Russian Baptist denominational, pastoral, and educational leaders (all males). The reason for the selection of this particular population is that, due to the Baptist Union's hierarchical structure and a fairly high power distance in Russian culture in general, leaders tend to be perceived as spiritually superior to those they lead.[20] From this perspective, the leaders of the denomination are the most important bearers of the Russian Baptist tradition from the past and its most influential shapers in the present.

---

20. Fernandez et al., "Hofstede's Country Classification"; Thelen and Coulson, "Russian National Character"; Prasnikar, Pahor, and Svetlik, "Are National Cultures Important?"

In selecting the sample, the researcher followed the logic of non-probability, or purposive, sampling that focuses on "information-rich" participants.[21] Among the thirty interviewees, ten represent the top denominational leadership of the RUECB (the president; the vice-president; the president's assistants in the areas of mission, social service, public relations, and education; and regional superintendents from five regions: the city of Moscow, the Central Federal District, the Volga Federal District, the Siberian Federal District, and the Southern Federal District). These regions historically have had the largest number and density of Baptists in the Russian Federation. The eight educational leaders include presidents and/or deans of five schools: Moscow Theological Seminary, St Petersburg Christian University, Novosibirsk Theological Seminary, the Samara School of Preaching, and the North Caucasus Bible Institute. These particular seminaries were chosen because, according to the official website of the RUECB, they are the leading schools of the union.[22] The remaining twelve participants are either lead pastors or mission pastors from some of the largest Baptist churches in the RUECB.

In the dissertation, the participants are not identified by either name or position. In order to encourage greater openness in their responses to the interview questions, a promise was made to them that their identities would not be revealed. The table in appendix 3 presents a breakdown of the research sample by age, spiritual formation (grew up in a Baptist home or not), education (general and/or theological), vocation (denominational, pastoral, or educational), ministry experience, and ministry context (rural, town-based, or urban).

Research Procedures

Interviews and data collection were conducted during May and June of 2016. Potential participants were contacted via email, telephone, or mutual acquaintances to gain their consent to participate in the research and to schedule an interview. At the beginning of each interview, the purpose of the research

---

21. Merriam, *Qualitative Research*, 78; cf. Earl R. Babbie, *The Practice of Social Research* (Belmont, CA: Thomson Wadsworth, 2010), 193.

22. "Spisok Uchebnykh Zavedenii EKhB. Vysshee Professional'noe Obrazovanie [The List of Educational Institutions of ECB. Higher Vocational Education]," accessed 20 June 2017, https://baptist.org.ru/education.

was explained and permission to record the interviews was requested and granted. The semi-structured interviews were guided by the interview protocol (appendix 2) and lasted between fifty and ninety minutes. The first three interviews served as a pilot project to refine the interview questions to ensure that they would uncover information relevant to the research questions. The point of saturation in data collection was reached by August 2016 after thirty interviews had been conducted, including the three pilot interviews. Most interviews were conducted in person, but in five cases via Skype. Two key participants agreed to be interviewed only in written form by filling out and sending their responses to the interview questions to the researcher.

All interviews were transcribed, analyzed, and coded with the purpose of identifying the "recurring patterns that characterize the data."[23] Codes were generated inductively by observing reappearing themes in interviews. At a later stage, the codes were grouped into broader categories that were organized into separate Microsoft Word document files. These broad categories then, as a rule, became separate sections in the presentation of findings in chapters 5 and 6. These chapters are structured as a combination of thick description in the form of quotations from data and of interpretive comments by the researcher which note patterns discovered in the data or help the reader make connections between the details of findings.[24] Since all interviews were conducted and analyzed in Russian, the quotations as well as any other original citations from Russian sources referred to in this dissertation were translated into English by the author at the stage of research and writing.

Validity and Reliability

Merriam admits that "reliability in the social sciences is problematic, simply because human behavior is not static."[25] In fact, the assumption that reality is ever-changing and not "a single, fixed, objective phenomenon waiting to be discovered" is one of the differences between qualitative and quantitative research approaches. Nevertheless, she does suggest three strategies for

---

23. Merriam, *Qualitative Research*, 24.

24. F. Erickson, "Qualitative Methods in Research on Teaching," in *Handbook of Research on Teaching: A Project of the American Educational Research Association*, ed. Merlin C. Wittrock (New York: Macmillan, 1986), 149.

25. Merriam, *Qualitative Research*, 220; cf. Babbie, *Practice of Social Research*, 328.

ensuring internal validity and reliability in basic qualitative research: triangulation, respondent validation, and adequate engagement in data collection.[26] To establish triangulation, the researcher used several approaches. First, he wrote memos and observations during the interviews about the participants and their answers. Second, the actual words of the participants were used whenever possible to support each finding. Third, the researcher attempted to obtain an *emic* perspective by attending worship services, fellowship gatherings, and ministry events during the research period. Fourth, he consulted church documents, such as official RUECB statements, both historical and contemporary, mission statements, academic curricula, and several relevant sermons and presentations by the participants that are available online in order to determine the missiological convictions of Russian Baptist leaders.

With regard to respondent validation, the researcher was able to ask for feedback from a few of the interviewees as the findings were emerging to avoid misinterpreting them due to his personal biases. In terms of adequate engagement, the researcher followed the basic rule that the data and findings should feel saturated, which was achieved after thirty interviews and the gathering of some additional material.[27]

Research Delimitations

Given the fact that the subject of mission theology is a very broad field, the conceptual framework presented earlier set the limits of this study, restricting it to the four foundational concepts in Christian mission. In terms of the population, the research focuses on the mission thinking of the denominational, educational, and pastoral leadership of the RUECB and does not aim at evaluating the distribution of these ideas among the general membership of Baptist churches in Russia. Finally, the research is limited to the study of theological concepts behind the denomination's mission practices, with only secondary attention given to how those views have played out in daily activities in local churches.

---

26. Merriam, *Qualitative Research*, 217–219.
27. Merriam, 219.

Research Limitations

The findings of this study can be generalized with caution only to the leaders of the RUECB and, with even greater caution, to the leaders of two other, smaller Baptist groups which share much of the common history (the union is the largest of three Baptist denominations in the country). A large portion of the findings are not applicable to other evangelical groups in Russia, especially those planted by Western missionaries after 1991. The findings of the research also indicate gaps and opportunities for further research.

Research Bias

The researcher is neither Russian nor Baptist. As a Ukrainian missionary in Russia from 2001 to 2012, he had the privilege of working in a Bible institute associated with the Russian Baptist Union and was part of a Russian Baptist church and of two ministry boards during the same period, which gave him at least a partial understanding of internal realities. At the same time, his Western education, a more post-denominational stance, and his political orientation can bring certain perspectives to his perceptions of the findings that might not necessarily be shared by many of the participants.

CHAPTER 5

Research Findings, Part I: The Participants' Views on the Theology of Mission

Introductory Comments

This chapter is based on the participants' answers to the first research question and summarizes their perceptions of the four key missiological concepts: the gospel, the church, cultural engagement, and holistic mission. The analysis of findings suggests that, based on their views, the participants can be loosely divided into three groups. In the presentation below, the first group will be identified as "traditionalists." As we will see, the views of the participants in this group, with some modifications, largely correspond with the late-Soviet escapist micro-paradigm of mission. The second, and opposite, group will be called "innovators," because it consists of those whose mission theology has moved away considerably from the traditional concepts. The number of key proponents with the most articulated and consistent views is about the same in both groups – between six and eight (for the proponents' demographic information see appendix 3). The divide between the two conceptions of mission seems to be significant enough that their proponents can be said to hold to two different theological paradigms rather than merely exhibiting superficial differences.

The views of the third group, or the "moderates," fall on the continuum between the two extreme positions. The variety of views in this middle group cannot be reduced to a single position. What unites them with the innovators is their tendency to criticize certain aspects of the traditional understanding and practice of mission and their willingness to use methods of evangelism and church planting that are similar to those of the innovators. Yet at the level of the "basic presuppositions and underlying principles,"[1] many of them seem to perceive little need to reconsider the most fundamental traditional assumptions related to how they understand the gospel, the church, culture, and mission. From the perspective of this research, the members of the middle group are less theologically consistent than those in the other two groups: while they tend to "sew a patch of unshrunk cloth on an old garment," many of them can be safely placed within the same late-Soviet theological micro-paradigm as the traditionalists.

It should be added, however, that none of the groups (especially the third one) represents a well-formed set with sharp boundaries. For many participants it is common to agree in certain respects with the traditionalists and in other respects with the innovators. Perhaps it would make sense to employ Paul Hiebert's application of mathematical sets to missiology and to describe the first and second groups as "centered sets."[2] In other words, only two distinctive missiological paradigms are recognizable in the findings, and they are represented by the views of the most articulate and consistent traditionalists and innovators. The views of the rest of the participants are farther from or nearer to one of these reference points, or are moving toward one or the other. For this reason, in the presentation of findings below I will deal primarily with the views of the traditionalists and the innovators.

The Contours of Russian Baptist Mission Theology

The Nature of the Gospel

Perhaps the most common form of gospel presentation revealed in the interviews can be summarized as follows: it starts with the problem of human sin and condemnation and moves to its solution provided by God's love in the salvific work of Christ. Acceptance of Christ's sacrifice by faith results in salvation for those who believe (twelve out of the thirty respondents). The two quotations below are representative of this understanding:

---

1. Bosch, *Witness to the World*, 21.
2. Hiebert, *Anthropological Reflections*, 107–136.

> [The gospel] is the good news of salvation. In essence, we are sinners and Christ is our savior. The gospel tells us how he came and how he died and was resurrected. He saves sinners from eternal condemnation. Through him we have forgiveness, peace with God, and eternal life.[3]

> Every person is born a sinner, is a slave to sin, and is destined to perish. God sent his own Son to take our sins on himself and nail them to the cross... By his death he overcame death and redeemed us from eternal condemnation. Salvation is liberation from the power of sin and death and the gift of eternal life in heaven. It is a return to the Garden of Eden, a return to personal fellowship with God.[4]

Within this general view some variations with slightly different emphases can be discerned. Several participants tend to begin with the love of God rather than the problem of sin. They find the essence of the gospel in texts such as John 3:16. A smaller group of respondents emphasizes spiritual regeneration as the primary work of the gospel. For these leaders, the gospel is not only a *message* or information, but is the regenerating *power* working in the hearts of those who accept it by faith. The gospel is, first and foremost, what "gives new life" that enables sinners to overcome their "self-centeredness and the power of sin."[5] One participant described this power as the "sacramental work" of the gospel within human hearts.[6]

The ultimate purpose of salvation is expressed in terms of two primary images: entry (or transition) into heaven (or sometimes "the kingdom of heaven") and intimate fellowship with God. The goal of the gospel is "a person's return to God" so that believers "will see God ... face to face and have eternal fellowship with the Triune God and the saints."[7] A commonly used description of the afterlife is the word "eternity" which includes all of the blessings of salvation. Eternity is synonymous with "heaven" or "paradise":

---

3. P2 (hereinafter, refer to appendix 3 for the details of interviewee designations).
4. P12.
5. D7.
6. D4.
7. P9.

"Eternity in the traditional sense, as we inherited (sic) it from our parents, is [what Paul experienced] when he was taken up to the third heaven; it is a totally new life, as designed [by God] in the very beginning."[8]

In this model, the hope of salvation is usually connected with the expectation of the "church's rapture," when Christ will come "to take his church to himself."[9] The resurrection of the body does not feature prominently in the interviews (although, when asked, the participants affirm it), and the renewal of the cosmos usually comes into the picture only after a follow-up question. Both doctrines are accepted as biblical, yet there is a discernible uncertainty as to how they fit into the concept of future salvation. In fact, the common tendency is to identify the new earth with "paradise," or "the third heaven." One participant ironically states: "Yes, there also will be a new earth, but who is going to live there? . . . Maybe, Jehovah's Witnesses will. But we will be living in heaven."[10]

This belief is typically accompanied by the strong conviction, affirmed by almost everyone among the traditionalists, that the material creation will be destroyed. This view is based primarily on 2 Peter 3:10 (RST: "the earth and all the deeds on it will be burned up"). Some respondents understand this in the sense that the first creation will be "transformed into immaterial, or spiritual, things."[11] When asked how they reconcile this view with the total annihilation of matter seemingly implied by the RST translation, one of them explained that a temporary restoration of creation would take place only during the time of the millennial kingdom, but not in the eternal kingdom.[12] When prompted to comment about the Cape Town Commitment's affirmation of the cosmic aspects of the gospel, a regional supervisor summarized a common reservation as follows:

> I am not convinced that we should broaden the gospel so much as to include even ecology . . . Perhaps this reflects some

---

8. D5.

9. P9; some leaders also speak of a "minor rapture," meaning one's death as a personal transition to heaven, should it take place before Christ returns (P10).

10. P3.

11. D7.

12. Another participant adds that the millennium will be "for the Jews and the church, but [that] heaven is for the church only," which reflects a rather common view (P9).

contemporary trends. I do not deny that Christ will restore nature and human relationships in the millennial kingdom, but it is something peripheral . . . Our residency is in heaven. The earth and everything on it will be burned up.[13]

When it comes to the innovators, however, their conception of the gospel sets them apart from the rest of the group. Perhaps the main difference is that they tend to see the gospel as God's plan that "embraces both humanity and the world."[14] For them, it is "the story of the redemptive work of God" in the world as a whole.[15] The most coherent and consistent expression of this view came from a Moscow pastor and church planter, who first explained the reasons behind his dissatisfaction with the traditional understanding of the good news: "The gospel I grew up with, just as I believe you did, was this: God loves you. You are a sinner. God can forgive you if you repent. Then, if you live righteously, you have a chance to get to heaven . . . The essence of this faith was to wait for Christ's return, to remain faithful to him [until his coming], and to keep our clothes clean."[16]

As this man entered ministry, he gradually came to the conclusion that at least three aspects of this understanding of the gospel needed to be reevaluated in light of Scripture: its legalistic ethos, its otherworldly orientation, and its lack of "wholeness" or "completeness." Although "we got saved by the gospel, we lived our lives by the law." This version of the gospel "provided little incentive to engage with the world in order to change one's environment or even to evangelize others . . . In fact, 'others' were rather our enemies, 'Canaanites' or 'Chaldeans' who prevented us from keeping our clothes clean." Its otherworldly orientation greatly contributed to a massive emigration of Russian Baptists to the West in the 1990s, because they "did not see themselves as citizens of this country, nor did they identify with its people or view themselves as agents of redemption within it." Addressing the issue of "wholeness" or consistency, this pastor asked rhetorically: "Yes, the cross of Christ stands at the very center of the gospel. But *why* was he crucified? *What* was all that for? . . . We just declare many slogans which we have not thought through

---

13. D7.
14. P8.
15. P1.
16. P1.

very well." He then described his personal journey: "After several years as a Christian, I began feeling some incompleteness. [Theological] books helped me gain a fuller picture of God's work in the restoration of the sin-broken world." This completely transformed his view of the church's relationship to the world: he now sees Christians as "agents of God's redemption." Among the factors that have kept Russian Baptists from having a fuller view of the gospel, this pastor listed their past social isolation and the "scarecrow of the social gospel," which features prominently in the teaching of Western fundamentalists who are influential among evangelicals in Russia.

Other participants in the same group, while not as radical in their criticism of the traditional understanding, emphasized similar themes in their presentations of the gospel. One pastor expressed his view of the gospel in the following words: "It is, through the work of Christ, a blessing for humanity – not only in eternity but even now, here on earth. The gospel transforms us and the world around us. Redemption includes restored relationships with God, the world, and creation."[17] The lack of appreciation for the final restoration of all things is a major reason why many Christians today are "immersed in their petty lives." They do not see how the future hope shapes our lives in the present: "[Cosmic and cultural] restoration is an integral part of the gospel. But because we don't have a clear understanding of this, we do not really strive to achieve it or value it."[18]

In addition to a broader, cosmic understanding of the gospel, another aspect of the gospel that unites participants in this group is their conviction that the blessings of the gospel are available already in this life. One educator formulated the gospel in terms of the presence of the kingdom of God in the present:

> I have understood the gospel differently over the course of my Christian life. Today, I put emphasis on the fact that it is about the kingdom of God that has come near. It is the message about God who has drawn near, so that we can and should have

---

17. P8.
18. P1.

fellowship with him. This opportunity is available to everyone, and that is why this message is good news.[19]

A denominational leader added that the gospel has to do "not [only] with knowing about, and preparing for, the future," but also with "living here on earth [as citizens of] the kingdom of God."[20] A key blessing (and responsibility) in connection with this is the opportunity to be used by God to accomplish his purposes in the world. As a pastor in a large city put it: "The gospel is about the new creation. It is the understanding that Christ is for me, in me, and, as it were, through me . . . If you see what Christ has done for you and what he is doing through you – that he wants to use you – you will be ready for every task God sets before for you."[21] One seminary leader added: "The point is not to hold on until you reach heaven, but to realize your mission. God has a dream or plan for you here."[22]

In response to a question about the ultimate end of salvation, one denominational leader said,

> We keep hearing that it is life eternal. But I am convinced that the gospel is not only about life eternal. It is [also] about a true, real, holy, and joyful life on earth – life in obedience to God. It is about the realization of your new status in the Lord, about having the power of God in the Holy Spirit, about the knowledge of God's truth, and about sharing the gospel with the world around us.[23]

From the perspective of another pastor, Russian Baptists as a whole still think within the framework of the traditional understanding of the gospel: "So far, there has not been a reconsideration of the gospel message."[24] In fact, he affirms that Baptists "confess the gospel but do not live by it. We think in religious terms and have replaced the gospel with our traditions."

---

19. E4.
20. D3.
21. D5.
22. E1.
23. D10.
24. P1.

The Kingdom of God

The common thread running through most of the responses was that the kingdom of God involves Christ's lordship or kingly power in the life of a Christian. This idea was often further explicated in one of three additional motifs: (1) an "internal state of paradisal bliss," or "love, joy, and peace in the Holy Spirit"; (2) a "living fellowship with God and the ability to see his work in our lives"; or (3) personal spiritual guidance by the Holy Spirit, as he guides believers "in their heart" in the process of sanctification and of decision-making.

From this perspective, to "seek the kingdom of God and his righteousness" (Matt 6:33) is understood in terms of individual piety and personal submission to God. In everyday life it means to "seek his rule so that he may reign over us."[25] Most participants see this reign in terms of the Christian's personal holiness or victory over sin. One participant explained "seeking the kingdom" in more positive terms as an aspiration to "measure up to the level of love in relationships that is characteristic of heaven."[26] With very few exceptions, the social or political implications of the kingdom's righteousness are not emphasized, or are even openly rejected: "I don't think Jesus is speaking about social justice here. The world is under the control of sin. All have sinned and fall short of the glory of God . . . In this context [the seeking of God's kingdom has to do] primarily with the internal condition of a person. To seek the kingdom is to let it fill me, so that my heart will be righteous."[27]

When asked to describe the location of the kingdom, participants in this group typically spoke about its two dimensions. First, in the present age it is found "in the heart of the believer" as a "spiritual realm in which God's laws and freedom from sin are at work."[28] The primary text supporting this conviction is Luke 17:21: "The kingdom of God is within you." The second aspect of the kingdom is its future reality in heaven (hence the term "the kingdom of heaven") which Christians will enter either at the moment of death or in the rapture, when Christ comes to take them where he is now. In the present life, Christians enjoy fellowship with God as a foretaste of its

---

25. D7; E7.
26. E8.
27. E7.
28. P12; D7.

future and indescribable fullness, and prepare for the future "transition into the heavenly kingdom."[29]

As far as the innovators concerned, there is a discernible thread in their responses that sees the present work of the kingdom as going beyond the internal state of the believer. As one pastor put it, the kingdom is "the core within you that changes you and everything around you."[30] It is "an active force that transforms my person and my walk, and then, as a chain reaction, works around me."[31] The emphasis thus falls not so much on the eschatological realm into which the Christian will one day enter, but on the fact that "God's kingly power . . . has already come here."[32] One leader describes the relationship between the present and future aspects of the kingdom as follows: "Since I believe that everything will be a thousand times better there [than here], I am aspiring to share about it [and] to show that a life of fullness in God's image and likeness already begins here. This is much more important for me [than eschatological speculation]."[33]

Another emphasis recognizable among the members of this group is their more communal, or congregational, understanding of the nature of the kingdom's presence and witness in the world today. As one denominational leader put it: "[Seeking the kingdom] means capturing as many people as possible through sharing the gospel. The lordship of Christ is then extended and manifested in the totality of people, the church."[34] Overall, the gospel of the kingdom is more than a message of future salvation. The emphasis falls on its present power to produce "a Christlike life, a character that is transformed into Christ's character, and obedience to Christ."[35] The purpose of the gospel is seen in terms of God's righteousness in every area of life. The practical realization of this intention in Baptist communities, however, is fraught with difficulties, largely because of "the tragic divide between the spiritual and secular realms in our thinking."[36]

---

29. P10.
30. P8.
31. D9.
32. D10.
33. D9.
34. D10.
35. D10.
36. D8.

The Identity and Purpose of the Church

Four aspects of the church's identity are recognizable in the participants' views: the church as the gathered people of God, the church as God's temple, the church as the body of Christ, and the church as the custodian of God's truth. The concept that is usually mentioned first is that of the people of God. Specific descriptions include "the community of believers," "the totality of souls who believe in Jesus Christ," "the society of people who love God and have made their choice to follow Christ," "the gathering of saved persons washed by the blood of Jesus in whom the Spirit of God resides," "the community of people who confess God and love him, who have accepted Christ's sacrifice," "the *ecclesia* of the elect," "the gathering of spiritual people," etc. The emphasis on the church as community has been important for Russian Baptists, whose history is rooted in the Anabaptist tradition. They have cherished their alternative communal life against the background of the societal collectivisms of both Russian Orthodoxy and Communism.

This communal understanding of the church is often combined with the idea of its sacramental nature. This mystical aspect of the church is rooted in the fact that God is present amidst his people: it is "a community of believers, but at the same time it is a mystery, because God created it; it is the house of God, his temple."[37] One educator develops this point in more detail: "The church is where humans and God meet, where humans worship Christ. A church without Christ is not a church. Today this emphasis is being increasingly lost as we tend to become program-centered."[38] A vice president of the Baptist Union who admits to being strongly influenced by Russian Orthodox literature describes the church as "the mysterious . . . meeting place of humans and God." Due to its sacramental dimension, the church is God's representative on earth, his "embassy" in the world. Through the church (that is, through a gathered, worshipping community) humans can experience, in an anticipatory form, personal fellowship with God.[39]

The third major image of the church is that of the body of Christ. For some, this means primarily the church's connection to Christ: it is a "living organism

---

37. P7.
38. ED5.
39. D4.

in which we work together with God,"[40] and to "accomplish his will on earth."[41] For others, the key idea of this image is the connection of believers to one another and an interdependence that finds expression in their "mutual and joint service of a common purpose."[42] Most participants combine these two aspects, as does the pastor of a large traditional city church who said: "The church is the body of Christ, of whom Christ is the head . . . We all need one another, and a hand cannot tell a leg, 'I do not need you.'"[43]

The fourth common view of the church is taken from 1 Timothy 3:15, where the church is described as "the pillar and foundation of the truth." Based on RST's translation of the word "foundation" as *affirmation*, the church is seen primarily as a community authorized by God to preserve and proclaim his word. "The Holy Spirit gives the church a consensus to affirm spiritual truths," says a denominational leader.[44] A pastor adds: "The church proclaims in a down-to-earth form what God is doing and is about to do. It is the place where God's truth is announced."[45]

When it comes to the calling of the church, Baptist leaders generally agree that it exists for three main purposes: worship, evangelism, and sanctification. One pastor describes these tasks as three "vectors" or "directions": "worship is directed toward God, evangelism is directed toward outsiders, and sanctification is directed inward."[46] The pastor of a large church summarizes them as "up, in, and out – to glorify God, to make disciples of all nations, and to teach believers to obey everything Jesus commanded us."[47] An educational leader believes it is helpful to distinguish between the church's calling and its duty. The calling is "to glorify God just as the people of God did in both Old and New Testament times. This is what we will be doing for all eternity.

---

40. P10.
41. ED2.
42. D3.
43. P2.
44. D1.
45. P3.
46. P12. Some ministers reduce these tasks to two: "I am convinced that the church exists basically for two things: corporate worship through which believers are edified, and spreading the gospel in the world. There are no other tasks" (E3). A regional leader agrees with this thinking and describes these two tasks as "two wings by which the church soars in the world, or two oars by which she floats through the sea of life" (D7).
47. P12.

The latter is to make disciples. Everything else the church does is simply different forms of making disciples, whether it is evangelism, discipleship, personal mentoring, etc."[48]

Despite general agreement in theory, a difference in emphases becomes visible when it comes to the practical expression of these tasks. The traditionalists emphasize that the church's primary calling is to "show Christ" to people, or to make him visible. From this perspective the recent emphasis on evangelism is sometimes seen as detrimental:

> Some people have been telling us that the exclusive task of the church is to evangelize . . . As a result, back in the 1990s we focused only on "the Great Commission," pushing the church's great assignment to the side . . . But I am convinced that the church exists to make God visible, to show his glory on earth . . . Christ demonstrated the image of God in himself; he made God known. In the same way, we are called to manifest the image of our Savior, just as an obedient child reflects the image of his father. I am convinced that this will only strengthen our evangelistic work.[49]

When asked for clarification, these leaders define "making Christ visible" as individual sanctification resulting from the life of discipleship within a church community:

> Since the beginning of the *Perestroika* era there has been much emphasis on church planting, and little on sanctification. But we live in the Laodiceian period of the church when so many Christians need counseling. To start a new church is not a problem; it is much harder to lead it further. There are plenty of teachers, but few fathers. We need fathers . . . So the church's mission cannot be reduced to evangelism and church planting.[50]

While no respondents in this group deny the need for evangelism or church planting, there is a strong tendency to overemphasize the need for

---

48. E3.
49. P7.
50. P2.

personal sanctification, because, in their opinion, this value has been threatened by extensive mission work, with its focus on outsiders. Instead, the traditionalists believe that the church's primary means of witness is in *being* a different people. This conviction defines the primary purpose of individual Christian lives as well: "The main goal of our lives is the transformation of our inner being into the character of Jesus Christ . . . Everything that God does in your life he does with this one goal in mind – to help you know Christ and live by him. Here is the power of Christianity. As soon as you divert from it, there is only an empty religion without God's power."[51]

In contrast, the innovators strongly emphasize missional purpose of the church in every area of its life. Certainly, no one in this group rejects the need for personal holiness, yet for them it is never an end in itself. Rather, it is always connected to the church's primary purpose of being God's instrument in mission: "Any holiness that is torn away from the fulfilling of God's [Great] Commission is not holiness at all; it is a form of selfishness. On the other hand, to share the gospel of the kingdom without having the righteousness of the kingdom is nonsense. Therefore, these two are parts of a single whole."[52] They also understand missional living in broader terms than just evangelism and church planting: "The church was not left here to wait for her salvation, [because] we have already received salvation . . . [The church was left here] for a life of fullness and completeness on earth. God left the church here to do what Adam was not able to do, namely, to live in obedience to God in these difficult spiritual and moral conditions."[53]

Cultural Engagement

Answers to this section of the interview revealed the highest degree of diversity and were the most challenging part of the findings to analyze and systematize. Separation into the three groups also became most pronounced in this section. The first group of informants strongly holds to the traditional model of cultural engagement (or rather, disengagement). The second group views cultural engagement in very different, sometimes opposite terms. The middle group is open to relationships with people outside the church, both

---

51. P7.
52. D9.
53. D10.

individually and congregationally, but their openness is rather pragmatic in the sense that it is motivated by the need to share the gospel. When assessed theologically, it becomes clear that the participants in this group tend to share the views of the first group in terms of how they understand church and culture.

The traditional model is represented largely by pastors of larger and older churches. Its basic tenet is that the church is "not called to meddle in the things of the world."[54] Three leaders explicitly ground this belief in the faith of their Baptist forerunners.[55] One of them says: "We just teach what our fathers taught: it is not our task to transform the world or to change society. Our task is to be a light attracting people, to be transformed personally, and to transform those who have been attracted."[56] Sometimes this conviction is connected to another: if the church truly makes Christ visible, the society around it will naturally change for the better: "We should manifest God, and the Lord himself will influence [the world] through us."[57] Another pastor adds: "When we don't accept the form of the world, when we don't love the world or anything in it, God himself will spread the aroma [of Christ] – the smell of death for some and the fragrance of life for others."[58]

From this perspective, the reason for the lack of growth of the Baptist movement in Russia is seen exactly in its attempts to engage culture. This very desire is denounced as the "social gospel" and as "syncretism":

> I do not approve of the social gospel . . . The recent trend since *Perestroika* has been that of integration into society. I see no point in that. In the final analysis, it leads to a "symphony" with the state, when church simply becomes an ideology, a political power, and is exploited . . . We are a kingdom that is not of the world. So I am against syncretism and confusion [or blending] of the church and culture.[59]

---

54. P2.
55. ED2; P2; P3.
56. ED2.
57. P2; P7.
58. P3.
59. P2.

Instead, Baptists should insist on separation from culture, which will ultimately strengthen their witness and, perhaps, result in the transformation of society: "In order to actively influence the world, we should come out of the world. Our intentions to become like they are, to be noticed, to be popular, are simply cheap tricks. True influence will be possible [only] when we don't love anything in the world. Then the salt and light will do their work in the world."[60] This logic is supported by analogies with Old Testament Israel:

> We had always believed that to protect a city you have to build walls. The current fashion is to destroy walls. We think that Gentiles must be given access to the Most Holy Place . . . We tell them: you do not need to be circumcised . . . Instead of lifting them to the level of holiness, we step down to their Chaldean level. But God says, "I will break down its wall, and my vineyard will be trampled." When we tear down walls, we are simply devastated. We do not win anyone; we just become emptied, like them.[61]

When asked to clarify the meaning of "walls," the participants in this group tended to identify them as traditional Baptist forms of worship, ethics, dress, and congregational life. One denominational leader said: "I believe in Christian culture, in the special people of God, as Scripture teaches. The prophet says, 'I see a people who live apart and do not consider themselves one of the nations' (Num 23:9)."[62] This specific Baptist culture is thought of as an alternative to worldly cultures, as *the* Christian culture that must be protected at all costs, lest the work of Baptists in Russia be fruitless:

> We are like Ahab who said to Naboth, "Let me have your vineyard to use for a vegetable garden." So we attempt to remake the vineyard [of God] into a vegetable garden. But Naboth said: "The Lord forbid that I should give you the inheritance of my fathers." The inheritance of our fathers was what we received,

---

60. P3.
61. P3.
62. ED2.

what we imbibed. I don't think we should destroy it. This vegetable garden is not going to bear fruit.[63]

This position does not necessarily endorse a complete separation from society or an outright neglect of its needs. As we will see in the section on holistic mission, all participants believe in the need to show mercy toward outsiders. The church should respond to the needs of society, but "she is not called to solve them. We should not be diverted and carried away [by them]."[64] Whatever number of good deeds believers could ever do, these deeds "are not going to change society."[65] As a regional superintendent put it, the church's involvement "should be limited to those social problems that stem from sin or are direct effects of sin."[66] The concept of sin here includes only personal sins, such as crime, prostitution, drug addiction, or alcoholism. "We should help a person's soul and body," he continued, but as for "economic or political issues, they are not effects of sin and so are outside the realm of our calling."

Soteriological, eschatological, and moral factors contribute greatly to this understanding of cultural engagement. A quotation from a sermon by a regional leader illustrates the way this view is rooted in popular eschatology:

> The list of the most important vocations in this world is widely known. It includes such vocations as politicians, medical doctors, teachers, soldiers, farmers, etc. But all of these vocations, while important and necessary, share one serious flaw: the results of their work will be nullified with time . . . The Bible says that one day "the earth . . . and the works therein shall be burned up." Hence, all the efforts by these people will be reduced to zero. Yet there is one vocation the results of which will never amount to nothing and will remain forever. It is the work of saving human souls.[67]

The same sermon also fairly well summarizes the traditional view of salvation: "You know, the soul is the most important part of a human being.

---

63. P3.
64. ED2.
65. D5.
66. D4.
67. D7.

The body is mortal; the soul is immortal. And after this temporary life, souls will inherit one of the two realms: either paradise or hell . . . To help people turn from the path to hell and find the way of salvation – this is the calling of saving human souls."

Another regional leader elucidates with a specific example the moral concerns of cultural engagement:

> What would I do if a new Christian in my church was an actress? Well, I would not prohibit [her from doing] that. But I would tell her that it will be difficult for her to remain there. The world of the arts, if you look at it, is an abomination. I would not like my children to become, say, professional athletes or actors. Even when they were learning how to play the piano at music school, I kept telling them that this was not so that they would become professionals. I wanted them to serve God with these gifts, playing in worship services. That's it. The world of sports or the arts – this is all outrageous, with fornication and divorces . . . However, if a person finds the strength to remain within such a context and still live a holy life, it is a matter of their conscience and choice.

One more important factor that keeps coming to the surface in the responses of this first group is an *a priori* conviction of the inevitability of rejection of the church by most outsiders: "Society will reject the true, living church, because by her own life and deeds the church is condemning this world. The dead and the living are irreconcilable."[68] Another pastor added: "The world loves the things of its own. Israel was a special people, uncomfortable to other nations. That is why the surrounding nations were at war with it. When you speak about repentance, about human sinfulness, people don't like this."[69]

The second group, the "innovators," is comprised mostly of educational and denominational leaders, many of whom are also church planters in large cities. As a rule, these people have developed coherent theological positions underlying their views of cultural engagement. They are also quite vocal in

---

68. P12.
69. P7.

expressing their dissatisfaction with the traditional paradigm, seeing it as a barrier to missional engagement with the culture: "It is the raw spot of our churches – maybe not all of them, but definitely of many. They have isolated themselves. They have built walls. Theirs is a temple-centered Christianity [that insists] that people should come to them [rather than that we should be going to them]. It is now so deeply embedded in our DNA that it creates a problem."[70]

Another leader looks back at Baptist history in Russia for the roots of this attitude:

> A deep trauma has been inflicted on our brotherhood by the idea that all secular things, all things simply human, whether in the family or in society, must be moved outside the range of interests of both believers and the church. All of that was filled with negative content and . . . characterized as sinful, whether [certain types of] clothes, music, fellowship, family relationships, political activities, [or] civic responsibilities.[71]

Those well acquainted with Baptist history in Russia also stress that this mentality did not always dominate in the past. They correctly see it as rooted in the social and political pressures of the late Soviet epoch. As one educator put it:

> The current post-Soviet Baptist tradition is really very different from the way Baptists were back in the 1920s . . . Hymns that were produced at that time and musical instruments that were used were relevant for that time . . . It was a serious breakthrough in contrast to the traditions they had come from. Everything was used to evangelize outsiders. The church spoke the same language that unbelievers did or were used to. They even used Soviet, pro-socialist terminology, as seen in Prokhanov's rhetoric.[72]

He proceeded to reflect on how this tradition was changed: "The Bolsheviks saw [the church] as a threat. They marginalized our brotherhood to the status

---

70. P6.
71. D9.
72. E3.

of a sect whose main concern was survival. Unfortunately, after the collapse of the USSR, the church, at least the majority of it, was not able to move away from this model." A large-city pastor agreed:

> The Soviet form of Baptist faith was not the same as its initial form. This largely accounts for why we have not been able to use wisely the freedoms we received . . . Our attitude toward the world became quite different, and we even held to a different version of the gospel [than did the early Baptists]. We pretty much became like the Jews of Jonah's day: 'Here is a holy nation; come to us.'[73]

The participants in this group also noted that the traditional theology of culture was nurtured by a specific type of eschatology. One denominational leader put it as follows:

> What complicates our relation to the world is that we see it as already condemned, [so] we just need to wait until it is burned in the flames. This, however, is where our schizophrenia comes from. When we live spiritual lives and talk about spiritual things, it is one kind of talk. But when we go back to secular life, we hold to another set of values. We cannot connect the two, because what is there during the week is sinful, and yet we have to spend our lives and our energy on it. If we could, we would rather be singing and worshiping all week long.[74]

When seen from this perspective of eschatological annihilation, cultural activities simply have no intrinsic value: "The very concept of 'culture' is somewhat alien to us – I mean everything humans do, the fruit of their creative capacities. If 'everything will be burned up,' why waste time and energy [on it]?"[75]

A seminary dean connected this view to another factor, namely, Baptist ecclesiological primitivism: "The early church initially saw itself as a temporary institution, not designed to exist in this world for many centuries. Everything was going to end very soon. We who believe we have inherited

---

73. P1.
74. D8.
75. D8.

this model of the early church have inherited both its blessings and its problems." Among other things, it means that "we are not [mentally] prepared to solve the problems related to the church's living in the world . . . The reason we so easily accepted the idea of the 'rapture' is because we are not part of this world. In fact, all of the events that were happening seemed to indicate that. So we opted for the sentiment: 'O Lord, come very soon and take us away from here.'"[76]

Thus, the leaders in the second group tend to agree that the idea of cultural isolationism is "inherently misguided."[77] While they generally refrain from condemning their forerunners for adopting it, they also believe that biblical faithfulness today requires Christians to move beyond it. While it is true that Soviet Baptists were "forced to live in a ghetto in which it was really difficult to remain open to society," they suggest that what the Baptist churches in Russia need today is to recover the fullness of the biblical witness about the relationship between church and culture.[78]

Several elements can be identified in how these leaders understand this witness. First, the innovators intentionally qualify certain traditional Baptist concepts, such as the separation of church and state and the injunction not to love the world: "Separation from the state is not separation from society. It was meant to keep the state from meddling in the church's affairs, but not the church from participating in the life of society,"[79] and "Not to love the world means to reject its depraved, sinful system of values, [but] not [to reject] people or the world as such."[80] A big-city pastor affirms that "to the contrary, we are called to love the world: to love people, nature, animals, to love and enjoy all of it."[81] In fact, he believes that cultural expressions (e.g., city architecture) can actually become a channel for the gospel: "As a matter of fact, culture is not a product of evil. If [culture] is [utilized] for the glory of Christ, life in this city would be healthier, more joyful, and happier."

---

76. E6.
77. P4.
78. P4.
79. D1.
80. P1.
81. P1.

Second, their more positive view of culture as potentially redeemable calls on Christians both to participate fully in it, while, at the same time, not to be "regulated by or submitted to the vicious values of the world."[82] Instead, as "agents of redemption," they are to "bring positive gospel values into culture."[83] From the perspective of this pastor, Christianity is more than a way to escape the final judgment or merely a religious alternative to the ways of the world. Rather, "Christianity is, in essence, an effective alternative, enabling a contemporary person to live an authentic life here and now ... It is an effective alternative for the cynicism of society, for its damaged ideals and ideas. It is an alternative model of humanity ... an amazing community of people united around their faith in Christ."[84]

Third, this view of Christianity and culture has an important implication for evangelism: "People must first encounter a different model of life that raises the question: why do they walk like this? ... I teach believers to be enemies of sin, not of the world, and to show others how different your life can be when God is at the center."[85] Among other things, this includes "not being a sectarian, always seeking an opportunity to interject a word about God. Instead, you [should] treat others generously, do your work responsibly, share your food, [and] encourage and help others [at your job]." At the same time, sharing the gospel verbally is equally important: "The gospel is ... a story which, if received, changes the life of a person. But it cannot be told [only] by what you do; it [must also] be told in words."[86]

Participants in this second group would agree with the traditionalists that confrontation between the gospel and worldly values might take place, but they do not see this as inevitable. On the one hand, there "will be opposition to the gospel because it upholds different values. This confrontation sometimes takes the form of a cold war, sometimes of a hot war."[87] On the other hand, they tend to ridicule the fear of constant persecution expressed by older ministers: "We immediately lose heart. [We say that] no one needs

---

82. E7; E4.
83. P1.
84. D9.
85. P1.
86. P1.
87. E4.

us, [that] everyone persecutes us! But this is complete nonsense! In reality, [society] is open enough; it is a competitive environment."[88] What Baptists must recognize is that their marginalization is, to a large degree, self-inflicted:

> A professor back in my university class once asked me: 'But where are your writers? Philosophers? Thinkers? Artists? Where are they?' ... We do not feel like we are part of this society, its history and its culture. We voluntarily snatch ourselves out of this space. There is a psychological pattern: first, outsiders persecute you. Then insiders themselves reinterpret this persecution from a positive perspective. You explain to yourself that since Jesus was just a carpenter, there is no need for you to get an education.[89]

Theologically, there are three primary convictions underlying the innovators' model of cultural engagement. The first is based on a form of the creation mandate: "Isolationism stems from a false view of holiness which declares everything to be sinful. However . . . Scripture says, 'Subdue the earth, work it, and take care of it.' Everything was given [to us] with God's blessing. It was God's work. He is present in the whole process [of the creation of culture]."[90] Another leader adds: "I believe [God] is interested in everything I do: not only in what concerns eternity, but also in what I plan here. I believe he works in me to act not only in spiritual things, but in things material as well."[91] From the cultural mandate follows the idea of partnering with God in history: "Who creates history? Fundamentalists say that God does. Liberals say that humans do. I am convinced that we both do. While we cannot initiate social movements that change the course of history, there is a small share of responsibility which each of us has to fulfill."[92]

The second theological foundation is Christ's incarnation and his example of living a righteous life among sinners. Properly understood, this neutralizes moral objections to Christian engagement with culture: "It is wrong to

---

88. D8.
89. D8.
90. D9.
91. D8.
92. P8.

think that our holiness will fade if we find ourselves among ungodly people. God himself came to this earth in human flesh. Christ was in the presence of Satan himself, and no stain of darkness desecrated him. Separation means that when they sin, I don't."[93] In fact, instead of producing holiness, isolationism "kills faith, turns our minds into a monastery, and fills us with a pharisaical spirit, taking away the power of life. A congregation [starts] eating itself. It teaches itself, encourages itself, convicts itself of sin ... It makes the church fruitless and powerless; it makes its faith strained and dismal." Instead, the Christian cultural and civic responsibilities are "exactly those holy functions in the world that extend the boundaries of the kingdom. Godly life in their apartment building, in the neighborhood, in a civic position, in business relations – these are exactly those things in which Christians should show themselves as Christians. These areas are not sin, and we should teach this."[94]

Third, Christian separation from the sinful world should be understood as spiritual and moral, not as physical or relational: "We have already been set apart in the Spirit, because no one will enter the church without the work of the Spirit. But [the] invisible church interacts with the world through a visible, local church."[95] For a congregation to isolate itself from society and to make its "self-perfection an end in itself" is a gross mistake because, first, moral perfection is unattainable in principle, and second, it betrays the church's primary calling.[96] Therefore, the church must teach new believers that "they have two poles in their lives," i.e., the church and culture – and that Christians are both "called out from the world, and sent back into it."[97]

In a younger pastor's summary, a Christian stance toward general culture must be defined by both "solidarity and alternative."[98] This requires important skills of critical discernment, because, on the one hand, some cultural values are compatible with the Christian message – the gospel "was in the world

---

93. D9.

94. D9.

95. D10.

96. Additionally, it puts formidable pressure on young Christians who, having grown up within a specifically Baptist subculture, enter society for education, a job, or family life: "They are not prepared for living in that territory, they have few skills, [and] they experience a crisis because they have been taught that whenever they leave the church, they enter a sinful world ... They lose orientation, and their ties to their church and parents can be severed" (D9).

97. D9; P10.

98. P8.

before we came here; it has imbibed some aspects of culture and human souls"[99] – while on the other hand, culture is fallen, and without practicing discernment, Christians will not be able to avoid sin. This pastor proceeds to give an example related to the issue of emerging Russian nationalism: "In this respect, I will tell you, we must not show solidarity with society. Yes, it provides an opportunity to identify with our people, to demonstrate that we are part of [our nation]. But it dehumanizes other peoples. Gospel values are different and we cannot lead a double life . . . So our solidarity must be selective."[100]

A few words must be said now about the views of the third group, the "moderates." Theologically, they typically have much in common with the first group, the traditionalists. At the same time, they tend to support the church's openness toward outsiders in order to be able to proclaim the gospel and invite people to join the community of faith. (This group includes four active missionaries and church planters.). The church should "open [itself] up to such an extent as to be able to save sinners, but close [itself] against the world's value system and its culture, or rather, lack of culture."[101] As pastors of local communities, these participants call on their members to intentionally develop friendships and relationships with unbelievers outside the church. For this to happen, they stress the need for each individual Christian to recognize his or her "calling to be a missionary at the place where one already is."[102]

These ministers actively use "non-standard" approaches to evangelism, such as parachute jumps, hikes, meals together with unchurched family members, etc. They see little need to avoid associating with unbelievers for moral or soteriological reasons: "If we understand that holiness is God's gift to us, we should have the strength to proclaim the gospel to outsiders."[103] At the same time, unlike the members of the second group, they display little incentive to strive to transform society or culture because of their supposedly irredeemable nature: "No matter how much good we might do, we can't really influence society, because 'the whole world lies in wickedness.' But what we

---

99. P8.
100. P8.
101. P12.
102. D3.
103. P10.

can do is influence individuals. When we preach the gospel, God changes the hearts" of those who are then incorporated into the church.[104]

Holistic Mission

The participants' responses in this area generally manifest more agreement than in the previous one, although some differences between the traditional understanding and more recent developments are evident. As mentioned in chapter 2, below I follow Lausanne Occasional Paper 21 in its division of holistic mission into two aspects: acts of mercy (or social service) and working for social justice (or social action). With regard to social service, most respondents in all groups agree that it is an important element of the church's mission. Some noted that in this respect post-Soviet Baptists have made a measure of progress: "For a church to serve its society is one of the principles of the kingdom of God. I believe that our churches increasingly realize the importance of this ministry, for initially we were focused on evangelism [only]."[105] Absolutely all participants reject the idea of "using" good deeds as "bait" for more successful evangelism. An educational leader recalls his seminary experience: "I was taught that they [i.e. good deeds] were bridges for reaching people with the gospel. But I have come to the conclusion that social service is sufficient in itself. It is an aspect of [what] God's kingdom [is all about]. The kingdom is broader than evangelism; it is a holistic reflection in this life of the laws that underlie the kingdom."[106]

The primary reason behind the rejection of this view of good deeds is that it turns charity into "manipulation" and "dishonesty." Instead, Christians should be "sincerely interested in people as persons"[107] and should "truly wish good for all people."[108] Whether the beneficiaries come to Christ or not ultimately does not depend on these efforts: it is "their own choice which we can never attempt to purchase."[109] Moreover, to use good deeds as "bait" is

---

104. D5.
105. E4; P11.
106. E1; E4; E8.
107. D7.
108. D10.
109. P9.

actually counterproductive: two pastors shared stories of "rice Christians" who left their churches as soon as regular distributions of aid stopped.[110]

At the same time, most participants emphasize that good deeds must be accompanied by the proclamation of the gospel: "The Orthodox Church is now taking up this [kind of] ministry, supported by state funding. They receive millions of rubles. But the problem is that they do not teach the gospel, and without it social ministry is not effective."[111] While Christians should understand that they "won't save anyone with a piece of bread," if they truly love people, they should "come with both bread and the word."[112] A specifically Christian motivation for doing acts of mercy, therefore, should not be concealed; instead, believers should openly declare that they are doing them in the name of Christ. God, in his sovereignty, is "able to use [acts of mercy] for [the beneficiaries'] salvation."[113] From this perspective, as one pastor points out, "the whole polemic [of evangelism vs. social involvement] is artificial."[114]

Theologically, three primary motives for doing acts of mercy are mentioned in the interviews:

Good deeds are the fruit of new life and should proceed naturally from a "reborn heart."[115] We have been created in Christ Jesus to do good works, so loving people is a mark of a Christian just as "apples are produced by an apple tree."[116]

The need to imitate Christ: "Jesus acted in this way, and so we are called to demonstrate what he did – he fed, he cared for [people's] needs."[117] Christians should have "the same attitude as that of Christ" (Phil 2:5) and are called to act like Jesus did. It is "a way to show God's love and the nobility of his character."[118]

Direct commandments in Scripture such as admonitions about "pure and faultless religion" (Jas 1:27) and Jesus's parables of "the sheep and the goats" (Matt 25:32–46) and of the Good Samaritan (Luke 10:30–37). These

---

110. D6; P7.
111. D7.
112. D8.
113. E7.
114. D9.
115. D9.
116. D3.
117. D5.
118. ED2.

commands are binding for Christians even if, as one pastor put it, "we understand that in most cases suffering results from punishment for [personal] sins."[119]

One denominational leader pointed out an additional motive: good works are an instrument of believers' spiritual formation: "We ourselves need this because it shapes and enriches us spiritually. Otherwise we tend to become hard-hearted. Perhaps this is why God allows problems to come – so that we don't become like beasts."[120]

Despite this broad consensus, however, two participants from the traditionalist group openly challenged recent developments in the way mission is understood.[121] The following quotation reveals their concerns very well:

> When they began advertising social ministry, I had a feeling that something was wrong. Of course, what they do is no sin . . . But I just cannot see any biblical foundation for this focus on social service. I don't see that the church should be committed to it. The only clear injunction in Scripture is that the church should care for its own members.[122]

It is important to note here that this minister does not reject holistic mission as such; rather, he is concerned that social service is emphasized at the expense of gospel proclamation and the work of sanctification. The other minister, however, is more strongly opposed to basically any form of social involvement: "We should not be involved in social service, nor should we step down to the level of merely social organizations. We must not buy into lowly, earthly purposes. The state should view us as an organization that has completely different goals."[123] He then elucidates his point further: the church's only business in the world is religious, and its task is that of saving souls for eternity.

When it comes to the innovators, the primary difference between their position and that of the other two groups is twofold. First, they see social

---

119. ED2.
120. ED2.
121. P3; P7.
122. P7.
123. P3.

service not only as mandated by individual texts of Scripture or as a practical necessity arising from the needs of society, but as an integral part of the church's mission: "Works of mercy are an integral part of the kingdom and [a responsibility] of its people. If we use them only to win people, the question arises: are we really kingdom people?"[124] A seminary leader agrees: "Mission cannot be reduced to verbal proclamation of the gospel. Our actions can also serve as our witness, as 1 Peter says. Mission is the manifestation of God through the church's words, deeds, and life."[125]

Second, they believe that social service must be integrated into the life of local churches not only theologically, but structurally and financially. Local churches should set apart a certain percentage of their budget for works of mercy and/or should have mercy teams with leaders responsible for this type of ministry. In general, these participants represent local communities that have passed from an almost complete absence of social involvement to theological acceptance of a holistic gospel and its organizational integration.

Things became more complicated, however, when discussion moved from acts of mercy to issues of social justice. Given Russia's underdeveloped civil society and the tight governmental regulation of independent social activities, this question typically led to the theme of the Christian view of the state. In this respect, all thirty participants agreed on the following three points.

The obligation to obey state laws and to fulfill one's civic obligations by supporting any social good that comes from those in power.[126] This obedience begins with personal integrity in small things such as paying taxes, utility bills, etc. In principle, to obey the authorities is not difficult if we "obey the law of God" and are "guided by God's principles."[127] The primary texts used to support this view are Romans 13:1–8 and 1 Peter 2:13–15.

The Christian obligation to pray for those in power, asking for God's guidance and blessing as they serve the people. Some ministers repeatedly used the cliché phrase, "to bless the powers," but when asked to explain its

---

124. E1.

125. E7.

126. In fact, Christian obedience to the state is hailed as one of the "major Christian virtues." So also in the official "Statement of Social Responsibility of the RUECB" adopted by the Baptist Union of Russia in 2014.

127. D5.

meaning, they usually boiled it down to the issue of prayer as commanded in 1 Timothy 2:1–4.

All respondents potentially acknowledged the possibility of civil disobedience if the requirements of the state conflict with those of God's word. The primary text used for this is Acts 5:29. The only legitimate purpose of such action, however, is to protect religious freedom, but never to overthrow the existing powers in a coup d'état.

The differences among the groups began coming to the surface when I asked the participants to elaborate on the nature of power as established by God (Rom 13:1). The traditionalists normally explain this text in the sense that specific political *leaders* are assigned by God for specific times. This does not mean that they approve everything the powers do, nor do they see the state as somehow sacred or divine. Yet they are convinced that God actually *wills* these specific persons to be in power: "They are his servants, the scepter of the One who controls everything."[128]

The innovators, on the other hand, believe that God *allows* specific persons, including those who are grossly godless or immoral, to penetrate the good system of power he established. From the perspective of this group, God has ordained the principle of subordination rather than specific rulers: "What is ordained by God is the institution of state, not the quality of people who use or abuse it . . . Those who concern themselves with the country's well-being properly belong to the structure of the divine institution. But those who [wield power] for their selfish ends are parasites, abusing the structures."[129] From this perspective, there is no contradiction between the idea of power as coming from God and its demonic manifestations. At least four interviewees in this group described the current authorities as openly inimical to God's purposes.[130] One of them said:

> The world today . . . claims to be Christian, but in reality this government is demonic. This government is hostile toward God because it attempts to take from me the God-given right [to the free exercise of faith and mission]. And we agree with [what

---

128. ED2.
129. D10.
130. D9; D10; E3; D7.

> they are doing], saying that 'all power comes from God.' Does it really? The devil told Christ that all kingdoms are his and that he gives them to whomever he wishes. God did not *establish* the powers that be; he *allowed* them to be . . . It is spiritual warfare, but we have chosen [to hide behind] a nice picture of "living peaceful and quiet lives."[131]

The practical significance of this difference becomes visible when it comes to the issues of legitimate reasons for civil disobedience and the prophetic role of the church. Two respondents[132] believe that it is legitimate to disobey the government not only when it prohibits Baptists from freely engaging in religious activities, but that believers are also "not under obligation to obey any laws that contradict [their] conscience or generally recognized divine principles and rules."[133] In other words, in cases of some "obvious social injustices"[134] Christians can challenge the authorities and refuse to comply with their directives. This strongly contrasts with the majority view that holds that the sole reason for disobedience is the restriction of religious liberty for Baptist community (i.e. prohibition to conduct worship services).

With regard to the issue of the church's prophetic role, three clearly defined positions are recognizable in the findings. The largest group (about two-thirds of participants) strongly rejects the very idea of the church's prophetic ministry. Here are some of the most representative quotations:

> I think it is not the church's function to interfere with the life and actions of the authorities. This is God's prerogative. The church should devote itself to the salvation of human beings, to their spiritual nature . . . To criticize the powers and meddle in politics is absolutely not the church's business.[135]

> We believe in the separation of church and state. The church is not part of the state and so it must not interfere with the state's business. It must not take upon itself any prophetic role. It should fulfill its obligations before God and people, and then

---

131. D9.
132. D9; D10.
133. D10.
134. D5.
135. P7.

God himself will act through her life. This includes [his influence on] the state.[136]

A prophetic role ultimately leads to the concept of a "symphony [between the church and the state], as we can observe in the Orthodox Church. But we hold to the separation of church and state. The church should engage in church work, and the state should deal with state business. There are plenty of sinners for the church to work with and preach the gospel to."[137]

Upon further discussion, however, some of the leaders in this group qualified their position in two respects. First, they see the proclamation of the gospel in itself as a prophetic ministry: the church is called to preach a generic message of sin and personal salvation to every person, including those in power. It is the "Holy Spirit's work is to convict them of [their personal] sin, but who am I to take it on me?"[138] Moreover, unless sinners experience spiritual regeneration, pointing out their sins may only harden them. Therefore, the church "fulfils its prophetic ministry when it loves" sinners.[139] Second, the church's prophetic role is exercised through her moral purity and holiness. By being holy, she exposes the unrighteousness of society. In cases of injustice, Christians must respond with acts of mercy and prayers for justice and peace. Yet in the final analysis, working for social justice is "not our prerogative; I can only fight for it through prayer. I believe it is God who sets up [rulers] and deposes them."[140]

It is important to note some of the theological bases on which this position rests. The first and most common is the idea that society is unredeemable and cannot be morally improved: "To change the world by creating Christian political parties with the hope of somehow influencing it is a futile work."[141] One regional leader put it rather bluntly:

---

136. P12.

137. ED5. One educational leader rejects the prophetic ministry of the church on the ground of cessationism rather than the separation of church and state: "I don't think the church has any prophetic role. The time of prophets belonged to the past when they laid the foundation of the church. Today, since there are no prophets, there is no such function in the church" (E7).

138. D2.

139. E8.

140. D4.

141. P7.

> I don't believe in [the possibility of true] freedom or of just government here on earth. When anyone gives the example of some other country [being just], for me it is all merely anecdotes . . . It is fighting windmills. One sinner in power will be replaced by another sinner. This brings only disasters. I don't believe in earthly well-being, and I see no sense in the church working for it.[142]

One educational leader followed basically the same line of thought: "I don't think the church can really influence society [for good]. Any power will simply digest the church and spit it out . . . It is the old Constantinian temptation. There are no pure democracies; everything is just a different form of manipulation."[143]

The second theological basis is that the church's engagement with powers is usually counterproductive. Moreover, it tends to corrupt the church: "History teaches us that the church loses its moral authority and sinks into the same sins and problems that the state does."[144]

Third, fighting for justice would mean that the church has lost both its trust in God and its moral orientation: "The essence of Christianity is not about reacting to injustice; it is about forgiveness."[145] This minister continued: "In the past some Baptists got involved in politics, and a result they had to rely on man rather than on God. They wrote letters to the UN or the European Court. But trusting in princes is a sign of weakness. They should have trusted in God, and he would have brought it to pass."

The fourth theological basis is that neither Christ nor the apostles ever called on Christians to be involved in the struggle for justice:

> Jesus never criticized political powers. He did criticize religious leaders, but these two [belong to] completely different kingdoms. The prophetic role is nothing but [mere] philosophy. The [real] prophecy is this: get ready for his coming, be alert, and watch for what happens. Live a holy life. Some [powers] win today;

---

142. D4.
143. E3.
144. P7.
145. ED2.

others will win tomorrow. But Christians are to go through all these changing systems without being contaminated.[146]

Finally, three respondents indicated the fear of persecution as another reason for their position. A regional leader applied Amos 5:13 to believers living in a totalitarian state: "The prudent man keeps quiet in such times, for the times are evil."[147] An educational leader added: "If you are in a certain position of power, your conviction may be accepted. If you are not, they will simply squash you."[148] A seminary leader commented: "The 'tsar' is cleaning up the country – those who bring in 'strange fire.' All those who are not for him will be cleaned up . . . But we must protect the church. One way is by preaching Christ, not [having] political ambitions. Ours is a message about Christ, not a message about politics."[149]

At the same time, about one-third of the participants affirmed the need for the church to be God's prophetic voice in society – to "raise a voice for those who have no voice,"[150] and, as citizens, to "evaluate the work of the government [and] not simply pay taxes."[151] This affirmation, however, was qualified with several conditions. First, the respondents in this group strongly agreed that working for justice should not be the work of the church as an institution, but rather of individual Christians who are called to and prepared for this task. The church should emphasize its non-involvement in politics. This will help not only to keep the church on track in its primary mission but also to protect it from persecution: "Our primary purpose is to proclaim the gospel, for the sake of which it is better to neglect what can get in the way. By attempting to correct the uncorrectable we give ungodly people enough reasons to take away our opportunities for evangelism. Only God can correct [injustice], and we must wait."[152]

Second, prophetic denouncements of injustice must be focused more on the moral side of issues than on their political side. This includes avoiding

---

146. ED2.
147. D7.
148. E3.
149. ED5.
150. D8.
151. D7.
152. D7.

the risk of identifying with specific political parties, movements, and ideas: "Whenever the church takes a specific political position, its political opponents become the opponents of the church itself."[153]

Third, the church's criticism should be directed at specific actions, and not at persons. In other words, it must voice its concerns without attacking the authorities and those in power.

Finally, the church should not only point out societal injustices and vices, but also suggest constructive, biblically informed ways of improving the situation at hand. As one educational leader put it, "It is important not so much to convict as to offer prescriptions. A good doctor gives hope and suggests treatment."[154]

In sum, on the issue of social justice Baptist leaders seem to continue searching for satisfactory theological solutions. As the church is learning to live outside her former "ghettos," and as the changing political and social realities raise new questions and shatter her once-and-for-all accepted beliefs, they are forced to go back to Scripture and learn from the experiences of other Christian groups. An educator summarizes the current state of the debate:

> There is a [biblical] teaching that all power comes from God – that he is in control, so there is no need to worry about what is happening in the political realm . . . Then again, [there is a teaching that] the church is not to support evil. As a result, the temptation is either to become overly involved, losing focus on the things God has called us to do, or to withdraw because those in power will always be sinners anyway. Since our church has been politically and socially weak, we have preferred the latter option. But this [issue] requires a theological evaluation. Some attempts at it have been made here and there, yet no clear answers have yet been developed.[155]

---

153. E8.
154. ED5.
155. E4.

CHAPTER 6

Research Findings, Part II: The Need for Revisions to Traditional Missiological Views and Ways of Introducing Them

This chapter summarizes the participants' responses to the second research question: What missiological revisions, if any, do they deem necessary in the current socio-political and religious context of Russia? As part of their response to this question, the interviewees were asked to reflect on the adequacy of the traditional formulations of mission theology over the twenty-five years of religious freedom since 1992, with special attention to the factors that have either contributed to or hindered the success of Baptist mission efforts. Finally, they were asked to propose specific areas and issues that require theological reconsideration and suggest some constructive ways of introducing these revisions.

As noted in the last chapter, based on their responses to the first research question the participants were divided into three distinct groups, and those groups remained largely stable with regard to the way they responded to the second question. While not all members of each group agreed among themselves on all matters, there were two clearly identifiable core groups (with six to eight leaders in each) whose members have a similar view of mission theology within their group, but hold to a very different, and even opposing, missiological trajectory than the members of the other group. The members of the third group, "the moderates," were usually closer theologically to the first group and yet shared many ideas that are more in line with those of the second group. The report below, as in the previous chapter, consists of two sections with one focusing on the views of the traditionalists and the other on those of the innovators.

It is important to note that the members of the first group, in contrast to those in the second group, had much less to say about potential missiological revisions, largely because many of them do not see any serious issues with the current paradigm. For this reason, more space below will be given to the exposition of the more consistent and detailed views of the innovators.

Group One: Revisions in the Traditionalist Perspective

Reflections on the Experience of Baptist Mission in Russia

As they looked back at the years of almost unrestrained religious freedom and activism, participants in this group usually acknowledged that Baptist mission efforts have not been very effective. In fact, one regional leader summed it up as follows: "We have to admit that our experiment with mission has been a failure" (immediately adding, however, that still much was achieved).[1] When asked to account for this lack of success, the members of this group typically suggested reasons that are outside of the church's control. Based on their responses, these reasons could be divided into two primary categories: (1) social factors, or the condition of the "soil," and (2) spiritual and eschatological factors.

In particular, the traditionalists regularly observed that, despite the high level of curiosity about Christianity after the demise of Communist ideology, a specifically *spiritual* quest was not really very common. People were "looking for solutions to their own financial or family problems; they [were] not interested in God per se."[2] Many were coming because of humanitarian aid: free food, medication, clothes, etc. But as soon as the economic situation started improving in the early 2000s, few of these visitors remained in the church.[3] This is even more true today: "The general atmosphere in the country is such that . . . society is more interested in its earthly well-being and

---

1. D4.
2. P10.
3. D4; P10.

comfort. No one needs anything [spiritual]; everyone says they are Orthodox. Despite whatever we strive to do, people are not hurrying to our churches."[4] Sometimes, participants in this group contrasted the current social conditions with those of the 1920s when Baptists experienced consistent growth. At that time, the "soil was different. We did not experience as much turmoil as they had experienced during WWI. Besides, the [Communist] government restrained the Orthodox Church."[5]

Another social factor that has kept outsiders from joining Baptist communities is the fear of loss of reputation due to association with a "sectarian" group: "Socially, it is not advantageous to be an evangelical. [Only] those who are not afraid to be [part of a] minority come."[6] This is especially true for educated and well-to-do members of society. As one pastor put it, "I don't think [the problem is] that we do not know how to speak to them. It is more that they do not want to speak to us. They are complacent and self-sufficient. Whom they reject is not us, but God. That is why we, like Paul, go to those who know they are perishing."[7] In fact, this is not a new reality: "It has always been like this under the sun. People hear the gospel, they come, and they leave . . . You can attract them through contemporary tricks, but they leave when they come to understand the price of discipleship."[8]

The second category of reasons is more spiritual than social in nature. True revival when multitudes come to faith is seen as depending exclusively on the work of God. One denominational leader commented: "I disagree that revivals depend on social factors. They are a special work of the Holy Spirit. No social factors can pose a barrier for the Spirit. [Revivals have taken place because] there were people anointed with the power of the Spirit."[9] Switching from history to the current period, he continued: "There are also periods of spiritual stagnation. Alas, it appears that we are in the middle of one of them." Another influential regional leader backed up a similar conclusion eschatologically:

---

4. P3.
5. P2.
6. ED2; E4.
7. P3; D9.
8. P3; ED2.
9. D7.

> We used to go [with the gospel] to public schools, military divisions, prisons, etc. But everything is being closed now because the eschatological falling away is coming. People are not searching for God today. They don't have it in their hearts, which is why doors are being closed. "What else should I do for you?" [says the Lord]. It is not the church's fault; it is their own spiritual condition. We should not be pointing fingers at [i.e., blaming] the saints.[10]

Some respondents in this group did mention certain factors within the church that may have hindered the success of mission. In particular, they noted the lack of experience with public evangelism, the shortage of finances both for the rental of facilities for follow-up classes and for the support of discipleship leaders, the poor level of preaching, and the inadequate pastoral care of new converts. However, discussion of these elements was typically short circuited with comments or rhetorical questions such as these: "It is the law of life. It has always been like that. Christ chose seventy disciples but was left with [only] eleven. So I would not measure [success] numerically."[11] Or, "Did Christ ever attempt to keep those people [who left him]? Why did he not fight for their souls then?."[12] It was also quite common for the participants in this group to refer to Christ's parables of seed falling on rocky places (Matt 13:5) and of the bad fish outnumbering the good ones (Matt 13:48).

The issue of the Baptist subculture (in particular, Baptist forms and elements of worship, aesthetics and dress code, patterns of relationships and leadership, etc.) was also brought up. While some in this group admitted that newcomers have often had "a hard time bearing our subculture that was shaped during Soviet times,"[13] the idea of rejecting or reconsidering the traditional forms is generally not acceptable for these leaders. In fact, the most radical members of this group see contemporary worship styles as nothing but a compromise with worldly culture, and so the rejection of traditional Baptist distinctives is for them a syncretistic "removal of the ancient landmarks" set

---

10. P3.
11. P10; D4.
12. P7.
13. D4.

up by the fathers.[14] Moreover, when some Baptists were "enticed by freedom and rushed to use all possible opportunities," in reality this "desire to be understood" worked in the opposite direction. Changing "our order of things, our statement of faith, in order to attract people" not only led these communities to the gradual loss of "[their] own culture and identity," but also seriously weakened their spirituality.[15]

This last point deserves more attention. The traditionalists typically complain that contemporary Russian Baptists in general have become very different from their predecessors who were characterized by "true godliness and the fear [of God], eschatological expectations [of the imminent rapture], and sound spirituality."[16] Their "treasures were not on this earth."[17] In the final analysis, it was lack of deep spirituality that negatively affected the missionary potential of Baptists after 1992. If the church of today had the same characteristics which the early Russian Baptists had, she would be able to bear spiritual fruit despite any social or political conditions she finds herself in: "Freedom comes and goes, but . . . mission does not depend on the social situation . . . All these changes are nothing but 'the basic principles of the world' that we should not walk after. [Even] in the USSR new believers were baptized, because of the presence of [spiritually] healthy ministers."[18]

A denominational leader in this group was less radical and admitted that the traditional subculture is "neutral" and that it was shaped into what it is "for objective reasons."[19] At the same time, he agreed with the rest of the group that attempts to modify it in order to retain newcomers were a serious mistake. On the one hand, it is true that traditional Baptist "choir singing" is "no more biblical" than contemporary Western worship styles. On the other hand, it is "ours; it is rooted in a thousand years of Orthodox culture; it is in our DNA, in our blood." Contemporary worship songs "impoverish liturgics," but from his perspective "liturgics is more important for us than preaching, because it tunes your heart rather than just speaking to your mind. When a

---

14. P3; ED2; P7; P2.
15. P3; ED2.
16. ED2; D6.
17. P3.
18. P3.
19. D4.

person comes to a temple [church building], they first look for the altar, not the pulpit." The examples of those communities that abandoned traditional forms of worship and experimented with new ones only prove that they were wrong. Although they "discarded all the traditions and even moral norms in order to retain people," they too "have not been filled with multitudes."[20]

A similar critique is directed against some concepts of mission work imported from the West. Three aspects of Western missiology in particular fell under severe criticism: (1) the hiring of gifted young people by Western agencies, which has contributed to the "professionalization"[21] of missionary service and the impoverishment of churches; (2) planting churches in large cities by splitting existing churches, which did not produce the results promised by Western mission strategists;[22] and (3) the Western pragmatic approach that sees mission as "business that can be managed: you invest certain amounts, you develop a plan, and you expect effects that can be measured in numbers. But often it does not work this way."[23]

Overall, Western missionaries, while bringing much good, have "not been able to teach local Christians how to evangelize Russians."[24] What these Western brothers have taught Russian Baptists was "not spirituality, but management theories"[25] and "American religious technologies."[26] Baptist history in Russia, however, already demonstrated that such approaches would not have long-term effects. A regional leader compares today's situation with that of the 1920s: "Prokhanov was also swept away with social projects and ecumenical ties, seeking to partner with Orthodox Christians. But this is all

---

20. When his attention was directed to the strong growth of charismatic churches over the same period, he responded: "I am not impressed with these numbers. So many people have become disappointed in Christianity [after joining those churches]. Although there are some sincere believers there, as well, I call it a 'vaccination against Christianity,' [because of their] loud scandals and psychological manipulation of the audience."

21. That is, it created the impression that only those who get paid and are "on staff" should do missions, which negatively impacted the motivation of church members to get involved in the work of evangelism.

22. While the number of churches has grown, the overall number of believers has decreased. Instead of "one strong church, a city can now have several weak churches that cannot afford a strong choir or well-developed youth and children's programs" (D4).

23. D5.
24. D4.
25. ED2.
26. E6.

wrong. Although he achieved a lot by his [human] enthusiasm, when persecutions came, everything was crushed. Only what was inside survived."[27] In this view, Stalin's persecutions "immediately revealed who was following Christ and who was simply buckled [that is, loosely attached to the church]."[28]

Instead, what Baptists should have been doing is "teaching the gospel to those who came."[29] For this minister, the gospel includes an "honest catechization" into Baptist church culture. Rather than having churches "adapt to the comfort of newcomers," in most cases it is newcomers who "should accept [our culture]."[30] Those who are called by God will not see traditional forms as a barrier, but "will accept them with joy."[31] The fear of losing people is unfounded because those who truly seek God will stay:

> Based on our experience, those who truly came to God ... felt comfortable and interested, because they came not [merely] to gain some knowledge; they came to Christ. When they come to a church service, they come to worship God. Our church service is not a lecture or entertainment time to satisfy the needs of listeners. It is a time of worship.[32]

Accordingly, whenever people choose not to stay in the church, it is "their own personal problem – their lack of faith or commitment to Christ."[33] The failure of Baptist mission endeavors, therefore, is not the church's fault; it is largely the effect of the spiritual condition of society.

Suggested Missiological Revisions

This question caused some degree of perplexity with many of the participants in this group. Some initial answers included the following: "This is the most difficult question [in the interview so far]. I realize something must change, but I just don't know what"[34] and "I cannot answer this question. Perhaps only

---

27. ED2.
28. D6.
29. P7; ED5.
30. D4.
31. P7; P3.
32. P7.
33. P10.
34. D4.

God knows exactly what must be done."[35] Upon further reflection, however, these ministers typically focused on what all of them consider to be the key factor in the success of Baptist mission in Russia: the spiritual renovation of the church. They believe that "what we need is spiritual revival. We need to go back to our spiritual beginnings. First, a revival of God's people [must take place]; only then will there be a revival among [the Russian] people [as a whole]. Spiritual tasks must be achieved with spiritual means."[36]

From the perspective of these leaders, Baptists need first of all to go back to what historically was their distinctive mark in a nominally Orthodox environment: "The evangelical movement attracted people because believers lived according to what they preached. This is how we should live. Then there will surely be people who will observe this and come."[37] Outsiders, in small numbers, were joining the church even during the time of intense pressure by the atheistic Soviet state because "believers demonstrated the light of God in their personal lives."[38] Unfortunately, this is largely not the case today: "As it is written, 'They will glorify God when they see the purity and reverence of your lives.' Sadly, there is so much nominal [Christianity] in our midst today."[39] Christians have become "freedom lovers and lightweights."[40]

Theological education has proven unable to adequately equip Christians for this task because "knowledge does not result in the fear of God: 'Knowledge shall increase,' but lawlessness shall increase too."[41] Although more and more people are getting theological degrees today, "'Knowledge puffs up, and love builds up'; you might get someone interested in your theology for a few days, but they will soon figure out whether you love them or not."[42] Instead, what the church needs these days is to "be filled with Christ and infect others with him"[43] and to "raise the level of love for God and neighbor."[44] This can hap-

---

35. ED5.
36. ED2.
37. D4.
38. P7.
39. P2.
40. D6.
41. P3; D4.
42. E8.
43. ED5.
44. E8.

pen only through a "living connection to God – through prayer, not through textbooks."[45] If Baptists should "preserve the image of the letter of Christ" in the future[46], they can count on the "natural success of evangelism." But, ultimately, "only God knows whether the numbers will be large or small."[47]

This emphasis on spirituality goes hand in hand with the perceived need to preserve and protect the unique Russian Baptist subculture. Since the coming of religious freedom, many changes have been "imported from the West," so that Baptists have "largely lost our canons (sic) and liturgics, which is our doctrine."[48] This idea comes up in the interviews again and again: Baptists "looked to the West with our mouths open, adopting their forms, but they don't work here because our culture is different."[49] Western forms reflect the cultural values of "secularism, of a worldly, ungodly culture."[50] As a result, "We now have people who have become Christians externally but whose worldview remains secular. Their philosophy [of life] is worldly."[51] All of this negatively affects Baptist convictions, behavioral patterns, outward appearance, worship and music patterns, etc. Worse still, it affects their ethical standards: "Pragmatic approaches prevail. We began living according to worldly standards, paying bribes to solve problems . . . Christian standards of faithfulness to God, integrity, honesty, reliability, humility, and chastity are disappearing."[52]

The response to this challenge is found in protectionism: "To attract people, we need to build walls; otherwise we are going to be devastated."[53] To begin with, the very "idea of giving the Gentiles free access to the holiest place was demonic." Moving "our fathers' boundary stones" or doing away "with the inheritance of our fathers" means to "forsake things of our own for

---

45. P3.

46. This is an allusion to 2 Corinthians 3:3, where the "letter from Christ" has traditionally been understood by Russian Baptists to refer to the personal godliness of believers.

47. P7.
48. P2.
49. P2.
50. ED2.
51. P3.
52. ED2; P3.
53. P3.

someone else's, losing the respect of others."[54] The Orthodox Church can be looked upon as a model in this regard: "Orthodox [believers] are our example in this. They have not changed their liturgy for so many centuries, unlike us who constantly adjust it back and forth. I don't really understand this."[55] In mission and discipleship, this type of "syncretism" will not produce genuine conversions, even if it may "attract and entice people with some [updated] methods."[56] Moreover, without the "railroad" of tradition new believers will succumb to pluralistic relativism: "They see that everybody is a believer now and that each person believes in a different way."[57] The traditional heritage is the answer to both problems.

In this discussion, the text of Hebrews 13:7 plays an important role. Russian Baptists should be "directed by the history of the brotherhood and by imitating the faith of deceased [believers]."[58] At the same time, tradition should not be strongly imposed on new believers. Ministers should with love "strive to explain from our history why this particular set of forms has taken shape." It is important for a newcomer to "gradually understand why we do what we do," rather than to be "forced to accept it humbly." The whole process works best when the "original meaning [of the traditional forms is] . . . understood."[59] Ultimately, for those who have been called by God, this will not constitute a serious problem: "If a person is truly seeking God . . . they will accept our lifestyle, our customs and culture. They will adapt to them so that it all will become natural for them."[60]

The key role in this process should belong to raising up proper spiritual leadership: "There is a great need for leaders who will be led by the Spirit in shaping the church."[61] Baptist churches toady, however, are experiencing a serious leadership crisis: many pastors "simply conduct services and funerals; they don't understand that their task is to shepherd and oversee and to teach the difference between the holy and the common, the clean and the

---

54. P3.
55. P2.
56. ED2; P3.
57. ED2.
58. P2.
59. D4.
60. P7; P10.
61. P3.

unclean."⁶² Again, seminaries are unable to fill the vacuum because this type of wisdom, value system, and experience can be received only "in the church, through the succession" of tradition. Schools simply "cannot give what they promise; moreover, graduates [often] cannot be integrated into church life afterwards, or [worse still] they bring some 'strange fire.'" The crisis is exacerbated by the fact that *Perestroika* resulted in many "old ministers being allured and extorted" to the West, whereas "new types of churches, with new forms of church life, have been rigorously planted with the help of Western donors' money." The succession, therefore, has been largely broken: emigration "played a huge role in making the brotherhood shallow." As to those who joined the church in the 1990s their young years were "wasted in the world so that they cannot give anything [to the youth now]."⁶³

In keeping with this emphasis on leadership, the members of this group typically look to the central office of the Baptist Union in Moscow for guidance. Their hopes for restoration are connected to the agenda the office can potentially suggest, and to its leadership. The pastor of one large church put it as follows:

> They keep telling us to take it to the local level, but we are not ready for that. We Russians are used to having a center. It is not that the center decides everything, but vision and ideas come from the center . . . They tell us about the autonomy of the local church. Yes, we are autonomous, but with regard to doctrine, forms, and [overall] direction, these are impossible without a center.⁶⁴

Another denominational leader referred to this function of denominational leadership as "apostolic": "The [bonds of the] brotherhood keep us from demoralization and fragmentation."⁶⁵ From this perspective, several leaders raised concerns about the current lack of centralization within the union: "I am concerned over this localization, when decentralization becomes a substitute for a strong center, when regional superintendents are [primarily]

---

62. P3.
63. P3.
64. P2.
65. ED2.

concerned about things in their [own] regions."[66] Anxiety about weak leadership coupled with the fear of potential doctrinal divisions raises worries about the future of the union as a centralized denomination.[67] A seminary leader revealed his heart: "I am seriously afraid that Russian Baptists are facing the threat of losing their distinctive identity as we have known it – the threat that it will take some other form and shape. This doctrinal atomism can one day lead to a moment when churches will go their separate ways: 'Every man to his tent, O Israel!'"[68]

Preserving unity requires a certain type of personality in the position of the union's president. Representatives of this group tend to see the central office as some kind of suprachurch and the union's president as the pastor over other pastors. A regional leader commented: "One of the most serious problems is [the question of] what kind of president we need. I say openly: we need a father. We do not need programs, we need someone who will caress us and bring us together so that we can become like one family."[69] Another former denominational leader who now pastors a large church adds: "I believe no programs or methods can save us. We need God's work. This would be possible if God found a person whom he could use mightily, in his power."[70]

On the whole, the participants in this group largely tended to be rather pessimistic about the prospects for Baptist mission in Russia: "I don't know if it is possible to change the church's degrading condition. Even the external appearance [of Christians] is changing [for the worse]."[71] Another leader adds: "For a revival to happen there should be two conditions: The seeking of God among the people, and the readiness of Christians to lay down their souls for the sake of sinners. Sadly, today neither of these is present."[72] Yet some others are guardedly optimistic: even though the current situation

---

66. E6.

67. The primary doctrinal threat from the perspective of this group comes from the movement of the so-called "biblical" churches planted under the inspiration of John MacArthur and the Master's Seminary. These churches usually hold to a version of Reformed soteriology and define themselves largely over against the traditional Arminian theology of Russian Baptist churches.

68. E6.
69. D6.
70. P12.
71. P3.
72. P12.

might not be the best time for missions, Baptists have to focus on the inner development and maturation of their communities, leaving the results in God's hands. What they need is to "work on what we were charged to do, minding our own business, and whether the numbers increase or decrease is not up to us."[73] A key area that needs attention today is the launching and development of counseling programs in seminaries and local churches. As one educator observed, "Counseling is the most popular program today in our school, which speaks volumes about the immaturity within our churches – emotional, physical, and spiritual. But we must serve where the need is, and the changes will happen gradually over time."[74]

What all the leaders in this group seem to agree on is that, in the final analysis, Christians cannot produce or control church growth. One pastor put it as follows: "Looking into the future, I am convinced that the process of church growth is under God's control. If we try to intrude into it today, [the result] will be an unnatural, artificial phenomenon."[75] It is the Holy Spirit who builds the church, not our methodology: "There are multiple methodologies, such as psychology, 'purpose-driven church' approaches, etc. These might produce numerical growth, but how many of the people reached will be *living* souls? Perhaps [only] two or three will."[76] Numerical growth is "not correlated with [God's] blessing."[77] To support this claim, the informants often referred to Christ's model of ministry: he "was not pursuing numbers; but focused on twelve, not [even] three thousand or five thousand."[78] In fact, the current period may be a time of God's purification of his church:

> There have been different periods in church history, so I accept the situation today as it is. I look at this conservatively: Let God's will be done. I am for a church that is perhaps a little flock, but Christ is in it. I am even glad that the church is being cleansed of those who came just to get some aid or to join a good

---

73. P12.
74. ED5.
75. P7.
76. P3.
77. P3.
78. ED5.

company of non-drinking people, but who did not experience regeneration.[79]

Therefore, instead of pursuing some missionary agenda or strategy, Baptists should "simply live." They need to "leave the bravado behind" and realize that "pioneering in an Orthodox country is wrong, as if we were the first Christians here." What Baptists need is "a revelation [from God] on how to live and work in this country." For this, they should "admit their weaknesses, come together, be obedient and faithful in abiding in God's calling, and pray," asking God for direction, and "sooner or later he will hear us and respond."[80] Finally, it is also very important to remember the now-neglected, but reliable path to church growth that helped Baptists expand their communities even during the time of repression: "The primary factor in church growth is healthy, large families, the heritage of the saints from the Lord. This is the main factor [that will define] the future of the church."[81]

Group Two: Revisions from the Innovators' Perspective

Reflections on the Experience of Baptist Mission in Russia

The leaders in this group agreed with the traditionalists that Baptist mission efforts in Russia over the past quarter of a century have not been overly successful. They also point to several objective, or social, factors that have affected the work of the gospel. In particular, massive religious curiosity following the breakup of the Soviet Union was not deeply spiritual in nature. Rather, it was stimulated by the ideological vacuum following the collapse of Communist ideology and curiosity about formerly prohibited religious ideas and practices. Post-Soviet people suddenly found themselves in a situation with "no meaning, no 'bright future,' no [meaningful] present: Who am I? Where am

---

79. ED5; D7.
80. D4.
81. P3; D4. A top denominational leader concurred with this thinking: "The whole idea that it is great to have many children so that we can bring them to the Lord is gone. We stopped encouraging it; we said that we needed missions to bring people from the world. But almost nothing has worked there for us anyway" (D4).

I? Total confusion."[82] But when those seekers discovered what Christianity was all about, they were not necessarily attracted to it.[83]

Second, the participants in this group largely agreed with the traditionalists that many were attracted to Baptist churches because of the humanitarian aid that was offered during the time of economic collapse following the breakup of the USSR, and that many of these people left as soon as the economy more or less stabilized. Some leaders mentioned a third important factor: genuine freedom for the open proclamation of the gospel in reality did not last long.[84] By 1997, the state-controlled media reverted to the old Soviet language of "cults and sects." Once again it became difficult to secure property for new church buildings or to rent facilities for church services.

Finally, the participants conceded that since "we live in an Orthodox country," it is simply a matter of fact that when someone "begins their search [for God], they first go to the Orthodox Church."[85] Given the fact that "these days in some [Orthodox] parishes there are biblical preaching, social services, and non-standard approaches" to evangelism, this is not necessarily bad. Yet there is the general recognition of the fact that the revitalization of Orthodoxy has diminished general interest in the evangelical faith among the Russian population.

At the same time, all the members of this group strongly rejected the suggestion that Russians are no longer interested in the gospel or that they have entered a time of eschatological "falling away." In fact, the innovators dismiss such ideas as "merely excuses."[86] They are convinced that Baptist mission efforts in Russia have not been successful primarily because of the way, consciously or unconsciously, Baptists have engaged in mission over the last quarter century. Eight primary factors that negatively affected the missionary potential of Baptist church emerged from the interviews.

---

82. D9.
83. D9.
84. D7.
85. P6.
86. D5; D10.

Lack of Spiritual, Intellectual, and Organizational Preparation

The time of freedom caught most of the church unawares. In the 1980s, the emphasis in preaching and teaching in local churches was on "correct beliefs" and "spirituality."[87] Baptists lived in "survival mode as [they] waited expectantly for Christ's return."[88] Consequently, there was "no thought or preparation" for what was to happen in society in the coming years. There were also "no materials on how to work with converts nor were enough brothers prepared to do so."[89] Organizationally, the union as a centralized structure proved ineffective either in "inspiring or organizing a strong movement to save sinners and plant churches."[90] The "power vertical"[91] was simply not able to either suggest a general strategy for missions or to encourage local initiatives necessary for successful mission engagement.[92] As a result, "most [church planting] movements [in Russia] were ignited by individuals who went against the prevailing ignorance and traditions."[93]

An Inward-Focused Church Life

All participants in the second group were strongly critical of Baptist self-absorption. An educator identified it as an "entrenched Christianity" which prefers to stay in its comfort zone and lacks love for sinners.[94] A pastor noted that the church-focused piety that developed in social isolation nurtured a number of "deep-seated reflexes as to what a good Christian and a good church should look like."[95] The most valuable asset for Baptist congregations

---

87. E7. One leader listed three primary sermon topics that were dominant when he was growing up: "The need to keep your clothes clean, readiness for Christ's coming [i.e., the rapture], and the return of prodigal sons [children from Christian families who had left the church]" (D2). Another leader admitted that the quality of preaching in many churches was "weak and ignorant" – not because of the church's failure, he added, but because this was "historically conditioned" (E1).

88. D2.

89. D7.

90. E7.

91. D8; P11.

92. In the words of one participant, the "habit of looking up at the superiors" when people "waited for their decision" often led to the loss of "personal self-sufficiency in ministry" (P11).

93. D10.

94. E8.

95. P4.

was a Christian whose concerns were in heaven and whose primary commitment was to his or her local church. A denominational leader commented:

> For seventy years they forced us behind a religious fence, [into] the realm of the "religious." They forced us to exercise our religious rites within the constraints of our buildings, never allowing us to take [our Christianity] outside. Christians have adopted this philosophy [as their own] . . . We focused on temple [church] worship, choirs, internal organization, improvements within, [and] beautiful buildings, having forgotten that this is not what we were saved for.[96]

He added that during the period of persecution, the concept of "brotherly fellowship" became one of the highest values for the church. As a result, when freedom came, Baptists saw it, first of all, as an opportunity for fellowship, not for outreach: "We used [freedom] to build more comfortable 'barns' for the saved [and] 'vacation houses' and 'resort places' for the church, rather than fishing facilities."

Some participants observed that initially leadership in many churches discouraged evangelism outside the church building.[97] Despite these bans, however, some "individual odd 'freaks' immediately got involved [in evangelism], although this was a very limited number of people."[98] The fact that the work of mission is still limited to just a few individuals is seen as "the primary paralysis of the evangelical movement in our country today." Had Baptists "reoriented ourselves from temple-focused service and the Baptist liturgy to evangelism, there would be many more churches today."[99]

Later, when more congregations became involved in evangelism, the model of mission that many churches adopted was naturally centripetal: the idea was that "they should come to us if they want the gospel."[100] In one participant's

---

96. D10.
97. "I was repeatedly told on many occasions that it was not the time to evangelize. They were persuading me to leave the streets . . . I am not even talking about forms of evangelism; the very idea of it was met with a less-than-positive attitude in many cases" (D3).
98. D10.
99. D10.
100. D10.

observation, Baptists "became like the Jews of Jonah's[101] day."[102] When few evangelists began planting new churches for converts who had grown up outside the Baptist subculture, this was often met with misunderstanding and criticism. Protectionist pastoral concerns outweighed evangelistic ones. One missionary leader shared:

> When we tried to incorporate newcomers into existing churches, we lost most of them. The fact is that [only] when a new church was intentionally planted did we retain more newcomers. But I was asked [by leaders of existing churches]: "Why new? Do you mean we are old? Are we not good enough for a church?" The regional leader actually said that new churches were "the work of the devil."[103]

Expressing frustration, most leaders in this group added that the centripetal model of mission has largely remained in place until today. As one educator observed: "Ideas [about mission] are around, courses are available, but [a mission mindset has] not been firmly planted within the evangelical culture. Information is available, but the worldview [of Baptists] has not been significantly transformed."[104] A denominational leader agreed that "mission has not yet become the whole church's work, as our budgets amply testify . . . Our first concern [is] self-feeding, church buildings, staff, and inside-the-church activities."[105] Another leader added: "Some [pastors] still think the work of God is to consume God's money with pomp, music, and [expensive] equipment. This is nothing but comfort and self-service."[106]

Lack of Follow-up and Discipleship

As seen by the members of this group, another major reason for the lack of substantial church growth was the churches' inadequate approaches to discipleship. In one regional leader's words, "We proved to be wonderful

---

101. What he was referring to was the Jewish religious ethnocentrism and contempt for Gentiles that is reflected in Jonah's attitude toward the Ninevites in the biblical book of Jonah.
102. P1.
103. D3.
104. P8.
105. D10.
106. D9.

evangelists, but poor pastors, counselors, and mentors."[107] Six primary aspects of this problem emerge from the data. First, the initiative for evangelistic campaigns often came from Western short-term missionary teams. The Westerners' approach, however, "was project-oriented; they proclaimed the gospel and then left."[108] This contributed to the impression that a presentation of the gospel was all people needed. A pastor observes that "for Paul, proclamation and discipleship together were both part of evangelism. But we somehow managed to separate one from the other."[109]

Second, the content of the proclamation often consisted of catchy slogans promising fast relief from personal or family problems. What should have been made clear was that the emotion-driven "sinner's prayer" following a passionate sermon was only the first step in the journey of faith – not a "miraculous spell" that breaks a person free from all their problems.[110] One pastor noted regarding many who left the church: "They might have been 'revived,' but they were not regenerated."[111]

Third, there was a lack of well-developed follow-up materials. An educator described the level of theological teaching he received after joining a Baptist church in the early 1990s: "It was more like the repeating of anecdotes received from earlier generations of preachers."[112] A regional leader added: "We told them, 'Your sins will be forgiven,' and they came forward and repented. What's next? Well, now attend church and perhaps one day you will reach heaven."[113] Another pastor complained that "we were not able to provide answers to their existential questions."[114]

Fourth, there were very few avenues for intentional discipleship, such as small groups or personal mentoring. In the Baptist "parish model" it was "assumed that the Sunday service was enough."[115] There were "almost no home Bible study groups where these people would receive care and [be

---

107. ED2.
108. ED5.
109. P1.
110. D1; E4.
111. P12; D6; D5.
112. E7.
113. P1.
114. ED2; D5.
115. D7.

helped to] grow. Even now there are very few [churches with a small group network]."[116] The lack of personal mentoring hindered new converts in developing deeper personal relationships with, and in becoming more involved in, their congregations. A regional leader said: "We conducted services but had little [by way of] personal relationships with them. But unless you let them into your life, the chances are high they will leave. They need to [be able to] observe a different [kind of] life and relationships."[117] One educator who himself became a Christian in the early 1990s commented that "there were, and still are, very few opportunities to get involved. As you prepare to be baptized, you go to classes. But after your baptism, you are left to yourself and must be equipped from sermons . . . [But] it is when you serve others that you grow. When you just sit in a pew, it becomes routine."[118] What made the integration of newcomers even more problematic was the fact that in Baptist communities there typically were strong family and business ties among the insiders, making it difficult for new attendees without a Baptist "pedigree" to move beyond their outsider status.[119]

Fifth, the overwhelming majority of participants in this group pointed out that discipleship, in most cases, was little more than acculturation into the specifically Baptist subculture. For decades, the "only known form of conversion was that of children who were growing up in Baptist families."[120] When such persons became Christians, they "simply became like others in the community. Their external conformity to the standards of the community was how [other members] evaluated [the authenticity of] their conversion."[121] When outsiders began joining Baptist churches en masse, mission-minded leaders discovered that "our people were simply unable to absorb [them]."[122] Newcomers were often met with suspicion because many of them had hard time acculturating into what they saw as a strange and narrow subculture. In fact, the pressure to conform often was a defensive reaction on the part of

---

116. D3.
117. P9.
118. E3; E7.
119. E7.
120. P4.
121. P4.
122. D3.

church leaders who feared that letting in many converts might pose a serious threat to the church's identity. These leaders "knew very well how to preserve themselves," but they were not prepared to accept people who reflected "worldly culture." As a result, "only the most determined and [spiritually] thirsty were able to digest our forms."[123] Many others "turned back . . . on our legalistic set of rules . . . and left for Orthodox or charismatic churches, or even for their homes."[124]

Lastly, the issue of disrespectful treatment of people repeatedly came up in the interviews. Unfortunately, public shaming or disrespect for individuals were not uncommon in Baptist churches. Sometimes during membership meetings the details of a person's private life or marriage relationship were publicly discussed. While this was done out of a perceived need for biblical holiness, it often resulted in the frustration and estrangement of members. An educational leader commented: "Our problem is that the Bible simply became the letter [of the law] for passing sentence."[125] One pastor admitted that "we failed to see the diversity of persons and cultures as part of God's design."[126]

Unwillingness to Adjust Worship Expressions

All the respondents in this group emphasized the fact that there was little, if any, inclination among Baptists to adjust their worship forms in order to make them more understandable to outsiders. One denominational leader explained: "We got used to our forms, and, I would say, viewed them as sacred, not caring about the way we were viewed from the outside. We thought that the forms and the meanings were the same."[127] A missionary leader added: "We sowed the gospel in a Baptist shell . . . without distinguishing between its cultural and spiritual aspects."[128] During the Soviet epoch, Baptists "created . . . a lower-than-average level culture which normal people found difficult to enter."[129] This subculture "is too complex; it adds too much to the gospel . . . [it] is encumbered with [merely] human views and ideas." Unlike

---

123. B10.
124. P1.
125. E6.
126. D10.
127. D10.
128. D2.
129. D10.

the traditionalists, the innovators tend to believe that an honest look at "the Christian culture" reveals that "there is no such thing: there is a small Baptist 'ethnicity' that created its own version of a closed culture within its narrow group." As a result, Baptists "became captive to their own past" and "spoke their own language" with society.[130]

Two participants in this group tried to explain Baptists' attitudes toward their worship forms by nothing but "egotism." They believe that some pastors were "simply comfortable without new people and wanted to retain their comfort."[131] Overall, this "valuing our forms more than the gospel" has seriously inhibited missional engagement with society.[132] A denominational leader summed up this concern as follows:

> By our worship forms and our ways of presenting the gospel, we have created a peculiar and very narrow stream [for people to become part of] the church. We have detached ourselves from the largest part of society, the middle class; our proclamation is not tuned for them – I mean a growing sector of the population who will never become very rich but are neither alcoholics nor drug addicts. We have nothing to offer them.[133]

A related factor that played a role in alienating potential members was the conviction of many Russian Baptists that their form of Christianity was "the true faith" and "the pure gospel."[134] It was not uncommon for Baptist preachers to denounce Orthodox Christians (or, for that matter, almost any other Christian groups) as "idolaters" or "false teachers." In one leader's words, Baptists "were preaching their denomination, but this pushes seekers away."[135] Moreover, whenever newcomers stayed in the church long enough, they would discover that the life of Baptist communities was often characterized

---

130. D10. One educational leader pointed out that in the 1920s Baptists were unencumbered by traditions and felt free to experiment with evangelistic forms and worship expressions (E3).

131. D2.

132. D3.

133. D10.

134. D5.

135. D6.

by power struggles, divisions over petty issues, or unresolved conflicts. A denominational leader was rather straightforward about it:

> We demanded that new believers be holy, but we ourselves were far from holy in the true sense of the word. [It is no wonder that] these demands caused aversion and resistance. What they heard from the pulpit were high-flying declarations, but the community itself was "regular," with its own shortcomings and failures, with an obvious lack of general culture, and with chummy manners.[136]

Attitudes toward the Outside Culture

Another important issue that seriously affected Baptist mission was their general perception of the culture of the society around them. One pastor who, before joining a Baptist church, directed the production of documentaries on state television shared his story to illustrate the effects of these attitudes in his own life:

> I knew that the brothers did not go to universities . . . They knew that the gospel was the core [of everything], and so they thought God did not need culture or anything. Everything will be burned up anyway. When I tried to disagree, they would tell me: "Don't you know your Bible? Take it and read again." And I agreed with them that perhaps it was my pride boiling in me. I wondered: When I stand before God, why would I bring into his presence perishable things? Does he really need them?[137]

He quit his job at the state television network, but today, fifteen years later, he is leading the only Christian school of video evangelism in Russia. A turning point for him was a conversation he had with a well-known Orthodox priest and intellectual, Benjamin Novik (1946 - 2010), who confided that he had considered joining a Baptist church during his spiritual quest. However, the primary reason he did not do so was that "Baptists do not like their own Russian culture."

---

136. D10.
137. E8.

For another pastor of a growing church, the turning point was when, as a student at a state university, he was given an assignment to read a portion of John Calvin's *Institutes* on the Christian view of secular vocation. He was rather shocked:

> Why did I never hear this from the pulpit? The whole idea that a believer is called to be a good smith or craftsman, or that he is to strive to make his city cleaner and beautiful – I just never heard this. What I was taught was that you don't need to get an education because Christ is coming soon. "Keep your soul clean, or he won't take you with him!"[138]

In response to a follow-up question about factors that shaped such attitudes, several leaders in this group pointed to the inability to bring together the spiritual and secular realms, rooted in Baptists' social isolation during the Soviet era. This dualism became ingrained in the traditional Baptist view of the world. A denominational leader observed: "Sometimes the world a pastor creates in his head is so small that others feel too tight in it. This alone can push out someone whose world is larger and broader."[139] An educator connected this with the prevailing social composition of Baptist communities: "Of course, social context plays into it as well. Baptists have been 'unschooled and ordinary men' on average, blue collar people and peasants. This is another inheritance of the Soviet era."[140]

Two other factors were mentioned: the eschatological doctrine of the imminent rapture and Baptists' restorationist ecclesiology. According to a seminary leader, both contributed to the development of a "short historical perspective" which is not conducive to cultural engagement. The length of time between Christ's first coming and his *parousia* "proves to be complex for those who aspire to restore the model of the early church. We are simply unprepared to think deeply about how we are supposed to live in the world until Christ comes again."[141] A denominational leader agreed: "We live one day at a time: if we have food and clothing, thanks to God. As soon as you

---

138. P1.
139. D8.
140. E6.
141. E6.

start talking about some greater goals, you face 'theological' arguments that we 'know neither the day nor the hour.' That is why our aspirations are so limited."[142] As a result, "We don't care about culture, although it could become a link connecting us with unbelievers."[143]

A related factor is that it has become habitual in many congregations "not to prepare thoroughly for worship services, or to conduct them in a shabby manner. [We think] why care if we sing in a sloppy manner, if everything is for God's glory anyway?"[144] He continues: "Intelligentsia would not feel comfortable in many of our churches due to the quality of our worship or the vocabulary of our preaching." When touching upon the fact that in many churches today new members are added primarily through rehabilitation centers for alcoholics and drug addicts, an educator voiced his concern:

> Perhaps it is our uneasiness about evangelizing the broader society and our lack of ability to do so [effectively]. Our format is more attractive to risk groups where things are black and white, where people are on the brink, and where they experience their salvation in the strongest terms."[145]

Social Marginality

Several ministers in this group agreed with the traditionalists that another significant reason for the lack of missionary success was the perceived social status of Baptist churches. The "pressure of the minority complex," as one leader put it, was especially hard to bear for "students, young professionals, or those working in tight groups."[146] Yet unlike the traditionalists, the participants in this group suggested that Baptists themselves tended to accept outsiders' views of themselves as if they were true. In the words of a denominational leader: "We, of course, dressed it in a spiritual explanation. But in practice it does not matter. The main thing is that we have accepted

---

142. D8.
143. E8.
144. D6.
145. E6.
146. P1.

[the view] that we are a foreign community here, that we are not part of our people. We do not proclaim it, but we agree with it on the inside."[147]

Another denominational leader added: "We do not see ourselves as part of this society, its history and its culture. We are tearing ourselves away from this space."[148] In fact, in the context of freedom it was rather internal (that is, self-imposed) aspects of marginalization that have hindered Baptists from growing as rapidly as, for instance, charismatic churches did in Russia:

> [Their members are] yesterday's converts with no past. They did not have this internal limitation factor, so they openly and confidently got involved in business or the government. They had never seen themselves as "enemies of the people"; rather, they were an organic part of [society]. That is why they were able to integrate easily, without internal stresses . . . Our specific view of the world was the primary thing that held us back.[149]

Lack of Qualified Missionary Leaders

A pastor from Moscow shared that after the 1992 Billy Graham "Revival" crusade in Moscow, about one hundred groups of converts were started in the city.[150] But there were simply not enough committed and qualified people, as well as not enough worship facilities for developing these groups into church plants. Emigration to the West was always mentioned first in the list of reasons for this situation: "We lost good, active, and capable people."[151] Not only active, but many potential leaders as well "used the open doors to leave."[152] At the same time, unlike the participants in the first group, the innovators emphasized that there was a positive side to emigration. As one educator put it: "We must admit that our missionary potential was significantly undermined by the emigration. Yet on the other hand, it rid congregations of the most

---

147. D10.
148. D8.
149. D10.
150. P11.
151. D3.
152. E3.

numbed, stiff, and conservative members which gave us an opportunity to pour in some new wine."[153]

Another important reason behind the lack of qualified leaders was the breach of generational succession that took place in many congregations with the coming of freedom. New opportunities to evangelize created two opposite drives among Baptist leaders: some rushed to use them, leaving the "entangling" church traditions behind, "diving into freedom," and "breaking free from the roots."[154] Many older-generation leaders, on the contrary, were "terrified" as they watched these "experiments." They perceived them as a "threat" and "took them with hostility." Often, breaches in relationships between "mature leaders with pastoral experience" and "dynamic young leaders with energy" followed. As a result, the preparation of new missionary leaders had to be "reduced" to academic education in newly established theological schools run by diverse Western mission organizations, sometimes with "conflicting agendas and philosophies of education."[155]

In addition, religious freedom brought with it a "job fair of ministry opportunities" offered by foreign mission agencies. They extended many young leaders tempting invitations to "self-realization," which, in one leader's assessment, "turned Christianity into a decent business."[156] All of the above factors contributed to the decrease in the quality of leadership and, in the end, to weakening Baptist mission efforts.

Financial Issues

The final factor behind the lack of mission success, according to the innovators, had to do with the issue of finances. An educator from this group expressed their sentiments as follows:

> We must admit that in the 1990s the impetus toward mission came from foreign missionaries, and that the whole enterprise

---

153. E6. One minister compared emigration with the events surrounding Israel's exodus from Egypt: "The people with a slave mentality died out in the wilderness. In our case, [the Lord] sent them to America, because he knew they would not be able to use the time of freedom [productively]" (P11). This evaluation may be too strong, yet it reflects the general tone in most of the interviews. Emigration "swept out and cleaned out the church, so that the places [of those who left] could be filled by others" (D3).

154. P4.

155. P4.

156. E6.

was financed from abroad. This was a tremendous blessing, but we lost [the] financial self-sufficiency [we had before that time]. Plus, we never actually asked until recently: what can we ourselves do for the sake of our mission?[157]

Paradoxically, where there was much foreign support, the work "did not really advance."[158] This was especially true when pastors and missionaries received regular salaries from foreign agencies. In these cases, their churches "did not care much about their ministries because they did not invest in them from their own pockets."[159] In fact, many of them "are still barely interested, because [they] hardly sacrifice anything for either mission or social service." A denominational leader agreed: "The negative side [of Western financial help] was that they did not pass along the idea that we had to contribute as well – [the idea] that they were [only] sowing what we should then have watered."[160] Worse still, there have been cases when Western funding sometimes corrupted ministers who were tempted to propose fake projects that might interest donors.

A denominational leader through whom large amounts of foreign aid were channeled concluded: "Baptists did not grow because of wrong approaches to leadership, including the absence of teaching about the church's need to achieve financial self-sufficiency."[161] While outside support was, perhaps, indispensable for large one-time projects such as the purchase or construction of facilities or the publishing of literature, it did not encourage local ownership and created long-term dependencies. Therefore, the "everyday day life of a [local] church and its evangelistic outreach, these should be supported by the church itself."[162]

Suggested Missiological Revisions

In keeping with their understanding of the reasons for the lack of missionary success, the innovators identified several areas that need to be reconsidered if

---

157. E6.
158. D3.
159. D5.
160. D10.
161. P11.
162. D10; D6; D5.

Baptist mission in Russia is to achieve more going forward. Their suggestions are summarized in ten broad categories below.

Rediscovering the Church's Missional Calling

All the respondents in this group expressed in various ways the conviction that Baptist congregations need to recover the primary purpose of their existence, namely, mission. Due to historical influences, Baptists "reduced [this purpose] to catering to [their] own spiritual needs."[163] Even after twenty-five years of freedom, many "have not yet begun to see [them]selves as God's voice [and] his instrument for taking the message of salvation" to the Russian people.[164] Baptists should learn to "think of Russia as our mission field, to dream of something bigger and more impossible than maintaining our own little flock."[165] Another minister burst out rather emotionally: "Stop fattening yourselves and go to the world! Bring in your neighbor and dilute your church's blood with outside people. Turn the ministry paradigm inside out."[166]

A pastor of a large urban church suggested that underlying Baptists' introversion was a failure to grasp the broader meaning of the good news: "This all comes from a lack of understanding of the gospel. Until we understand who we are as representatives of the kingdom, we won't see who we are and what we exist for."[167] The reality is that "introvert[ed congregations] will not grow."[168] In fact, they won't grow spiritually either because "faith grows in us when we sow it widely." A denominational leader summarized his view of the connection between mission and the church's health in the following way:

> If a church has no purpose, it is destined to become sick. Quarrels will arise. The more you feed them, the more they will become sick, because a person who only eats and does not work inevitably gets ill – physically, spiritually, and emotionally. Only when a church is busy serving can it thrive. Otherwise, it

---

163. D2.

164. D10. Sometimes this self-absorption was described in vivid and strong language: "We have coated our 'ark of salvation' with pitch inside and out and are suffocating inside from the stink of our own socks" (D3).

165. D1.

166. P11.

167. D5.

168. D2.

will be like a mammoth that is heading for extinction, no matter how large it is.[169]

This outward turn needs to have several dimensions. First, Baptists should be intentional and proactive: "We must go to people . . . We must learn to initiate conversations, to invite people. Our people are afraid of unbelievers."[170] Second, mission should become each Christian's calling in every area of their personal, family, and public lives: "Individual evangelists can set a good example, but they won't change the big picture. Mission should be planted in each person's heart."[171] Another minister added, "We tend to think that the preaching of the gospel happens [only] from the pulpit. But God has [given to each of] us a responsibility for our home, our school, and our work." The task is to "make every Christian a minister wherever they are."[172] Admittedly, not every believer is a gifted evangelist. Yet, each "can participate . . . through their prayers, through godly living, or financially," by supporting either "short-term trips or long-term missions."[173]

Third, the concept of mission itself needs reconsideration so that the emphasis is placed on the missional calling of a local church in its own environment. One leader said:

> When we hear the word "mission" we immediately think of somewhere out there, Cambodia [perhaps]. We should [instead] emphasize mission in *our* city, in *our* neighborhoods: your church must be a church for *your* neighborhood . . . God has been growing your church as a beacon for some people in your city who need to come to the Lord. Who are these people? Start praying and you will see them.[174]

Fourth, this outward turn requires a willingness to relinquish control of newly planted churches – not only with regard to leadership, but sometimes

---

169. D10.

170. D3; D2; D5.

171. E3.

172. Again and again in the innovators' interviews this idea of making "every Christian a missionary," or a witness for Christ, came to the fore as the most important prerequisite for successful Baptist mission in Russia.

173. P10.

174. D10.

even with regard to doctrinal teaching or denominational allegiance. One leader said: "We erroneously think: why be divided[175] if there are only 100,000 people in our city? It is not that I encourage divisions; I just say that we should not hinder the growth of what God is building up. Bless them instead, and let them gather separately."[176]

Fifth, the innovators typically emphasized that, in addition to a desire to change, structural and institutional adjustments may be needed. One pastor thinks that active believers are too overloaded with "church activities – choir practices, committee meetings, prayer gatherings, and weekly worship gatherings." What is needed is the "setting apart of a special time" for engaging with outsiders.[177] A denominational leader suggested that, perhaps, some sort of general, all-union strategy of mission needs to be adopted by all, or most, churches in the RUECB.[178]

A Fresh Look at the Content of the Gospel Presentation

Two of the respondents in this group shared their convictions that the most important aspect of Baptist mission that needs revision is the way the gospel is understood and proclaimed. Baptists "try [again and again] to preach it according to a certain formula we once learned," but their presentation of the gospel "suffers from oversimplification [such as] the Four Spiritual Laws: Christ died for you, you are saved, hallelujah – with very little effort to explain how all of it works."[179] One missing element is the emphasis on the relevance of the gospel for one's present life in this world: "the key thing for the Reformers was abiding in Christ, that is, how to be connected to him and how to live out *his* life [here and] now."[180] Another problem is that the traditional gospel message does not encourage Christian involvement in

---

175. That is, to plant a new church by letting a group of members worship in a different place.

176. D2.

177. P9.

178. D10. A proposal of such a strategy is currently being discussed by the union leadership. The strategy begins with the intentional involvement of every Christian in personal evangelism (M1), moves to regional church planting by the common efforts of the churches in that region (M2), and then moves still further to the establishment of a mission society at the union level for intercultural mission in Russia and beyond (M3).

179. E7.

180. P1.

society either: "In addition to [our] gospel, our understanding of human life is [also] oversimplified."

One result of this is that Baptist preaching tends to attract those who already feel alienated from society for personal reasons. A denominational leader put it rather bluntly:

> The gospel we proclaim is for . . . wimps, because all we preach is God's comfort and love. Rarely do we preach a gospel that challenges people; a gospel that is beautiful and engaging, calling people to make every effort to reach the height of their human potential; a gospel of a person in Christ; a gospel of victory."[181]

In fact, in his view this is the main reason why Baptists have so many "hapless, divorced, disadvantaged women" in their ranks. "A 'primitive' gospel," he continued, "does not work for 'normal' people." A less radical, but pointed analysis from an educational leader goes along similar lines: "We say that we need to go to universities, but what message will we take there? What kinds of questions will we raise there, and what answers do we have to offer there?" In fact, drug rehabilitation ministries work, because "people who go there have a specific need, a burning issue. Are we aware of the burning issues and needs in the broader society?"[182]

The above considerations also highlight the urgency of contextualization. Without it, Baptists won't be able to engage their society: "To be accepted, we must be understood. What we preach today is often simply incomprehensible." But the gospel message is "beautiful if understood."[183] An educator concluded that the early evangelical movement in Russia grew mainly because its members "spoke in the language of their time and went to where people were rather than waiting for them to come; their worship forms, their music, and even the pro-socialist terminology they adopted were relevant for their time."[184] The church today also must learn to "understand society and people's needs and adapt its [presentation of the] gospel to them."[185] This process

---

181. D10.
182. E4.
183. D10.
184. E3.
185. D1.

involves more than purely intellectual efforts, however: "We need both the ability to adapt to the [current] situation and the spiritual ability to listen to God as [he reveals to us] where he is leading us."[186]

A related issue has to do with methods of evangelism. An often-heard comment in this group was that "no single method will change everything; instead, we should advance in all directions."[187] In other words, Baptists should be "looking for contemporary ways and forms of sharing the gospel, for quality materials, and for high-quality evangelistic ministries." What counts is both "holiness *and* professionalism, faithfulness *and* creativity."[188] The specific examples some ministers provided revealed their preference for informal – that is, interpersonal and relational – approaches to evangelism: "Play chess; go fishing and hunting with them. The average person needs someone to be friends with."[189] Another pastor argued that "it is better to instruct youth in how to engage in a [spiritual] conversation in a café than to plan an evangelistic concert. We baptize many more people after the former than after the latter."[190]

Generally, the innovators agreed that traditional approaches to evangelism that are focused on proclamation alone would not produce church growth. Many of them suggested that in the current situation some of the most effective evangelistic approaches could be identified as pre-conversion discipleship methods. In other words, the goal is not "simply to hand out a tract and invite [someone] to a church service," but to initiate a "prayerful, personal mentoring that helps lead a person to a relationship with Christ." It takes "walking alongside them from [the beginning], sharing the gospel, going with them through the struggles of conversion, counseling and caring for them."[191] Reorienting local congregations toward adopting these methods, however, will require time and intentional efforts: "Mentoring others to Christ should be in every believer's DNA, but [teaching] this [approach] will require five

---

186. D1.
187. E1.
188. E1.
189. D10.
190. P1.
191. P6; D8. One missionary leader described this approach as the "222" method, which refers to his understanding of 2 Timothy 2:2 ("And the things you have heard me say in the presence of many witnesses entrust to reliable men who will also be qualified to teach others.")

or ten years of intensive work, plus another ten years for every year when we do not do anything."[192]

Holistic Approaches to Mission

For the innovators, expressions of social care tend to have intrinsic value as an integral part of the church's mission. The significance of social service does not really depend on whether it can serve as an opportunity for evangelism; rather, it is viewed as a natural extension of the kingdom's life beyond the church's boundaries.[193] From this perspective, a denominational leader expressed his regrets that "this ministry is not among the chief priorities" at the level of the union.[194] When asked to name some social ills for which evangelicals could possibly provide solutions, the participants in this group included alcoholism, drug addiction, the high divorce rate, large number of orphaned children, growing numbers of prisoners, etc.

A top denominational leader participant suggested that Baptists have a potential go beyond acts of mercy toward engaging with social, cultural, and even political issues. He asked rhetorically:

> Where are our Daniels and Josephs who could speak wisely in order to end violence or ethnic strife? . . . [Why is] the level of our claims, requests, and decisions mostly restricted to our personal concerns, our families, and our narrow circles? Because this is how we think of Christianity . . . But I would strive toward an increasingly higher level of problems to which we could dare to suggest our answers.[195]

In reality, what hinders Baptists' involvement with the outside world is a lack of theological reflection on things outside of the ecclesiastical issues: "It is necessary to speak about developing worldviews which would embrace more sizable tasks. The solution lies, in part, in the area of education." Therefore,

---

192. P6.
193. E1; E4; E7.
194. D5.
195. D8.

he continued, "If I could, I would make it obligatory for every pastor to have both theological and general higher education."[196]

The Need for More Robust Discipleship Approaches

The participants in this group regularly expressed the need for more intentional approaches to discipleship. Two pastors made participation in spiritual accountability groups mandatory for new converts: "If you don't participate in a group, you cannot become a member in my church,"[197] and "We don't baptize anyone who does not regularly attend a group."[198] Discipleship should go beyond the basics of Christian life and the teaching of doctrine: "The church must teach systematic theology. Believers in local communities [often] function on the basis of [their] emotions, not on the convictions of faith."[199] Another important element of discipleship is teaching the missional identity of the church and the missionary calling of individual believers:

> In this teaching there should sound a striking chord: you are God's instrument for spreading the gospel – through your personal relationships at your workplace, through being sent, or through donating funds, etc. We need to start preaching the gospel in its full scope, changing the consciousness of believers: we do not exist just to die in the pews. This must change radically.[200]

As a result of these efforts, "missionary consciousness" should become "the internal conviction of every believer." It is not just "an idea for some freaks"; anyone who has accepted Christ "should become a missionary in the broad sense of the word."[201]

Openness to Society and Culture

Among the participants in this group there is an awareness of the need for more intentional social and cultural engagement: "We close ourselves up from the world not because outsiders want us to, but because *we* are not able

---

196. So far, neither has been a requirement for ordination and most likely will not be in the foreseeable future.
197. D3.
198. D10.
199. D10.
200. D10; P1.
201. D10.

to work with them. We and they speak different languages. We need to open the church doors."²⁰² Historically, Baptists "lost their social links. The world is here, but we live as if we were on another planet. We are hardly interested in them, and they are hardly interested in the gospel."²⁰³ Engaging with culture could become a vital "connecting link" for bridging this divide, because a large part of "culture does not contradict [the gospel] and, in fact, complements it."²⁰⁴ Unfortunately "the very word 'culture' is almost foreign to us."²⁰⁵

To overcome their anti-cultural heritage, Baptists should work on "getting educated" and on "meriting the respect and trust of society" by their involvement with other people.²⁰⁶ Since Baptists are "not easily welcomed in society, [they] should work twice as hard to be heard."²⁰⁷ They need to become "curious" people who "read, understand, and are understandable, and who speak in contemporary idiom rather than in the language of liturgy," which many don't comprehend.²⁰⁸ Theologically, this engagement is rooted in the fact that "Christ is the Savior both in eternity and here," and that he "cares about everything [we] do on earth."²⁰⁹ Through his Spirit, he works within us "holy strivings toward both spiritual and material things."²¹⁰ In practice, this requires that ministers themselves "grow continually, because otherwise they will pull those around them down to their own [level]."²¹¹

Biblically based cultural engagement will allow Baptists to "enter into dialogue" with diverse social groups, as well as to carry their mission into all areas of life.²¹² A denominational leader identified several "eyes" through

---

202. P11.

203. E8.

204. E8.

205. D8.

206. D1.

207. D8.

208. D5; D1.

209. D8.

210. D8. When asked how this understanding is compatible with the version of annihilationist eschatology that the Russian Synodal Translation seems to uphold, this leader said: "Well, [the Bible] does say that everything will eventually be burned up. But until then people can benefit from our cultural [involvement]. It has been like this for twenty centuries already, and no one knows when the end will come. [Besides,] while the world will be burned up, we will remain. The most important thing, therefore, is who we become in the process."

211. E8.

212. E8.

which society "perceives the world": the media, culture, sports, leisure, etc.[213] When Baptist presence is discernible there, it "demonstrates that we are not sectarians." Another pastor calls these areas the "doors through which we can enter people's lives."[214] In particular, Baptists could intentionally study and use the riches of Russian culture (e.g., writers such as Dostoevsky and Tolstoy) when sharing the gospel with "cultured" people: "If they [secular Russians] honor Dostoevsky, I will study him in order to open up a dialogue and to make the gospel interesting to them. In this way . . . they can see that what Dostoevsky said has everything to do with the gospel."[215] But cultural engagement should also embrace mundane things that are the concern of the average person. One leader put it ironically: Baptist "preaching is often emasculated . . . and churchly . . . because preachers do not interact with unbelievers on the street . . . [They] would hardly even notice if a nuclear explosion happened outside."[216]

Attitudes toward the Baptist Subculture

Every participant in this group commented on the need to reevaluate the traditional Baptist subculture. The pastor of a growing urban church said: "We tend to think like religious people, in terms of maintaining our tradition rather than in terms of the gospel. I personally struggled with my religiosity in order to remold my DNA into a more gospel-shaped form."[217] One aspect of this "reshaping of one's DNA" involves a willingness to welcome and accept changes that newcomers with little or no church background bring to the table of worship and ministry. This starts with a respectful stance toward the work of the Holy Spirit in them:

> Every individual has a [unique] personality; they are a temple of the Holy Spirit. Each person uniquely refracts the Scriptures in themselves. So each one can both receive something *from* me and also give something *to* me – especially when they are

---

213. D1.
214. D10.
215. E8.
216. D2.
217. P1.

highly educated persons or professionals. This was how the early church was enriched.[218]

Respecting the work of the Spirit in newcomers may also mean injecting more personal testimonies into traditional, monologue-style worship services. Even those who have not yet formally become members but faithfully attend the church deserve to be "given a voice in the church."[219] This respect is also manifested in a gentle and reasonable approach to things such as dress styles, the use of cosmetics, jewelry, etc. An experienced pastor and denominational leader said: "Don't disturb her for wearing a miniskirt. Teach her the fear of God and after a month she herself will change her dress. You will be amazed at how everything changes in her."[220]

Admittedly, these approaches will inevitably transform the local church, with both positive and negative effects being a possibility. One pastor said: "There is nothing bad in the fact that [newcomers] see things differently than I do. I believe they won't bring anything bad, because they fear God and love him just as [I do]."[221] Other participants took a somewhat more cautious stance: "The main thing is that we do not distort the gospel."[222] To ensure that the gospel is intact, critical discernment is needed with respect to both cultural trends and internal church culture. Pastors should "teach their people to evaluate things critically. This is something we have a hard time with. We should not be afraid to approach things from a critical angle, whether it is in our sermons, in our understanding of the Bible, or in life around us." This process requires "the minister's education, his boldness, and his responsibility."[223]

Unlike the traditionalists, the respondents in this group normally did not see any conflict between the guidance of the Spirit and theological knowledge. In fact, serving God requires both: "Preparation must be at the highest level, so that our services will provide visitors with genuine spiritual food. We need

---

218. D9.
219. D10.
220. D10.
221. P8.
222. D3.
223. E4.

the Holy Spirit as well as knowledge, skills, and competence."[224] Unfortunately, the value of theological education is not yet recognized in many local churches. An educational leader complained:

> You go to a church and listen to the preaching there. Young brothers, obviously talented, come forward and . . . talk pure nonsense, [which they think they received] by "revelation." What amazes me most is that people respond with prayers. Perhaps the language is familiar for everybody, and there is little demand for something deeper.[225]

According to the innovators, this attitude has to change if Baptist mission work is to be successful in Russia. The mere "reproduction of a hundred-year-old ritual and plaintive songs will attract only a small percentage of individuals – people who are willing to embrace such a form of religion. We won't ever reach the bulk of the population."[226] Baptists need to "leave behind the routine, the beaten path, and the comfort zone of tradition; we need to start living by the gospel."[227] Some of the most commonly recommended changes in worship services include (1) moving beyond ritualism and formalism; (2) avoiding insincerity and quasi-spiritual pomp; and (3) aiming worship services at broader social groups, especially youth and men. Traditionally, they have been largely "designed for grandmothers."[228]

Openness toward Other Christian Denominations

Members of this group expressed willingness to work together and build bridges of fellowship with Christians of other denominations. The pastor of a recently planted urban church said that it is "difficult and actually unnecessary to prove the superiority of one denomination over another."[229] Each group has its own "unique strengths that can be adopted [by others]. Remain

---

224. E1.
225. E3.
226. E1.
227. D2.
228. D10.
229. P11.

within your own [denomination], but see what you can learn from others."[230] This denominational leader took his point one step further:

> The boundaries between different denominations are gradually being erased, and the difference between nominal, or traditional, believers and true believers in any group is becoming more and more visible. It is the latter who will become the instrument of any [future] revival in Russia."[231]

One implication of this openness is that Baptists should learn how "to think about the kingdom in broader terms: not only to convert more people to the Baptist faith, but to see a greater presence of the kingdom in society and in the world."[232] An educator put his concern as follows:

> While we should work to see more people join our churches, the belief in our exceptionality is a disturbing symptom ... Our purpose is not simply to recruit people into our ranks. Of course, we need to know why we are called by this name [Baptists], just as we need to value our heritage. But sometimes, when we think that our only purpose is to make them come to us, these narrowly conceived denominational interests tend to predominate over the interests of the kingdom of God.[233]

Open-mindedness toward the broader Christian community inevitably invites a re-examination of Baptists' own identity and uniqueness. An educational leader commented: "Whether we like it or not, there are other Christians here ... What is our [unique] place? It seems to me that we have no answer [to this question], or it has not been formulated clearly enough. This is where we should direct our efforts."[234]

---

230. D2.
231. D2.
232. E6.
233. E6.
234. E4.

Institutional Dynamics

Several participants in this group pointed to institutionalism as a major obstacle to the effectiveness of Baptist mission work in Russia.[235] From their perspective, the union is struggling with problems common to many organizations. An educator offered the following explanation to the lack of mission success in comparison to the explosive growth of Baptist congregations in the 1920s with: "Perhaps this is the 'three generation' thing: pioneers are followed by interpreters, who are in turn followed by nominal members, who do things by inertia. Perhaps we have entered the third stage."[236] Some other interviewees commented that "Christ created a movement, not an institution,"[237] whereas "we have built the institution of the Baptist denomination."[238] As a result, institutional dynamics "hinder our mission," making Baptist churches "inflexible."[239]

One way in which institutionalism has become an obstacle to Baptist mission is seen in the fact that structures focus on their own survival: "We have become a self-sufficient structure that keeps perpetuating its own existence."[240] A former denominational leader who is now a pastor illustrated the effect of this in his own life: "I left my work at the union's office because I did not want to waste my life with never-ending trips and non-essential meetings."[241] Another aspect of the problem is that there is little understanding of what specific role the administrative structure must fulfill at this time. A seminary leader commented, "Initially, the union was created to help churches evangelize. Later it supported them during persecutions. Now its role is not clearly defined."[242]

Further, the top-down way the union is structured tends to stifle initiative at the grassroots level. An educator observed: "The union was designed to function in a way that was parallel to how the Soviet apparatus worked.

---

235. P1; D2; D3; D7.
236. E3.
237. D2.
238. D10; P1.
239. D2.
240. E1.
241. P1.
242. E7; P1.

Today external conditions have changed, but the structure remains basically the same, which does not encourage effectiveness."[243] A primary concern is that the union has become "a hierarchy-centered, not church-centered, structure."[244] As such, it "restricts and hinders our efforts" in mission. For instance, "Although we are not Orthodox, unless [senior] brothers have blessed me, I won't do [some specific] work [of ministry] . . . We thus sanctify the structure more than the gospel."[245]

Lastly, some participants pointed out that the work of the Baptist Union is subject to organizational life cycles: "A stone thrown up stops and remains still before it begins falling down."[246] From a more radical perspective, "No president [of the union] has been able to admit the bankruptcy of the system, which means that it is not susceptible to resuscitation; we just have to wait for the death of the system."[247] However, most participants take a more moderate position in this respect. The following comment expresses their views: "Based on management theories, we have already moved to the stage of dying, not just that of stagnation. But there are some steps that still can be made – steps that are more or less radical."[248]

The innovators suggested several avenues that might catalyze institutional renewal. First, a clear guiding vision should be developed as the basis for unity and partnership. The problem today lies "precisely in the absence of such ideology."[249] This vision should be mission-focused rather than maintenance-focused: "The administrative structure [must] be subjugated to the spiritual, and evangelism [must] saturate all the departments [of the union]."[250] The union's vision should also be broad enough to embrace the growing diversity of Baptist churches while protecting their essential identity. One pastor spoke of the need to put together a statement of Baptist identity analogous to *The Book of Concord* in Lutheranism.[251]

---

243. E7.
244. P1.
245. D2.
246. D3.
247. P12.
248. P1.
249. P1.
250. P10.
251. P1.

Second, the central office in Moscow should stop seeing itself as a governing body and start seeing its role in coordination and representation. In fact, this model corresponds more closely with Baptists' belief in local church autonomy than a form of "an episcopalian system." As a superstructure, the union should "serve churches rather than use them for *its* projects."[252] Unlike the traditionalists, the participants in this group tend to see the president of the union not as a fatherly figure, but as a visionary leader. A Moscow pastor commented:

> To have a [spiritual] father is great, but as you grow you need a leader with whom you want to work alongside. When you have problems, you need a father. But a thoughtful leader will develop others to maturity rather than to dependency. What we need is a strategic leader, a colleague.[253]

Overall, Baptists need to "return to the priority of the local church." In the final analysis, only churches "give birth to churches; structures give birth to nothing." In fact, "all structures worldwide are tending to become looser rather than tighter." Therefore, there is "no point in strengthening what is not going to last; individuals and churches are what really matter."[254] The existing administrative structure, however, can be of much help if it becomes a platform for dialogue and the sharing of resources. A regional leader said: "There is little by way of a working dialogue. Our congresses are more like official celebrations characterized by formalism."[255] Another pastor added: "What we need is not an administrative center, but rather a base that connects regional associations of churches to one another. We are not poor and could easily enrich one another, depending on who has the abundance of what: some [have] musicians, some have literature, some have other gifts."[256] In the end, "the stronger local churches are, the stronger the union is."[257]

---

252. P1.
253. P1.
254. P1.
255. D6.
256. D5.
257. P1.

Baptists as an Alternative Community

Several participants suggested that Russia might soon experience a strong backflow from the semi-official Orthodox Church caused by mass frustration with the repressive approaches of its leadership.[258] In this connection, the idea of the Baptist (or, more broadly, evangelical) community as an alternative society kept recurring during the interviews. A seminary leader, looking back at Baptist history, affirmed that "in Soviet times, evangelicals represented an alternative view of the world. While definitely not politically dissident, intellectually it was an alternative vision [of society]."[259] A pastor added that this was one of the reasons people flocked to evangelical churches immediately after the collapse of the Communist state.[260]

These days, however, evangelical leaders are "trying to become as much like the Orthodox Church as possible, saying, 'We are not sectarians, and we also have a history here.'" The problem with these attempts is that "we have lost the vision of what it means to be a social alternative," which may "damage our ministry in the long run."[261] Three main areas in particular were suggested by the participants in this group in which evangelicals could serve as a genuine alternative to the dominant church. These are: (1) healthy marriage and family life; (2) respectful leadership styles; and (3) responsible service in the larger society for the common good.

As Russian society is experiencing a severe marriage crisis,[262] it desperately needs "tangible examples of strong families, of the mutual responsibility of spouses, and of raising obedient children."[263] Baptist families can be such examples provided that they do not conform to their society in this respect. When it comes to the issue of leadership, it must begin with deep respect for every person: "Christ gives back to each of us our human dignity . . . We should strive for . . . sensitivity to and respect for others. People want to be

---

258. D3; D2; D9.

259. E6.

260. D7.

261. E4.

262. According to the United Nations, between 2004 and 2008 Russia had the highest divorce rate of any nation. United Nations Statistics Division, "Demographic and Social Statistics," accessed 27 August 2017, https://unstats.un.org/unsd/demographic/products/dyb/dyb2008.htm.

263. D5.

accepted no matter what their past may have been. We need to respect the personhood of every individual."[264] Another pastor contrasted this approach to leadership with the predominant treatment of individuals in Russian society:

> We are still in that Soviet system in which an individual was [merely] a cog in a machine . . . Serfdom is still present; it is in human heads and hearts. "The master will come and decide." Our task as the church is to allow individuals to be free, to enable them as agents who can express themselves and contribute [to the church] – not to humiliate them [in response to] their past sins, but to trust them. In this way we will be truly needed in this society.[265]

Given their heritage of authoritarian leadership, Baptists will "need to reconsider their 'power vertical' approach and start searching for other leadership models."[266] Instead of "beating [members] on their heads by exposing their every fault," leaders need to "change their tone of voice from that of bosses to that of trainers who teach people about the love and power of Christ amidst the realities of life."[267] This can help solve the leadership crisis within Baptist churches. One problem that causes it is that many leaders largely "gather obedient executers around themselves; they don't know how to work together with other able leaders."[268] As a result, there are "plenty of potential leaders in local churches, but we tend to press them into a specific mold." Instead, we should allow them "to develop according to the way God is leading each of them" personally. This requires "trust, delegation, and opportunities to contribute."[269]

Finally, a commitment to work for the common good of society, starting at the neighborhood level, would be perceived as a genuine alternative to the currently atomized state of Russian society. In the words of one pastor:

---

264. D2. Literally, he said, "We must respect the human being in every human being."
265. D5.
266. P11.
267. D8.
268. P1.
269. D2; D5; D10.

Russians generally don't like to accept personal responsibility for their lives. They like to be dependent [on the authorities]. If we believers took it on ourselves, we could demonstrate to the world that something can be changed [for the better]. What it takes is to view ourselves as representative of God's kingdom on the earth. Then it [would be] quite possible to influence society.[270]

Prayer and Partnering with God in Mission

Some leaders in this group confessed Baptists' "conspicuous lack of prayer" for reaching their fellow countrymen: "We pray too little about it; perhaps we have become callous and do not see how God is working" or "where he wants to lead us." God wants believers to remain "sensitive to his actions in [their] lives" and to be able to "listen spiritually to God."[271] At the same time, the participants in this group generally tended to disagree with the traditionalists that spiritual revival comes unilaterally from God. Besides prayer, Christians need to learn how "to work together with God."[272] What Baptists need today is an "emphasis on *both* holiness *and* professionalism, *both* righteousness *and* creativity."[273] The work of the Holy Spirit does not cancel the need for "knowledge, skills, abilities, and competence."[274] Likewise, a lack of visible results does not necessarily mean that God is not pleased with evangelical ministries: "If we choose to focus on the work [of mission], obstacles will come. We need committed Christians, even if they are few. And God will bless [their work] spiritually."[275]

Finally, this group's thinking reflects a cautious optimism regarding evangelical mission in Russia. They passionately reject the idea that Russians today have little or no interest in the gospel. One denominational worker said: "I am hearing this all the time, but this is just an excuse. The gospel works everywhere and all the time."[276] A pastor added: "Some say it is a sign of the

---

270. D5.
271. D1.
272. P6.
273. E1.
274. E1.
275. P9.
276. D1.

times or is how people are today. But I believe the gospel is the same; the key is in knowing how to apply it."[277] They also tend to discard the "nostalgic" idea of persecution as the catalyst of church growth: "My experience tells me that the church does not grow under persecution."[278] Instead, "Let's learn the secret of serving Christ when [conditions are] peaceful."[279]

Overall, the innovators express a reserved hope that Baptist communities will eventually realize their missional potential, even though "there will be no quick changes."[280] A minister commented: "Our task is to turn the ideals we proclaim into reality. Is it possible? I believe it is. Nothing 'super-spiritual' is needed . . . Wherever top leaders understand that church planting is *their* responsibility and become participants in this process, it will really work."[281] Therefore, the church "must prepare to receive people unless we want to repeat [the experience of] the 1990s. To know how to accept five hundred people tomorrow, you need to accept fifty today."[282]

The Innovators on the Process of Revision

Although one top denominational leader suggested a "top-down" approach, in which "we must strictly require [pastors to] live according to the gospel,"[283] most participants in this group rejected such approaches. First, they understand that many Baptist pastors simply feel little or no need to reconsider their convictions about mission. One participant complained that in many "established churches things just go on as usual. The problem is simply not recognized. [They say] 'What are you talking about? Everything is going the way it did under our fathers.'"[284] In these communities, there is "no demand for rethinking reality from another perspective. If you point to membership decrease, you'll hear: 'Do not be afraid, little flock,' and all the questions are [supposedly] resolved."[285]

---

277. D10.
278. D7.
279. D8.
280. P6.
281. D10.
282. D1.
283. D10.
284. D8.
285. D8.

Second, the innovators realize that the acceptance of a new missional outlook is a deep personal experience, which cannot be imposed from the outside. A few participants recalled their own journey toward discovering a new perspective on mission.[286] Typically, it had been precipitated by a crisis either in their personal spiritual life or in their ministry. Four short testimonies below illustrate this important point. The "paradigm shift" for one pastor of a large church began at seminary: "It was a painful experience, almost like the crushing of my faith."[287] He had to come to the realization that there is "certain [degree of] relativity with all theological formulations." In other words, it was first an "epistemological shift" before it became a theological one. Today, this "uncertainty and relativity does not scare me anymore, because theology is only an avenue to experiencing a relationship [with God]." Another pastor recalls how, after several years of ministry, he "began feeling some incompleteness . . . and literature helped [him] get a fuller picture of God's work of redeeming this sin-broken world."[288] Some of this literature was reading assignments for a class at a state university.

Still another pastor said that his former views had to change when he became actively involved in evangelism:

> When you truly start sharing Christ with people, God will necessarily transform you in the process. Through involvement with unbelievers I was becoming more of a believer myself. If each of us led one person a year to Christ, our philosophy of the Christian life would drastically change from self-gratification and self-cultivation to [serving] others.[289]

Finally, a big-city pastor admitted that he had to reconsider his approach to mission when a group of eleven youth, including his teenage daughter, left his church. Unfortunately, none of these young people attends any church today. The pastor said: "They wanted to start a [worship] group, but we said no; they wanted to start a café and a club to engage unbelievers, and we said no. Our hearts were not set on them. As a result, we lost them from our

---

286. P6; E8; P1; P8.
287. P8.
288. P1.
289. D10.

church. The whole generation! It was a catastrophe."[290] After experiencing ministry "burnout," this pastor and his team had to start looking for fresh ways of engaging youth. Through this painful experience "God began changing us," he concluded.

The four strategies of introducing missiological revisions that the innovators suggest below grow out of such experiences. The first strategy is education, both the formal theological training of pastors and the informal teaching by pastors in local-church settings. "By means of teaching," the task is "to turn the ship of the church in the direction of fulfilling its primary calling."[291] This process should be undertaken, however, through "gradual formation by systematic exposition and not by shattering their convictions."[292] It is important to teach future pastors the provisional nature of all theology as "constantly being revised" and of worship forms as "neutral and having an instrumental value."[293]

Second, fruitful ministry examples modeling new missional paradigms are crucial. The participants generally agreed that "appeals and slogans will not work."[294] Neither is there an expectation that the existing centralized structure can turn the institution as a whole into a movement again. Rather, the hope is that some "strong leaders and alternative movements will naturally spring up, whether in church planting, youth ministries, etc. They will rise in different locations, and they might potentially renew the life of the union. But the structure itself will have less and less influence."[295]

Third, it is highly important for church leaders (at all levels) themselves to be involved in mission. Several participants in this group pointed out that "unless pastors take part in mission, their members will remain passive."[296] In particular, involvement in short-term mission trips could significantly transform ministers' outlook: "There can hardly be personal commitment to mission if a person has never been there. Every pastor must go on a short-term

---

290. P6.
291. D10.
292. P8.
293. P8.
294. P9; P1.
295. P1.
296. P9.

mission trip at least once in their lifetime. This will give them a missionary spirit." Another participant added: "I would recommend that every pastor do some work outside their church at least once a year – perhaps as a security guard at a parking lot near a mall, or in some other role where you mean nothing and can simply relate to people."[297]

Finally, several participants expressed the need for strategic thinking based on accurate research and honest dialogue of all who want to see Baptist missional renewal happen. Research would help Baptists "identify those false ideas that we have come to believe so that they can be replaced by true ones: first in our thinking, and then in our practice." The dialogue must be open and frank, without "traditional Soviet doubletalk, pleasantries, and generalizations."[298] As a fresh concept of Baptist mission in Russia gradually takes shape, the task of church leaders should be "to speak it, to show it, to prove it, in order to affect as much as possible every person in the church, so that the church as a whole will start turning from a static position toward [becoming] a movement once again."[299]

---

297. E8.
298. D8.
299. P1.

CHAPTER 7

Conclusions and Implications

The purpose of this research has been twofold: (1) to investigate the selected Russian Baptist leaders' perceptions of the gospel, the church, culture, and mission in their present socio-political context; and (2) to explore these leaders' views regarding the need for, the potential of, and specific ways of introducing possible revisions to traditional Russian Baptist mission thinking. The principal background for both the formulation of the research questions and the evaluation of the participants' answers is found in how these issues are framed in contemporary global evangelical mission theologies working within the general framework of the Lausanne movement. This chapter draws together the essential findings of the entire dissertation and presents some of my own thinking on the subject matter.

Summary of the Chapters

In chapter 1 I described the research problem, formulated the research questions, provided a brief overview of evangelical history in Russia, and outlined the socio-political and religious contexts in which Russian Baptist communities exist today. In chapter 2, I focused on the historical development of global evangelical mission theology since 1910. During most of this period evangelical mission thinking as reflected in the Lausanne movement and the World Evangelical Alliance developed in dialectical tension with ecumenical Protestant missiology. While taking a primarily defensive stance against it, it also reinterpreted and adopted from it some valuable biblical insights. In particular, these include the *missio Dei* concept, the missionary nature of the church, and the need for social and cultural involvement. Another vital development during this period was the growing role of the global church, a factor that is vividly illustrated by the Lausanne movement. The Cape Town Commitment demonstrates that current evangelical missiology has moved from being an exclusively Western effort to a truly global reflection on the church's mission in our increasingly globalized world.

As a result of these developments, the traditional evangelical paradigm of mission has been giving way for a new model of holistic or *integral* mission. More specifically, understanding the gospel as the message of the kingdom has brought to light the cosmic and communal aspects of salvation with their rich implications for social participation and cultural renewal. The salvation of the soul is now understood as being not exclusively future and spiritual in nature, but as involving the whole person, both in the future and in the present. With regard to ecclesiology, the emphasis shifted from seeing the church as a repository of the saved to being the sign, instrument, and foretaste of the kingdom. The church is both "called out" from, and "sent" back into, the world to continue the mission of Israel and Jesus in its words, deeds, and total life. The scope of its mission is therefore as broad as God's own mission, embracing individuals, society, culture, and ecology. As the model of a renewed human society, the church is called to reveal God's comprehensive plan for the restoration of creation. This calling presupposes its involvement with culture in both affirmation and critique, solidarity and alternative.

In chapter 3 I looked at the development of Russian Baptist mission thinking from the inception of the movement in 1867 up to the collapse of the USSR in 1991. The diverse roots and experiences of Russian Baptists in their particular context shaped a specific understanding of mission which, while not always explicitly articulated, has been the guiding vision for their mission efforts. From the Plymouth Brethren, Baptists inherited a pietistic view of personal salvation; from the Anabaptists, the value of communal life; and from Orthodoxy, a liturgical service as the core of their church life. In the 1910s and 1920s they were also influenced to some extent by postmillennial social-gospel teaching, and conversely, by Anglo-American dispensationalism. During different historical periods certain of these influences came to the fore while others were pushed to the background or even completely suppressed.

Based on a review of the literature in chapter 3, I suggested that three distinctive missiological micro-paradigms were dominant in the history of

Russian Baptists. The actual story is obviously more complex, but I believe this heuristic device is nevertheless legitimate in that it demonstrates that during each period Baptist mission theology had its own unique configuration with corresponding chief emphases. I identified these models as follows:

1. Revivalist Pietism (1867–1905)
2. Transformationist Pietism (1905–1930)
3. Escapist Pietism (1944–1991)

During the stage of Revivalist Pietism, Russian evangelicals emphatically spoke about having a *personal* relationship with Christ in a country where religious affiliation was based on the circumstance of one's birth. They focused on personal prayer, Bible reading, communal worship, fervent evangelism, and charity work. Originally, these believers did not see themselves as a separate religious confession, but rather as a renewal movement *within* the Russian Orthodox Church. The vision of a Russian reformation was born within the St Petersburg wing of the movement whose leaders expected the gospel gradually to transform the spiritual, cultural, social, and political life of the entire nation.

During the second period, this transformationist thread came to the fore and reached its climax under the new socio-political conditions. Leaders such as Ivan Prokhanov and Vasily Pavlov adopted Bolshevik vocabulary and spoke about the need for social justice and equality which they believed could be achieved through spiritual revolution. They openly articulated their political vision and expectations. Prokhanov advanced a view of the gospel that renews the whole of human life: personal morality and family life, neighborhoods and cities, education and science, arts and architecture, politics and ecology. Evangelicals actively promoted solutions for poverty through communal workshops, artisan cooperatives, and agricultural collectives. Much of this work echoed Bolshevik initiatives.[1] Similar terminology, however, concealed vast ideological differences: while the Communists taught that social evil is rooted in class-based animosities driven by private property, the Baptists emphasized personal sin and the need for spiritual transformation through faith in Christ.

---

1. Wanner, *Communities of the Converted*, 33.

After the years of bloody persecutions, Baptists entered the third period in which they gradually forged a view of mission characterized by a form of eschatological escapism. Several important developments became definitive for shaping this missiological micro-paradigm. First, dispensational eschatology completely superseded the vestiges of postmillennial thought. The kingdom of God was limited to its individual, ecclesial, and future aspects. Second, the theology of suffering developed earlier by Ivan Kargel came to the fore: persecutions and tribulations were now seen as having positive value as God's instruments in the process of sanctification. In a situation in which the church's social and political involvement was made technically impossible by the state, these two theological developments became the theological rationalizations for the state of affairs that prevailed at the time. Both solidified a pessimistic view of the world and directed the inclinations of the righteous into the otherworldly, heavenly realm. Faithful believers were now to look ahead to the day of the rapture, preparing themselves to meet the Lord in the air.[2]

Finally, in keeping with the intentional strategies of the authorities, the formalization of the leadership selection process, the standardization of worship forms and doctrinal formulations, the development of the internal Baptist subculture insulating believers from the outside world, and the intentional discouragement of evangelistic efforts and social involvement gradually shaped a religious institution that lost its original characteristics of a spontaneous movement. By the end of the 1980s Russian Baptists represented a theologically uniform, sociologically homogeneous, and culturally idiosyncratic denomination that had developed a distinctive understanding of the gospel, church, culture, and mission.[3]

A helpful comparison between chapters 2 and 3 can be made at this stage. Despite the fact that Russian Baptists were largely isolated from developments in Western mission theology, their missiological paradigm by the end of the

---

2. Russian Baptists could be said to have developed a version of what Wolterstorff calls an *avertive* religion as opposed to a *world-formative* one. The former term describes a spirituality that sees as its fundamental goal a "turning away from a lower reality and . . . establishing . . . a closer relation with a higher reality." Wolterstorff, *Justice and Peace*, 5. For its adherents, this physical world is not their home. They are "aliens here, just traveling through. It is a reality ultimately unworthy of [them], the inferior of another reality to which [they] have access – the world of the eternal, the immutable, the incorruptible, the imperishable. [Their] true happiness lies in becoming united with that supreme reality, God." Wolterstorff, 4.

3. Panych, "Soviet Baptism," 142.

1980s was in many respects parallel to that of conservative evangelicals in the West.[4] Although Russian Baptists' specific experiences were different (the enforcement of militant atheism by a totalitarian state vs denominational liberalism, the fundamentalist-modernist controversy, the Scopes trial, etc.), the social forces of radical modernism were pushing them, like their fellow believers in the West, into cultural isolationism and legalism. Given this parallelism, the character of traditional Russian Baptist mission theology can be summarized, with some qualifications, using the same three adjectives Goheen uses to describe the traditional evangelical understanding of salvation in the West: *otherworldly, dualistic,* and *individualistic*.[5]

Goheen defines *otherworldly* as focusing "on escaping this world when you die and going to heaven."[6] As we have seen, Russian Baptists' view of salvation in the late Soviet period leaned heavily toward this understanding when they developed a form of "ahistorical existence."[7] The term *dualistic* in relation to the conservative evangelical view of salvation means that the church surrendered to the Enlightenment's separation of private religion from public life.[8] Russian Baptists adjusted to the pressures of militant modernism in similar, but more radical ways – by splitting their view of reality itself into the spiritual and secular realms and turning away completely from the secular sphere. The cultural and social order outside the church was seen as designed and ruled by the powers that oppose God, a view that was reinforced daily by their experience of living in the atheistic Soviet society. From this perspective, God was not interested in *all* of reality, but only in those aspects of it that he would ultimately redeem, that is, human souls. The church as the gathering of "saved souls" was seen as the locus of God's work. In this way, Russian Baptists' ahistorical existence was also strongly *asocial* and *acultural*.

Finally, Goheen defines *individualistic* as "limited to introducing Jesus as Savior to individual people who can find forgiveness . . . and go to heaven to

---

4. Perhaps it is fairer to say that it had many similarities with conservative evangelical theology prior to 1947, the year that Carl Henry published his book *The Uneasy Conscience of Fundamentalism*, challenging evangelicals to rethink their attitudes toward social action and cultural engagement.
5. Goheen, *Introducing Christian Mission Today*.
6. Goheen, 1436.
7. Sergienko, "Baptisty i Obshcestvo [Baptists and Society]."
8. Goheen, *Introducing Christian Mission Today*, 1674.

live with God when they die."⁹ While evangelizing individuals is essential for the Russian Baptist view of salvation, they have always connected the salvation of individuals with a community of faith. In the nineteenth century, pietism brought with it a valuable emphasis on individuation in a highly collectivist society, yet the strong Anabaptist influence kept Russian Baptists from falling into individualism. Their understanding of salvation, therefore, has been *personal,* but can hardly be described as *individualistic.* Perhaps, a better designation would be *church-centered* or focused on an alternative community.

In chapter 4, I described the conceptual framework of research, its methodology, and the sample. In the next two chapters, I proceeded to present the research findings based on the analysis of thirty interviews with prominent Baptists workers in academic, pastoral, and denominational leadership. In chapter 5, I summarized their understandings of the four aspects of mission theology, and in chapter 6, I outlined their perceptions of the need for revisions to the Russian Baptists' theology of mission and of possible ways to introduce these revisions. As was noted, the analysis of the findings suggests that two distinct conceptions of mission theology can be discerned in the data, especially in the views of the most articulate and consistent participants. The differences between the two models appear to be significant enough to justify the conclusion that we are dealing here with two different theological paradigms, and not merely with superficial variations.

Based on their responses, the first group was identified as "traditionalists" and the second as "innovators" (both included between six and eight particularly articulate representatives; see appendix 3). The views of the third and largest group, the "moderates," fall between the two distinctive "poles." The variety of views in this middle group cannot be reduced to a single position. Rather, it is common for many in this group to agree in certain respects with the traditionalists and in other respects with the innovators. In other words, the first and second groups can be seen as "centered sets" with loose boundaries. For this reason, in the presentation of the findings I focused primarily on the views of the traditionalists and the innovators.

---

9. Goheen, 1494.

The Answers to the Research Questions by Those Espousing the Traditionalist Paradigm

The first research question explored the contours of Russian Baptist mission theology as espoused by the interviewees. More specifically, it focused on their understandings of the gospel, the church, the principles of cultural engagement, and holistic mission. The second question dealt with their convictions regarding the need for revising traditional Baptist missiological views in light of the current Russian context. The answers of the traditionalist group are summarized below.

The Contours of Russian Baptist Mission Theology

The gospel. A typical presentation of the good news in this paradigm is cast mainly in *negative* terms as salvation from eternal condemnation in hell. As a rule, it begins with human sin, moves to the person and work of Christ – especially to his substitutionary death on the cross as the reason for his incarnation – and then culminates in a call to personal repentance and faith. The ultimate purpose of salvation is seen as enabling people to enjoy eternal bliss in paradise, or the heavenly kingdom. In the interim, as corrupt humanity is waiting for its condemnation and the material creation for its final annihilation, the task of the saved is to be continuously sanctified in preparation for meeting the Lord in the air at the moment of the rapture.

The church. The church as the gathering of the saved is the locus of God's salvific work. Its first and foremost purpose is to worship God. Second, it exists for the continuing and ever-deepening process of the personal sanctification of its members. The third major task of the church as the custodian and dispenser of God's truth is the verbal proclamation of the gospel. The emphasis typically falls on *being* the church: in the final analysis, the Christian *life* is a stronger form of witness than *words*. In fact, an overemphasis on evangelism at the expense of sanctification can be detrimental to the calling of the church in the world. As the community of God's people, the church represents him through the individual lives of its members in society. Therefore, it should focus primarily on the edification of its members to be the temple of God through the Spirit.

Cultural engagement. Based on a number of soteriological and eschatological arguments, the traditional model does not presuppose any *intention* to change or transform the world. The church and the world belong to two different and opposing kingdoms, and the Christian is called not to conform to worldly culture. The desire to engage with culture leads to spiritual and theological compromises which are the primary reason why the church's mission work sometimes produces little or no fruit. The emphasis falls on separation ("building the walls of the vineyard") and dissimilarity in essentially all aspects of culture: values, behavior, outward appearance, music styles, etc. There is also an *a priori* conviction of the inevitability of tensions in relationships with the world and of the resulting persecution of believers. In fact, in its extreme version, this view affirms that religious freedom is harmful for mission because when the church is not persecuted it tends to lose its purity.

At the same time, some proponents of this view do not rule out the possible transformation of certain aspects of culture if Christians are truly able to live as the light of the world and the salt of the earth. Nor do they rule out cautious involvement in society with acts of mercy and service. Nevertheless, any transformation is seen more as an unintended consequence than as an aim of the Christian life. Ultimately, no number of good deeds can significantly change fallen society or culture as a whole.

Holistic mission. This portion of my report on the findings was divided into two sections: social service (or acts of mercy) and social action (or acts of justice). With regard to the former, most respondents agreed that this is one of the church's obligations. Apparently, this is one area in which a significant shift from the late Soviet paradigm can be noticed. At the same time, only few participants in this group see the need for structural changes in either their local communities or the denomination as a whole that would move this form of ministry beyond occasional response to social crises. Moreover, some traditionalists within the group tend to completely discard social service as a non-biblical digression from the church's primary calling. For them, biblical injunctions to take care of physical needs are limited to their fellow Baptist church members.

With regard to social action as political involvement, the proponents of the traditional paradigm strongly reject the idea of the church's participation in politics as an institution. Their belief that God ordains specific persons as political rulers (based on Rom 13:1) precludes essentially any thought of civil disobedience – with a single exception: if the authorities prohibit them from engaging in worship. The idea of the church's prophetic role in society is either completely denied or is explained as preaching the gospel of repentance to everyone, including those in power. Biblically, the only two legitimate instruments the church has in its desire to see a more just society are prayer and the proclamation of the gospel.

Overall, this perspective displays deep pessimism concerning the possibility of social and cultural change. Even if many human hearts were regenerated by the Spirit through faith in Christ, there can be no lasting moral improvement or genuine social justice until Christ returns. The purpose of the Christian life on earth is therefore not to change structures, but to pursue personal sanctification and to proclaim the kingdom of heaven. Unjust treatment and suffering, should they return, must be seen as God's tools to help believers grow in Christlikeness.

Potential Missiological Revisions

The suggested revisions by the participants in this group are based on their perception of the reasons for the lack of mission success after 1991. The traditionalists tend to emphasize external or "objective" factors which lay outside the church's control (e.g., the quality of the "soil," or the hardened spiritual condition of society; flawed Western mission approaches; signs of eschatological apostasy, etc.). Among internal factors they typically point to the church's compromises with worldly culture and the weakening of traditional Baptist spirituality. Given the external factors, the church can do little to catalyze spiritual revival; ultimately, this is the sovereign work of the Spirit. What the church should work on instead is its own spiritual renewal: Baptists must focus on the inner development of their communities and the maturation of their members, leaving the results in God's hands.

In practice, this primarily means solidifying and protecting the traditional Baptist subculture. The cases (or "experiments") when traditional Baptist spirituality has been compromised to keep newcomers in the church have proved counterproductive. The focus therefore should be on discipleship, counseling, and building strong families which, after all, have historically been the primary source of members for Baptist communities. Generally, for theological and practical guidance these leaders look to the central office of the union in Moscow as their spiritual direction-setter.

The Answers to the Research Questions by Those Espousing the Innovative Paradigm

This section summarizes the second group's theological understandings and their convictions regarding possible revisions of traditional views.

The Contours of Russian Baptist Mission Theology

The Gospel. For the members of this group, the gospel tends to begin *positively* with the creation rather than with sin. The gospel is the good news of God's redemption and restoration, embracing both humanity and the world. The cross of Christ as the climax of the biblical story extending from the creation to the new creation generally takes on a meaning broader than being the means of individual salvation. In fact, the "innovators" tend to emphasize Christ's resurrection and the availability of the blessings of the kingdom to believers even now in the present age: belief in the gospel is seen as the source of a real, joyous, and productive life on earth. The power of God's kingdom is not limited to inner or future realms; it is already changing the world. The purpose of Christian existence is typically thought of in transformationist terms: believers are God's agents of redemption for the sake of the world.

The church. The concept and imagery of the church among the members of this group generally correspond with those of the traditionalists, with one important difference. This group tends to prioritize the *missional* purpose of the church over its other tasks. The church is therefore seen primarily as God's *instrument* of mission. From this perspective, an excessive emphasis on holiness and personal sanctification apart from the fulfillment of this purpose leads to a distortion of God's intentions for the church. In fact, it is little more than a form of Christian selfishness.

Cultural engagement. It is in this area that the sharpest differences between the two groups become manifest. The "innovators" strongly criticize the idea of "temple [church]-centered" Christianity which, in their view, is so dear to the traditionalists. Some of them identify this focus on purely religious matters as *the* weakest aspect of the Baptist movement in Russia. While they understand the historical reasons for the cultural and social isolation of Baptists, they see this as both unbiblical and contradictory to the practice of the early Baptist believers in Russia.

The innovators usually point out that in addition to external pressures, certain internal factors have contributed to the development and perpetuation of the prevalent attitude of cultural indifference. Among these they list such beliefs as ecclesiastical primitivism and the eschatological annihilation of the material creation. From the innovators' perspective, biblical faithfulness requires active, even if cautious, cultural engagement. Being God's agents of redemption means that they are called to bring into culture gospel convictions and values. This task presupposes loving God's world and believing in the possibility of its transformation. Some of the innovators add that Christian influence in the world goes beyond individual witness: the church is called to be an alternative community that demonstrates how the gospel shapes its responses to cultural questions and challenges.

Holistic mission. Two important convictions stand out among the members of this group in contrast to the members of the first group. First, they consider social service to be an *integral* part of Christian mission, that is, one of the church's obligations, in contrast to engaging only in occasional acts of mercy in response to crises. Accordingly, these leaders are willing to make structural and budgeting changes in churches and organizations in order to incorporate this ministry as a regular aspect of the church's service in the world.

Second, in relation to social action, they tend to operate on the conviction that Romans 13 speaks about God's establishment of the *principle* of authority and subordination, not about the ordination of specific rulers. This opens the possibility of prophetically critiquing those in power whenever their actions or legislation conflict with biblical principles or state laws. They also encourage Christians who are gifted in and called to minister in the political sphere to do so, either within state structures or in NGOs. At the same time, they tend to agree with the first group that the church as an institution should not entangle itself in political affairs, because it has a different task: to prepare Christians for responsible service in the world. The innovators also agree that Christians should never become agents of violent structural change, even if the intention is to create more just structures. God's purposes in the world can be accomplished only by God's means.

Potential Missiological Revisions

The participants in this group attribute the lack of success in Baptist mission over the last twenty-five years to a combination of both external and internal factors. In particular, they note that the initial spiritual hunger stimulated by the ideological vacuum of the early 1990s was soon satisfied by the emerging civil religion, as Russians rediscovered their traditional identity and began returning (nominally) to the Russian Orthodox Church. At the same time, they strongly reject the idea that Russians are no longer interested in the gospel. Instead, the primary reasons for the lack of success in mission were *internal* factors within the Baptist churches themselves. These include the lack of spiritual and organizational preparedness; an inward-focused church life; poor approaches to follow-up and discipleship; unwillingness to adapt worship expressions; negative attitudes toward the general culture; the need for newcomers to adjust to the specific subculture of Baptist communities, which did not always have a biblical foundation; the social marginality of Baptist cultures; and the inability or unwillingness of local churches to finance mission work.

The innovators proposed several major revisions. They believe that Baptists need to (1) rediscover an understanding of the gospel as the comprehensive message of the kingdom; (2) develop a missional self-consciousness as being God's instrument in the redemption of the world; (3) see value in the general culture and actively engage with it; (4) reassess their own subculture in dialogue with the general culture and with other Christian traditions; (5) understand the restrictive effects of institutionalization and the limitations of a centralized hierarchical structure; and (6) strive to be a culturally embodied but alternative community. Unlike the passive reliance of the traditionalists on God to produce spiritual revival, the proponents of this model believe in the need for God's people to partner with him in preparing the conditions for revival. At the same time, they realize there will be no quick or easy changes, whether within the church or in society.

With regard to possible ways of introducing revisions, most of them reject the idea of top-down attempts at renewal. What might work is the personal involvement of ministers in evangelism and missions, helping people to recognize the value of education (both formal and informal), and calling attention to viable examples of successful missionary work. They also underscore the importance of strategic thinking that is based on the objective analysis of both social and ecclesiastical dynamics. Finally, they see the need for both theological dialogue and missional partnership with other Christian groups that are reaching Russians for Christ.

Conclusions

Based on the findings of this research, the following conclusions can be made:

The missiological thinking of the current Russian Baptist leadership – academic, denominational, and pastoral – reflects two distinct theological paradigms, which in this research are identified as "traditionalist" and "innovative."

The traditionalist paradigm closely corresponds to the late-Soviet model of eschatological escapism as summarized at the end of chapter 3. Since 1991, this otherworldly, dualistic, and church-centered paradigm has been modified in three main ways: (1) stronger emphasis is placed on evangelism outside the church; (2) appreciation of the need for social service has increased; and (3) the attitude toward the general culture has largely changed from outright rejection to neglect/indifference.

The innovative paradigm emphasizes the comprehensiveness of the gospel as the message of God's kingdom, the missionary calling of the church, active cultural engagement based on biblically informed discernment, and a more holistic view of mission. In many respects, this model is parallel to recent developments in global evangelical mission theology, which apparently reflects decades of international partnership, Western theological education, the growing availability of missiological literature, etc.

A larger number of the participants tend to hold to the traditionalist model, although only about one-fourth of them firmly espouse and consistently voice that model. Another one-fourth are consistent and articulate adherents of the innovative paradigm. Many other participants are open to borrowing views on and methods of mission from the innovators and to reconsidering aspects of the traditionalist model that they find unsatisfactory in their own ministry experience.

Based on demographic information (appendix 3), the following observations can be made: the pastors of older churches that were planted in the Soviet or pre-Soviet epoch as well as those who minister in small cities and towns tend to hold to the traditionalist paradigm. The proponents of the new paradigm, on the other hand, are found among those who have been active in evangelism and church planting, live in urban areas, and have been exposed to Western mission thinking through their study abroad, missiological literature, or international partnerships.[10]

A crucial factor in creating an openness to the reconsideration of traditional perspectives appears to be close personal involvement with unbelievers through evangelism and church planting and the resulting struggles with issues of the gospel and culture. (In Kuhn's terms, these struggles become the "anomalies" that the traditional model cannot explain.) Neither having or not having grown up in a Baptist family, nor age, nor education per se seem to be decisive factors in determining which missiological paradigm one tends to adopt.

The data demonstrates that, as far as the traditionalist paradigm is concerned, its core theological convictions (about salvation and the kingdom, church and eschatology, sanctification and cultural isolation, socio-political pessimism and state powers, etc.) have remained basically intact. The fact that this model remains strong several decades after the social pressure that engendered it is gone suggests that it is held at the level of worldview assumptions and, apparently, is adopted by new generations of ministers more through the processes of socialization/acculturation than through conscious theological deliberation.

One evidence of this comes from the statements of the traditionalists themselves. Unlike the innovators, they made practically no reference to theological or missiological literature, social research, the historical experience of the church across cultures, etc. Instead, they referred to the traditional interpretations of certain biblical texts that are usually taken as self-evident, and on occasion they said such things as "as our fathers believed," "as it was in the past," "as I was taught in my church," etc. As a rule, these interviews did not reveal signs of personal ministry crises that could spur a search for different models of ministry. At the same time, these participants often expressed their dissatisfaction with the threats to traditional Baptist identity

---

10. The growing body of missiological literature in Russian includes texts of David Bosch, Lesslie Newbigin, Christopher Wright, N. T. Wright, Michael Goheen, Tim Keller, and some others.

that have resulted from diverse cultural and theological influences over the last two decades.[11]

Finally, it is worth noting some of the deeper level presuppositions that have perpetuated the traditional paradigm, and most likely will continue to do so in the future. Underlying this worldview seems to be a form of radical supernaturalism shaped in response to the atheistic culture of the Soviet state. Basic to it is the antithesis between "things human" and "things divine." Human agency (in biblical interpretation, theology, or culture in general) is, at best, irrelevant, and at worst, fleshly and inimical to God's work. In particular, here are several ways in which this type of thinking often comes to the surface in preaching and popular theologizing, including some of the interviews conducted for this research:

- The Bible is seen as strictly the product of divine revelation to which human dimension is essentially denied. What is needed to understand its message is the work of the Spirit, not the study of the culture and history of biblical times.[12]
- Theology is seen as a set of truths revealed once and for all, not as a continuing dialogue between the gospel and changing human cultures.[13]
- The concept of the cultural mandate by which "we mirror God's own generative act . . . as [creatures] made in his likeness" is almost completely absent.[14] Cultural activity is, at best, irrelevant to the true essence of human nature and redemption.

---

11. The social nature of the traditionalist paradigm is also observed by Olga Bokova in her research: "In the contemporary ECB churches . . . traditionalism and conservatism dominate . . . These communities can hardly provide a breeding ground for the spread of the new type of Protestantism." By the "new type" of Protestants she has in mind those believers within Baptist communities who are "active in [the] socio-economic arena, who pursue the achievement of goals, who have a developed sense of political and legal consciousness, who have a strong desire to bring change in the world, and who have a positive attitude toward culture." Bokova, "Sovremennye Rossiyskie Evangelskie Khristiane-Baptisty: Sotsialnaia Struktura i Ideologiia [Contemporary Russian Evangelical Christians-Baptists: Social Structure and Ideology]," 37.

12. Ales Dubrovsky describes this conviction as a "new docetism." Dubrovsky, "Bogoslovskii Fundamentalism Kak Tormoziaschiy Faktor v Razvitii Evangel'skikh Tserkvey Postsovetskogo Perioda [Theological Fundamentalism as a Constraining Factor in the Development of Evangelical Churches in the Post-Soviet Period]," 29–34.

13. cf. Tiénou and Hiebert, "Missional Theology."

14. Hunter, *To Change the World*, 3.

- In popular Christology, the emphasis falls heavily on Christ's divinity. The value of his humanity is seen primarily in enabling him to die in the place of sinners.
- In ecclesiology, the social dimension of the church is either unrecognized or is disconnected from the larger social context. The church is seen as a supernatural creation for which non-spiritual understandings of human interaction play no real role. Accordingly, insights from social studies are irrelevant for planting or managing a church.[15]
- In evangelism, there is hardly any need to understand contemporary culture. What matters is the preaching of the "pure Word of God" which minimizes human agency. Contextualization from this perspective tends to be seen as a compromise.[16]
- In the work of mission, spiritual revival is thought to result not from a combination of spiritual and social factors, but is completely dependent on the Holy Spirit. Basically, the only way one can contribute to this process is to work on his or her own devotion and holiness.

In Paul Hiebert's terminology, this worldview can be seen as a case of "spiritual reductionism," in which all problems are attributed to spiritual causes.[17] Methodologically, the search for solutions is reduced to a single explanatory system; the potential contribution of social sciences, rooted in a theological understanding of general revelation, is disregarded. As a result, important dimensions of truth are either denied or unrecognized. When it comes to mission involvement, this view inescapably nurtures introversion and isolationist tendencies within the church.[18] By now, this model has

---

15. For instance, in pastoral counseling, so-called "biblical" approaches are dominant, and there is strong opposition to borrowing almost any ideas from psychology.

16. cf. Mikhailo Mokienko, "Evangelizatsiino-Misionerska Diial'nist Piznikh Protestantiv v Ukraiini [Evangelism and Mission Work of the Late Ukrainian Protestants]," in *Dvatsat' Let Religioznoy Svobody i Aktivnoi Misii [Twenty Years of Religious Freedom and Active Mission]*, ed. Mikhaiil Cherenkov (Kiev: Dukh i Litera, 2011), 307.

17. Hiebert, *Gospel in Human Contexts*, 128–129; cf. "spiritualism" in Michael E. Wittmer, *Becoming Worldly Saints: Can You Serve Jesus and Still Enjoy Your Life?* (Grand Rapids, MI: Zondervan, 2015).

18. Often, these tendencies are further reinforced by an emphasis on the sort of moralistic introspection that results from divorcing sanctification from God's missionary purposes for

become an essential part of the Russian Baptist tradition which, with minor adaptations, tends to reproduce itself in the next generation of ministers. Furthermore, given the general conservative trend in current Russian culture, we are likely to see this paradigm become even stronger in the future.

Implications

Virtually all the participants in this research agree that Baptist mission efforts in Russia since 1991 have not been as successful as was hoped for, even if their specific assessments vary from "a complete failure," to "an era of missed opportunities," to "we have done what we could." I tend to believe that the primary reason for this lack of success is to be found in the traditional theological understanding of mission more than in anything else. As Yuchkovski profoundly observes, when religious freedom took Baptists by surprise, they "found themselves bound by their eschatological views . . . [as they] waited for another direct divine intervention."[19] While Baptists in Russia passionately looked to God for a miraculous change of the status quo, they did not expect it could come in the form of opportunities to share the gospel openly and to initiate change themselves. Their apocalyptic agenda did not presuppose any vision for mission in society, let alone strategic planning for long-term missionary involvement.

As a result, Baptists had to follow the lead of Western Christians who took initiative in mission immediately after the fall of the Iron Curtain.[20] Despite all of their tremendous help with finances and other resources, the flood of American and other missionaries into Russia in the 1990s proved in many cases to be a mixed blessing. First, during this era many churches experienced splits as more progressive views entered and created conflicts with traditionalists.[21] Typically, these splinter groups were not integrated into the RUECB

---

the church and making it an end in itself.

19. Yuchkovski, "Comparison of the Evangelical Movement," 111; cf. Mary Raber, "Discerning Joy from Sorrow: Reflecting on Changes among Ukrainian Evangelicals Since Independence," 2004, 1, http://www.eastwestreport.org/articles/ew12101.html.

20. Mark R. Elliot, "Theological Education after Communism: The Mixed Blessing of Western Assistance," *The Asbury Theological Journal* 50 (1995): 67.

21. Bokova, "Teologia Rossiiskikh Evangel'skikh Khristian-Baptistov Na Rubezhe XX i XXI Vekov [Theology of Russian Evangelical Christians-Baptists at the Turn of the Twenty-First Century]," 15.

and remained non-denominational or joined other similar groups.[22] This process of separation was often accompanied by bitter conflicts which tended to make older churches antagonistic toward new approaches in mission and to insulate them from the influence of more "progressive" churches. Second, the dominance of Westerners in public evangelism tended to confirm the stereotype in the mass consciousness of Baptists being adherents of a "foreign faith." Third, active Western "proselytism" caused serious concerns and uneasiness among Orthodox clergy and state officials and eventually led to the passing of stricter legislation, such as the law on traditional religions of 1997 and, recently, the anti-missionary law of 2016. Finally, outside financial support resulted in a situation in which, after Westerners ended their projects and took their money with them, many mission initiatives came to a halt.

But, perhaps, the weakest aspect of Baptist mission has been their acultural and asocial conceptions of the gospel. As Coleman profoundly observes, many seekers after the fall of Communism were not only in search of "new ways to understand their individual journeys on this earth, but [they were] also looking for alternative models of community and identity to replace Soviet ones."[23] For these people, the Baptists' otherworldly and dualistic understanding of Christianity with an anti-intellectual flavor did not have much to offer. Likewise, many Western missionaries, despite their best intentions, often had a superficial understanding of Russian culture and used stereotyped methods of evangelism that did not address those questions either.[24] At the same time, the Orthodox resurgence was gaining momentum with its more holistic outlook and strong ties to Russian history and culture. As a result, after the initial curiosity of unbelievers faded out, many lost interest

---

22. The tragedy of many such groups was that after the Western missionaries completed their terms and returned home, the new Christians were often left without proper pastoral care. One of the umbrellas that has recently attempted to unite such communities is the All-Russian Fellowship of Gospel-Christians, which claims to continue the tradition of the RUGC prior to 1944. "All-Russian Fellowship of Gospel-Christians," accessed 25 August 2017, http://moskva.drevolife.ru/denominaciya/vseh.

23. Coleman, *Russian Baptists and Spiritual Revolution*, 1.

24. Harris, "Historical Perspectives;" Yuchkovski, "Comparison of the Evangelical Movement."

in Protestant evangelistic appeals. By the end of the 1990s the growth rate of the churches generally declined to that of the Soviet period.[25]

It can be added that some other, seemingly non-theological, factors noted by the participants as affecting Baptist mission such as expensive construction projects, massive emigration, and the absence of mission budgets in local churches, had in reality much to do with Baptist mission thinking. Indeed they can be seen as expressions of Baptists' convictions about the centrality of worship; their inward-focused, church-centered spirituality; and their weak emotional attachment to the "earthly" motherland. Bokova observes that even new churches that were planted largely as daughter churches of the older communities sooner or later socialized new converts into the traditional Baptist view of Christianity.[26] Overall, therefore, it seems safe to conclude that many of the beliefs that had successfully helped the Baptist denomination in Russia to maintain its identity during the time of state-sponsored atheism, have become major constraining factors in its mission in the new situation of freedom.

Today, objections to the dualistic supernaturalism underlying the traditional paradigm are commonly looked upon as unorthodox, which complicates the possibility of revising this assumption in light of Scripture. One problem with this worldview is that naïve biblicism it espouses displays little critical awareness of the cultural-historical conditioning of the process of theological construction. As such, it simply has a very weak theoretical foundation for distinguishing between a text and the way it has traditionally been understood, or as Ales Dubrovsky puts it, between *Sola Scriptura* and

---

25. Golovin, "Missing Dimension." It is instructive to see that some Russian Orthodox thinkers note a similar one-sidedness in the current Orthodox message: "The affirmed 'vulgarity' of the church does not allow her to express adequately many implications of the gospel that people need today. Through church routine and rituals we talk a lot about obedience, submissiveness, humility, following the will of God, etc., but [we say] practically nothing about the royal dignity of man, the high calling for which he was created, the freedom with which he was endowed, and the talents he needs to develop." Iliukovich, "Krestyianstvo Ili Khristianstvo: Sotsialnye Aspekty Sovremennogo Pravoslaviya [Peasants or Christians: Social Aspects of Contemporary Orthodox Faith]."

26. Bokova, "Sovremennye Rossiyskie Evangelskie Khristiane-Baptisty: Sotsialnaia Struktura i Ideologiia [Contemporary Russian Evangelical Christians-Baptists: Social Structure and Ideology]," 37.

traditionalism.[27] Puzynin adds that the Soviet school system with its belief in naïve realism and objective scientific methods contributed to the tendency among Russian evangelicals to equate their theological understanding with biblical revelation itself.[28]

Another related problem is that after the collapse of the USSR theological partnerships between Russian Baptists and Western right-wing evangelical groups have had the effect of strengthening the traditional paradigm, actually giving it a stronger biblical legitimization. As Puzynin observes, in the post-Soviet period it was Western evangelical fundamentalism that has played the most influential role in shaping the "identity, theology, and practices of the [Baptist] tradition."[29] Again, naïve biblicism may serve as a reliable safeguard against those who bluntly deny biblical authority, but sometimes it dramatically lacks critical discernment with regard to the teachings of those groups that utilize the high view of Scripture to develop their one-sided discourse. Their appeals to biblical texts tend to conceal the historical and contextual contingency of their interpretations.[30]

Arguably, John MacArthur of the Master's Seminary has wielded the greatest influence among Russian Baptists since 1991. For many of them he has become the Bible teacher and theologian *par excellence* as they highly appreciate his emphasis on expository preaching and his uncompromised commitment to biblical authority and traditional moral teachings. An extension of the Master's Seminary was launched in Russia and several other schools have depended on its theological (and financial) resources, mediated through a Western missionary organization. Dozens of his books and commentaries were translated into Russian and widely distributed (often free of charge), including his study Bible. With regard to mission theology, however, his influence has tended to perpetuate the traditional paradigm. For instance, he confidently states that "God's purpose in this world – and the church's

---

27. Dubrovsky, "Bogoslovskii Fundamentalism Kak Tormoziaschiy Faktor v Razvitii Evangel'skikh Tserkvey Postsovetskogo Perioda [Theological Fundamentalism as a Constraining Factor in the Development of Evangelical Churches in the Post-Soviet Period]," 35.

28. Puzynin, *Tradition of the Gospel Christians*, 248.

29. Puzynin, 283. He suggests that the inherent fundamentalist type of reasoning was a major reason why Baptist theology after the collapse of the USSR leaned toward Western fundamentalism in the first place. Puzynin, 183.

30. Sergienko, "Nevyuchenyie Uroki Proshlogo [Unlearned Lessons of the Past]."

only legitimate commission – is the proclamation of the message of sin and salvation to individuals, whom God sovereignly redeems and calls out of the world."[31] Obviously, from this perspective the "moral, social, and political state of a people is irrelevant to the advance of the gospel. Jesus said that His kingdom was not of this world."[32]

While MacArthur upholds many indispensable biblical truths, he interprets the gospel as a message of individual salvation, not as the story of the restoration of all creation under God's reign. This interpretation of salvation, as Bosch points out, "dangerously narrows the meaning of salvation, as if it comprises only escape from the wrath of God and the redemption of the individual soul in the hereafter" and makes an "absolute distinction between creation and new creation, between well-being and salvation."[33] The resultant understanding of mission naturally focuses on the personal and ecclesiastical aspects of redemption and basically ignores its cosmic, cultural, sociopolitical, and ecological dimensions.

The irony is that while this kind of theology claims to be Reformed, it tends to disregard important aspects of the Reformers' heritage that are highly relevant in the former Soviet countries, namely, the lordship of Christ over every sphere of creation and a comprehensive vision of cultural renewal by equipping Christians to faithfully carry out their callings in the world. In its best expressions, Calvinism has called on the church to "shine its light out through its windows to areas far beyond, illuminating all the sectors and associations that appear across the wide range of human life and activity."[34] From this comprehensive perspective, what the fundamentalist groups offer looks more like a theological hybrid of Reformed soteriology and a dualistic, sectarian view of cultural engagement.

Another aspect of the problem is that their theologies were shaped in a foreign context in response to different challenges. When brought to Russia in ready-to-use packages, they import artificial theological problems which

---

31. MacArthur, *Vanishing Conscience*, 12.
32. MacArthur, *Government Can't Save You*, 11–12.
33. Bosch, *Transforming Mission*, 390.
34. Abraham Kuyper, "Common Grace," in *Abraham Kuyper: A Centennial Reader*, ed. James D. Bratt (Grand Rapids, MI: Eerdmans, 1902), 194.

tend to threaten evangelical unity over non-essential matters.[35] In the context where modernist-fundamentalist debates have never been an issue, their polemical stance against the straw men of "liberalism" and the "social gospel" also tends to lock Russian Baptists onto the traditional conservative end of the evangelical theological spectrum. This raises needless barriers against the appreciation of the theological convergence in much of global evangelical missiology today and does not help Russian Baptist community in developing their own holistic responses to the challenges in context. In the long run, therefore, these non-native theologies may inhibit the Russian church's ability to become self-theologizing in its own context.[36]

This is why the emergence of a new paradigm among Russian Baptist leaders is so important and encouraging. While the proponents of the new paradigm do not agree on all matters and speak from diverse ministry contexts, many common threads are observable. In fact, in its most mature versions, this model approximates the theology of mission found in the Lausanne primary documents and in much recent global evangelical missiology. For this reason, a broader and more intentional dialogue between Russian Baptists and the global evangelical community could bring into clearer focus what Russian Baptist leaders have already been arriving at. Ultimately, it could help them rediscover the fuller story of the gospel for their context and facilitate a transition from the paradigm of eschatological escapism to that of a holistic, missional evangelicalism.

In my view, this transition is indispensable if Baptist mission is to achieve more going forward. The experience of the last twenty-five years, I believe, strongly suggests that "ahistorical" (i.e. asocial and acultural) communities have little chance of becoming mediators of spiritual revival for their own people. Rather, they are more likely to remain small, sectarian type communities that attract people with a similar outlook or those who have also become asocial (although in a very different way) through an existential crisis of some sort, such as drug addiction, alcoholism, imprisonment, etc. Undeniably, the

---

35. Some examples of these foreign dichotomies are election vs human choice, biblical inerrancy vs human authorship, preaching the gospel vs social involvement, the sufficiency of Scripture vs social studies, etc.

36. Paul G. Hiebert, *Anthropological Insights for Missionaries* (Grand Rapids, MI: Baker Book House, 1985).

ability of evangelical churches to effectively reach such groups in Russia is one of their strengths, but an exclusive focus on them, as it sometimes happens today, would mean confining the universal gospel of salvation to only a few groups of Russian population.

Having outlined this need for a paradigm shift, I believe two comments must be added at this stage. First, the example of Lausanne suggests that this shift will not come without a lot of dialogue, and that everyone will not agree in the end. It has been a messy process for the global evangelical community, and it might be a messy process for Russian Baptists as well. They might have to go through their own debates on many important and thorny issues, such as the gospel and culture, evangelism and social responsibility, etc. In fact, it would be surprising if they do not. Second, I do not mean to claim that Lausanne "has everything right" and so Russian Baptists simply need to adopt its theology. Rather, my point is that there is a missiological conversation going on, and this is where the consensus seems to be moving. I want to advocate openness to a dialogue more than a specific solution to the issue of social involvement or cultural engagement. Debates continue, but the problem is that the Russian Baptists are not part of them, and as a result are missing opportunities to be enriched by the exchange, as well as, perhaps, to enrich others in the process.

In the rest of this chapter, I suggest five theological themes from global evangelical missiology which I believe can facilitate the transition of Russian Baptists to a more comprehensive missional paradigm. These themes are as follows: (1) a critical realist theological epistemology, (2) a fuller view of the gospel, (3) missional ecclesiology, (4) critical cultural engagement, and (5) holistic living as an alternative community. In what follows, I briefly outline these five areas and reflect on what their application might look like in the specific context of Russian Baptist communities today.

Five Themes from Global Evangelical Missiology
1. Critical Realism as an Epistemological Foundation

Paul Hiebert points out that disagreements in theology often "have less to do with the contents of theology than with its epistemic nature."[37] In particular, he observes that some young evangelicals who are aware of the shifts in

---

37. Hiebert, *Epistemological Shifts*, 103.

Western epistemology "have moved from the old position of naïve realism to that of critical realism, while remaining evangelical in theological content."[38] Roger Olson also exposes the polarity among evangelicals in the West between what he identifies as "conservative" vs "post-conservative" styles of doing theology. He ascribes the latter approach primarily to its "constructive use of some aspects of postmodernity."[39] Apparently, some of the tensions between the two missiological paradigms among Russian Baptists also stem from different epistemological assumptions. The Soviet educational system promoted a type of rationality that was based on naïve realism with its belief in the inductive method and "objective scientific" knowledge.[40] But as general Russian culture increasingly displays signs of the so-called postmodern turn, some evangelicals, just as some of their fellow believers in the West have done, are tending to drift in their theology from naïve to more critical realism.

According to Hiebert, critical realism is the helpful middle way between the optimism of modernity and the pessimism of postmodernity. In this approach knowledge is seen as "based on symbols, models, and analogies" rather than as factual and literal.[41] David Bosch uses the terms "modified" or "tempered" realism which he describes in similar terms as "a road between Enlightenment optimism and anti-Enlightenment pessimism." The alternative to modernity's claims of objectivism and absolutism is not found in subjectivism or relativism; rather, one must remain aware of the "contextuality of convictions."[42] Among other things, this means that the authentic Christian

---

38. Hiebert, *Anthropological Reflections*, 31.

39. Roger E. Olson, *Reformed and Always Reforming: The Postconservative Approach to Evangelical Theology* (Grand Rapids, MI: Baker Academic, 2007), 16. Olson compares the main characteristics of the two styles as follows: conservative theology emphasizes the propositional nature of revelation, tends to view evangelicalism as a bounded-set category, is inimical to postmodernity, and is suspicious of the constructive task of theology. It assumes that theology can be done relatively uninfluenced by history and culture. One of its major driving forces is the fear of liberal theology. Postconservative theology, on the other hand, tends to see the enduring essence of Christianity in spiritual experience and relationships rather than in doctrinal beliefs, perceives evangelicalism as a centered-set category, and considers transformation more than information to be the purpose of revelation. Theology is seen more as a "pilgrimage" than a "conquest." There is also dissatisfaction with the conservative reliance on modernistic modes of thought and an openness to the constructive task of theology. Olson, 22–26.

40. Puzynin, *Tradition of the Gospel Christians*, 283.

41. Hiebert, *Epistemological Shifts*, 20, 98; Hiebert, *Gospel in Human Contexts*.

42. Bosch, *Transforming Mission*, 350–351.

position with regard to the human ability to know the truth completely should be one of humility and self-criticism.[43]

Adopting a version of critical realist epistemology could positively impact Russian Baptists' mission thinking and practice on multiple levels. First, in addition to their high view of Scripture, it could give them a greater appreciation for context, both biblical and cultural.[44] This is simply indispensable if they are to move from naïve biblicism to reading Scripture "contextually, culturally and theologically."[45] With regard to the communication of the gospel, an appreciation of the context and of the conceptual framework of the hearers could open new avenues for contextualizing the gospel.[46] Second, the contextual nature of all theology implies the need to critically re-examine traditional understandings of and commitment to biblical faith.[47] As is the case with any other church tradition, Russian Baptists face the danger of "absolutizing and universalizing its historically contingent form of life."[48] But the epistemology of critical realism views theology as understandings of divine revelation in particular contexts which cannot be equated with Scripture.[49]

Third, the critical realist perspective could lead to a less combative and more dialogical approach to other theological views, whether within or outside of one's own denomination. Sergienko notes that the stance of some fundamentalist groups in Russia is often characterized by "categorical exclusivism, ideological agendas, and claims that theirs is the only true interpretation of the text."[50] The problem is that their opponents are often equally exclusive. Much of this schismatic spirit and judgmentalism could be eliminated if both parties would keep in mind that theological constructions are not exact descriptions of revealed truth but rather analogical models that approximate

---

43. Bosch, 351.
44. Hiebert, *Anthropological Reflections*, 70–72.
45. Noll, "Peril and Potential," 55.
46. cf. Charles Howard Kraft, *Worldview for Christian Witness* (Pasadena, CA: William Carey Library, 2008), 71–73.
47. Roger E. Olson, *How to Be Evangelical without Being Conservative* (Grand Rapids, MI: Zondervan, 2008).
48. Puzynin, *Tradition of the Gospel Christians*, 287; cf. Hiebert, *Epistemological Shifts*, 115.
49. Hiebert, *Gospel in Human Contexts*, 183.
50. Sergienko, "Nevyuchenyie Uroki Proshlogo [Unlearned Lessons of the Past]."

or represent truth.⁵¹ This perspective suggests the need to adopt a posture of epistemic humility rather than dogmatism on theological issues. When it comes to dialogue with other Christian traditions, many Baptists might need to start thinking of the "brotherhood" in a broader way – one that includes the faithful from other denominations in Russia and abroad.

Overall, the critical realist approach is an essential prerequisite for coping with the challenges of pluralism in the increasingly "post-truth" social, political, and religious contexts. It is possible that much of the traditionalists' nostalgia of the former unity and spirituality stems from a measure of confusion in the face of cultural and theological diversity. In the past, the boundaries between the church and the world were clear and unambiguous, and external pressures resulted in much stronger ties within and between the Baptist communities. Traditionalism today may be seen as a natural defensive reaction against the dissolution of the past uniformity.⁵² But in the interconnected, globalized world with its electronic media, it can hardly solve the problem of the availability of diverse theological and cultural expressions of Christianity. The question is how to develop biblical responses that will enable the church to live and serve faithfully with the challenges of pluralism. Among other things, this might require drawing afresh the lines between the essential truths of the gospel and culturally and historically conditioned *adiaphora*, and developing a more inclusivist view of global Christianity.

2. Rediscovering the Fullness of the Gospel

David Bosch observes that one's theology of mission is "always closely dependent on one's theology of salvation."⁵³ As we have seen, in contemporary

---

51. Grant R. Osborne, *The Hermeneutical Spiral: A Comprehensive Introduction to Biblical Interpretation* (Downers Grove, IL: IVP Academic, 1991), 11, 310; Kraft, *Worldview for Christian Witness*, 69.

52. Puzynin observes that the simplicity and clarity of fundamentalism give many evangelicals "the feeling that they are standing on firm ground with clear safety boundaries in the dizzying vortex of socio-political and cultural motion." Puzynin, *Tradition of the Gospel Christians*, 248. Simplistic solutions for complex issues, however, tend to attract people who prefer the psychological comfort of simple answers over accepting the complexity of the world. This tends to perpetuate the notorious anti-intellectualism and emotional spirituality of Baptist churches. cf. Bokova, "Sovremennye Rossiyskie Evangelskie Khristiane-Baptisty: Sotsialnaia Struktura i Ideologiia [Contemporary Russian Evangelical Christians-Baptists: Social Structure and Ideology]," 41.

53. Bosch, *Transforming Mission*, 385.

global evangelical mission theologies the gospel is seen as a message about the restoration of the whole creation and of all of human life in Christ. The cross and resurrection are cosmic events by which the old age was defeated and the kingdom of God inaugurated. God's ultimate purpose is seen as the "ultimate reconciliation of all creation" and "creation-wide, culture-wide renewal."[54] Having outlined this vision of the gospel, the Cape Town Commitment makes a strong appeal to Christian workers everywhere: "We urge church leaders, pastors and evangelists to preach and teach the fullness of the biblical gospel as Paul did, in all its cosmic scope and truth. We must present the gospel not merely as offering individual salvation, or a better solution to needs than other gods can provide, but as God's plan for the whole universe in Christ."[55]

From this perspective, mission that focuses exclusively on verbal proclamation of the gospel and individual salvation is "truncated and misses the trajectory of divine intention for humanity."[56] Rather, the scope of the church's mission is defined by the comprehensive mission of God himself:

Integral mission means discerning, proclaiming, and living out, the biblical truth that the gospel is God's good news, through the cross and resurrection of Jesus Christ, for individual persons, and for society, and for creation. All three are broken and suffering because of sin; all three are included in the redeeming love and mission of God; all three must be part of the comprehensive mission of God's people.[57]

This more holistic understanding of the gospel could greatly enrich Russian Baptist mission thinking. First, it could help overcome the traditional dualistic mindset by nurturing a coherent biblical worldview. The basis for developing such a worldview is found in the gospel when it is understood as the Bible's "overarching narrative."[58] When Scripture is understood as the true story of the world, it provides the context for understanding the meaning of human lives in all their personal, social, cultural, political, and economic dimensions. A holistic biblical worldview therefore validates attempts

---

54. The Lausanne Movement, "The Cape Town Commitment"; Goheen, *Introducing Christian Mission Today*, 1482; Wright, *Mission of God*.

55. The Lausanne Movement, "The Cape Town Commitment."

56. Ross Hastings, *Missional God, Missional Church: Hope for Re-Evangelizing the West* (Downers Grove, IL: IVP Academic, 2012), 1666.

57. The Lausanne Movement, "The Cape Town Commitment."

58. The Lausanne Movement.

to integrate theology with social studies and other fields of knowledge.[59] In Newbigin's words, when we as Christians "indwell" the biblical story, while "focally attending" to the world, we become able "confidently, though not infallibly, to increase our understanding of it and our ability to cope with it."[60]

Second, a fresh appreciation of the gospel could provide a biblical foundation for a positive, holistic ethics. When divorced from the missional thrust of the biblical narrative, ethics tends to turn moralistic and is motivated by fear and guilt, which, in the end, stifles the believer's spiritual and creative potentials. Besides, in the escapist paradigm the concept of holiness tends to be understood negatively as avoidance of evil rather than as positive work for the common good.[61] Discipleship becomes focused on cognitive models that see information obtained through participation in worship services as the main (if not the only) means of spiritual growth. The "church-centered" or "classroom-centered" forms of the Christian life, in turn, inevitably affect missional engagement with culture.

On the other hand, when Christians view themselves as part of the cosmic drama of redemption, sanctification gains a more positive meaning.[62] It is seen not so much as an escape from the world, but as the restoration of human life in it in keeping with God's purposes for both. This renewal happens through relationships with God, humans (within and outside the church),

---

59. Carson, *Christ and Culture Revisited*; Hiebert, *Gospel in Human Contexts*; Hunter, *To Change the World*.

60. Newbigin, *Gospel in a Pluralist Society*, 38. In recent social studies it has become common to underscore the role of so-called master narratives in generating and sustaining a culture's worldview and moral order. Christian Smith affirms that "people . . . most fundamentally understand what reality is, who they are, and how they to ought to live by locating themselves within the larger narratives which they hear and tell, which constitute what is for [them] real and significant." Christian Stephen Smith, *Moral, Believing Animals: Human Personhood and Culture* (New York: Oxford University Press, 2003), 64; cf. Jeffry R. Halverson, H. Lloyd Goodall, and Steven R. Corman, *Master Narratives of Islamist Extremism* (New York: Palgrave McMillan, 2011); Haidt, *Righteous Mind*.

61. Bosch points out that an individualistic gospel "couches conversion only in micro-ethical terms" neglecting politics, racism and structural injustice. Bosch, *Transforming Mission*, 409. Goheen adds that an individualistic version of the gospel "socializes new converts into a misunderstanding of the nature of the Christian faith . . . [and] profoundly weakens robust discipleship from the beginning." Goheen, *Introducing Christian Mission Today*, 3919.

62. In the famous words of Alasdair MacIntire, "I *can* only answer the question 'What am I to do?' if I can answer the prior question 'Of what story or *stories* do *I find myself* a part?'" Alasdair C. MacIntyre, *After Virtue: A Study in Moral Theory* (Notre Dame, IN: University of Notre Dame Press, 2007), 216.

and the rest of creation.[63] Apart from involvement in all these relationships as intended by the Creator, separation from sin can hardly by itself produce holiness.[64] As the proponents of a missional hermeneutics have reminded us, spiritual formation requires a "missional location" of the Christian community, that is, its participation in God's purposes for the world.[65] From this perspective, missional living may be seen as a *means* of spiritual growth, not just its *fruit*. Bosch profoundly observes that "no church that is involved in true mission ever remains unchanged . . . [It] discovers new dimensions of truth, new depths of discipleship."[66] If so, the opposite must also be true: where there is little missional involvement, there can be little transformation.

Finally, a more comprehensive gospel can provide adequate theological foundations for cultural engagement and holistic mission. Since the fall of the Soviet Union, some Baptists, with different levels of success, have attempted to engage with the cultural, social, and even political arenas. However, without a strong biblical basis these attempts have generally lacked consistency and have been limited to a few individual enthusiasts.[67] The problem is that, due to their tendency to neglect creation and the cultural mandate, dualist conceptions of the gospel can hardly offer a positive theology of culture. In H. Richard Niebuhr's words, dualists tend "to move [the doctrines of] creation and fall into very close proximity and in that connection to do less than justice to the creative work of God."[68]

I believe that rediscovering the fullness of gospel is crucial for Russian Baptists if they are to adopt the full scope of God's mission as the basis for

---

63. Michael J. Gorman, *Reading Paul* (Eugene, OR: Cascade Books, 2008), 45; Tiénou and Hiebert, "Missional Theology"; Keller, *Center Church*.

64. Tim Keller identifies these four relationships as "four ministry fronts" that are essential for every Christian community, and he insists that engaging with all of them "is required by the nature of the gospel." Keller, *Center Church*, 291.

65. George R. Hunsberger, "Proposals for a Missional Hermeneutic: Mapping the Conversation," 2009, https://gocn.org/library/proposals-for-a-missional-hermeneutic-mapping-the-conversation/; Michael Barram, "The Bible, Mission, and Social Location: Toward a Missional Hermeneutic," *Interpretation*, no. 61 (2007): 52; David Guder, "Biblical Formation and Discipleship," in *Treasure in Clay Jars: Patterns in Missional Faithfulness*, ed. Lois Y. Barrett (Grand Rapids, MI: Eerdmans, 2004), 62.

66. Bosch, *Transforming Mission*, 210–211.

67. Bokova, "Teologia Rossiiskikh Evangel'skikh Khristian-Baptistov Na Rubezhe XX i XXI Vekov [Theology of Russian Evangelical Christians-Baptists at the Turn of the Twenty-First Century]."

68. Niebuhr, *Christ and Culture*, 188.

their own mission in society. While for Western churches the concept of *missio Dei* was needed to refocus attention from anthropocentric activism in mission, for Russian evangelicals it can serve as a way to discover the breadth of God's redemptive purposes. If for Western evangelicals it was needed to overcome their Christendom mentality, for Russian Baptists it is needed to overcome the vestiges of their "fortress mentality."

3. Missional Ecclesiology

The concept of the church's missionary nature flows from the logic of the gospel. With his ultimate goal of creation-wide renewal in mind, God "chooses a community to embody and make known that future, calling individuals to join this community and play their role in the bigger story."[69] This makes the church missional in its very nature. As Dean Flemming puts it: "We don't simply do mission. 'Mission' is who we are. We are a people called by God for the sake of the world."[70] Conversely, whenever the church tries to order its life simply in relation to "its own concerns and for the purposes of its own continued existence, it is untrue to its proper nature."[71] From this perspective, withdrawal from the world is no less a denial of the church's calling than becoming conformed to it.[72]

With this view of the church in mind, Newbigin calls on Western churches to "renounce their introverted concern for their own life," and recognize that they "exist for the sake of those who are not members, as sign, instrument, and foretaste of God's redeeming grace for the whole life of society."[73] As we have seen, Russian Baptists in late Soviet period almost completely lost their orientation to the world. The church was seen as an isolated community in which the faithful encourage each other as they wait for their rescue from this perishing world. To renew their missional encounter with culture, Russian Baptists today need to nurture an understanding of themselves as a body taken up in God's redemptive work and sent into the world to continue the mission of Jesus.

---

69. Goheen, *Introducing Christian Mission Today*, 1483; Gorman, *Reading Paul*, 45.

70. Dean E. Flemming, *Recovering the Full Mission of God: A Biblical Perspective on Being, Doing, and Telling* (Downers Grove, IL: IVP Academic, 2013), 258.

71. Newbigin, "Local Church Truly United," 154.

72. Stott, "Lausanne Covenant," 9.

73. Newbigin, *Gospel in a Pluralist Society*, 233.

The most powerful instrument for nurturing this missionary consciousness is the Bible itself when presented as "the story that tells of the mission of God and the formation of a community sent to participate in it."[74] In addition to a hermeneutics that focuses on doctrinal and pastoral concerns, Baptists need to develop a missional reading of Scripture. In clarifying the specifics of the church's orientation to the world, the theological resources of the missional church movement can be found helpful. In particular, the following three emphases of that movement could enrich Russian Baptists' views of the church:

- A broader view of God's redemptive purposes understood as humanization.[75]
- An incarnational ecclesiology which assumes that the church "seeps into the cracks and crevices of a society in order to be Christ to those who don't yet know him."[76]
- The mandate to exercise "loving stewardship over creation through work and in all aspects of the human endeavor."[77]

Adopting a missional view of the church might also catalyze organizational and structural change. Goheen points out that building a missional church requires leadership that "constantly challenges the selfish introversion that seems to be the default mode of congregations."[78] Van Engen adds that missionary congregations must have "an administrative system which explodes outward into the world."[79] Frost and Hirsch suggest adopting a form of "apostolic leadership" in accordance with the fivefold pattern of Ephesians 4:7, 11 ("apostles . . . prophets . . . evangelists . . . pastors and teachers").[80] They believe that missional leadership is "one of the most significant aspects needed

---

74. Craig Van Gelder and Dwight J. Zscheile, *The Missional Church in Perspective: Mapping Trends and Shaping the Conversation* (Grand Rapids, MI: Baker Academic, 2011), 97.

75. Hastings, *Missional God, Missional Church*, 1666.

76. Michael Frost and Alan Hirsch, *The Shaping of Things to Come: Innovation and Mission for the 21st Century Church* (Peabody, MA: Hendrickson, 2003), 12.

77. Hastings, *Missional God, Missional Church*, 1665; Van Gelder and Zscheile, *Missional Church in Perspective*, 125.

78. Goheen, *Introducing Christian Mission Today*, 4166.

79. Van Engen, *God's Missionary People*, 116.

80. Frost and Hirsch, *Shaping of Things*.

for the transition . . . to a missional mode of the church."[81] In fact, without this "charismatic ministry pattern" a local church cannot mature.[82]

4. Critical Cultural Engagement

Being a sign, foretaste, and instrument of the kingdom of God presupposes the church's involvement in human society and its engagement with culture. Historically, Russian Baptists developed a protective acultural stance which helped them to maintain their identity in an environment of militant atheism. Today, many Baptist leaders and church members continue to hold a view of culture that, at best, ignores social and cultural developments outside the church walls. As a result, over the past quarter century there have been very few consistent attempts to propose a biblical and contextual theology of culture.[83] In fact, since much of the Russian Baptist tradition was shaped in a cultural ghetto, its own resources may not be sufficient for this task.

The reality is that some of the most important theological motifs for thinking about culture from a biblical perspective are virtually absent in the traditional paradigm. These themes include (1) the cultural mandate and stewardship of creation as aspects of the *imago Dei;* (2) culture as an expression of both human nature and God's common grace; (3) the comprehensive nature and the "already" of the kingdom; and (4) the eschatological renewal of creation and the continuity of cultural efforts in the new creation. For developing a working theology of culture, Russian Baptists might need to draw on the resources of global evangelicalism and especially on those of the Reformed tradition.[84]

In particular, the following recent developments in evangelical theology might be found helpful. First, D.A. Carson suggests that a theology of culture

---

81. Frost and Hirsch, 165.

82. Frost and Hirsch, 169.

83. One serious attempt to develop such a theology was the so-called "Statement of Social Responsibility of the RUECB," published by the central office in Moscow in 2014. Unfortunately, this anonymous document has never been publicly promoted or discussed, either prior to or after its publication. In fact, from my interviews it became clear that most participants had never read it, and some were simply unaware of its existence.

84. Abraham Kuyper, *Lectures on Calvinism* (Grand Rapids, MI: Eerdmans, 1931); Herman Bavinck, *The Philosophy of Revelation* (New York; London: Longmans, Green & Co., 1909); Hoekema, *Bible and Future*; Wolterstorff, *Justice and Peace*; Wolters, *Creation Regained*; Carson, *Christ and Culture Revisited*; Hunter, *To Change the World*; Plantinga, *Engaging God's World*; Keller, *Center Church*.

should be constructed within the framework of a biblical theology that focuses on the turning points of the Scriptural narrative. This allows the church intentionally to hold together the realities of creation, fall, redemption, and restoration.[85] Second, the comprehensive nature of the kingdom of God allows Christians to see redemption in Christ as "creation regained" and helps overcome false dualities in their view of God's world.[86] In Howard Snyder's words:

> God's kingdom means that all things are within the sphere of God's sovereignty, and, therefore, of God's concern. No room for compartmentalized thinking here. Economics, ecology, politics, the arts, social and family life – all these are kingdom topics. So kingdom Christians bring a Jesus perspective to every area of life.[87]

Third, the eschatological tension between the "already" and the "not yet" of the kingdom provides a basis for critical discernment between what is creationally good and the "negative fingerprints" of sin.[88] A hard-to-achieve, but necessary biblical balance between the *affirmation* and *antithesis* or the *indigenizing* and *pilgrim* principles helps the church to navigate between the temptations of both cultural syncretism and withdrawal in its context.[89] Fourth, for this task a biblical theology of culture requires not only responsible biblical exegesis, but also a deep phenomenological study of culture. The goal is to think biblically about God's universal mission in the "context of the world here and now, in all its particularities, paradoxes, and confusions."[90] Finally, a theology of culture will greatly benefit from taking into account the global church's responses in different historical and cultural contexts.[91]

---

85. Carson, *Christ and Culture Revisited*, 59; cf. Craig G. Bartholomew and Michael W. Goheen, *The Drama of Scripture: Finding Our Place in the Biblical Story* (Grand Rapids, MI: Baker Academic, 2004); Wright, *Mission of God*; Wright, *Surprised by Hope*.

86. Wolters, *Creation Regained*.

87. Snyder, *Models of the Kingdom*, 154.

88. The Lausanne Movement, "The Cape Town Commitment."

89. Hunter, *To Change the World*, 237; Walls, *Missionary Movement*, 14.

90. Tiénou and Hiebert, "Missional Theology," 227; Robert J. Priest, "'Experience-near Theologizing' in Diverse Human Contexts," in *Globalizing Theology: Belief and Practice in an Era of World Christianity*, ed. Craig Ott and Harold A Netland (Grand Rapids, MI: Baker Academic, 2006), 181–195.

91. Shenk, "Recasting Theology of Mission," 131; Hiebert, *Anthropological Reflections*, 35.

Methodologically, a helpful approach for thinking biblically about culture can be found in Paul Hiebert's critical contextualization model.[92] In his later writings, he emphasized that contextualization is not limited to dealing with immediate cases or customs at hand, but rather should be understood as a "longer range reflection on underlying issues."[93] From this perspective, contextualization is a comprehensive and ongoing task of the church to respond biblically to personal, cultural, and social issues with the ultimate purpose being "to reflect the kingdom of God on earth."[94]

Developing biblical theologies of culture could have a positive effect on several aspects of Russian Baptists' mission in society. First, it is hard to see how they can begin to overcome their inherited social marginality if they continue neglecting culture. The innovators, in my view, correctly see much of Baptist marginality as self-imposed "psychological defense mechanisms" and "habitual behavior models."[95] In his analysis of the phenomenon among post-Soviet Slavic evangelicals, Konstantin Teteryatnikov identifies three key theological beliefs that tend to perpetuate this mindset:

- The irredeemable nature of culture: "The present reality is seen as an unchangeable negative reality which cannot be either transformed or taken away; what is left is to be internally isolated from it."
- A form of regenerationist soteriology that sharply contrasts the "new nature" Christians receive through the act of regeneration with the sinful nature and deeds of other persons.
- Repentance (i.e., the initial act of coming to faith) implies that a person rejects his or her former life experiences, education, and skills, and stops striving toward the "rubbish" of "worldly things."

---

92. Hiebert, "Critical Contextualization."

93. Hiebert, *Gospel in Human Contexts*, 32.

94. Hiebert, *Anthropological Reflections*, 92; cf. Moreau, "Contextualization That Is Comprehensive."

95. Mikhail Dubrovsky, "Obretenie Sebia: Puti Formirovaniia Novoi Identichnosti [Finding Ourselves: The Ways of Shaping a New Identity]," in *Dvatsat' Let Religioznoy Svobody i Aktivnoi Misii [Twenty Years of Religious Freedom and Active Mission]*, ed. Mikhaiil Cherenkov (Kiev: Dukh i Litera, 2011), 398.

> This practice inevitably weakens the social networks of Baptist believers and their communities.[96]

As we have seen, the traditionalists tend to perceive attacks against these and other traditional views as a threat to Baptist identity itself, and so fight to protect them despite the fact that these beliefs may hinder their mission. The common perception of these convictions as biblical can only be challenged when they are explicitly articulated and then evaluated against the background of a biblical theology and the theological reflection of others in the evangelical camp.

Second, developing biblical theologies of culture could help the Baptist movement to guard against cultural syncretism. Whenever a church fails to evaluate culture biblically and respond with biblically informed understandings and practices, it tends to uncritically accommodate to cultural currents.[97] With regard to the issue of nationalism in particular, Hiebert observes:

> If our deepest identities are ethnicity, culture, and nationalism, we can gather on the surface for worship, fellowship, and mission, but we know that when problems arise the underlying differences will emerge and will divide. If, on the contrary, we are one at the deepest level of our identities, we can celebrate ethnic, cultural, and gender differences, knowing that when problems arise we will pull together.[98]

Unfortunately, within the Baptist community Russia's "hybrid war" against Ukraine since 2014 has given expression to some implicit beliefs which have made it painfully obvious that many believers, including church leaders, are susceptible to nationalistic ideologies and the animosities they produce. In some cases the reasons for the uncritical approval of the government's actions might have included a particular understanding of Romans 13, fear of rejection by the majority, or the desire to "show their loyalty and patriotic

---

96. Konstantin Teteriatnikov, "Tserkov' Vchera i Segodnia [The Church Yesterday and Today]," in *Dvatsat' Let Religioznoy Svobody i Aktivnoi Misii [Twenty Years of Religious Freedom and Active Mission]*, ed. Mikhaiil Cherenkov (Kiev: Dukh i Litera, 2011), 182–183.

97. Hiebert, *Gospel in Human Contexts*, 32.

98. Hiebert, 193.

spirit."[99] But for many this approval seems to have been based on a sincere belief in the official interpretations of the conflict and the narratives constructed by the official media. This suggests a lack of a critical awareness of the messages believers receive and of the worldviews behind them. Unless dominant cultural trends are tested against a biblical worldview, the result can be a compromised witness to the gospel.[100]

Third, a biblical theology of culture could help Baptists extend their mission to every area of life. Today, unlike thirty years ago, talented Baptist youth have opportunities to fulfill themselves basically in every sphere outside the church: education, business, the public square, the media, the arts, etc. Without a clear theological understanding of how to view work missionally, these opportunities can be perceived merely as individual self-actualization, a means of making a living, or even as a "necessary evil." A biblical theology of culture could help Christians bridge the dualistic divide between the "secular" and the "sacred" and bring together faith and work. The Cape Town Commitment identifies this divide as a "major obstacle to the mobilization of all God's people in the mission of God."[101] A theological understanding of cultural engagement could encourage believers to view even mundane tasks as part of their mission to reflect the kingdom of God in every area of life.[102]

5. *Holistic Living as an Alternative Community*

Thanks to the influence of Lesslie Newbigin,[103] it has now become common in evangelical missiology to talk about the church's "missionary encounter with culture."[104] According to Michael Goheen, making this vision a reality presupposes two essential tasks: first, the church should live fully in the

---

99. Roman Lunkin, "A Reaction of Russian Churches on Ukrainian Crisis: A Prophecy of Democracy," in *Religion, State, Society, and Identity in Transition: Ukraine*, ed. Rob van der Laarse et al. (Oisterwijk: Wolf Legal Publishers, 2015), 454.

100. Hiebert, *Gospel in Human Contexts*, 32.

101. The Lausanne Movement, "The Cape Town Commitment."

102. Keller, *Center Church*, 331–332. Recently, Mission Eurasia (based in Wheaton, Illinois) launched the so-called Next Generation Professional Leaders Initiative with the goal of equipping Christians in the former USSR to "boldly share Christ and demonstrate biblical values . . . in the workplace with clients, colleagues, patients, students, and co-workers." "Mission Eurasia," accessed 23 June 2017, https://missioneurasia.org/. Their resources are increasingly being used by Russian Baptist youth as well.

103. Newbigin, *Foolishness to the Greeks*.

104. Shenk, *Write the Vision*; Goheen, *Introducing Christian Mission Today*.

biblical story and interpret its culture in the light of that story. Second, the church is called to offer the gospel as "a counterstory, as a credible alternative way of life," by which it will inevitably challenge the idolatrous cultural story. As a result, the lives and words of those in the Christian community will be a "call for radical conversion, an invitation to understand and live in the world in the light of the gospel."[105]

From this perspective, for the Baptist (or more broadly, evangelical) movement to be an alternative community in Russia means something more than holding to higher moral standards or being doctrinally distinct from the dominant church. In many parts of the country, Baptists have already been known for strong families, mutual help, a responsible work ethic, and resilience in difficult circumstances. They are also perceived (whether negatively or positively) as a religious alternative to the Orthodox Church in that they reject its hierarchical structure and sacramentalism, do not practice an elaborate ritual with visible objects of worship, and strive to build their faith on the Bible rather than on historical traditions. These characteristics have been important aspects of Baptist witness, yet from the standpoint of the missionary encounter with culture, evangelicals, in their individual and communal lives, are called to reflect the ways the gospel "deals with all of life as a whole and transforms all of life under the lordship of Jesus Christ."[106] In other words, evangelicals are called to be *a visible and comprehensive sample of what Russian society might look like if transformed by the gospel.*

This poses a number of challenges to Russian Baptists, both theological and pastoral. Theologically, the gospel needs to be made the foundation for understanding life in all its fullness. Balanced biblical responses to the current challenges facing Russian society should be formulated. Pastorally, members need to be encouraged and instructed regarding specific ways the gospel transforms their personal and social lives. In the words of the Cape Town Commitment, the global church today needs "intensive efforts to train all God's people in whole-life discipleship, which means to live, think, work,

---

105. Goheen, 4919.

106. Ed Stetzer, "Monday Is for Missiology," 2010, https://www.christianitytoday.com/edstetzer/2010/march/monday-is-for-missiology.html.

and speak from a biblical worldview and with missional effectiveness in every place or circumstance of daily life and work."[107]

In the current socio-political context of Russia, three areas in particular stand out in which evangelicals could model a viable social alternative.[108] First, in their communal life they could become working models of healthy social relations. As communities based on "voluntary membership, democratic organization, and intellectual egalitarianism," they could exemplify a social space where individuals make choices based on their convictions, yet in harmony with others in their community.[109] When properly understood and practiced, such evangelical convictions as the priesthood of all believers and the church as the body of Christ have multiple implications for the broader society. In particular, they could help engender an understanding of social life that is different from both Western liberal models of secular individualism and the Russian authoritarian tradition which has historically suppressed individual expression for the "good" of the collective.[110]

According to Cyril Hovorun, much of the current political unrest in the post-Soviet countries can be explained by the conflict between a "neo-Soviet interpretation of citizenship built on paternalism and an imperial mindset, and an anti-Soviet thinking that focuses on the themes of personal freedom and responsibility." He affirms that Christianity "teaches individuals to leave paternalism behind and take responsibility for the[ir] lives and [for] society. This is how the . . . churches could contribute to the development of the civil society."[111] As was shown in chapter 3, the early Baptists contributed significantly to the creation of a public sphere and civic culture in tsarist Russia.[112] Today, when the very idea of democracy is often dismissed as a fraud

---

107. The Lausanne Movement, "The Cape Town Commitment."

108. In this primary text on missional ecclesiology, Goheen suggests several important ways in which the church can be an alternative society in the West. Bartholomew and Goheen, *Drama of Scripture*. Most of his points are directly applicable to Russian evangelicals as well. Here I want to outline some areas that are more relevant specifically for the Russian context.

109. Coleman, *Russian Baptists and Spiritual Revolution*, 3, 223.

110. cf. Olson, *How to Be Evangelical*, 184–199.

111. Hovorun, *Ukraiinska Publichna Teologiia [Ukrainian Public Theology]*, 21–22.

112. Deryck Lovegrove observes that religious voluntarism in totalitarian contexts tends to raise issues regarding "the extent of the [state's] power over the conscience of the individual believer, and the precise basis of its authority, whether prescriptive or derivative." Deryck W. Lovegrove, *Established Church, Sectarian People* (Cambridge: Cambridge University Press, 2009), 5.

in Russian public discourse, evangelical communities have an opportunity to demonstrate working examples of corruption-free and manipulation-free democratic communities. What this presupposes, however, is respect for the personal dignity of members in their own communities, mutual accountability, and leadership models rooted in the biblical value of "an inverted hierarchy" rather than in the cultural idea of the sacred legitimization of authoritarianism.[113]

Second, Baptists could demonstrate a social alternative by their voluntary commitment to the common good. It has been repeatedly said that one of the serious weaknesses of Russian society is a lack of horizontal connections and self-organization beyond nuclear family ties.[114] The result is a widespread indifference toward what is going on beyond the door of one's house, weak volunteer movements, underdeveloped human rights activism, etc. Yet this situation gives Baptists multiple opportunities to serve actively for the good of all, provided they choose not to focus on their own needs or narrowly understood ecclesiastical concerns. Ott and Wilson stress the need for local churches to be "churches with kingdom impact," that is, communities that influence all their relationships by "reflecting and advancing . . . righteousness, compassion, justice, and [the] restoration of all things under Christ's reign."[115]

Tim Keller comments that such churches will be distinctively different from both secular and traditional religious communities:

> If the Christian faith is to have any impact on culture, the time must come when it is widely known that secularism tends to make people selfish, while general religion and traditional morality make people tribal (concerned mainly for their own), but the Christian gospel turns people away from both their

---

113. Hiebert, *Gospel in Human Contexts*, 191.

114. Akhiezer, Klyamkin, and Yakovenko, *Istoriia Rosii: Konets Ili Novoye Nachalo? [History of Russia: The End or A New Beginning?]*; Kovalyova, *Unlearning the Soviet Tongue*; Bobrov, "Pochemu Rossiiskii Politicheskii Rezhim Prevraschaet Grazhdan v Iskliuchionnykh [Why Russian Political Regime Deprives Citizens of Their Rights]."

115. Craig Ott and Gene Wilson, *Global Church Planting: Biblical Principles and Best Practices for Multiplication* (Grand Rapids, MI: Baker Academic, 2011), 395; Miroslav Volf, *A Public Faith: How Followers of Christ Should Serve the Common Good* (Grand Rapids, MI: Brazos Press, 2011); Sider, Olson, and Unruh, *Churches That Make a Difference*.

selfishness and their self-righteousness to serve others in the way that Jesus gave himself for his enemies.[116]

For this to happen, Russian Baptists will need to overcome their deep-seated habits of cultural withdrawal and passivity.[117] Miroslav Volf speaks of two "malfunctions" Christianity can exhibit in its relationship with society: coerciveness and idleness.[118] The former is hardly a temptation for the small Baptist minority in Russia. Furthermore, they are well aware of the Orthodox Church's historical reliance on the state to achieve the "victory of the theocratic dream" with its bitter fruits of imperial conquests and cruel persecution of minorities.[119] In fact, these experiences seem to have predisposed many Baptists to believe that the only faithful alternative to the Constantinian temptation is found in isolation and quietism. Today, this conviction is being reinforced once more by the renewed attempts of Orthodox fundamentalists to control the public square and to justify political violence on the basis of the Christian faith.

On the one hand, I firmly believe that Russian evangelicals should openly and unambiguously distance themselves from any coercive form of Christianity. A proper understanding of the gospel and of the cross would make it impossible for Christians to use power to oppress.[120] In the final analysis, what post-Soviet societies need today is not so much another "moral institution from above" that speaks from a position of superiority, but rather a "place of hope from below" that is there to serve.[121] As Volf points out, this attitude of service does not require political power: "Christian communities [should be] more comfortable with being just one of many players, so that

---

116. Keller, *Center Church*, 235.

117. Russian historian and sociologist Igor Bobrov, who is more interested in the social aspects of Protestantism in Russia than in its mission, argues that "the future of Christianity in a new Russia" will depend on the choice between "political conformism and a more articulate civic position" which Russian Protestants face today. Bobrov, "Pirrova Pobeda [A Pyrrhic Victory]." What he seems to imply is that in the absence of alternatives to the authoritarianism of the Orthodox Church, Russians might en masse turn to secularism.

118. Volf, *Public Faith*, 23–54.

119. Schmemann, *Historical Road*, 313; Meyendorff, *Byzantine Theology*, 217.

120. Volf, *Public Faith*, 53–54.

121. Fedor Raychinets, "Est' Li Sotsial'naia i Politichskaia Positsiia u Evangel'skikh Tserkvei Ukrainy? [Do Evangelical Churches of Ukraine Have a Social and Political Position?]," in *Dvatsat' Let Religioznoy Svobody i Aktivnoi Misii [Twenty Years of Religious Freedom and Active Mission]*, ed. Mikhaiil Cherenkov (Kiev: Dukh i Litera, 2011), 327.

from whatever place they find themselves – on the margins, at the center, or anywhere in between – they can promote human flourishing. . . ."[122]

On the other hand, if Russian Baptists are to be committed to the common good, they *must* leave their self-absorption behind and become actively involved in their communities. James Hunter suggests that the model for the church's engagement with the world is found in Christ's mediation of God's "faithful presence" with humanity.[123] When faithfully present in the world, the church will not strive to coercively impose a Christian political or moral agenda on society. In the final analysis, politicization, or the proclivity to engage culture in political terms, does not usually achieve its intended purpose of cultural change. Rather, the church must seek to strengthen the world's healthy qualities and humbly criticize and subvert its most destructive tendencies.[124] Therefore, unlike some recent developments in the dominant church in Russia, evangelical involvement should be markedly *different*: active but humble, and brave but without compulsion or manipulation.

The third area in which evangelicals could become a viable social alternative has to do with the issue of reemerging Russian nationalism. As was shown in the first chapter, the current upsurge in national consciousness has a strong religious dimension that is rooted in the outlook of the Russian Orthodox hierarchy. On the popular level, it takes various forms of religious and cultural ethnocentrism and militant anti-Westernism. What space these diverse visions of the civilizational struggle leave for the social role of evangelical Christianity is not yet clear at this stage. However, the increasingly suspicious public attitude toward evangelical mission work[125] and legal restrictions of it create the impression that this role is supposed to be limited to the internal life of their communities (with the possible exception of social service among the poor and addicted).

---

122. Volf, *Public Faith*, 79.

123. Hunter, *To Change the World*, 87.

124. Hunter, 285.

125. According to Russian sociologist Boris Dubin, 57 percent respondents in 1989 believed that "sect members can be left to do their own thing," whereas 10 percent wanted to have them "removed or isolated from society." By 2003, these numbers had changed to 24 percent and 54 percent respectively. Dubin, "Pravoslavie i Natsional'naia Identichnost: Neotraditsionalistskoe Znachenie Very [The Russian Orthodoxy and National Identity: A Neo-Traditionalist Meaning of Faith]," 42.

Few attempts have been made so far to respond to these ideological developments from an evangelical perspective in Russia. One strong voice has been that of Andrei Puzynin, who called on the evangelical church not to take part in "the current political battles between the Orthodox and Western civilizations" and to resist the "waves of Ukrainian or Russian nationalism" that accompany them.[126] He argues that evangelicals in Russia have historically tended to adjust their narratives of self-identity to the changing political and social currents. As a result, their self-identity has depended on the "fluctuations in the geopolitical force field . . . at the meeting point of the tectonic plates of the Western and Soviet (later Orthodox) civilizations." This led the evangelical tradition in Russia into a deep theological crisis it is experiencing today. The solution is to be found in "the cross of Christ and in the creative reconstruction of the narratives and practices of this historically contingent tradition in light of the cross."[127] Rather than accommodating to its context, the church should strive to be "an eschatological community that demonstrates the life of Christ's victory over the powers."[128]

One can hear in this proposal echoes of the neo-Anabaptist theological tradition represented primarily by such thinkers as John H. Yoder and Stanley Hauerwas. While this tradition cherishes the important biblical emphases on Christian community, on its countercultural identity, and on spiritual formation, I suspect that by itself it might not be sufficient to provide the theological resources needed to undergird the renewal of the Russian Baptists' missionary encounter with their culture. Unfortunately, Puzynin never unpacks his important concepts of "resisting" or of living "in light of the cross," but as they stand, they create the impression of an enlightened version of the traditional eschatological escapism. Unless accompanied by a positive social agenda rooted in a holistic biblical worldview, these negative concepts can only further encourage the habit of self-absorption within Russian Baptist communities. The church indeed *is* an eschatological community, but it is also God's primary *agent* of his redemptive mission for the sake of the world.[129]

---

126. Puzynin, *Tradition of the Gospel Christians*, 279.

127. Puzynin, 278–279.

128. Puzynin, 278.

129. In theory, the concept of the church as "a social program" that by its very existence becomes a challenge to the fallen powers seems attractive and theologically consistent. Hauerwas

I believe that in order to model a biblical alternative to nationalism, the evangelical church, first of all, needs to attempt to understand and scripturally evaluate the narratives, sentiments, and traumas behind the phenomenon. Second, it should articulate and bring to public consideration alternative visions of social life rooted in a biblical worldview and biblical values. Finally, evangelicals need to embody these visions in their own communal and social life. As the Cape Town Commitment puts it, "God's plan for the integration of the whole creation in Christ is modeled in the ethnic reconciliation of God's new humanity."[130]

Tim Keller emphasizes that contextualization of the gospel strives both to deconstruct the idols of a culture and to highlight its aspirations and ultimate values. In other words, the gospel not only confronts, but also completes and fulfils each society's "baseline cultural narratives."[131] From this perspective, Russian evangelicals need both to expose the underlying stories of nationalism and to seek to persuade Russians that the true healing of their traumas and the true answer to their deepest longings can be found in Christ. It has been observed that a mature ideology usually presumes to be a "false revelation of creation, fall and redemption" in the sense that it claims to be rooted in a comprehensive, cosmic narrative which explains the origin of, and provides the solution for, the current plight.[132] As such, it opens itself to evaluation from the vantage point of the Bible's cosmic story – not only in light of the cross, as Puzynin puts it, but in light of the whole narrative extending from creation to redemption to the ultimate restoration and fulfillment of creation (Rom 8:19–23).[133]

---

and Willimon, *Resident Aliens*, 81. However, Russian Baptist history strongly suggests that when effectively marginalized by the authorities, disparaged by the media, and ignored by most of society, the church may hardly present any challenge at all. Moreover, believers tend to internalize and theologically rationalize the status quo. It seems, therefore, that not all ethics is social, as the authors want to believe. For an evangelical community to be a visible moral alternative apparently requires a measure of social and symbolic capital that is more characteristic of traditionally Protestant societies than of Russia with its historic dominance of the Orthodox Church.

130. The Lausanne Movement, "The Cape Town Commitment."
131. Keller, *Center Church*, 90.
132. B. Goudzwaard, *Idols of Our Time* (Downers Grove, IL: IVP Academic, 1984), 25.
133. In Puzynin's neo-Anabaptist approach, the (exclusive) focus on the cross seems to suggest the need for Russian evangelicals to distance themselves from burning cultural issues. Puzynin, *Tradition of the Gospel Christians*, 278–279. But evangelicals have not only

To offer credible alternatives to nationalism, the Russian evangelical church might also have to consider the issue of its *contextual* identity in addition to its theological identity. Mikhail Dubrovsky invites evangelicals to develop a complex self-understanding that "does not fit into a standard niche" in that it intentionally attempts to bridge the historically painful East-West division:

> We are the fruit of both the Reformation and Russian "God-seeking" over the centuries. In the search for our identity we need to keep both focal points in view . . . Only then can we find the answer to the question of our mission and calling in the religious, social, and political spheres of our countries, and . . . offer an indigenous way for our peoples [that is] different from the Byzantine route.[134]

Among other things, this requires that evangelicals formulate their own answers to "the specifically Russian questions that have been so deeply raised in both Russian literature and philosophy."[135] Vladislav Bachinin suggests that for this evangelicals need to see their faith as a holistic, comprehensive worldview that is different from the worldview of Byzantism with its historic monopoly on spiritual programs for Russian society.[136] Without such deep engagement with the issues of Russian history and culture from the perspective (and vast resources) of the evangelical tradition, Russian evangelicals

---

been a legitimate part of their society for a century and a half; they, in fact, *should be* for the sake of their mission. Given their hybrid identity, the tendency to "fluctuate" between their Slavic and Western roots is not necessarily a theological compromise in itself. The question is how to distinguish between genuine contextualization and syncretism that distorts the gospel. This question can only be answered, however, from within biblical (and contextual) theologies of culture that intentionally hold together the realities of creation, fall, cross, and consummation. Oliver O'Donovan, *Resurrection and Moral Order: An Outline for Evangelical Ethics* (Leicester, England; Grand Rapids, MI: IVP Academic; Eerdmans, 1986); Carson, *Christ and Culture Revisited*.

134. Dubrovsky, "Obretenie Sebia: Puti Formirovaniia Novoi Identichnosti [Finding Ourselves: The Ways of Shaping a New Identity]," 396.

135. Dubrovsky, 397.

136. Vladislav Bachinin, *Vizantizm i Evangelizm: Genealogiia Russkogo Protestantizma [Byzantism and Evangelicalism: The Genealogy of Russian Protestantism]* (St Petersburg: SPGU, 2003), n.p. The concept of "Byzantism" was first introduced by the Russian thinker Konstantin Leontiev in 1875 and further elaborated by Vladimir Solovyov in 1896. They described it as a culture that Russia inherited from the eastern Roman Empire which focuses on the autocracy, the Eastern Orthodox faith, collectivism, and traditionalism.

can neither free themselves from their theological dependence on the West nor overcome their deeply internalized inferiority complex in relation to the Orthodox Church.[137]

In sum, as Russian society is experiencing the emergence of a new (and old) public ideology that is rooted in the totalitarian outlook of Byzantism, Baptist communities could learn to openly articulate the cultural and sociopolitical implications of the gospel from an evangelical perspective. While the resultant social stance might in many respects be close to the principles that underlie Western civilization, it cannot be written off as merely "Western," because it would also draw on the rich heritage of Russian humanist writers and thinkers and intentionally distance itself from Western post-Christian liberalism. Rather than siding with either of the two conflicting powers that Patriarch Kirill envisions in his version of "civilizational struggle," this position would:[138]

- Challenge the idolatrous cultural stories of *both* secular liberalism with its anthropocentrism and amorality, *and* of religious traditionalism with its ethnocentrism, judgmental self-righteousness, and xenophobia.
- Nurture a lifestyle that is not compromised by the ethnic pride exhibited by a large number of Russians. As the community of

---

137. Slavic Baptists often complain about the "theological crisis" of their tradition, meaning the virtual absence of native theologies and their intellectual dependence on Western sources. Alexander Negrov, "Pochemu v Rossii Otsutstvuet Sobstvennaia Protestantskaia Teologia? [Why Is There No Indigenous Protestant Theology in Russia?]," *Mirt [Myrtle]* 1 (1997): 4–5; Nikolai Kornilov, "Evngel'skiie Khristiane-Baptisty Na Istoricheskom Perelome, 1991–1997 [Evangelical Christian-Baptists at the Historical Turning Point, 1991-1997]," in *Dia-Logos* (Moscow: Istina i Zhizn,' 1997), 171–179; Kornilov, "Kakogo Roda Bogoslovie Nam Nuzhno? [What Kind of Theology Do We Need?]"; Puzynin, *Tradition of the Gospel Christians*. But as Viktoria Liubaschenko profoundly comments, "Shaping 'our theology' has to do not so much with the accumulation of new [doctrinal] content as with its integration with local historical and cultural realities . . . The goal is not to formally bring together Protestant [theologies] and local factors, but to cultivate that only ground from which the growth of 'our theology' is possible – the discovery of the wealth of native history, culture, [and] traditions . . . in light of a Protestant worldview." Viktoria Liubaschenko, "Otechestvennaia Shkola Bogosloviia: Metodologiia, Problemy, Perspectivy [Development of a Native Theological Scholarship: Methodologies, Problems, and Prospects]," in *Bogoslovie i Bogoslovskoye Obrazovanie v Sovremennom Obschestve: Aktualnye Voprosy Teorii i Praktiki [Theology and Theological Education in the Contemporary Society: Current Issues of Theory and Practice]*, ed. EAAA (Odessa: BOE, 2002), 43; cf. Priest, "'Experience-near Theologizing.'"

138. Kirill, , *Freedom and Responsibility*.

God's people, the church "transcends all cultures [and] social or political systems."[139]

As a final point, it is worth noting that some Russian sociologists observe, especially among educated urban dwellers and youth, a growing dissatisfaction in Russia today with the authoritarian tendencies of the state and with the support it receives from the dominant church.[140] Many are searching for alternative forms of religious and social life rooted in the gospel and individual freedoms.[141] If Baptist presentations of the gospel avoid important cultural issues and focus exclusively on "spiritual" matters, or if they uncritically accommodate to the socio-political thinking of the majority church, the likelihood is that many such seekers will bypass Baptist communities in their search. Michael Cherenkov rightly points out that the place of a "temple-centered," liturgical Christianity has already been successfully taken by the Russian Orthodox Church. What is noticeably absent in society, however, is a holistic biblical worldview that

> connects Christianity in the church with Christianity in the world, blesses work and creativity and family and society, and sanctifies life in all its multidimensional fullness. If Baptists choose to represent a narrow, inward-focused type of Christianity, they consent to the [prescribed] place of a sect within the Orthodox tradition and, in this way, lose their uniqueness and special calling.[142]

---

139. Timothy C. Tennent, "Lausanne and Global Evangelicalism: Theological Distinctives and Missiological Impact," in *The Lausanne Movement: A Range of Perspectives*, ed. Lars Dahle, Margunn Serigstad Dahle, and Knud Jørgensen (Eugene, OR: Wipf & Stock, 2014), 48.

140. Zorkaia, "Pravoslavie v Bezreligioznom Obschetve [The Orthodox Church in a Secular Society]"; Gribanova, "Ethnic and Religious Relations."

141. Within the Orthodox Church itself there are emerging movements of believers who are dissatisfied with the growing reliance on, and de facto merger of their church with, the state. Due to their informal nature, these movements do not have centralized leadership, but some key thinkers who are shaping alternative visions of church and society are the priest Sergei Chapnin, deacon Andrey Kuraev, and Bible scholar Andrey Desnitsky. Russian Orthodox artist Maxim Kantor has proposed the idea of a "Christian humanism" which is distinctively different from mainline Orthodox fundamentalism, and can possibly bring together Christians from different traditions for social initiatives and projects in the country. Maxim Kantor, *Uchebnik Risovaniia [A Textbook of Drawing]*. Vol. 1 (Moscow: OGI, 2006).

142. Mikhaiil Cherenkov, "Otkrytaia Evangel'skaia Identichnost [An Open Evangelical Identity]," in *Dvatsat' Let Religioznoy Svobody i Aktivnoi Misii [Twenty Years of Religious Freedom and Active Mission]*, ed. Mikhaiil Cherenkov (Kiev: Dukh i Litera, 2011), 22. It is

Approaches to Missiological Revisions

Rooted in the way people understand God and the world, theological paradigms apparently do not easily succumb to change. David Bosch observes that people often resist the challenges a new view brings with "deep emotional reactions, since those challenges threaten to destroy their very perception and experience of reality, indeed their entire world."[143] As a result, "power blocs" emerge during a paradigm war, each arguing on its own terms that the other paradigm is not merely weak but totally false and misleading. Institutional dynamics and the power of tradition tend to add to the tension, especially in cultural contexts with high power distance, low tolerance of ambiguity, and strong positivist epistemological assumptions.[144] If my analysis of the interviews in this research more or less correctly reflects the typical situation among Russian Baptist leaders, it shows the existence of two potential "power blocs," serious tensions among which may potentially threaten the unity of the denomination. What might be some irenic ways to facilitate missiological revisions among the leaders of the union?

Formal and informal theological education. The educational network of the union comprises about a dozen theological schools,[145] most of which are part of a centralized system due to their affiliation with Moscow Theological Seminary of the RUECB. The current educational models go back to the first schools in the FSU established by North American and German mission agencies, and have largely followed the fourfold pattern of biblical studies, church history, systematic theology, and practical theology.[146] The available

---

instructive to note how Alexander Prokhanov, the founder of the nationalist Izborsk Club (and who happens to be a grandnephew of the leader of the Gospel Christians, Ivan Prokhanov), perceives Baptists after paying a visit to a congregation in Moscow recently: "Baptists do not distinguish themselves from the Orthodox. They believe that the Russian mentality is very close to them. The only difference between us has to do with [liturgical] rites." Andrew Mel'nikov, "Alexander Prokhanov: 'Baptisty vo Mne Vidiat Plot" i Krov' Svoego Verouchitelia" [Alexander Prokhanov: "The Baptists See the Flesh and Blood of Their Teacher in Me"]," 2017, http://www.ng.ru/ng_religii/2017-08-16/9_426_prohanov.html.

143. Bosch, *Transforming Mission*, 173.

144. Keller, *Center Church*, 341; Bosch, *Witness to the World*.

145. This number is not constant as some schools open or close based on need and on the availability of financial support.

146. Mark R. Elliot, "The Current Crisis in Protestant Theological Education in the Former Soviet Union," in *History and Mission in Europe: Continuing the Conversation*, ed. Mary Raber and Peter F. Penner (Schwarzenfeld, Germany: Neufeld Verlag, 2011), 230.

programs focus primarily on biblical studies, theology, pastoral leadership, Christian education, and worship. Missiology has not been a priority; in fact, *none* of the seven leading seminaries of the union offer any program in missions or missiology.[147] In addition, a strong pastoral presence on the boards of many of these schools has tended to informally censor the curricula, with the purpose of preserving the theological and cultural identity of the union. As a result, safeguarding the traditional life of the "brotherhood" has often been the central concern of the Baptist educational system.

Since the leadership of each school participates in the annual conference of the Council for Coordination in Education at the central Baptist seminary in Moscow, this platform may be a good ground for a gradual refocusing of educational priorities around the theme of *missio Dei*. Discussing the Lausanne primary documents together could be the first step – especially the section on mission and education in the Cape Town Commitment. It is important that the educational leadership seriously consider one of its key principles: "The mission of the Church on earth is to serve the mission of God, and the mission of theological education is to strengthen and accompany the mission of the Church."[148] In particular, conferences could be held on several of the specific strategies the authors of the Commitment suggest for making education intentionally missional, such as conducting a "missional audit" of seminary curricula, structures, and ethos, and developing partnerships with various forms of missionary engagement.

Ideally, the Cape Town Commitment calls on theological educators to "recenter" the missional study of the Bible as "the core discipline in Christian theology . . . permeating all other fields of study and application."[149] The goal is to make *missio Dei* the integrative theme for classes in all four areas of a

---

147. These seminaries have been recently listed on the education page of the official website of the RUECB at "Spisok Uchebnykh Zavedenii EKhB. Vysshee Professional'noe Obrazovanie [The List of Educational Institutions of ECB. Higher Vocational Education]." The only school in this list that offers several online courses in missions as part of its pastoral or leadership programs is the distance-learning seminary in Kursk. "Trinity Video Seminary," accessed 20 June 2017, http://en.tvseminary.org/.

148. The Lausanne Movement, "The Cape Town Commitment." Bosch offers several helpful insights on how biblical studies, church history, and systematic theology can be taught from a missiological point of view. Bosch, *Transforming Mission*, 487–490. Priest suggests using the social sciences and actual social realities as dialogue partners in constructing systematic theologies. Priest, "'Experience-near Theologizing'"

149. The Lausanne Movement, "The Cape Town Commitment."

typical seminary curriculum: biblical, theological, historical, and practical studies. In the Russian Baptist context, this would require, at the very least, the addition of new classes focusing on a holistic missional reading of the Bible and on the integration of theology and the social sciences (a typical curriculum at a Russian Baptist school today tends to ignore both social studies and current developments in Russian society). Wherever such restructuring or expansion of the curriculum is technically or financially impossible at present, Baptist seminaries could consider adding at least one missiological class to existing pastoral programs (see appendix 4 for a diagram representing a version of a missional philosophy of education in contrast to the traditional fourfold model).

On an informal level, there is a need for pastoral conferences, retreats, and focus groups that present and popularize important missiological topics, such as the cosmic and communal aspects of God's salvific purpose, the missional nature of the church, the theology and ethics of cultural engagement, holistic mission, God's heart for the nations, missionary calling as a distinctive ministry, mission history, principles of intercultural communication and contextualization, strategic aspects of missions, etc. It is important, however, that any attempts to revise the traditional view proceed from a biblical-theological foundation. Citing trusted voices closer to the traditional position (such as D.A. Carson who has taught at several Baptist conferences in Russia) could alleviate the ever-present suspicion of liberal infiltration. Finally, the effect of these seminars would be greatly enhanced if they were combined with the leaders' personal involvement in mission through short-term mission trips inside or outside the country.

Mission in Russian Baptist history. In the current context of growing anti-Westernism, there is a tendency among many leaders to reject what they see as "Western" approaches to mission. However, as the survey of Russian Baptist history in chapter 3 demonstrates, their own past, when presented from a missiological perspective, could offer many valuable lessons for today. In the turmoil of social and political transitions, Russian Baptists experienced times of incredible growth when they were socially and culturally active, and when they creatively contextualized their mission approaches. Russian Baptists do not need to adopt "Western" models; what they need is to rediscover their own heritage. Besides, a greater familiarity with their own history and heroes could help both "demythologize" certain quasi-spiritual stereotypes that are hindering missional engagement today and rekindle genuine passion for reaching their compatriots for Christ.

Successful models of mission work in the new paradigm. Missiologists often observe that planting new churches can become a catalyst for the renewal of existing churches.[150] During my interviews, some participants strongly disagreed with this statement, based on their experience of planting new churches by dividing old ones. Despite assurances by Western missionaries, this approach in many places did not result in growth; it only weakened the existing churches. The problem here seems to stem from a somewhat mechanical understanding of church planting as the reproduction of the existing models. What is needed, however, is not merely *new* churches, but *new kinds* of churches: viable models of communities and ministries that follow a missional model and are led by missional leadership.[151] Successful cases can create a thirst for change and significantly lower the tension between the two "power blocs." Russian Baptists therefore need many indigenous sparks of life that can demonstrate the possibility of a transition from the institutional self-maintenance of the denomination to the spontaneously growing kind of movement it initially was.

Concluding Thoughts

Along with other members of their society, Russian Baptists today find themselves in the midst of perhaps the most sweeping political and social changes since 1991. The era of post-Soviet experimentation with democracy is apparently coming to an end, and a number of signs suggest that Russia could be entering into another cycle of enforced ideology and totalitarianism.[152] The place left vacant after the collapse of Communist doctrine is gradually being occupied by religiously based traditionalism which, paradoxically, is remarkably similar to the former in its alleged cultural superiority, militaristic isolationism, state-centered collectivism, and intolerance to dissent. The

---

150. Ed Stetzer and Daniel Im, *Planting Missional Churches: Your Guide to Starting Churches That Multiply* (Nashville, TN: B&H Academic, 2016); Keller, *Center Church*; Ott and Wilson, *Global Church Planting*.

151. cf. Murray, *Church Planting*, 25; Ott and Wilson, *Global Church Planting*, 235.

152. Sakwa, "Bringing the People Back In," 292.

practically unlimited freedom of religion of the 1990s has been effectively reduced to mere toleration of the adherents of so-called "non-traditional religions." As they adjust to the changing landscape, Baptists might be compelled to negotiate their identity and rethink their approaches to mission.

In this process it is quite natural to resort to historical memory and draw on past resources. The late-Soviet period of Russian Baptist history bequeathed to them several different models of mission in society. Which of the following will become their default mode in the years to come: escapist quietism focusing on purely religious matters, which characterized much of the church during the Soviet period, or the sort of active accommodation that was demonstrated in the past by much of the top Baptist leadership? Will they now seek to present themselves as uncritically supportive of the government and willing to accommodate to the socio-political outlook of the "older brother," meaning the leaders of the Russian Orthodox Church? Or will they instead lean toward a form of total rejection of society with its culture, as is the case with some of the splinter Baptist groups?

Based on the results of this research, I believe that conforming to any of the above models will in the long run mean for Russian Baptists a failure to fulfill their mission. While social isolationism or conformism may have been legitimate survival strategies in the past, they deeply affected Baptist theological thinking which, in turn, largely defined the nature of their missional engagement with society during the recent years of freedom. Under the pressure of modernistic ideology Baptists focused on the salvation of the soul, separation from culture, and the preservation of their traditional understanding of Christian spirituality. When the society around them underwent radical changes and Baptists were given an opportunity to share the gospel, they proclaimed a message of eternal salvation that invited seekers to leave the corrupt world behind and socialize into their inward-focused communities with their peculiar culture. Of course, in this they simply followed the logic of their understanding of the gospel. Yet the result was that, unlike their forerunners a century before, post-Soviet Baptists generally were not able to offer their society-in-transition a convincing biblical vision for the whole of life based on the gospel of the kingdom of God.

For this reason, I believe that a more comprehensive understanding of the gospel, rooted in a more holistic approach to the theological logic of the biblical story, is the key to the renewal of Russian Baptists' missionary encounter with culture. Setting the gospel message in the cosmic and communal contexts of Scripture is the prerequisite for nurturing personal and ecclesiastical lifestyles that are neither acultural, anti-cultural, or culturally syncretistic, but rather *countercultural* in that they strive to demonstrate a genuine biblical and contextualized alternative to the reigning story in all areas of life. A renewed appreciation of the good news of the kingdom might help Russian Baptists recover the lost dimensions of their proclamation – the message that had once made them a vibrant and dynamically growing movement before the Communists forced them into a ghetto. Whether undeservedly forgotten or even intentionally discredited, this model of mission is also a part of their heritage that I believe needs to be reclaimed today.

In light of the present research, I have suggested that to be an alternative community, Russian Baptists need to add several other important elements of a missionary encounter to their existing strengths (of being a *biblical* movement that holds to high *moral* standards). Negatively, this would mean distancing themselves from the coercive methods of the majority religion that relies on the power of an authoritarian state, and refusing to conform to cultural ethnocentrism, xenophobia, and aggressive nationalism. Positively, it would mean engagement with Russian history and culture, both classic and contemporary, from the perspective and resources of the evangelical tradition, a selfless commitment to the common good, and the modeling of communities in which group goals do not suppress the dignity and unique callings of individuals. All of the above, however, presupposes that Baptists need to abandon their "stepchild complex" and intentionally nurture a missionary consciousness of themselves as a people of God who have a distinctive and relevant message to share with their compatriots.

Christopher Wright reminds us that when a dissenting group challenges the idolatry of the dominant story, the powers quite naturally lash back in order to hold the cultural community together.[153] For a time, a holistic evangelical position might go against the social currents and be perceived (both outside and inside the church) as the view of a tiny minority. Yet, given that Russian history has tended to move back and forth between the extremes of

---

153. Wright, *Mission of God's People*, 239.

authoritarianism and democratization, Baptists may again find themselves in a new missionary situation in the more or less distant future.[154] One pertinent implication of this research, I believe, is as follows: if Baptists today choose to accommodate themselves to the pressures of the emerging civil religion and reduce their distinctiveness to purely liturgical or dogmatic differences from the established church, or if they turn away from burning cultural issues and limit their view of the gospel to otherworldly salvation and/or help in personal crises, the chances are high that their message will remain largely overlooked again, just as it happened after the collapse of the Soviet regime.

Certainly, our sovereign God is in full control of history. In spite of current trends, things could turn around quite unexpectedly tomorrow, opening vast missionary and social opportunities for the evangelical community in Russia. Whatever the future brings, I am convinced that the way forward is to be found neither in an uncritical accommodation to the status quo, nor in cultural withdrawal or resistance conceived largely in negative terms. Rather, it is to be found in becoming communities that "embody an alternative story" through their faithfulness to the comprehensive implications of the gospel.[155] Among other things, this task necessitates the articulation of biblical and contextual theologies of mission. In light of the present research I have suggested five themes for theological conversation with the global evangelical community, the members of which are seeking to answer similar questions in their own specific locations. My hope and prayer is that this dissertation will contribute to the growing discussion of, and ultimately to the greater success of evangelical mission in Russia.

---

154. Akhiezer, Klyamkin, and Yakovenko, *Istoriia Rosii: Konets Ili Novoye Nachalo? [History of Russia: The End or A New Beginning?]*.

155. Michael Frost and Christiana Rice remind us that "Some of the most prophetically charged world-changing movements throughout history were catalyzed not by charismatic leaders taking the world by force, but by small groups of faithful people on the fringe of society who chose to embody an alternative story to that of the prevailing culture around them." Michael Frost and Christiana Rice, *To Alter Your World: Partnering with God to Rebirth Our Communities* (Downers Grove, IL: IVP Academic, 2017), 108.

APPENDIX 1

Informed Consent Form

Dear Participant,

My name is Andrey Kravtsev, and I am conducting a study for the completion of a PhD at Trinity Evangelical Divinity School. I appreciate your willingness to be interviewed for this research. My purpose is to investigate the current understandings of the gospel, church, and mission that prevail among the denominational, pastoral, and educational leadership of the RUECB. In this interview you will be asked a series of questions on how you personally understand these theological themes. Your participation in this research is completely voluntary, and you are free to withdraw at any time during this study.

The interview will last around sixty minutes. I am asking your permission to digitally record it and transcribe for later analysis. Please be assured that all your personal information and identity will be kept confidential and used exclusively for the purpose of research. Your name will not appear in connection with any statements without your expressed permission. Audio recordings of the interview will be deleted after they are transcribed.

"By signing this consent form, I acknowledge that I have read and understood the above information, and that I willingly agree to participate in this study."

Name: _____ Date: _____

APPENDIX 2

Interview Protocol

1. Short demographic information:
   - Age
   - Spiritual background (Baptist heritage or raised outside of the tradition)
   - Education (secular and theological)
   - Ministry experience and ministry context today (town, city, megacity)

2. Understanding the gospel
   - How would you concisely express the meaning of the gospel?
   - What is salvation? What is saved and from what? When does salvation happen?
   - What is the ultimate purpose of salvation? What is the kingdom of God?
   - How have you arrived at these conclusions?

3. Understanding the church
   - How would you define "the church"?
   - What are the purposes of the church, and which one is primary?
   - How are the kingdom of God and church related?
   - How are the church and society related?

4. Understanding mission
   - What do you understand by the term "mission"?
   - What does it include and exclude?
   - What is the relationship between evangelism and social service?
   - Is social action for justice part of mission?

5. Cultural engagement in the current socio-political context
    - What specific stories, beliefs, and developments in culture today should be especially challenged by the gospel?
    - What should be the church's institutional role in society, politics, and ecology?
    - How do you teach your people to individually connect to society and culture?

6. Interaction with alternative evangelical views on the gospel, church, and mission
    - What do you agree or disagree with in these specific statements, and why?
    - What aspects would you reject, modify, or possibly adopt for teaching in your church?

7. Missiological revisions
    - Do you feel that Baptists have realized their full missionary potential over the last twenty-five years? Explain your answer.
    - Do you see any need for Baptists to reconsider their theology of mission? If so, what specific beliefs and/or practices should be adjusted for more successful mission in the future?
    - What would be some of the productive and less controversial strategies for introducing these theological changes?

APPENDIX 3

Participants' Demographic Information

Abbreviations:
D – Denominational leader
E – Educational leader
P – Pastoral leader

The settlement hierarchy as accepted here:
- Town – between 1,000 and 20,000 people.
- Large town – between 20,000 and 100,000.
- City – between 100,000 and 300,000.
- Large city – between 300,000 and 1 million.
- Megacity – more than one million people

Interviewee Designation	Age	Spiritual Formation (upbringing)	Education	Ministry Vocation	Ministry Context
E1	41	Non-Baptist	Secular & theological	Pastor 6 years, educational leadership	Megacity
P1	40	Baptist	Secular & Theological	Pastor 12 years, church planting denominational work	Megacity
D1	46	Baptist	Secular & theological	Pastor 5 years, denominational work	Megacity
D2	54	Baptist	Theological	Church planting 24 years, denominational work	Megacity
ED2	62	Non-Baptist	Secular & theological	Pastor 25 years, denominational work	Megacity
E3	43	Non-Baptist	Theological	Education 20 years	Large town
P2	62	Non-Baptist	Theological	Pastor 24 years	Megacity
P3	54	Baptist	None	Pastor 21 years	Town
D3	59	Baptist	Secular & theological	Missions for 25 years	Megacity
P4	53	Baptist	Theological	Pastor for 15 years	City

Interviewee Designation	Age	Spiritual Formation (upbringing)	Education	Ministry Vocation	Ministry Context
P5	53	Baptist	Secular & theological	Pastor 18 years	Town
P6	47	Non-Baptist	Secular	Pastor 14 years	Megacity
D4	45	Baptist	Theological	Pastor 18 years, denominational work	Town
P7	66	Baptist	None	Pastor 25 years	City
P8	37	Baptist	Theological	Pastor 10 years	Large town
D5	55	Baptist	Theological	Pastor 20 years, missionary leadership, denominational work	Megacity
E4	44	Non-Baptist	Secular & theological	Educational leadership, pastor 7 years	Megacity
D6	56	Baptist	Secular	Pastor 25 years	Large town
P9	56	Baptist	Theological	Pastor 21 years	Large town
ED5	57	Baptist	Secular & theological	Pastor 25 years	Megacity
P10	40	Non-Baptist	Theological	Pastor 15 years	Large city
D7	65	Baptist	Theological	Pastor 36 years	Megacity
P11	68	Baptist	None	Pastor 45 years	Megacity
E6	58	Baptist	Secular & theological	Pastor 15 years, educational leadership	Megacity
D8	41	Baptist	Secular & theological	Pastor 15 years, missionary and educational leadership, denominational work	Megacity
D9	61	Baptist	Courses in theology	Pastor 31 years, denominational work	Megacity
D10	61	Baptist	Courses in theology	Pastor 25 years, denominational work	Megacity
P12	65	Baptist	Secular & theological	Church planting work and pastor for 25 years	Large city
E7	43	Non-Baptist	Secular & theological	Pastor 8 years, educational leadership	Megacity
E8	58	Non-Baptist	Secular	Pastor 17 years, educational work	Large city

APPENDIX 4

A Missional Model of Theological Education

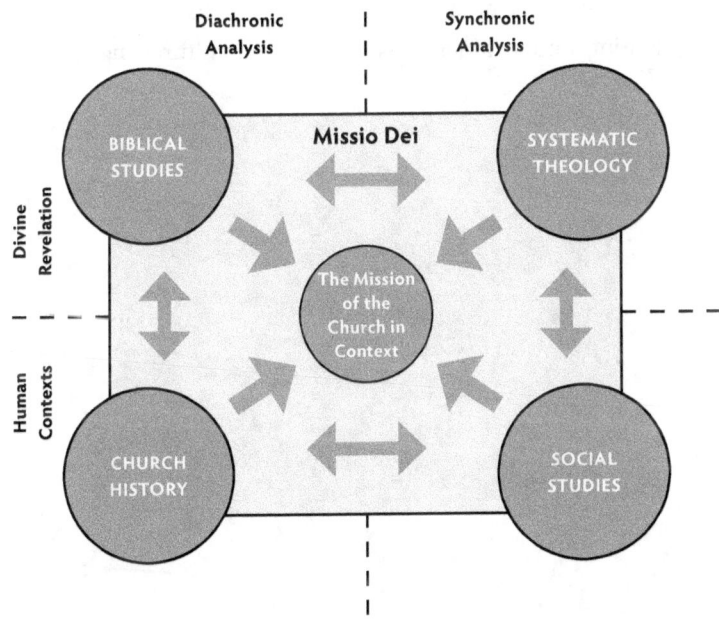

Explanation:
1. This model is based on an adaptation of Paul Hiebert's diagram of Missiology and Related Disciplines.[1]
2. The concept of *missio Dei* provides the general context and becomes the integrative theme for teaching classes in all of the five disciplines.

---

1. Hiebert, *Gospel in Human Contexts*, 34.

3. In addition to the four classical elements of curriculum, social studies are introduced. The discipline includes both the discussion of methodological frameworks and the analysis of specific issues in the context.
4. The two disciplines in the upper half of the diagram focus on the study of God's revelation, and the two in the lower deal with human contexts. The two disciplines on the left employ diachronic methodologies, whereas the two on the right practice synchronic analysis.
5. The focal point of the curriculum is found in the discussion of the church's mission in its specific situation. The mission is understood in a broader sense than evangelism and church planting, and includes holistic social and cultural engagement.

Bibliography

Ad Hoc Group. "Theology and Implications of Radical Discipleship." In *Let the Earth Hear His Voice: International Congress on World Evangelization, Lausanne, Switzerland*, edited by J. D. Douglas, 1294–1296. Minneapolis, MN: World Wide Publications, 1975.

"Adopted Documents and Statements." World Council of Churches. Accessed 26 June 2017. https://www.oikoumene.org/en/resources/documents/assembly/2013-busan/adopted-documents-statements.

Akhiezer, Alexander, Igor Klyamkin, and Igor Yakovenko. *Istoriia Rosii: Konets Ili Novoye Nachalo? [History of Russia: The End or A New Beginning?]*. Moscow: Liberalnaya Missiya, 2013.

"All-Russian Fellowship of Gospel-Christians." Accessed 25 August 2017. http://moskva.drevolife.ru/denominaciya/vseh.

Andornoviene, Lina, and Parush R. Parushev. "Church, State, and Culture: On the Complexities of Post-Soviet Evangelical Social Involvement." *Theological Reflection* 3 (2004): 194–212.

Anikin, A., P. Arseev, A. Belavin, S. Gulev, and V. Zakharov. "O Metodakh Nauchnogo Issledovaniia i Dissertatsii V.R. Medinskogo [About the Research Methodology and Dissertation of V.R. Medinsky]," 2016. https://www.kommersant.ru/doc/3127495.

Arnold, Victoria. "Russia: 'Anti-Missionary' Punishments Full Listing," 2017. http://www.forum18.org/archive.php?article_id=2306.

AUCECB. "Verouchenie Evangel'skikh Khristian-Baptistov [The Confession of Faith of Evangelical Christians-Baptists]." *Bratskii Vestnik [Brotherly Herald]* 4 (1985): 33–49.

Babbie, Earl R. *The Practice of Social Research*. Belmont, CA: Thomson Wadsworth, 2010.

Bachinin, Vladislav. *Vizantizm i Evangelizm: Genealogiia Russkogo Protestantizma [Byzantism and Evangelicalism: The Genealogy of Russian Protestantism]*. St Petersburg: SPGU, 2003.

Barram, Michael. "The Bible, Mission, and Social Location: Toward a Missional Hermeneutic." *Interpretation* 61 (2007): 42–58.

Bartholomew, Craig G., and Michael W. Goheen. *The Drama of Scripture: Finding Our Place in the Biblical Story*. Grand Rapids, MI: Baker Academic, 2004.

Baryshnikov, Valentin. "For the Church, Violence Is the Norm," 2017. https://therussianreader.com/tag/juvenile-justice/.

Bavinck, Herman. *The Philosophy of Revelation*. New York; London: Longmans, Green & Co., 1909.

Bears, Max. "Homo Sovieticus: Twelve Traits of a Soviet Man," 2014. http://bearsandvodka.com/homo-sovieticus.

Bebbington, David. *Evangelicalism in Modern Britain: A History from the 1730's to the 1980's*. New York: Routledge, 1989.

———. "Introduction." In *Evangelicalism: Comparative Studies of Popular Protestantism in North America, the British Isles, and Beyond, 1700–1990*, edited by Mark A. Noll, David Bebbington, and George A. Rawlyk, 3–18. New York: Oxford University Press, 1994.

Berdyaev, Nicolas. *The Origin of Russian Communism*. Ann Arbor, MI: University of Michigan Press, 1960.

Berkhof, Hendrikus. *Christian Faith: An Introduction to the Study of the Faith*. Grand Rapids, MI: Eerdmans, 1979.

Bevans, Stephen B., and Roger Schroeder. *Constants in Context: A Theology of Mission for Today*. Maryknoll, NY: Orbis Books, 2004.

Beyerhaus, Peter. "World Evangelization and the Kingdom of God." In *Let the Earth Hear His Voice: International Congress on World Evangelization, Lausanne, Switzerland*, edited by J. D. Douglas, 283–302. Minneapolis, MN: World Wide Publications, 1975.

Birdsall, Doug, and Lindsay Brown. "Foreword." In *The Cape Town Commitment: A Confirmation of Faith and a Call to Action*, edited by Julia Cameron, 4–6. Peabody, MA: Hendrickson, 2011.

Blauw, Johannes. *The Missionary Nature of the Church: A Survey of the Biblical Theology of Mission*. New York: McGraw-Hill, 1962.

Bobrov, Igor. "Pirrova Pobeda [A Pyrrhic Victory]," 2017. http://www.igorbobrov.com/2017/07/blog-post_4.html.

———. "Pochemu Rossiiskii Politicheskii Rezhim Prevraschaet Grazhdan v Iskliuchionnykh [Why Russian Political Regime Deprives Citizens of Their Rights]," 2017. http://www.igorbobrov.com/2017/07/blog-post.html.

Bokova, Olga. "Sovremennye Rossiyskie Evangelskie Khristiane-Baptisty: Sotsialnaia Struktura i Ideologiia [Contemporary Russian Evangelical Christians-Baptists: Social Structure and Ideology]." *Gosudarstvo, Religiia, Tserkov v Rossii i Za Rubezhom [State, Religion and Church in Russia and Abroad]* 3 (2009): 35–46.

Bibliography

———. "Teologia Rossiiskikh Evangel'skikh Khristian-Baptistov Na Rubezhe XX i XXI Vekov [Theology of Russian Evangelical Christians-Baptists at the Turn of the Twenty-First Century]." PhD diss., St Petersburg State University, 2011.

Bolotov, Sergey. "Mitropolit Illarion Posovetoval Rossii Absolyutnuyu Monarkhiyu [Metropolitan Hilarion Advised Russia an Absolute Monarchy]," 2017. https://www.ridus.ru/news/256104.

Bolshakoff, S. *Russian Nonconformity: The Story of "Unofficial" Religion in Russia.* Philadelphia: Westminster, 1950.

Bosch, David J. *Believing in the Future: Toward a Missiology of Western Culture.* Valley Forge, PA: Trinity Press International, 1995.

———. *Transforming Mission: Paradigm Shifts in Theology of Mission.* Twentieth anniversary edition. Maryknoll, NY: Orbis Books, 2011.

———. *Witness to the World: The Christian Mission in Theological Perspective.* Eugene, OR: Wipf & Stock, 1980.

Brandenburg, Hans. *The Meek and the Mighty: The Emergence of the Evangelical Movement in Russia.* New York: Oxford University Press, 1977.

Brubaker, Rogers. "Religion and Nationalism: Four Approaches." *Nations and Nationalism* 18, no. 1 (2012): 2–20.

Bychkov, A. M., and A. I. Mitskevich. *Dogmatika [Dogmatic Theology].* Moscow: VSEKhB, 1970.

Bychkov, Alexei. "Otchetnyi Doklad General'nogo Sekretaria VSEKhB A.M. Bychkov. [The Report by the General Secretary of the AUCECB A.M. Buchkov]." *Bratskii Vestnik [Brotherly Herald]* 1 (1975): 50–65.

Cameron, Julia, ed. *The Cape Town Commitment: A Confirmation of Faith and a Call to Action.* Peabody, MA: Hendrickson, 2011.

Carson, D. A. *Christ and Culture Revisited.* Grand Rapids, MI: Eerdmans, 2008.

Carter, Craig A. *Rethinking Christ and Culture: A Post-Christendom Perspective.* Grand Rapids, MI: Brazos Press, 2006.

Cherenkov, Mikhaiil. "Otkrytaia Evangel'skaia Identichnost [An Open Evangelical Identity]." In *Dvatsat' Let Religioznoy Svobody i Aktivnoi Misii [Twenty Years of Religious Freedom and Active Mission]*, edited by Mikhaiil Cherenkov, 17–26. Kiev: Dukh i Litera, 2011.

Chester, Tim. "Church Planting: A Theological Perspective." In *Multiplying Churches: Reaching Today's Communities through Church Planting*, edited by Stephen Timmis, 23–46. Fearn, Tain: Christian Focus, 2000.

Chistovich, I. A. *Istoriia Perevoda Biblii Na Russkii Iazyk [The History of the Russian Translation of the Bible].* Moscow: AFI, 2012.

"Church Spokesman: Russia Has Messianic Mission to Stop 'American Project.'" *The Moscow Times,* 2014. http://themoscowtimes.com/news/church-spokesman-russia-has-messianic-mission-to-stop-american-project-42577.

Clover, Charles. *Black Wind, White Snow: The Rise of Russia's New Nationalism.* New Haven: Yale University Press, 2016.

Coleman, Heather Jean. *Russian Baptists and Spiritual Revolution, 1905–1929.* Bloomington: Indiana University Press, 2005.

Colson, Charles W., and Nancy Pearcey. *How Now Shall We Live?* Wheaton, IL: Tyndale House, 1999.

Conn, Harvie M. *Evangelism: Doing Justice and Preaching Grace.* Grand Rapids, MI: Zondervan, 1982.

Corbin, Juliet M., and Anselm L. Strauss. *Basics of Qualitative Research: Techniques and Procedures for Developing Grounded Theory.* Los Angeles, CA: Sage, 2008.

Corrado, Sharyl. "The Philosophy of Ministry of Colonel Vasiliy Pashkov." MA thesis, Wheaton College, 2000.

Corrie, John. "Kingdom of God." In *Dictionary of Mission Theology: Evangelical Foundations,* edited by John Corrie, Samuel Escobar, and Wilbert R. Shenk, 195–199. Nottingham, UK; Downers Grove, IL: IVP Academic, 2007.

Costas, Orlando E. *Christ Outside the Gate: Mission Beyond Christendom.* Maryknoll, NY: Orbis Books, 1982.

———. *The Church and Its Mission: A Shattering Critique from the Third World.* Wheaton, IL: Tyndale House, 1974.

Creswell, John W. *Qualitative Inquiry and Research Design: Choosing Among Five Traditions.* Los Angeles, CA: Sage, 2007.

Cullmann, Oscar. "Eschatology and Missions in the New Testament." In *The Theology of the Christian Mission,* edited by Gerald H. Anderson, 42–54. Nashville, TN: Abingdon, 1961.

De Chalandeau, Alexander. *The Theology of the Evangelical Christians-Baptists in the USSR as Reflected in the Bratskii Vestnik.* Chicago, IL: Harper & Co, 1978.

De Jong, Sijbren. "Why Countries Are Not Rushing to Join Putin's Union," 2016. https://euobserver.com/opinion/133574.

DECR Communication Service. "VII Russian World Assembly Opens in St. Petersburg," 2013. https://mospat.ru/en/2013/11/04/news93676/.

DeYoung, Kevin, and Greg Gilbert. *What Is the Mission of the Church? Making Sense of Social Justice, Shalom, and the Great Commission.* Wheaton, IL: Crossway, 2011.

Dostoevskii, F. M. *Dnevnik Pisatelia Za 1876 g [A Writer's Diary for 1876].* 1879 ed. St Petersburg: Tipografiia Iu. Shtaufa, n.d.

Dubin, Boris. "Massovoe Pravoslavie v Rossii [The Mass Orthodoxy in Russia]," 2000. http://www.index.org.ru/journal/11/dubin.html.

———. "Pravoslavie i Natsional'naia Identichnost: Neotraditsionalistskoe Znachenie Very [The Russian Orthodoxy and National Identity: A Neo-Traditionalist Meaning of Faith]." *Vestnik Obschestvennogo Mneniia [Messenger of Public Opinion]* 71, no. 3 (2004): 35–44.

Dubrovsky, Ales. "Bogoslovskii Fundamentalism Kak Tormoziaschiy Faktor v Razvitii Evangel'skikh Tserkvey Postsovetskogo Perioda [Theological Fundamentalism as a Constraining Factor in the Development of Evangelical Churches in the Post-Soviet Period]." In *Dvatsat' Let Religioznoy Svobody i Aktivnoi Misii [Twenty Years of Religious Freedom and Active Mission]*, edited by Mikhaiil Cherenkov, 27–44. Kiev: Dukh i Litera, 2011.

Dubrovsky, Mikhail. "Obretenie Sebia: Puti Formirovaniia Novoi Identichnosti [Finding Ourselves: The Ways of Shaping a New Identity]." In *Dvatsat' Let Religioznoy Svobody i Aktivnoi Misii [Twenty Years of Religious Freedom and Active Mission]*, edited by Mikhaiil Cherenkov, 394–405. Kiev: Dukh i Litera, 2011.

Dugin, A. G. *Osnovy Geopolitiki [The Basics of Geopolitics]*. Moscow: Arktogeya, 1997.

Dukhonchenko, Y. K. "Prakticheskaya Khristianskaya Zhizn [Practical Christian Living]." *Bratskii Vestnik [Brotherly Herald]* 4 (1985): 27–33.

"Dukhovnyie Khristiane (Molokane) [The Spiritual Christians (The Molokans)]." Accessed 25 June 2017. http://molokan.narod.ru/index_long.html.

Durassoff, Steve. *The Russian Protestants*. Cranbury, NJ: Associated University Presses, 1969.

Dutkiewicz, Piotr, Vladimir Kulikov, and Richard Sakwa, eds. *The Social History of Post-Communist Russia*. London; New York: Routledge, 2016.

Dyck, Johannes. "Elements of Post-Gulag Mennonite Theology: View of an Eyewitness." In *History and Mission in Europe: Continuing the Conversation*, edited by Mary Raber and Peter F. Penner, 199–212. Schwarzenfeld, Germany: Neufeld Verlag, 2011.

———. "Zavisimost' Nezavisimosti: Obshchina v Zhizni Evangel'skogo Bratstva Rosii v Period Ego Stanovleniia, 1870–1887 [Dependence of Independence: The Local Church in the Life of the Evangelical Union of Russia at the Stage of Its Formation, 1870–1887]." In *Avtonomia Pomestnoi Tserkvi: Materialy Simposiuma [Local Church Autonomy: Proceedings of Symposium]*, edited by Sergey Sannikov, 275–294. Odessa: Dukhovnoe Vozrozhdenie, 2009.

Dyrness, William A. *Let the Earth Rejoice! A Biblical Theology of Holistic Mission*. Westchester, IL: Crossway, 1983.

Elliot, Mark, and Sharyl Corrado. "The 1997 Russian Law on Religion: The Demographics of Discrimination," 1999. http://www.eastwestreport.org/articles/ew07101.htm.

Elliot, Mark R. "The Current Crisis in Protestant Theological Education in the Former Soviet Union." In *History and Mission in Europe: Continuing the Conversation*, edited by Mary Raber and Peter F. Penner, 213–235. Schwarzenfeld, Germany: Neufeld Verlag, 2011.

———. "Theological Education After Communism: The Mixed Blessing of Western Assistance." *The Asbury Theological Journal* 50 (1995): 67–73.

Ellis, Geoffrey H., and L. Wesley Jones. *The Other Revolution: Russian Evangelical Awakenings*. Abilene, TX: ACU Press, 1996.

Engelsviken, Tormod. "*Missio Dei*: The Understanding and Misunderstanding of a Theological Concept in European Churches and Missiology." *International Review of Mission* 92 (2003): 481–497.

Eremin, Alexander, and Sergei Oscmachko. "The Education Activity of the Russian Orthodox Church in the Contemporary Transcultural Space of Russia." *Procedia* 237 (2017): 1475–1481.

Erickson, F. "Qualitative Methods in Research on Teaching." In *Handbook of Research on Teaching: A Project of the American Educational Research Association*, edited by Merlin C. Wittrock, 119–161. New York: Macmillan, 1986.

Escobar, Samuel. "Evangelical Missiology: Peering into the Future at the Turn of the Century." In *Global Missiology in the 21st Century: The Iguassu Dialogue*, edited by William David Taylor, 101–122. Grand Rapids, MI: Baker Academic, 2000.

Escobar, Samuel, and John Driver. *Christian Mission and Social Justice*. Scottdale, PA: Herald, 1978.

Fairbairn, Donald. *Eastern Orthodoxy through Western Eyes*. Louisville, KY: Westminster John Knox, 2002.

Felgengauer, Pavel. "Vostochnyi Flang Trebuet Peremen [The Eastern Wind Requires Changes]," 2017. https://www.novayagazeta.ru/articles/2017/07/01/72978-vostochnyy-flang-trebuet-peremen.

Fernandez, Denise R., Dawn S. Carlson, Lee P. Stepina, and Joel D. Nicholson. "Hofstede's Country Classification Twenty-Five Years Later." *The Journal of Social Psychology* 1 (1997): 43–54.

Flemming, Dean E. *Recovering the Full Mission of God: A Biblical Perspective on Being, Doing, and Telling*. Downers Grove, IL: IVP Academic, 2013.

Frost, Michael, and Alan Hirsch. *The Shaping of Things to Come: Innovation and Mission for the 21st Century Church*. Peabody, MA: Hendrickson, 2003.

Frost, Michael, and Christiana Rice. *To Alter Your World: Partnering with God to Rebirth Our Communities*. Downers Grove, IL: IVP Academic, 2017.

Furman, Dmitrii. "Ot Rossiiskoi Imperii k Russkomu Demokraticheskomu Gosudarstvu [From the Russian Empire to a Russian Democratic State]," 2010. http://polit.ru/article/2010/12/08/furman/.

Galstyan, Areg. "Third Rome Rising: The Ideologues Calling for a New Russian Empire," 2016. https://nationalinterest.org/feature/third-rome-rising-the-ideologues-calling-new-russian-empire-16748.

Gavrilyuk, Paul L. "The President and the Patriarch: An Alliance over Ukraine?," 2014. https://www.firstthings.com/web-exclusives/2014/04/the-president-and-the-patriarch.

Geifman, Anna, and Yuri Teper. "Russia's New National Identity under Putin's Regime." *BESA Center Perspectives Paper* 279 (2014). https://besacenter.org/perspectives-papers/russias-new-national-identity-putins-regime/.

Glasser, Arthur F. "The Evolution of Evangelical Mission Theology Since World War II." *International Bulletin of Missionary Research* 9 (1985): 9–13.

Glasser, Arthur F., and Donald A. McGavran. *Contemporary Theologies of Mission*. Grand Rapids, MI: Baker Book House, 1983.

Gnanakan, Kenneth Romesh. *Kingdom Concerns: A Biblical Exploration Towards a Theology of Mission*. Bangalore: Theological Book Trust, 1989.

Goble, Paul. "Moscow Archpriest Calls for New Death Squads to Destroy 'Traitor-Emigres.'" *Euromaidan Press* (blog), 2017. http://euromaidanpress.com/2017/03/11/moscow-archpriest-calls-for-new-death-squads-to-destroy-traitor-emigres-euromaidan-press/.

———. "'We Stopped Hitler and We Can Stop the Americans,' Aide to Patriarch Kirill Says," 2014. https://www.eesti.ca/we-stopped-hitler-and-we-can-stop-the-americans-aide-to-patriarch-kirill-says/article43959.

Gogin, Sergei. "Homo Sovieticus: Twenty Years after the End of the Soviet Union." *Russian Analytical Digest* 109 (2012): 12–15.

Goheen, Michael W. *A Light to the Nations: The Missional Church and the Biblical Story*. Grand Rapids, MI: Baker Academic, 2011.

———. *Introducing Christian Mission Today: Scripture, History, and Issues*. Kindle Edition. Downers Grove, IL: IVP Academic, 2014.

Golovin, Sergei. "The Missing Dimension of Evangelism in Post-Communist Society." *Religion in Eastern Europe* 28 (2008): 27–64.

Gorman, Michael J. *Reading Paul*. Eugene, OR: Cascade Books, 2008.

Gorshkov, Mikhail. "Twenty Years That Shook Russia: Public Opinion on the Reforms." In *The Social History of Post-Communist Russia*, edited by Piotr Dutkiewicz, Vladimir Kulikov, and Richard Sakwa, 95–129. London; New York: Routledge, 2016.

Goudzwaard, B. *Idols of Our Time*. Downers Grove, IL: IVP Academic, 1984.

Graham, Billy. "Why Lausanne?" In *Let the Earth Hear His Voice: International Congress on World Evangelization, Lausanne, Switzerland*, edited by J. D. Douglas, 23–36. Minneapolis, MN: World Wide Publications, 1975.

Gressel, Gustav. "Fellow Travelers: Russia, Anti-Westernism, and Europe's Political Parties," 2017. https://www.ecfr.eu/publications/summary/fellow_travellers_russia_anti_westernism_and_europes_political_parties_7213?utm_content=buffer72a49&utm_medium=social&utm_source=twitter.com&utm_campaign=buffer.

Gribanova, Galina. "Ethnic and Religious Relations in Russia Since the 1980s." In *The Social History of Post-Communist Russia*, edited by Piotr Dutkiewicz, Vladimir Kulikov, and Richard Sakwa, 209–228. London; New York: Routledge, 2016.

Grigoriev, Leonid. "Transformation: For the People or for the Elite?" In *The Social History of Post-Communist Russia*, edited by Piotr Dutkiewicz, Vladimir Kulikov, and Richard Sakwa, 81–94. London; New York: Routledge, 2016.

Grosby, Steven Elliott. *Nationalism: A Very Short Introduction*. Kindle Edition. Oxford: Oxford University Press, 2005.

Guder, David. "Biblical Formation and Discipleship." In *Treasure in Clay Jars: Patterns in Missional Faithfulness*, edited by Lois Y. Barrett, 59–73. Grand Rapids, MI: Eerdmans, 2004.

Gudkov, L., B. Dubin, and N. Zorkaya. *Postsovetskiy Chelovek i Grazhdanskoe Obschestvo [The Post-Soviet Person and Civil Society]*. Moscow: Moscow School of Political Research, 2008.

Gudkov, Lev. "Russian Cynicism: Symptom of a Stagnant Society," 2013. http://www.opendemocracy.net/od-russia/lev-gudkov/russian-cynicism-symptom-of-stagnant-society.

Haidt, Jonathan. *The Righteous Mind: Why Good People Are Divided by Politics and Religion*. New York: Pantheon Books, 2012.

Halverson, Jeffry R, H. Lloyd Goodall, and Steven R Corman. *Master Narratives of Islamist Extremism*. New York: Palgrave McMillan, 2011.

Harris, Mark J. "Historical Perspectives on the Evangelistic Theology and Methodology of Russian Baptists," 1999. http://cvi2.org/pages/harris/harris_russian_baptist_evangelistic_history_1999.pdf.

Hastings, Adrian. *The Construction of Nationhood: Ethnicity, Religion and Nationalism*. Cambridge: Cambridge University Press, 1997.

Hastings, Ross. *Missional God, Missional Church: Hope for Re-Evangelizing the West*. Downers Grove, IL: IVP Academic, 2012.

Hauerwas, Stanley, and William H. Willimon. *Resident Aliens: Life in the Christian Colony*. Nashville, TN: Abingdon, 1989.

Hebly, J. A. *Protestants in Russia*. Grand Rapids, MI: Eerdmans, 1976.

Hedlund, Roger E. *Roots of the Great Debate in Mission*. Madras, India: Evangelical Literature Service, 1981.

Heier, Edmund. *Religious Schism in the Russian Aristocracy 1860–1900: Radstockism and Pashkovism*. The Hague, Netherlands: Martinus Nijhoff, 1970.

Henry, Carl F. H. *The Uneasy Conscience of Modern Fundamentalism*. Grand Rapids, MI: Eerdmans, 1947.

Hesselgrave, David J. *Paradigms in Conflict: Ten Key Questions in Christian Missions Today*. Grand Rapids, MI: Kregel, 2005.

———. "Redefining Holism." *Evangelical Missions Quarterly* 35 (1999): 278–284.
Hibbert, Richard Yates. "The Place of Church Planting in Mission." *Evangelical Review of Theology* 33 (2009): 316–331.
Hiebert, Paul G. *Anthropological Insights for Missionaries*. Grand Rapids, MI: Baker Book House, 1985.
———. *Anthropological Reflections on Missiological Issues*. Grand Rapids, MI: Baker Book House, 1994.
———. "Critical Contextualization." *International Bulletin of Missionary Research* 11, no. 3 (1987): 104–112.
———. *The Gospel in Human Contexts: Anthropological Explorations for Contemporary Missions*. Grand Rapids, MI: Baker Academic, 2009.
———. *The Missiological Implications of Epistemological Shifts Affirming Truth in a Modern/Postmodern World*. Harrisburg, PA: Trinity Press International, 1999.
Hitchens, Peter. "The Cold War Is Over," 2016. https://www.firstthings.com/article/2016/10/the-cold-war-is-over.
Hoekema, Anthony A. *The Bible and the Future*. Grand Rapids, MI: Eerdmans, 1979.
Hoekendijk, Johannes Christiaan. "The Church in Missionary Thinking." *International Review of Mission* 41 (1952): 324–336.
———. *The Church Inside Out*. Philadelphia, PA: Westminster, 1964.
Horton, Michael S. "How the Kingdom Comes." *Christianity Today* 50, no. 1 (2006): 44–45.
Hosking, Geoffrey A. *The First Socialist Society: A History of the Soviet Union from Within*. Cambridge, MA: Harvard University Press, 1992.
Hovorun, Cyril. "Interpretiruia Russkii Mir [Interpreting the Russian World]," 2015. http://www.russ.ru/Mirovaya-povestka/Interpretiruya-russkij-mir.
———. *Ukraiinska Publichna Teologiia [Ukrainian Public Theology]*. Kyiv: Dukh i Litera, 2017.
Human Rights Watch. "Russia," 2017. https://www.hrw.org/europe/central-asia/russia.
Hunsberger, George R. "Proposals for a Missional Hermeneutic: Mapping the Conversation," 2009. https://gocn.org/library/proposals-for-a-missional-hermeneutic-mapping-the-conversation/.
Hunter, James Davison. *To Change the World: The Irony, Tragedy, and Possibility of Christianity in the Late Modern World*. New York: Oxford University Press, 2010.
Huntington, Samuel P. *The Clash of Civilizations and the Remaking of World Order*. New York: Simon & Schuster, 2011.
"Iiul'skie Reitingi Odobreniia i Doveriia [July Ratings of Approval and Trust]," 2015. https://www.levada.ru/2015/07/23/iyulskie-rejtingi-odobreniya-i-doveriya-6/.

Iliukovich, Ilya. "Krestyianstvo Ili Khristianstvo: Sotsialnye Aspekty Sovremennogo Pravoslaviya [Peasants or Christians: Social Aspects of Contemporary Orthodox Faith]," 2017. https://ahilla.ru/krestyanstvo-ili-hristianstvo-sotsialnye-aspekty-sovremennogo-pravoslaviya/.

Interfax. "Alexander Chepurin: 'Za Predelami Rossii Seichas Prozhivaet Okolo 30 Millionov Nashikh Sootechestvennikov' [Alexander Chepurin: 'About 30 million of Our Compatriots Live Outside of Russia Now']," 2010. https://www.interfax.ru/interview/131938.

International Missionary Council. *Missions under the Cross: Addresses Delivered at the Enlarged Meeting of the Committee of the International Missionary Council at Willingen, in Germany, 1952; With Statements Issued by the Meeting*. Edited by Norman Goodall. London: Edinburgh House, 1953.

Ivanov, I. G. "Tridtsat' Let Vmeste [Thirty Years Together]." *Bratskii Vestnik [Brotherly Herald]* 1 (1975): 18–24.

Ivanov, Mikhail. "Sovremennye Tendentsii v Bogoslovii Rossiyskikh Evangel'skikh Khristian-Baptistov [Contemporary Trends in the Theology of Russian Evangelical Christians-Baptists]." PhD diss., RANEPA, 2012.

"Izborskii Klub [The Izborsk Club]." Accessed 12 June 2017. https://izborsk-club.ru/.

Johnston, Arthur F. "The Kingdom in Relation to the Church and the World." In *Word and Deed: Evangelism and Social Responsibility*, edited by Bruce Nichols, 109–133. Exeter, Devon: Paternoster, 1985.

Johnston, Arthur P. *The Battle for World Evangelism*. Wheaton, IL: Tyndale House, 1978.

Kantor, Maxim. *Uchebnik Risovaniia [A Textbook of Drawing]*. Tom 1. Moscow: OGI, 2006.

Karetnikova, M. S. *Al'manakh Po Istorii Russkogo Baptizma [The Reader on the History of Russian Baptists]*. St Petersburg: Bibliia dlia vsekh, 1999.

Karev, A. V. "Doklad General'nogo Sekretaria VSEKhB [The Report of the General Secretary of the AUCECB]." *Bratskii Vestnik [Brotherly Herald]* 2 (1970): 19–46.

———. "Khristianin i Rodina [The Christian and the Motherland]." *Bratskii Vestnik [Brotherly Herald]* 3 (1970): 48–54.

———. "Rozhdenie Novogo Mira [The Birth of a New World]." *Bratskii Vestnik [Brotherly Herald]* 2 (1970): 5–7.

Kargel, Johann. *Sobranie Sochinenij [Collected Works]*. St Petersburg: Bibliia dlia vsekh, 1927.

———. "Verouchenie Evangel'skikh Khristian [The Confession of Faith of the Gospel Christians]." *Bratskii Vestnik [Brotherly Herald]* 4 (1966): 15–18.

Kasamara, V. A., and A. Sorokina. "Imperial Ambitions of Russians." *Communist and Post-Communist Studies* 45, no. 3–4 (2012): 279–288.

Keller, Timothy. *Center Church: Doing Balanced, Gospel-Centered Ministry in Your City*. Kindle Edition. Grand Rapids, MI: Zondervan, 2012.

Kirill. *Freedom and Responsibility: A Search for Harmony, Human Rights and Personal Dignity*. London: Darton, Longman & Todd, 2011.

———. "Interview," 2015. http://vlasti.net/news/209489.

———. "Russkii Mir eto Osobaiia Tsivilizatsiia Kotoruiu Neobkhodimo Sberech [The Russian World is a Special Civilization That Must be Preserved]," 2014. http://www.patriarchia.ru/db/text/3730705.html.

Kirk, J. Andrew. "The Kingdom of God and the Church in Contemporary Protestantism and Catholicism." In *Let the Earth Hear His Voice: International Congress on World Evangelization, Lausanne, Switzerland*, edited by J. D. Douglas, 1071–1080. Minneapolis, MN: World Wide Publications, 1975.

Kissinger, Henry A. "To Settle the Ukraine Crisis, Start at the End," 2014. https://www.washingtonpost.com/opinions/henry-kissinger-to-settle-the-ukraine-crisis-start-at-the-end/2014/03/05/46dad868-a496-11e3-8466-d34c451760b9_story.html?noredirect=on.

Knorre, Boris. "The Culture of War and Militarization within Political Orthodoxy in the Post-Soviet Region." *Transcultural Studies* 12, no. 1 (2016): 15–38.

Kolarz, Walter. *Religion in the Soviet Union*. London: Macmillan, 1961.

Kolesnikov, Andrei. "Russian Ideology after Crimea," 2015. https://carnegie.ru/2015/09/22/russian-ideology-after-crimea-pub-61350.

———. "The October Revolution in Post-Truth Russia," 2017. https://carnegie.ru/2017/03/28/october-revolution-in-post-truth-russia-pub-68456.

Kornilov, Nikolai. "Evngel'skiie Khristiane-Baptisty Na Istoricheskom Perelome, 1991–1997 [Evangelical Christian-Baptists at the Historical Turning Point, 1991–1997]." In *Dia-Logos*, 171–179. Moscow: Istina i Zhizn', 1997.

———. "Kakogo Roda Bogoslovie Nam Nuzhno? [What Kind of Theology Do We Need?]." *Put' Bogopoznaniia [Way of Knowledge of God]* 6 (2000): 5–17.

Kovalyova, Natalia. *Unlearning the Soviet Tongue: Discursive Practices of a Democratizing Polity*. London: Lexington Books, 2014.

Kraft, Charles Howard. *Worldview for Christian Witness*. Pasadena, CA: William Carey Library, 2008.

Kriuchkov, Gennady. *Tol'ko Khristos [Only Christ]*. Moscow: CCECB, 2001.

"Krizis Bogosluzheniia v Evangel'skikh Cerkviakh. Chto Dal'she? [The Crisis of Worship in Evangelical Churches. What's Next?]," 2009. https://baptist.org.ru/read/article/94462.

Kuhn, T. S. *The Structure of Scientific Revolutions*. Chicago, IL: University of Chicago Press, 1970.

Küng, Hans. *Theology for the Third Millennium: An Ecumenical View*. London: Harper Collins, 1991.

Küng, Hans, and David Tracy, eds. *Paradigm Change in Theology: A Symposium for the Future*. Edinburgh: T&T Clark, 1989.

Kuyper, Abraham. "Common Grace." In *Abraham Kuyper: A Centennial Reader*, edited by James D. Bratt, 165–201. Grand Rapids, MI: Eerdmans, 1902.

———. *Lectures on Calvinism*. Grand Rapids, MI: Eerdmans, 1931.

Kuznetsova, Miriam. "Early Russian Evangelicals (1874–1929): Historical Background and Hermeneutical Tendencies Based on I. V. Kargel's Written Heritage." PhD diss., University of Pretoria, 2009.

Ladd, George Eldon. *A Theology of the New Testament*. Grand Rapids, MI: Eerdmans, 1974.

———. *The Gospel of the Kingdom: Scriptural Studies in the Kingdom of God*. Grand Rapids, MI: Eerdmans, 1959.

Langman, Lauren. "The Social Psychology of Nationalism: To Die for the Sake of Strangers." In *The Sage Handbook of Nations and Nationalism*, edited by Gerard Delanty and Krishan Kumar, 66–83. London: Sage, 2006.

Laquer, Walter. "After the Fall: Russia in Search of a New Ideology." *World Affairs* 176, no. 6 (2014): 71–77.

LaRouche, Lyndon. "Colored Revolutions 'Illegal Warfare Under International Law and Federal Constitution,'" 2014. https://larouchepac.com/20141103/colored-revolutions-illegal-warfare.

Lausanne Committee for World Evangelization. "Evangelism and Social Responsibility: An Evangelical Commitment (LOP 21)." *Lausanne Movement* (blog), 1982. https://www.lausanne.org/content/lop/lop-21.

Lavrov, Sergei. "Remarks and Answers to Media Questions at the Primakov Readings International Forum, Moscow, June 30, 2017," 2017. http://www.mid.ru/foreign_policy/news/-/asset_publisher/cKNonkJE02Bw/content/id/2804842?p_p_id=101_INSTANCE_cKNonkJE02Bw&_101_INSTANCE_cKNonkJE02Bw_languageId=en_GB.

Leeman, Jonathan. "Soteriological Mission: Focusing in on the Mission of Redemption." In *Four Views on the Church's Mission*, edited by Jason S Sexton and Stanley N. Gundry, 17–45. Grand Rapids, MI: Zondervan, 2017.

Leskov, N. S. *Schism in High Society: Lord Radstock and His Followers*. Translated by James Y. Muckle. Nottingham: Bramcote Press, 1995.

Levada-Center. "Russia and the World," 2014. https://www.levada.ru/en/2014/10/22/russia-and-the-world/.

Levinson, Alexei. "Proektsiia Rosii Na Zapad [Russia's Projection to the West]," 2017. https://www.vedomosti.ru/opinion/columns/2017/04/11/685051-proektsiya-rossii.

Levy, Clifford J. "Welcome or Not, Orthodoxy Is Back in Russia's Public Schools." *The New York Times*, 2007, sec. Europe. https://www.nytimes.com/2007/09/23/world/europe/23russia.html.

Lindsell, Harold. "Philosophy of Christian Mission." In *The Theology of the Christian Mission*, edited by Gerald H. Anderson, 239–249. New York: McGraw-Hill, 1961.

Lints, Richard. *The Fabric of Theology: A Prolegomenon to Evangelical Theology*. Grand Rapids, MI: Eerdmans, 1993.

Lipman, Maria. "How Russia Has Come to Loathe the West," 2015. https://www.ecfr.eu/article/commentary_how_russia_has_come_to_loathe_the_west311346.

Little, Christopher R. "The Case for Prioritism." In *Controversies in Mission: Theology, People, and Practice of Mission in the 21st Century*, edited by Rochelle Cathcart Scheuermann, Kindle Edition, 11–28. Pasadena, CA: William Carey Library, 2016.

Liubaschenko, Viktoria. "Otechestvennaia Schkola Bogosloviia: Metodologiia, Problemy, Perspectivy [Development of a Native Theological Scholarship: Methodologies, Problems, and Prospects]." In *Bogoslovie i Bogoslovskoye Obrazovanie v Sovremennom Obschestve: Aktualnye Voprosy Teorii i Praktiki [Theology and Theological Education in the Contemporary Society: Current Issues of Theory and Practice]*, edited by EAAA, 37–43. Odessa: BOE, 2002.

Lovegrove, Deryck W. *Established Church, Sectarian People*. Cambridge: Cambridge University Press, 2009.

Lovelace, Richard. "Completing an Awakening." *The Christian Century* 98, no. 9 (1981): 296–300.

Lucas, Edward. "The Realism We Need," 2016. https://www.firstthings.com/web-exclusives/2016/10/the-realism-we-need.

Luhn, Alec. "Stalin, Russia's New Hero." *The New York Times*, 2016. https://www.nytimes.com/2016/03/13/opinion/sunday/stalinist-nostalgia-in-vladimir-putins-russia.html.

Lunkin, Roman. "A Reaction of Russian Churches on Ukrainian Crisis: A Prophecy of Democracy." In *Religion, State, Society, and Identity in Transition: Ukraine*, edited by Rob van der Laarse, Mykhailo Cherenkov, Vitaliy Proshck, and Tetiana Mykhalchuk, 43–76. Oisterwijk: Wolf Legal Publishers, 2015.

MacArthur, John. *The Vanishing Conscience: Drawing the Line in a No-Fault, Guilt-Free World*. Dallas, TX: Word Publishing, 1994.

———. *Why Government Can't Save You*. Dallas, TX: Word Publishing, 2000.

MacIntyre, Alasdair C. *After Virtue: A Study in Moral Theory*. Notre Dame, IN: University of Notre Dame Press, 2007.

Makarychev, Andrey. "The Russian World, Post-Truth, and Europe," 2017. http://www.ponarseurasia.org/memo/russian-world-post-truth-and-europe.

Mannteufel, Ingo. "Vladimir Putin's Post-Truth Year of Success," 2016. https://www.dw.com/en/opinion-vladimir-putins-post-truth-year-of-success/a-36914293.

Matthey, Jacques. "Missiology in the World Council of Churches: Update, Presentation, History, Theological Background and Emphases of the Most Recent Mission Statement of the WCC." *International Review of Mission* 90 (2001): 427–443.

McCarthy, Mark Myers. "Religious Conflict and Social Order in Nineteenth-Century Russia: Orthodoxy and the Protestant Challenge, 1812–1905." PhD diss., University of Notre Dame, 2004.

McGavran, Donald A. *Understanding Church Growth.* Grand Rapids, MI: Eerdmans, 1970.

McLaren, Brian D. *Everything Must Change: Jesus, Global Crises, and a Revolution of Hope.* Nashville, TN: Thomas Nelson, 2007.

Medinsky, Vladimir. "Interesnaia Istoriia [An Interesting Story]," 2017. https://rg.ru/2017/07/04/vladimir-medinskij-vpervye-otvechaet-kritikam-svoej-dissertacii.html.

Medvedev, Sergei. "Futurophobia," 2017. https://www.svoboda.org/a/28538329.html.

Mel'nikov, Andrew. "Alexander Prokhanov: 'Baptisty vo Mne Vidiat Plot' i Krov' Svoego Verouchitelia" [Alexander Prokhanov: "The Baptists See the Flesh and Blood of Their Teacher in Me"]," 2017. http://www.ng.ru/ng_religii/2017-08-16/9_426_prohanov.html.

Merriam, Sharan B. *Qualitative Research: A Guide to Design and Implementation.* San Francisco, CA: Jossey-Bass, 2009.

Meyendorff, John. *Byzantine Theology: Historical Trends and Doctrinal Themes.* New York: Fordham University Press, 1979.

———. *Catholicity and the Church.* Crestwood, NY: St Vladimir's Seminary Press, 1983.

Miliukov, P. N. *Russia and Its Crisis.* New York: Collier Books, 1962.

Minatrea, Milfred. *Shaped by God's Heart: The Passion and Practices of Missional Churches.* San Francisco, CA: Jossey-Bass, 2004.

"Mission Eurasia." Accessed 23 June 2017. https://missioneurasia.org/.

Mitrokhin, L. N. *Baptism: Istoriya i Sovremennost' [Baptists: History and Modernity].* St Petersburg: RKhGI, 1997.

———. "Izuchenie Sektanstva v Tambovskoi Oblasti [The Study of Sects in Tambov Province]." *Voprosy Filosofii [Issues of Philosophy]* 1 (1960): 143–148.

Mitskevich, A. I. "Derzhis' Obraztsa Zdravogo Ucheniia [Keep the Pattern of Sound Teaching]." *Bratskii Vestnik [Brotherly Herald]* 1 (1960): 52–55.

———. *Istoriia Evangel'skikh Khristian-Baptistov [A History of Evangelical Christians-Baptists].* Moscow: RSEKhB, 2007.

Moberg, David O. *The Great Reversal: Evangelism Versus Social Concern.* Philadelphia, PA: Lippincott, 1972.

Mokienko, Mikhailo. "Evangelizatsiino-Misionerska Diial'nist Piznikh Protestantiv v Ukraiini [Evangelism and Mission Work of the Late Ukrainian Protestants]." In *Dvatsat' Let Religioznoy Svobody i Aktivnoi Misii [Twenty Years of Religious Freedom and Active Mission]*, edited by Mikhaiil Cherenkov, 295–317. Kiev: Dukh i Litera, 2011.

Moreau, Scott. "Contextualization That Is Comprehensive." *Missiology: An International Review* 34, no. 3 (2006): 325–335.

Morozov, Evgeny. "Russia: Ideology Becomes a Mash-Up," 2008. http://www.opendemocracy.net/article/russia-theme/russia-ideology-becomes-a-mash-up.

Mosse, W.E. "Alexander II, Emperor of Russia," 2016. https://www.britannica.com/biography/Alexander-II-emperor-of-Russia.

Mouw, Richard J. *He Shines in All That's Fair: Culture and Common Grace*. Grand Rapids, MI: Eerdmans, 2001.

Movsesian, Mark. "Putin: Ideological, Not Irrational," 2014. https://www.firstthings.com/blogs/firstthoughts/2014/05/putin-ideological-not-rational.

Murray, Stuart. *Church Planting: Laying Foundations*. Kindle Edition. Scottdale, PA: Herald Press, 2001.

Nagirnyak, Alexander. *Podvizhniki Very [Devotees of Faith]*. Kiev: Knigonosha, 2014.

Nash, Manning. "The Core Elements of Ethnicity." In *Ethnicity*, edited by John Hutchinson and Antony D. Smith, 24–27. Oxford: Oxford University Press, 1996.

Negrov, Alexander. "Pochemu v Rossii Otsutstvuet Sobstvennaia Protestantskaia Teologia? [Why Is There No Indigenous Protestant Theology in Russia?]." *Mirt [Myrtle]* 1 (1997): 4–5.

Neill, Stephen. *Creative Tension*. London: Edinburgh House, 1959.

Netland, Harold. "The Cape Town Commitment: Continuity and Change." In *The Lausanne Movement: A Range of Perspectives*, edited by Lars Dahle, Margunn Serigstad Dahle, and Knud Jørgensen, 426–438. Eugene, OR: Wipf & Stock, 2014.

Nevolin, Michael. "Dvadtsat' Let Svobody: Dostizheniya i Problemy [Twenty Years of Freedom: Achievements and Problems]." In *Dvatsat' Let Religioznoy Svobody i Aktivnoi Misii [Twenty Years of Religious Freedom and Active Mission]*, edited by Mikhaiil Cherenkov, 8–16. Kiev: Dukh i Litera, 2011.

Newbigin, Lesslie. "Can the West Be Converted?" *International Bulletin of Missionary Research* 11, no. 1 (1987): 2–7.

———. "Ecumenical Amnesia." *International Bulletin of Missionary Research* 18, no. 1 (1994): 2–5.

———. *Foolishness to the Greeks: The Gospel and Western Culture*. Grand Rapids, MI: Eerdmans, 1986.

———. *The Gospel in a Pluralist Society*. Grand Rapids, MI: Eerdmans, 1989.

———. *The Open Secret: An Introduction to the Theology of Mission*. Grand Rapids, MI: Eerdmans, 1995.

———. *The Relevance of Trinitarian Doctrine for Today's Mission*. London: Edinburgh House, 1963.

———. "What Is a Local Church Truly United?" In *Growing Together in Unity: Text of the Faith and Order Commission on Conciliar Fellowship*, edited by Choan-Seng Song, 149–164. Geneva: Christian Literature Society, 1978.

Newman, Las. "Foreword." In *Holistic Mission: God's Plan for God's People*, edited by Brian Woolnough and Wonsuk Ma, ix–x. Eugene, OR: Wipf & Stock, 2010.

Nichols, Gregory L. "Pashkovism: Nineteenth Century Russian Piety." MA thesis, Wheaton College, 1991.

———. *The Development of Russian Evangelical Spirituality: A Study of Ivan V. Kargel (1849–1937)*. Kindle Edition. Eugene, OR: Pickwick, 2011.

Niebuhr, Helmut Richard. *Christ and Culture*. New York: Harper, 1956.

Nikol'skaia, Tatiana. "Istoriia Dvizheniia Baptistov-Initsiativnikov [The History of the Baptist Initsiativniki Movement]." In *History and Mission in Europe: Continuing the Conversation*, edited by Mary Raber and Peter F. Penner, 111–140. Schwarzenfeld, Germany: Neufeld Verlag, 2011.

Noll, Mark A. "The Peril and Potential of Scripture in Christian Political Witness." In *Christian Political Witness*, edited by George Kalantzis and Gregory W. Lee, 35–55. Downers Grove, IL: IVP Academic, 2014.

———. *The Scandal of the Evangelical Mind*. Grand Rapids, MI: Eerdmans, 1994.

O'Donovan, Oliver. *Resurrection and Moral Order: An Outline for Evangelical Ethics*. Leicester, England; Grand Rapids, MI: IVP Academic; Eerdmans, 1986.

Olema, Albert W. *History of Evangelical Christianity in Russia*. Dallas, TX: No Publisher, 1983.

Olson, Roger E. *How to Be Evangelical without Being Conservative*. Grand Rapids, MI: Zondervan, 2008.

———. *Reformed and Always Reforming: The Postconservative Approach to Evangelical Theology*. Grand Rapids, MI: Baker Academic, 2007.

Osborne, Grant R. *The Hermeneutical Spiral: A Comprehensive Introduction to Biblical Interpretation*. Downers Grove, IL: IVP Academic, 1991.

Osborne, Samuel. "Russia 'Weaponising Misinformation' to Create 'Post-Truth Age' and Destabilise the West, Defence Secretary Warns," 2017. https://www.independent.co.uk/news/world/europe/russia-weaponising-misinformation-destabilise-west-nato-cyber-attacks-michael-fallon-a7560481.html.

Osthold, Christian. "Nur Wenn Europa eine Voraussetzung Beachtet, Kann Seine Ukrainepolitik Erfolg Haben [Only if Europe Takes into Account One Prerequisite Can Its Ukraine Policy Succeed]," 2017. https://www.focus.de/politik/experten/osthold/ukraine-konflikt-nur-wenn-europa-eine-voraussetzung-beachtet-kann-seine-ukrainepolitik-erfolg-haben_id_7523140.html.

Ott, Craig. "Introduction." In *The Mission of the Church: Five Views in Conversation*, edited by Craig Ott, ix–xxxvi. Grand Rapids, MI: Baker Academic, 2016.

Ott, Craig, and Stephen J. Strauss. *Encountering Theology of Mission: Biblical Foundations, Historical Developments, and Contemporary Issues*. Grand Rapids, MI: Baker Academic, 2010.

Ott, Craig, and Gene Wilson. *Global Church Planting: Biblical Principles and Best Practices for Multiplication*. Grand Rapids, MI: Baker Academic, 2011.

Padilla, C. René. "Evangelism and the World." In *Let the Earth Hear His Voice: International Congress on World Evangelization, Lausanne, Switzerland*, edited by J. D. Douglas, 116–146. Minneapolis, MN: World Wide Publications, 1975.

———. *Mission Between the Times: Essays on the Kingdom*. Carlisle, UK: Langham Monographs, 2010.

———. "Response." In *In Word and Deed: Evangelism and Social Responsibility*, edited by Bruce Nicholls, 133–134. Grand Rapids, MI: Eerdmans, 1985.

Panych, Olena. "Soviet Baptism after World War II: Rethinking the Concept of Church." In *History and Mission in Europe: Continuing the Conversation*, edited by Mary Raber and Peter F. Penner, 141–160. Schwarzenfeld, Germany: Neufeld Verlag, 2011.

Parker, David, ed. "A Commentary of the 'Manila Manifesto.'" *Evangelical Review of Theology* 14 (1990): 236–253.

Pavlov, Pavel. "K Momentu [To the Moment]." *Slovo Istiny [The Word of Truth]* 1 (1917): 1–2.

Pavlov, Vasily. *Baptisty: Tzerkov i Gosudarstvo [Baptists: Church and State]*. Moscow: Logos, 2004.

Penner, Peter, Vladimir Ubeivolk, Ivan Rusin, and Ruslan Zagidulin, eds. *Novye Gorizonty Missii [New Horizons of Mission]*. Cherkassy: Colloquium, 2015.

Plantinga, Cornelius. *Engaging God's World: A Christian Vision of Faith, Learning, and Living*. Grand Rapids, MI: Eerdmans, 2002.

Plett, I. P. *Istoriia Evangel'skikh Khristian Baptistov s 1905 Po 1944 God [The History of Evangelical Christians-Baptists in 1905–1944]*. Moscow: ICCECB, 2001.

Pollock, John Charles. *The Faith of the Russian Evangelicals*. New York: McGraw-Hill, 1964.

Popov, Vladimir, and Piotr Dutkievicz. "A Time of Transition: Changes in Reality and Perceptions." In *The Social History of Post-Communist Russia*, edited by Piotr Dutkievicz, Vladimir Kulikov, and Richard Sakwa, 41–57. London; New York: Routledge, 2016.

Pospielovsky, D. *Russkaia Pravoslavnaia Tserkov' v XX Veke [The Russian Orthodox Church in the Twentieth Century]*. Moscow: Respublika, 1995.

Potapova, N. V. *Evnagel'skoe Khristianstvo i Baptism [The Gospel Christians and Baptists]. Tom 1.* Yuzhno-Sakhalisnk: SachGU, 2014.

Prasnikar, Janez, Marko Pahor, and Jasna V. Svetlik. "Are National Cultures Still Important in International Business? Russia, Serbia, and Slovenia in Comparison." *Management* 13, no. 2 (2008): 1–26.

Priest, Robert J. "'Experience-near Theologizing' in Diverse Human Contexts." In *Globalizing Theology: Belief and Practice in an Era of World Christianity*, edited by Craig Ott and Harold A. Netland, 181–195. Grand Rapids, MI: Baker Academic, 2006.

———. "What in the World Is Missiology!?," 2012. http://static1.squarespace.com/static/56dee43ee321400514f98522/t/575c3b17e707eb73521a574c/1465662232210/4+MISS+401+Mag+4.pdf.

Prokhanov, Ivan. *Ateism Ili Evangelie? [Atheism or the Gospel?]*. Moscow: VSEKh, 1933.

———. *In the Couldron of Russia: 1869–1933*. New York: All-Russian Evangelical Christian Union, 1933.

———. *Novaya Ili Evangel'skaya Zhizn [New Life in the Gospel]*. Moscow: Logos, 2009.

Prokhorov, Constantin. *Russian Baptists and Orthodoxy, 1960–1990*. Carlisle, UK: Langham Monographs, 2013.

Putin, Vladimir. "Address by President of the Russian Federation," 2014. http://en.kremlin.ru/events/president/news/20603.

———. "Annual Address to the Federal Assembly of the Russian Federation," 2005. http://kremlin.ru/events/president/transcripts/22931.

———. "Stenogramma [Transcript]," 2014. https://www.tvc.ru/news/show/id/37458.

———. "Vystuplenie na Zasedanii Valdaiskogo Kluba [The Speech at the Valdai Club]," 2013. https://rg.ru/2013/09/19/stenogramma-site.html.

Puzynin, Andrey P. *The Tradition of the Gospel Christians: A Study of Their Identity and Theology during the Russian, Soviet, and Post-Soviet Periods*. Kindle Edition. Eugene, OR: Pickwick, 2011.

Raber, Mary. "Discerning Joy from Sorrow: Reflecting on Changes among Ukrainian Evangelicals Since Independence," 2004. http://www.eastwestreport.org/articles/ew12101.html.

———. "Ministries of Compassion among Russian Evangelicals, 1905–1929." PhD diss., Wales University, 2014.

Raber, Mary, and Peter F. Penner, eds. *History and Mission in Europe: Continuing the Conversation*. Schwarzenfeld, Germany: Neufeld Verlag, 2011.

Ray, Julie, and Neli Esipova. "Russian Approval of Putin Soars to Highest Level in Years," 2014. https://news.gallup.com/poll/173597/russian-approval-putin-soars-highest-level-years.aspx.

Raychinets, Fedor. "Est' Li Sotsial'naia i Politichskaia Positsiia u Evangel'skikh Tserkvei Ukrainy? [Do Evangelical Churches of Ukraine Have a Social and Political Position?]." In *Dvatsat' Let Religioznoy Svobody i Aktivnoi Misii [Twenty Years of Religious Freedom and Active Mission]*, edited by Mikhaiil Cherenkov, 318–333. Kiev: Dukh i Litera, 2011.

Rommen, Edward. "A Sacramental Vision Approach." In *The Mission of the Church*, edited by Craig Ott, 69–90. Grand Rapids, MI: Baker Academic, 2016.

Roudakova, Natalia. *Losing Pravda. Ethics and the Press in Post-Truth Russia*. Cambridge: Cambridge University Press, 2017.

Sakwa, Richard. "Bringing the People Back In." In *The Social History of Post-Communist Russia*, edited by Piotr Dutkievicz, Vladimir Kulikov, and Richard Sakwa, 288–296. London; New York: Routledge, 2016.

———. "Nation and Nationalism in Russia." In *The SAGE Handbook of Nations and Nationalism*, edited by Gerard Delanty and Krishan Kumar, 410–424. London: Sage, 2006.

Sannikov, Sergey, ed. *Istoriia Baptizma [A History of Baptist Faith]*. Odessa: Bogomyslie, 1996.

Satter, David. "Putin Runs the Russian State – and the Russian Church Too," 2009. https://www.forbes.com/2009/02/20/putin-solzhenitsyn-kirill-russia-opinions-contributors_orthodox_church.html.

Savinskii, S. N. *Istoriia Evangel'skikh Khristian-Baptistov Ukrainy, Rossii, Belorussii: 1867–1917 [History of Evangelical Christians-Baptists of Ukraine, Russia, and Belarus: 1867–1917]*. St Petersburg: Bibliia dlia vsekh, 1999.

———. *Istoriia Evangel'skikh Khristian-Baptistov Ukrainy, Rossii, Belorussii: 1917–1967 [History of Evangelical Christians-Baptists of Ukraine, Russia, and Belarus: 1917–1967]*. St Petersburg: Bibliia dlia vsekh, 2001.

Savinskii, S. N., P. D. Savchenko, and I. P. Dik, eds. *Istoriia Evangel'skikh Khristian-Baptistov v SSSR [History of Evangelical Christians-Baptists in the USSR]*. Moscow: VSEKhB, 1989.

Sawatsky, Walter. "Review of Russian Baptists and Spiritual Revolution 1905-1929." Edited by Heather J. Coleman. *Religion in Eastern Europe* 26 (2006): 58–63.

———. *Soviet Evangelicals Since World War II*. Kitchener, ON; Scottdale, PA: Herald, 1981.

Sawatsky, Walter, and Peter F. Penner, eds. *Mission in the Former Soviet Union*. Schwarzenfeld, Germany: Neufeld Verlag, 2005.

Scherer, James A. "Church, Kingdom, and Missio Dei: Lutheran and Orthodox Correctives to Recent Ecumenical Mission Theology." In *Good News of the Kingdom: Mission Theology for the Third Millennium*, edited by Charles Van Engen, Dean S. Gilliland, and Paul Pierson, 82–88. Eugene, OR: Wipf & Stock, 1993.

Scherer, James A., and Stephen B. Bevans, eds. *New Directions in Mission and Evangelization*. Maryknoll, NY: Orbis Books, 1992.

Schindler, John R. "Putin's Orthodox Jihad," 2014. http://www.interpretermag.com/putins-orthodox-jihad/.

———. "Why Vladimir Putin Hates Us." *Observer* (blog), 2016. https://observer.com/2016/11/why-vladimir-putin-hates-us/.

Schmemann, Alexander. *The Historical Road of Eastern Orthodoxy*. Crestwood, NY: St Vladimir's Seminar Press, 1977.

Schreiter, Robert J. "From the Lausanne Covenant to the Cape Town Commitment: A Theological Assessment." *International Bulletin of Missionary Research* 35 (2011): 88–92.

Sergienko, Gennagii. "Baptisty i Obshcestvo [Baptists and Society]," 2011. http://www.mbchurch.ru/publications/articles/15/5892/.

———. "Nevyuchenyie Uroki Proshlogo [Unlearned Lessons of the Past]," 2011. http://gazeta.mirt.ru/stat-i/cerkov/post-1431/.

Shamgunov, Insur. "Listening to the Voice of the Graduate: An Analysis of Professional Practice and Training for Ministry in Central Asia." PhD diss., University of Oxford, 2009.

Shellnutt, Kate. "Russia Bans Jehovah's Witnesses as Extremists," 2017. https://www.christianitytoday.com/news/2017/april/russia-bans-jehovahs-witnesses.html.

Shenk, Wilbert R. *Changing Frontiers of Mission*. Maryknoll, NY: Orbis Books, 1999.

———. "Missionary Encounter with Culture." *International Bulletin of Missionary Research* 15 (1991): 104–109.

———. "Recasting Theology of Mission: Impulses from the Non-Western World." In *Landmark Essays in Mission and World Christianity*, edited by R. L. Gallagher and P. Hertig, 116–132. Maryknoll, NY: Orbis Books, 2009.

———. *Write the Vision: The Church Renewed*. Valley Forge, PA: Trinity Press International, 1995.

Shevkunov, Tikhon. *Everyday Saints*. Dallas, TX: Pokrov, 2012.

Shevtsova, Lilia. "Udar Po Modeli Suschestvovaniia Rossii [A Blow at Russia's Model of Existence]," 2017. https://nv.ua/opinion/shevcova/udar-po-modeli-sushchestvovanija-rossii-1209848.html.

Shweder, Richard A., Nancy C. Much, Manamohan Mahapatra, and Lawrence Park. "The 'Big Three' of Morality (Autonomy, Community, Divinity) and the 'Big Three' Explanations of Suffering." In *Morality and Health*, edited by Allan M. Brandt and Paul Rozin, 119–172. New York: Routledge, 1997.

Sider, Ronald J. *Good News and Good Works: A Theology for the Whole Gospel*. Grand Rapids, MI: Baker Book House, 1999.

Sider, Ronald J., Philip N. Olson, and Heidi Rolland Unruh. *Churches That Make a Difference: Reaching Your Community with Good News and Good Works.* Grand Rapids, MI: Baker Book House, 2002.

Sinichkin, Alexey. *Vozrozhdenie Vopreki Bezbozhiiu [Revival despite Godlessness].* Korosten, Ukraine: Triada, 2015.

———. *Vsio Radi Missii [Everything for the Sake of Mission].* Irpen: Dukhovnoe Vozrozhdenie, 2011.

Smart, Ninian. *Dimensions of the Sacred: An Anatomy of the World's Beliefs.* Berkeley: University of California Press, 1996.

Smith, Christian Stephen. *Moral, Believing Animals: Human Personhood and Culture.* New York: Oxford University Press, 2003.

Snyder, Howard. *Liberating the Church: The Ecology of Church and Kingdom.* Eugene, OR: Wipf & Stock, 1983.

———. "The Church as God's Agent in Evangelism." In *Let the Earth Hear His Voice: International Congress on World Evangelization, Lausanne, Switzerland,* edited by J. D. Douglas, 327–360. Minneapolis, MN: World Wide Publications, 1975.

Snyder, Howard A. *Models of the Kingdom.* Nashville, TN: Abingdon, 1991.

Solodovnikov, Vladimir. "Marginalizatsionnye Tendentsii v Sovremennom Rossiiskom Protestantisme i Perspektivy Ikh Preodoleniia [Tendencies Toward Marginalization in Contemporary Russian Protestantism, and the Prospects of Their Overcoming]." In *Krizisnye Iavleniia v Sovremennom Rossiiskom Protestantisme i Sposoby Ikh Preodoleniia [The Crisis Henomena in Contemporary Russian Protestantism and the Ways of Dealing with Them],* edited by Vladimir Solodovnikov, 7–20. Moscow: SEKhR, 2008.

Solovyov, Vladimir. *Freedom, Faith, and Dogma.* Edited by Vladimir Wozniuk. Albany, NY: State University of New York Press, 2008.

"Spisok Uchebnykh Zavedenii EKhB. Vysshee Professional'noe Obrazovanie [The List of Educational Institutions of ECB. Higher Vocational Education]." Accessed 20 June 2017. https://baptist.org.ru/education.

Steeves, Paul D. "The Russian Baptist Union, 1917–1935: Evangelical Awakening in Russia." PhD diss., University of Kansas, 1976.

Stepanov, V. A. "Sankt-Peterburgskii Syezd Evangel'skikh Veruiuschikh 1884 Goda: Mify, Facty, Uroki [The Congress of Evangelical Believers in St Petersburg in 1884: Myths, Facts, Lessons]," 2016. http://bit.ly/2lFHUYP.

Stetzer, Ed. "Monday Is for Missiology," 2010. https://www.christianitytoday.com/edstetzer/2010/march/monday-is-for-missiology.html.

Stetzer, Ed, and Daniel Im. *Planting Missional Churches: Your Guide to Starting Churches That Multiply.* Nashville, TN: B&H Academic, 2016.

Stott, John. *Christian Mission in the Modern World.* Downers Grove, IL: IVP Academic, 1975.

———. *Issues Facing Christians Today*. Grand Rapids, MI: Zondervan, 1984.

———, ed. *Making Christ Known: Historic Mission Documents from the Lausanne Movement, 1974–1989*. Grand Rapids, MI: Eerdmans, 1996.

———. "The Biblical Basis of Evangelism." In *Let the Earth Hear His Voice: International Congress on World Evangelization, Lausanne, Switzerland*, edited by J. D. Douglas, 65–78. Minneapolis, MN: World Wide Publications, 1975.

Stott, John R. W., ed. "The Lausanne Covenant with an Exposition and Commentary." In *Making Christ Known: Historic Mission Documents from the Lausanne Movement, 1974–1989*, 1–55. Grand Rapids, MI: Eerdmans, 1996.

———, ed. "The Manila Manifesto: An Elaboration of the Lausanne Covenant Fifteen Years Later." In *Making Christ Known: Historic Mission Documents from the Lausanne Movement, 1974–1989*, 225–248. Grand Rapids, MI: Eerdmans, 1996.

Taylor, William David, ed. *Global Missiology in the 21st Century: The Iguassu Dialogue*. Grand Rapids, MI: Baker Academic, 2000.

Tennent, Timothy C. *Invitation to World Missions: A Trinitarian Missiology for the Twenty-First Century*. Kindle Edition. Grand Rapids, MI: Kregel, 2010.

———. "Lausanne and Global Evangelicalism: Theological Distinctives and Missiological Impact." In *The Lausanne Movement: A Range of Perspectives*, edited by Lars Dahle, Margunn Serigstad Dahle, and Knud Jørgensen, 45–61. Eugene, OR: Wipf & Stock, 2014.

Teteriatnikov, Konstantin. "Tserkov' Vchera i Segodnia [The Church Yesterday and Today]." In *Dvatsat' Let Religioznoy Svobody i Aktivnoi Misii [Twenty Years of Religious Freedom and Active Mission]*, edited by Mikhaiil Cherenkov, 175–188. Kiev: Dukh i Litera, 2011.

The Lausanne Movement. "About the Movement." Accessed 25 July 2017. https://www.lausanne.org/about-the-movement.

———. "The Cape Town Commitment," 2011. https://www.lausanne.org/content/ctc/ctcommitment.

Thelen, Shawn, and Kevin Coulson. "Russian National Character: An Application of Clark's Comprehensive Framework." *The Marketing Management Journal* 12, no. 1 (2002): 19–31.

Tiénou, Tite. "Gospel and Cultures in the Lausanne Movement." In *The Lausanne Movement: A Range of Perspectives*, edited by Lars Dahle, Margunn Serigstad Dahle, and Knud Jørgensen, 157–169. Eugene, OR: Wipf & Stock, 2014.

Tiénou, Tite, and Paul G. Hiebert. "Missional Theology." *Missiology: An International Review* 2 (2006): 219–238.

Tikhonova, Natalya. "The Russian Roller Coaster: Changes in Social Structure in the Post-Communist Period." In *The Social History of Post-Communist Russia*, edited by Piotr Dutkievicz, Vladimir Kulikov, and Richard Sakwa, 130–150. London; New York: Routledge, 2016.

Tippett, Alan R. "Missiology, A New Discipline." In *The Means of World Evangelization: Missiological Education at the Fuller School of World Mission*, edited by Martin Alvin, 25–31. Pasadena, CA: William Carey Library, 1974.

"Trinity Video Seminary." Accessed 20 June 2017. http://en.tvseminary.org/.

Tsvirin'ko, Viacheslav. "Missiia Pervykh Evangel'skikh Dvizhenii v Rossiiskoi Iimperii i SSSR [Mission of the First Evangelical Movements in the Russian Empire and the USSR]." In *Novye Gorizonty Missii [New Horizons of Mission]*, edited by Peter Penner, Vladimir Ubeivolk, Ivan Rusin, and Ruslan Zagidulin, 189–205. Cherkassy: Colloquium, 2015.

United Nations Statistics Division. "Demographic and Social Statistics." Accessed 27 August 2017. https://unstats.un.org/unsd/demographic/products/dyb/dyb2008.htm.

Van Engen, Charles. *God's Missionary People: Rethinking the Purpose of the Local Church*. Grand Rapids, MI: Baker Book House, 1991.

———. *Mission on the Way: Issues in Mission Theology*. Grand Rapids, MI: Baker Book House, 1996.

———. *The Growth of the True Church: An Analysis of the Ecclesiology of Church Growth Theory*. Amsterdam: Rodopi, 1981.

———. "Theology of Mission." In *Evangelical Dictionary of World Missions*, edited by A. Scott Moreau, 949–951. Grand Rapids, MI: Baker Academic, 2000.

Van Gelder, Craig, and Dwight J. Zscheile. *The Missional Church in Perspective: Mapping Trends and Shaping the Conversation*. Grand Rapids, MI: Baker Academic, 2011.

VanDrunen, David. *Living in God's Two Kingdoms: A Biblical Vision for Christianity and Culture*. Kindle Edition. Wheaton, IL: Crossway, 2010.

———. "The Two Kingdoms and the Ordo Salutis: Life beyond Judgment and the Question of a Dual Ethic." *Westminster Theological Journal* 70 (2008): 207–224.

Vanhoozer, Kevin J. "May We Go beyond What Is Written After All? The Pattern of Theological Authority and the Problem of Doctrinal Development." In *The Enduring Authority of the Christian Scriptures*, edited by D. A. Carson, 747–794. Grand Rapids, MI: Eerdmans, 2016.

Verkuyl, J. *Contemporary Missiology: An Introduction*. Grand Rapids, MI: Eerdmans, 1978.

Vicedom, Georg F. *The Mission of God: An Introduction to a Theology of Mission*. Saint Louis, MO: Concordia, 1965.

Volf, Miroslav. *A Public Faith: How Followers of Christ Should Serve the Common Good*. Grand Rapids, MI: Brazos Press, 2011.

Walker, Shaun. "Russia Celebrates Anniversary of Crimea Takeover and Eyes Second Annexation," 2015. https://www.theguardian.com/world/2015/

mar/18/russia-celebrates-anniversary-crimea-takeover-eyes-second-annexation.

Walls, Andrew F. *The Missionary Movement in Christian History: Studies in the Transmission of Faith*. Maryknoll, NY: Orbis Books, 1996.

Walvoord, John F. "The Theological Basis for Foreign Missions." In *Facing the Unfinished Task: Messages Delivered at the Congress on World Missions*, edited by Mary Bennett, 244–250. Grand Rapids, MI: Zondervan, 1961.

Wanner, Catherine. *Communities of the Converted: Ukrainians and Global Evangelism*. Ithaca: Cornell University Press, 2007.

White, John E. "An Analysis of Factors behind the Surge in Ukrainian Evangelical Missionaries from 1989–1999." PhD diss., Biola University, 2016.

———. "Three Periods of Awakening in Eastern Slavic Lands." *Theological Reflections* Special Issue (2013): 244–258.

Whiteman, Darrell L. "Contextualization: The Theory, the Gap, the Challenge." *International Bulletin of Missionary Research* 21 (1997): 2–7.

Winter, Ralph D. "The Future of Evangelicals in Mission." In *Missionshift: Global Mission Issues in the Third Millennium*, edited by David J. Hesselgrave and Ed Stetzer, 164–191. Nashville, TN: B&H Academic, 2010.

———. "The Highest Priority: Cross-Cultural Evangelism." In *Let the Earth Hear His Voice: International Congress on World Evangelization, Lausanne, Switzerland*, edited by J. D. Douglas, 213–258. Minneapolis, MN: World Wide Publications, 1975.

Wittmer, Michael E. *Becoming Worldly Saints: Can You Serve Jesus and Still Enjoy Your Life?* Grand Rapids, MI: Zondervan, 2015.

Wolters, Albert M. *Creation Regained: Biblical Basics for a Reformational Worldview*. Grand Rapids, MI: Eerdmans, 2005.

Wolterstorff, Nicholas. *Until Justice and Peace Embrace*. Grand Rapids, MI: Eerdmans, 1983.

Woolnough, Brian E., and Wonsuk Ma, eds. *Holistic Mission: God's Plan for God's People*. Eugene, OR: Wipf & Stock, 2010.

Wright, Christopher J. H. "Holistic Mission," 2012. http://www.wycliffe.net/missiology?id=2723.

———. *The Mission of God: Unlocking the Bible's Grand Narrative*. Downers Grove, IL: IVP Academic, 2006.

———. *The Mission of God's People: A Biblical Theology of the Church's Mission*. Grand Rapids, MI: Zondervan, 2010.

Wright, N. T. *Surprised by Hope: Rethinking Heaven, the Resurrection, and the Mission of the Church*. New York: HarperOne, 2008.

———. *The Day the Revolution Began: Reconsidering the Meaning of Jesus's Crucifixion*. New York: HarperOne, 2016.

Yoder, John Howard. *The Politics of Jesus*. Grand Rapids, MI: Eerdmans, 1972.

———. *The Royal Priesthood: Essays Ecclesiological and Ecumenical*. Grand Rapids, MI: Eerdmans, 1994.

Yuchkovski, Alexander. "A Comparison of the Evangelical Movement in Russia in the 1920s and the 1990s." PhD diss., Oxford Centre for Mission Studies, 2014.

Zavalishina, Tatiana. "Vsevolod Chaplin: 'Ostanovili Gitlerovskii Proekt, Ostanovim i Amerikanskii!'" [Vsevolod Chaplin: 'We Stopped the Nazi Project and We Will Stop the American One!'], 2014. https://www.business-gazeta.ru/article/122025.

Zaychenko, Alexander. "Sila i Slabost' Sovremennogo Rossiiskogo Protestantisma [Strengths and Weaknesses of Russian Protestantism Today]," 2011. http://gazeta.mirt.ru/stat-i/obschestvo/post-1014/.

Zhidkov, M. Y. "Edinstvo vo Khriste [Unity in Christ]." *Bratskii Vestnik [Brotherly Herald]* 1 (1985): 50–53.

Zhidkov, Y. I. "Khristianin i Rodina [The Christian and the Motherland]." *Bratskii Vestnik [Brotherly Herald]* 1 (1945): 6–7.

———. "Nash Otchet [Our Report]." *Bratskii Vestnik [Brotherly Herald]* 1 (1947): 13–18.

———. "Nashi Prazdniki [Our Celebrations]." *Bratskii Vestnik [Brotherly Herald]* 2 (1946): 13–20.

———. "Staryi God i Novyi God [The Past Year and the New Year]." *Bratskii Vestnik [Brotherly Herald]* 1 (1949): 3–6.

———. "Vzglyad Nazad [Looking Back]." *Bratskii Vestnik [Brotherly Herald]* 1 (1948): 5–10.

Zhitenev, Artem. "Most Russians Feel Threat from External Enemies, Poll Shows," 2017. https://www.rt.com/politics/373929-most-russians-feel-threat-from/.

Zorkaia, Nataliia. "Pravoslavie v Bezreligioznom Obschetve [The Orthodox Church in a Secular Society]." *Vestnik Obschestvennogo Mneniia [Messenger of Public Opinion]* 100, no. 2 (2009): 65–84.

Langham Literature, with its publishing work, is a ministry of Langham Partnership.

Langham Partnership is a global fellowship working in pursuit of the vision God entrusted to its founder John Stott –

> **to facilitate the growth of the church in maturity and Christ-likeness through raising the standards of biblical preaching and teaching.**

Our vision is to see churches in the majority world equipped for mission and growing to maturity in Christ through the ministry of pastors and leaders who believe, teach and live by the Word of God.

Our mission is to strengthen the ministry of the Word of God through:
- nurturing national movements for biblical preaching
- fostering the creation and distribution of evangelical literature
- enhancing evangelical theological education

especially in countries where churches are under-resourced.

Our ministry

Langham Preaching partners with national leaders to nurture indigenous biblical preaching movements for pastors and lay preachers all around the world. With the support of a team of trainers from many countries, a multi-level programme of seminars provides practical training, and is followed by a programme for training local facilitators. Local preachers' groups and national and regional networks ensure continuity and ongoing development, seeking to build vigorous movements committed to Bible exposition.

Langham Literature provides majority world preachers, scholars and seminary libraries with evangelical books and electronic resources through publishing and distribution, grants and discounts. The programme also fosters the creation of indigenous evangelical books in many languages, through writer's grants, strengthening local evangelical publishing houses, and investment in major regional literature projects, such as one volume Bible commentaries like the *Africa Bible Commentary* and the *South Asia Bible Commentary*.

Langham Scholars provides financial support for evangelical doctoral students from the majority world so that, when they return home, they may train pastors and other Christian leaders with sound, biblical and theological teaching. This programme equips those who equip others. Langham Scholars also works in partnership with majority world seminaries in strengthening evangelical theological education. A growing number of Langham Scholars study in high quality doctoral programmes in the majority world itself. As well as teaching the next generation of pastors, graduated Langham Scholars exercise significant influence through their writing and leadership.

To learn more about Langham Partnership and the work we do visit **langham.org**

www.ingramcontent.com/pod-product-compliance
Lightning Source LLC
Chambersburg PA
CBHW070233240426
43673CB00044B/1775

"This is an excellent discussion of the vexed issue of Calvin and the extent of the atonement. It thoroughly and fairly reviews the works of others and itself reaches a judicious conclusion. It is to be wholeheartedly recommended and cannot be ignored by anyone in the future writing on the topic."

—ANTHONY N. S. LANE, Professor of Historical Theology, London School of Theology, author of *A Reader's Guide to Calvin's Institutes*; *Calvin and Bernard of Clairvaux*; and *John Calvin, Student of the Church Fathers*

"History can be messy indeed. It often doesn't fit neat and tidy categories. Paul Hartog has shown exactly this concerning John Calvin's own understanding of the extent of the atonement. Too often later ideas have been read back into Calvin. But Hartog does an excellent job of letting Calvin speak for himself. He has written a clear and concise piece of research that handles the primary sources judiciously."

—MARTIN FOORD, Lecturer in Systematic Theology, Evangelical Theological College of Asia (Singapore), author of *The 16th Century Protestant Doctrine of the Gospel in Systematic Theology*

"Historical theology at its best; well-researched, clearly written, and carefully reasoned.... It is essential reading for all who wish to know where Calvin stood on these issues."

—GARY L. SHULTZ, JR., Assistant Professor of Religion, Liberty University Online, author of *A Multi-Intentioned View of the Extent of the Atonement*

"This book is unsurpassed in its depth of research into primary and secondary sources. It analyzes the complex and much debated issue of Calvin's view of the atonement with fairness to all perspectives."

—JOHN SAMUEL HAMMETT, John Leadley Dagg Chair of Systematic Theology, Southeastern Baptist Theological Seminary (Wake Forest, NC), author of "Multiple-Intentions View of the Atonement" in *Perspectives on the Extent of the Atonement: Three Views*

"No issue in Calvin studies has generated more discussion than his view on the extent of the atonement. Hartog boldly enters the discussion with an impressive argument supported by careful research.... All who admire the great Swiss reformer will be grateful for the attempt to bring us closer to a satisfactory conclusion to this question."

—JEFFREY STRAUB, Professor of Historical Theology, Central Baptist Theological Seminary (Plymouth, Minnesota)

"In this well-documented work, Hartog shows how Calvin can and has been used to support both limited and unlimited atonement, but it cannot be both in an equivalent sense. I heartily recommend this work."

—Robert P. Lightner †, Professor Emeritus of Systematic Theology, Dallas Theological Seminary, author of *The Death Christ Died*

"There have been numerous articles, theses, and books on this topic, but in my opinion Paul Hartog's is the fullest and best.... All who study this topic must refer to this convincing research in future discussions. I am pleased to recommend it enthusiastically."

—Curt Daniel, Pastor of Faith Bible Church (Springfield, Illinois), author of *The History and Theology of Calvinism*